THE CODES
GUIDEBOOK
FOR INTERIORS

THE CODES GUIDEBOOK FOR INTERIORS

✦ ✦ ✦

Second Edition

Sharon Koomen Harmon, IIDA

Katherine E. Kennon, AIA

JOHN WILEY & SONS, INC.

New York   Chichester   Weinheim   Brisbane   Singapore   Toronto

The information in this book has been derived and extracted from a multitude of sources, including building codes, fire codes, industry codes and standards, manufacturer's literature, and personal professional experience. It is presented in good faith, but although the author and the publisher have made every reasonable effort to make the information presented accurate and authoritative, they do not warrant, and assume no liability for its accuracy or completeness or its fitness for any specific purpose. It is primarily intended as a learning and teaching aid, and not as a source of information for the final project design. It is the responsibility of the users to apply their professional knowledge in the use of the information presented in this book, and to consult original sources for current detailed information as needed in actual design situations. It should also be noted that many codes have more than one interpretation. The code officials in each jurisdiction have the authority to make all final decisions.

This publication is designed to provide accurate and authoritative information in regard to the subject matter covered. It is sold with the understanding that the publisher is not engaged in rendering professional services. If professional advice or other expert assistance is required, the services of a competent professional person should be sought.

Library of Congress Cataloging-in-Publication Data

Harmon, Sharon Koomen, 1964–
    The codes guidebook for interiors / by Sharon Koomen Harmon and
  Katherine E. Kennon.—2nd ed.
      p.   cm.
  Includes bibliographical references and index.
    ISBN 0-471-38134-9 (cloth : alk. paper)
    1. Building laws—United States. 2. Buildings—Specifications—United
States. 3. Interior architecture—United States I. Kennon, Katherine E.
II. Title.

KF5701 .H37 2001
343.73'078624—dc21   00-043813

Printed in the United States of America.

10 9 8 7 6 5

Dedication

RITA AND NICK KOOMEN

Who taught me about life's values, love, and the importance of discipline

MARGARET AND JOHN MULLEN, JR.

Who instilled in me a sense of dedication and determination

In special memory of

MARGARET MCDOWELL MULLEN, 1922–2000

CONTENTS

Preface   *xiii*

Acknowledgments   *xv*

HOW TO USE THIS BOOK   1

Definitions   1

The Organization   2

International Codes   3

Accessibility Regulations   4

Getting Started   4

Minimum Requirements   5

1 ABOUT THE CODES   7

A Brief History   7

Code Publications   8

    Building Codes   9

    Plumbing Codes   13

    Mechanical Codes   13

    Life Safety Code®   14

    Electrical Code   15

    Residential Code   15

Federal Regulations   16

    Americans with Disabilities Act   17

    Fair Housing Act   18

    Occupational Safety and Health Act   19

Standards Organizations   **19**

National Fire Protection Association   20

American National Standards Institute   20

American Society for Testing and Materials   22

American Society of Heating, Refrigeration, and Air-Conditioning Engineers   22

Underwriters Laboratories   22

Local Codes   **24**

Interior Codes Checklist   **24**

2   OCCUPANCY CLASSIFICATIONS AND LOADS   27

Definitions   **27**

Occupancy Classifications   **28**

Determining Classifications   29

List of Occupancies   31

Comparing the Codes   41

New Versus Existing   41

Mixed Occupancies   44

ADA Regulations   45

Occupant Loads   **48**

The Table   48

The Formula   50

Example   51

Mixed Uses or Occupancies   52

Multiple Uses or Occupancies   52

Fixed Seats   52

Means of Egress   53

Checklist   **54**

3   CONSTRUCTION TYPES AND BUILDING SIZES   57

Definitions   **58**

Construction Types   **58**

The Table   59

Comparing the Codes   61

Combustible Versus Noncombustible   63

Using the Table   64

Example   65

Mixed Construction Types   67

Occupancy Requirements   67

Building Height and Area 68
   The Table 68
   Example 70
   Height and Area Limitations 71

4 MEANS OF EGRESS 75

Definitions 76

Comparing the Codes 77

Types of Means of Egress 78
   Exit Accesses 81
   Exits 91
   Exit Discharges 95

Means of Egress Capacity 96
   Number of Exits 97
   Exit Widths 100
   Arrangement of Exits 106
   Travel Distance 108
   Dead End Corridors 111
   Common Path of Travel 114

Signage 114

Exit Lighting 115

Checklist 115

5 FIRE RESISTANT MATERIALS AND ASSEMBLIES 119

Definitions 121

Comparing the Codes 122

Fire Barriers 124
   Fire Walls 126
   Occupancy Separation Walls 127
   Tenant Separation Walls 128
   Corridor Walls 128
   Horizontal Exits 128
   Vertical Shaft Enclosures 128
   Room Separation 130
   Floor and Ceiling Asemblies 130

Smoke Barriers 132
   Wall Assemblies 132
   Vertical Shafts 133
   Vestibules 133

Opening Protectives 134
Fire Doors 134
Fire Windows 138
Rated Glazing 139

Through-Penetration Protectives 140
Firestops 141
Draftstops 142
Damper Systems 142

Test Ratings 144

Using Rated Materials 146

Checklist 149

6 FIRE PROTECTION SYSTEMS 153
Definitions 153
Comparing the Codes 154
Detection Systems 155
Smoke Detectors 157
Fire Alarms 158
Audio Systems 159
Accessible Warning Systems 159

Suppression Systems 159
Fire Extinguishers 160
Standpipes and Fire Hoses 160
Sprinkler Systems 163

Checklist 167

7 PLUMBING AND MECHANICAL REQUIREMENTS 171
Plumbing Requirements 172
Definitions 173
Quantity of Plumbing Fixtures 174
Types of Plumbing Fixtures 179
Toilet Facilities and Restrooms 182

Mechanical Requirements 186
Definitions 186
Code Considerations 187

Checklist 191

8 ELECTRICAL AND COMMUNICATION REQUIREMENTS — 195

Definitions — 196

Electrical Requirements — 198

    Electrical Panels/Rooms — 198
    Electrical Wiring and Conduit — 198
    Circuitry — 201
    Electrical Boxes — 201
    Junction Boxes — 203
    Grounding and GFIs — 204
    Light Fixtures — 204
    Emergency Electrical Systems — 205
    Standby Power Systems — 207

Communication Requirements — 207

    Communication Rooms — 208
    Low Voltage Wiring — 209
    Voice/Data Outlets — 211
    Security Systems — 211

Checklist — 214

9 FINISH AND FURNITURE SELECTION — 217

Definitions — 218

Types of Finishes and Furnishings — 219

Comparing the Codes — 220

Standards and Testing — 221

    Steiner Tunnel Test — 222
    Radiant Panel Test — 224
    Pill Test — 225
    Vertical Flame Test — 225
    Corner Test — 225
    Smolder Resistance Test — 226
    Smoke Density Test — 227
    Toxicity Test — 227
    Upholstered Seating Test — 228
    Mattresses — 229

Using the Codes — 230

    The Table — 230
    Example — 232

Obtaining Test Results — 235

    Pretested Finishes — 235
    Nontested Finishes — 238

Finishes Versus Furniture   239
Accessibility Regulations   242
Other Restrictions   243
Checklist   245

10 CODE OFFICIALS AND THE CODE PROCESS   249

The Code Officials   250
Code Enforcement   252
The Code Process   253
Initial Project Research   253
Preliminary Review   255
Appeals Process   256
Permit Process   257
Inspection Process   259
Certificate of Occupancy   261
Temporary Certificate of Occupancy   262
Certificate of Completion   262
Documentation and Liability   262
Construction Documents   265
Future Technology   266

Appendix A FAMILY RESIDENCES   269

Appendix B EXISTING AND HISTORIC BUILDINGS   275

Appendix C ABBREVIATIONS   279

Appendix D CODE RESOURCES   289

Appendix E ABOUT THE ADA   297

Bibliography by Topic   303
Glossary   309
Index   323

PREFACE

I am pleased to have Katherine Kennon as a co-author for this second edition. Not only is she knowledgeable about codes, as a design professional, but she also uses this book to teach college courses on interior design. Her experience has added a new dimension to the book.

Together we are proud of the design schools throughout the country. They have come a long way in the education of codes and standards. Six years ago when this book first came out, a class specifically about codes was almost unheard of. Now, colleges and universities everywhere have added courses on fire protection, codes and standards, and accessibility regulations. With the introduction of the international family of codes and the eventual use of one primary set of codes within the United States, it will become even easier for colleges and universities to include codes and standards in their curriculum.

We wrote the book for educators, students, and design and building professionals. We have tried to make the codes user-friendly and to provide a good overall understanding of codes, standards, and federal regulations. An understanding of the basics of the codes makes code research more efficient, which can save both time and money. The book also provides the necessary background required for code research and use. Below is a preview of what the book includes.

◆ Most building code publications incorporate interior, exterior, and structural codes. This book concentrates on codes that affect interior projects. Eliminating the less relevant chapters in each of the code publications cuts down on research time.

✦ Each of the main codes, standards, and federal regulations used in interior projects throughout the country are described. This information will help you determine which of these are required in the design of your project.

✦ The book combines the discussion of codes, standards, and federal regulations to explain when standards must be used in conjunction with the codes. This new edition includes code tables from the newest international codes. It also discusses the most common federal regulations, especially the *Americans with Disabilities Act* (ADA).

✦ Each code topic is presented in a logical order that corresponds to the design process. Each builds on the preceding one, thereby eliminating excessive research and cross-referencing.

✦ Learning the technical jargon of the code publications is a process in itself. This book explains the terms and concepts of the codes, standards, and federal regulations in a simple, organized format. Summary charts and helpful tips are included in each chapter to enhance understanding.

✦ Working with the code officials is an important part of using the codes. This book describes at which points research must be done and when code officials must be consulted.

✦ Summary checklists are included at the end of each chapter, which can be used on your interior projects or as a guideline to create your own checklists.

✦ As a design professional, it is important for you to put together your own code and standards library. This book will provide you with the information and resources to do so.

✦ This book uses real life design examples to explain how specific code and standards apply to a project.

✦ This book addresses a variety of building and project types—large and small. It even includes brief descriptions on residential, historical, and existing buildings.

We hope that this book is helpful to you. . . .

Sharon Koomen Harmon, IIDA

Katherine E. Kennon, AIA

ACKNOWLEDGMENTS

First and foremost we thank our husbands for their patience and constant support. We are grateful to the friends who read the manuscript and offered comments including Katherine Setser, Tim Sadler, and Ann McGauran. Thank you also to Brandy Johnson who helped with the internet research and to Amanda Miller, Executive Editor at John Wiley & Sons, Inc., for the continued support.

We owe a special thanks to our readers who continue to buy and recommend the book and who have gone out of their way to praise the book. Thank you for your comments and suggestions. And finally, thank you to all the various code jurisdictions and design professionals we have had the pleasure to work with through the years. You continue to give us inspiration.

HOW TO USE THIS BOOK

Codes are an essential part of designing building interiors. Whether you are space planning the interior of a new building or making some minor changes in an existing building, codes, standards, and federal regulations must always be taken into consideration. They should become a natural part of every project you design.

The Codes Guidebook for Interiors is designed to help you as the designer. If you are a design professional, such as an architect, interior designer, or an engineer, you must know the code. Most of the code publications deal with an entire building—exterior and interior as well as the structure of the building itself. This book concentrates on the codes that pertain to the interior of a building, helping you to minimize your research time. It will make the many interior codes, standards, and federal regulations user-friendly.

The best time to research codes and use this book is in the early stages of a design project, preferably in the schematic phase while the designs are still preliminary and before construction costs are estimated. This book will assist you in your code research, helping to eliminate costly and time-consuming changes in a project.

Note

This book deals with interior codes only. Unless otherwise noted, it is assumed that the exterior walls, including doors and windows, and the existing shell of the building are either existing or already determined.

DEFINITIONS

Below are some common terms used throughout this book. Additional definitions are provided in the beginning of each chapter and in the Glossary in the back of the book.

Note

All codes can be divided into two types: In the past most codes were considered *prescriptive type* codes. These codes require specific compliance with the code. Today, more *performance type* codes are being developed, which allow more than one solution to achieve the same results.

ACCESSIBLE: Unless otherwise noted, it refers to areas, products, or devices usable by persons with disabilities as required by the codes, the *Americans with Disabilities Act*, and accessibility standards.

CODES DEPARTMENT: A local government agency that enforces the codes within a jurisdiction. Some small jurisdictions may have a codes department that consists of only one person, while some large jurisdictions may consist of many different agencies and departments.

CODE OFFICIAL: Also known as a building official, an employee of a codes department who has the authority to interpret and enforce the codes, standards, and regulations within that jurisdiction. A code official can have a number of different titles, including fire marshal, plans examiner, and building inspector.

JURISDICTION: A determined geographical area that uses the same codes, standards, and regulations. Each jurisdiction passes a law specifying which codes and standards are required and how they will be regulated. A jurisdiction could be as small as a township or as large as an entire state. The jurisdiction of a project is determined by the location of the building.

THE ORGANIZATION

The first chapter gives a brief history of codes and provides some background on each of the main code publications, federal regulations, and standards organizations. New to this chapter is an introduction of the international codes and how they compare to the existing codes. (These new international codes are discussed throughout this revised edition of the book.) Chapter 1 is helpful in determining which publications are required for a project. The last chapter in this book discusses code officials and the code process—how they work and how to work with them.

The remaining chapters have been arranged with each chapter pertaining to a specific group of codes. They have been organized in the order that codes are typically considered during an interior project, beginning in Chapter 2 with the broad topic of occupancy classifications and ending in Chapter 9 with the final stages of finish selection and furniture placement. The fire protection chapter from the first edition has been divided into two separate chapters for better organization of information. Each chapter in the book includes the most current code tables, realistic design examples, summary charts, and helpful project checklists.

Like the code publications, most of the chapters in this book build and add to the preceding ones. For example, occupancy classifications in Chapter 2 are important because many of the other codes are based on the occupancy of a building. Therefore, it is suggested that the first-time user read this book in the order it is written and use it as a guide while referencing the actual codes, standards, and federal publications.

An Index is also provided in the back of the book so you can refer to specific topics of interest. As you become familiar with the codes, use the index and the table of contents to direct you to the section of the book that applies to your code situation. Then refer to the appropriate code publication to get the specific details.

Appendix A briefly discusses codes relating to the interior of private residences, referred to by the codes as "one- and two-family dwellings." Compared to the number of codes for commercial and public buildings, there are relatively few interior regulations for private residences. Since they have their own code publication, they have been addressed separately.

The interiors of existing and historical buildings are also discussed separately. Appendix B briefly describes these additional codes and regulations. Special consideration must be given to historical buildings, since they usually have additional regulations on a local level within the code jurisdiction or within the township of the building.

In this edition of the book, Appendix E has been replaced with a section on the *Americans with Disabilities Act (ADA)*. (See Accessibility Regulations on the following page.)

The last two appendixes are for your reference. Appendix C lists the many abbreviations or acronyms used throughout this book and the code publications. We have added web site addresses wherever they were available. Appendix D provides the addresses, phone numbers, and web sites of many code, federal, standards, and national organizations, as well as many bookstores throughout the country, so you can obtain your own code books and other reference material. The Bibliography in the back of this book has been organized by topic to help you start or add to your own personal reference library.

INTERNATIONAL CODES

Since the first publication of this book, the three main code organizations in the United States came together to create the first comprehensive set of codes that can be used anywhere in the

Note

When using the code tables, be sure to check all footnotes. The footnotes often specify extra conditions that can apply to your project.

Note

Many jurisdictions are already considering adopting the *International Building Code.* The first official adoption took place in May of 2000.

country. Known as the international codes, they are currently being published for the first time. As they gain popularity and as they are adopted by the various jurisdictions, the goal is for the existing regional model codes to be phased out. At this point in time, however, a code jurisdiction could be using any one of the available codes.

This edition of *The Codes Guidebook for Interiors* includes descriptions and code tables from the code publications of all four of the existing code organizations. (See Chapter 1.) If you are working in more than one code jurisdiction, it is important for you to know the differences.

ACCESSIBILITY REGULATIONS

Note

Accessibility regulations should not be used as an afterthought to comply with the laws, but rather as codes that are incorporated into your design from the initial concept.

In the past, accessibility standards were not always required in every jurisdiction. Some jurisdictions had created their own accessibility standards, while other jurisdictions used existing industry standards such as *ANSI A117.1*. But, with the passing of the *Americans with Disabilities Act (ADA)* as a federal law, accessible design is required for the majority of interior projects. (See Chapter 1.) Therefore, accessibility standards and the *ADA* are discussed throughout this book. For example, accessible toilet facilities are discussed in the plumbing chapter and accessible ramps are discussed in the means of egress chapter. To elaborate on compliance and enforcement issues of the *ADA* and the *ADA Accessibility Guidelines (ADAAG)*, Appendix E was added.

Like the codes discussed in this book, not every specific accessibility dimension and requirement has been mentioned. Instead, a general outline of the applicable accessibility regulations is discussed to aid you in your research. For the specific requirements and other additional information you must consult the *ADA* documents, the *ADA Accessibility Guidelines (ADAAG)*, specific chapters within the building codes, and any other accessibility regulations required by your jurisdiction.

GETTING STARTED

This book should be used as a guide to assist you in researching the codes and help you organize your projects. It is not a substitute or replacement for the actual code publications. It would be impossible to discuss all the specific codes, standards, and regulations in one book. In addition, each jurisdiction will have slightly different requirements. Therefore, this book must be used in conjunction with the code publications. You must still carry out a thorough investigation of the codes and standards and work closely with code officials, engineers, and other professionals as required by the scope of your project.

Before beginning a project you need to know which code publications must be referenced. Use Chapter 1 to help you get started. Determine which codes, standards, and regulations are required by contacting the codes department in the jurisdiction of your project. Ask the codes department to verify the publications that must be referenced and notify you of any required local codes. It is important for you to have the actual publications on hand during the project so specific codes can be referenced and verified.

Note

This book is not intended to be a substitute for any code, standard, or federal publication required by a jurisdiction. It should be used as a reference book to gain a better understanding of the codes and to guide you through the code process.

MINIMUM REQUIREMENTS

Always remember that codes, standards, and federal regulations have been developed as *minimum* requirements. There may be equivalent solutions, and there are often superior alternatives and solutions available. When designing a space, it is up to you to consider the project as a whole. By working with your client, the building requirements, and the budget of the project, you can make intelligent design decisions. Through the creative thinking process and working in conjunction with the code officials and other professionals, as the designer, you can develop the best design solutions for everyone.

Note

Rather than viewing codes as restrictive or as a burden, think of them as a way to help people reach their potential and keep them safe.

CHAPTER 1

ABOUT THE CODES

Codes are not the only requirements that regulate buildings and building interiors. A large number of standards and federal regulations play a major role as well. The most nationally recognized codes, laws, and standard organizations are described in this chapter. They are referenced and discussed throughout this book as they pertain to the interior of a building.

As you read about each of these codes, standards, and regulations, keep in mind that *not all of them will be enforced by every code jurisdiction.* (See Definitions in Introduction.) For example, *NFPA 101* can be used in conjunction with a building code, alone, or not at all. In addition, the code publication being used may not be the most current edition. Plus, each jurisdiction can make a variety of amendments that add to and/or delete clauses from the code. Each code publication also references certain standards. Other standards are widely used throughout the country or within an industry. However, not all standards are accepted by every jurisdiction. The only regulations that are consistent in every jurisdiction are the federal regulations that are made mandatory by law.

> **Note**
>
> **The newly published international codes and how they relate to the model codes are discussed in this chapter and throughout the book.**

A BRIEF HISTORY

The use of regulatory codes can be traced back as early as the 18th century BCE to the *Code of Hammurabi*, a collection of laws governing Babylonia. The *Code of Hammurabi* made the builder accountable for the houses he built. If one of his buildings fell down and killed someone, the builder would be put to death.

In the United States, the first codes addressed fire prevention. The first building law on record was in 1625 in what was then called New Amsterdam (now New York). It governed the types and locations of roof coverings to protect the buildings from chimney sparks. Then, in the 1800s, there were a number of large building fires, including the Chicago fire of 1871, which caused many fatalities. As a result, some of the larger U.S. cities developed their own municipal building *codes*. Many of these are still in existence today. In the mid 1800s, the National Board of Fire Underwriters was set up to provide insurance companies with information on which to base their fire damage claims. One of the results was the publication of the 1905 *National Building Code*—a code that helped spark the three model building codes in existence today.

Meanwhile, the federal government was also creating *regulations*. Many of these laws pertained to government-built and -owned buildings. Some were national laws that superseded other required codes. In 1973, in an attempt to control government intervention, Congress passed the *Consumer Product Safety Act* and formed the Consumer Product Safety Commission (CPSC). The goal of the commission is to prevent the necessity of federal regulations by encouraging industry self-regulation and *standardization*. This resulted in the creation of a number of new standards-writing organizations and trade associations.

Today, there are hundreds of separate codes in existence in the United States, a wide variety of federal regulations, and hundreds of standards organizations and regulatory and trade associations found in almost every industry. Only the most widely recognized have been described below. They will provide you with the groundwork as they are discussed throughout this book. (For more information refer to the resources in the Bibliography.)

Note

For a comprehensive list of the code organizations, federal agencies, standard organizations, and trade associations see Appendix C and Appendix D.

CODE PUBLICATIONS

Codes are a collection of regulations, ordinances, and other statutory requirements put together by various organizations. Each jurisdiction decides which codes it will follow and enforce. Once certain codes are adopted they become law within that jurisdiction. Most are commonly enforced on a local level. This allows the local municipalities to customize the code by amending certain sections of it. (See section on Code Enforcement, page 252.)

However, not every jurisdiction requires updating the codes on a regular basis. If a jurisdiction adopts a specific publication, it may not be enforcing the most recent edition. This is especially

CODE CHANGES

Each code and standards organization has its own procedure for changing the requirements in its publications. Each organization has a membership made up of a wide range of individuals. These members can typically propose changes in writing or in person at open public hearings. Some organizations allow nonmembers to propose changes as well.

These proposed changes are usually organized and reviewed by a committee. Some organizations allow the committee to make the approval or disapproval decisions, but most of the organizations hold open hearings where the proposals are voted on. Once a proposed code or standard change has passed the approval process, it is adopted by the organization. Usually once a year, or as needed, the organization will publish the most current changes in an addendum. When the next full edition of the code or standard publication is published, it incorporates all the changes into one text.

true with many of the smaller jurisdictions. As a result some states have issued a statewide code, usually based on one of the existing codes. This eliminates the discrepancies and creates uniform policies in each code jurisdiction throughout the state. It is important to check with the jurisdiction of your project to determine which codes you must follow. Some of the most common types of codes, as they pertain to interior projects, are discussed below.

Building Codes

Building codes stress the construction requirements of an entire building and place restrictions on hazardous materials or equipment used within a building. The principal purpose is to ensure public health and safety throughout a building. In the past, the three *"model"* building codes were the most common building codes used throughout the country. They are the *BOCA National Building Code (NBC)* published by the Building Officials Code Administrators International (BOCA), the *Standard Building Code (SBC)* published by the Southern Building Code Congress International (SBCCI), and the *Uniform Building Code (UBC)* published by the International Conference of Building Officials (ICBO). Typically, each state or jurisdiction either adopts one of these three model building codes or is covered by a state building code based on one of the model codes. (See Figure 1.1.) However, this is beginning to change.

In December of 1994, the International Code Council (ICC) was established. It consists of members from each of the three model building code councils—BOCA, SBCCI, and ICBO. They

Note

As of the year 2000, the model code organizations will no longer publish their separate code publications. Only the *IBC* will continue to be updated.

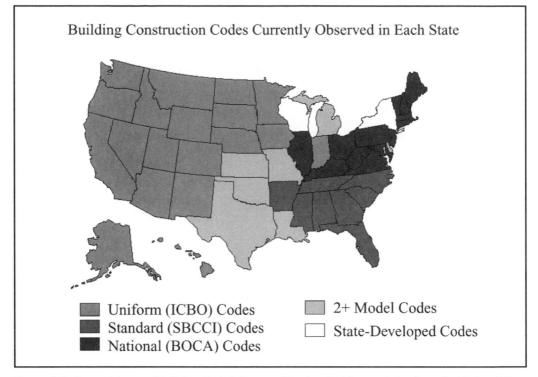

Figure 1.1. General Areas of Building Code Influence. (Reprinted with permission from the National Conference of States on Building Codes and Standards, 1999.)

joined together to develop a single set of code publications known as the "international" family of codes, which addresses the issues covered by the three individual model codes. The first *International Building Code (IBC)* was published in 2000. The *IBC* will be updated every three years and is eventually intended to replace the three separate model building codes.

New editions of the model building codes were published every three years as well. However, with the introduction of the *IBC*, the individual model codes will no longer be developed. The *NBC, SBC,* and the *UBC* will not be published past their 1999 editions and updates and will eventually be phased out. (1997 was the final edition of the *UBC*.) Yet, with the initial publication of the *IBC* in 2000, jurisdictions may not immediately choose to designate the *IBC* as their regulatory document. Some may choose to continue to use the building code that they have been using or update to a more current edition. Therefore, the existing model building codes will continue to be used. It is essential at the start of any project to determine which code and which edition of the code is being enforced in the jurisdiction of your project.

Although the building codes are very similar and cover most of the same issues, especially as they relate to the interior of a building, there are differences. Each region of the country has different climates and environmental issues to consider and needs specific code requirements. For example, California and its surrounding states need more restrictive seismic building code provisions to allow for the many earthquakes in that area, and the Northern states need codes to allow for long periods of below freezing temperatures. These regional differences affect which of the model building codes each jurisdiction chooses to enforce. Areas that have multiple characteristics may enforce more than one model code, make amendments to address additional issues, or develop their own state code based on one of the model codes. On the other hand, the new *IBC* has incorporated these regional differences into one building code. Until the *IBC* is enforced more consistently, designers who work on projects in various regions of the United States, must be familiar with multiple regulations for similar issues. It is important to know the specifics in each code.

Even though the requirements of the codes may vary, the organization of information is consistent throughout the building codes, including the *IBC*. This organization is called the CABO Common Code Format. Since 1994, chapter titles, general chapter contents, and the sequence of chapters are the same in each publication. Specific chapters pertain to the interior of a building. These have been listed below and are discussed throughout this book. Although certain projects may require referring to other sections of the building code, you should become the most familiar with these.

Use or Occupancy Classification
Special Use or Occupancy Requirements
Types of Construction
Fire Resistant Materials and Construction
Interior Finishes
Fire Protection Systems
Means of Egress
Accessibility

Another new development with the introduction of the *IBC* is the use of performance-based codes in addition to the typical prescriptive type codes. Generally, a prescriptive code tells you the precise requirement, such as the height of a handrail; a performance regulation will specify the goal that should be met but not provide a specific description as to how that must be achieved. The existing building codes are primarily prescriptive in the way

Note

With the introduction of the *IBC*, manufacturers are anticipating more affordable product development, since products do not have to meet varying guidelines.

Note

Chapter numbers and table numbers in each model building code were changed when the new *CABO Common Code Format* was incorporated so that each code is similarly organized. Editions published prior to 1994 do not follow this format.

they describe requirements. The new *IBC* is a combination of prescriptive and performance requirements. Allowances for alternative methods and materials are not as specific. The ICC is in the process of developing the *International Performance Code (IPC)* to work in conjunction with the *IBC*. In the future, some jurisdictions will adopt the *IPC* along with the *IBC*.

The purpose of performance codes is to allow for creative design solutions in the use of materials and systems of construction and to allow innovative engineering to solve code requirements in ways that can be specific to each project. In designing to meet the requirements of a performance code, the design solution should be discussed with the building official before construction. For the solution to be acceptable, the building official must agree with you that it meets the intent of the code. Performance codes are intended to allow for creativity in design and engineering while still providing for the necessary safety and welfare concerns of the code. (See inset titled *Using Performance Codes* for additional information.) Performance codes may be applied to any design project if allowed by the code official. However, they may be most effective in unique situations, including the use of new technology and reuse of existing buildings, which may not easily meet the strict requirement of the prescriptive codes.

USING PERFORMANCE CODES

Using performance codes can allow the use of innovative materials and unique design solutions for your project. It is the designer's responsibility to convince your client and the code official that the proposed situations meet the performance requirement of the code. You must take additional steps to prove that your design will provide equivalent safety to the same prescriptive requirements. A few of the steps you may need to take are to

✦ Acquire calculations from an engineer or other consultant
✦ Research the characteristics of a particular material (or assembly)
✦ Work with the manufacturer of a particular product
✦ Develop new research data to support your design solution
✦ Research similar uses or situations
✦ Make your case to the code official

As the performance codes begin to be used more as an alternative to prescriptive requirements, standards may be developed for the process of review. However, since their use is still new, you should work with the code official early in the design process to establish what criteria he or she will require for approval.

To cover as much as possible, the building codes frequently reference other codes and standards within their text. Each code organization publishes a number of other codes that may be referenced. These include a plumbing code, a mechanical code, a fire prevention code, and an existing structures code, some of which are described later in this chapter. In addition, nationally recognized standards organizations and publications are referenced by each of the codes. (See the section on Standards Organizations later in this chapter.)

Plumbing Codes

In the past, each of the three model code organizations had its own plumbing code: the *BOCA National Plumbing Code (NPC)*, the *Standard Plumbing Code (SPC)*, and the *Uniform Plumbing Code (UPC)*. In 1997, the International Code Council (ICC) published the first *International Plumbing Code (IPC)*, which replaced the three model code versions. Like the previous model plumbing codes, it will be revised every three years, with the newest edition being 2000. Most of the chapters in the plumbing code are geared toward an engineer and the professional plumbing contractor. In a project requiring plumbing work, you will often use the services of a licensed engineer to design the system.

The one chapter of the plumbing code considered in this book is the chapter on plumbing fixtures. (See Chapter 7 for more detail.) When designing interior projects, this chapter will be important to help you determine the minimum number and type of fixtures required for a particular occupancy classification.

> **Note**
>
> **The Uniform Plumbing Code (UPC) is actually published by the International Association of Plumbing and Mechanical Officials (IAPMO) and endorsed by ICBO. The Uniform Mechanical Code (UMC) is sponsored jointly by both organizations.**

Mechanical Codes

Similar to the plumbing codes, a mechanical code was originally published by each of the model code organizations and included the *BOCA National Mechanical Code (NMC)*, the *Standard Mechanical Code (SMC)*, and the *Uniform Mechanical Code (UMC)*. The first *International Mechanical Code (IMC)* was published by the International Code Council in 1997. The most current edition is 2000. Although some jurisdictions are still using one of the older model mechanical codes, the *IMC* will eventually replace them as the jurisdictions update their required codes. The mechanical codes are geared toward mechanical engineers and professional installers. Although you will very rarely have to refer to the mechanical codes, on interior projects you should be familiar with some of the general requirements and the terminology. (See Chapter 7 for more detail.)

Life Safety Code®

Note

Each of the model code organizations has its own fire code. They include the *BOCA National Fire Prevention Code,* the *Standard Fire Prevention Code,* and the *Uniform Fire Code Standards.* However, the *LSC* is the most widely known and is the only one discussed in this book.

The *Life Safety Code (LSC)* is one of the main standards published by the National Fire Protection Association (NFPA). It is also referred to as *NFPA 101®.* Like the building codes, the *LSC* is revised every three years. The most recent edition is 2000, yet many jurisdictions are still using the 1997 or 1994 versions. The *LSC* is not a building code. It is a life safety code that concentrates on problems involving the removal of all persons from a building fire zone. As stated in the *LSC,* the purpose of the code is to "establish minimum requirements that will provide a reasonable degree of safety from fire in buildings and structures." The 2000 edition of the *LSC* also includes alternative performance-based options to choose from, giving you the ability to select the requirements that best suit your project. (See inset titled *Using Performance Codes,* earlier in this chapter.) Like other codes, the *LSC* also references additional standard publications within its text. These are typically other NFPA standards, such as *NFPA 80: Standard for Fire Doors and Windows* and *NFPA 220: Standard on Types of Building Construction.* (See the section on the NFPA later in this chapter.)

The first part of the *LSC* concentrates on the broad topics of occupancies, means of egress, and fire protection. The remainder is divided into chapters by occupancy classification for both new and existing buildings. This distinction is made to provide older buildings with additional safety and protective devices so they are virtually as safe as newly constructed buildings. Once you know the occupancy classification of your project, most of your research will be limited to one section of the *LSC.* The requirements in the *LSC* are similar in scope to the requirements in the Means of Egress chapters in the building codes. If a jurisdiction requires the *LSC* in addition to a building code, you must satisfy both sets of requirements in your design. (See Chapter 4 for more detail.)

The *LSC* is the most widely used fire code. It is used throughout most of the United States and in several other countries. Yet, there are several states and cities in the United States that have established even stricter fire codes, often as a result of fatal fires. These include

Boston
California
Massachusetts
New Jersey
New York City
New York State

Life Safety Code® and *101®* are registered trademarks of the National Fire Protection Association, Inc., Quincy, MA 02269.

Boston, for example, has established the Boston Fire Code, and New York and New Jersey must comply with the standards set by the Port Authority. If you are working on a project in one of these jurisdictions, you should research the overlapping restrictions. Other cities or states may follow with similar fire codes in the future. The information in this book mentions some but not all of these special codes. Be sure to check the code jurisdiction of your project.

Electrical Code

The *National Electrical Code (NEC)* is published by NFPA and 1999 is the most current edition. Also known as *NFPA 70*, the *NEC* is the most used electrical code published, and is the basis for electrical codes in almost all code jurisdictions. Even the International Code Council (ICC) references the *NEC*. In 2000, the ICC published the *ICC Electrical Code—Administrative Provisions (IEC)*. Rather than creating a new electrical code, the *IEC* outlines the provisions required for the enforcement of the *NEC*, similar to the other international family of codes.

You will rarely, if ever, refer to the electrical code, since it is the responsibility of an engineer to design electrical systems. On the other hand, for an interior project you will typically specify the location of electrical outlets and fixtures. Therefore, it is important have a basic understanding of this code. The most common requirements are explained in Chapter 8.

Residential Code

The *International One and Two Family Dwelling Code (IOTFDC)* formerly known as the *One and Two Family Dwelling Code (OTFDC)* is the main code used for the construction of single and duplex family residences. (It is briefly discussed in Appendix A.) The most current *IOTFDC* was published in 1998. As the *OTFDC*, it was developed by the Council of American Building Officials (CABO), which is a national organization created by the three model code organizations. But in 1996 the development of the residential code was transferred to the ICC. The newest edition of the code is 2000 and has been renamed the *International Residential Code (IRC)*.

Other publications and programs supported by CABO have been transferred to the ICC, including the *Model Energy Code (MEC)*. The ICC is also assisting with the development of future editions of ANSI A117.1, as discussed later in this chapter. In the past, CABO was responsible for establishing the National Evaluation

Note

The *One and Two Family Dwelling Code* is now called the *International Residential Code* and is published by the ICC.

NATIONAL EVALUATION SERVICE

The National Evaluation Service (NES) is a program originally developed by CABO to evaluate new materials and methods of construction and testing as they become available. The program allows manufacturers to gain national recognition of a new product if it is reviewed and approved by NES. The NES evaluates the characteristics of the product or system, the installation of the product, and the conditions of its use in the evaluation. Currently, the NES is the only way manufacturers, code officials, and designers can determine whether products comply with the different building codes. Once the international family of codes, including the IBC, are readily enforced, this process may become easier.

Service (see inset above) and creating the CABO Common Code Format now used by the model codes.

FEDERAL REGULATIONS

A number of federal agencies and departments work with trade associations, private companies, and the general public to develop federal laws for building construction. These regulations are published in the *Federal Register (FR)* and the *Code of Federal Regulations (CFR)*. The *FR* is published daily and includes the newest updates for each federal agency. However, not all rules published in the *FR* are enforceable laws. Typically, a federal agency must review the regulations published in the *FR* and make a formal ruling. Once the regulations are passed into law, they are published in the *CFR*. The *CFR* is revised annually to include all permanent agency rules.

Note

When using federal regulations both the *FRI* and the *CFR* should be reviewed to determine the most current requirements.

The federal government plays a part in the building process in a number of ways. First, it regulates the building of its own facilities. These include federal buildings, Veterans Administration (VA) hospitals, and military establishments. Construction of federal buildings is usually not subject to state and local building codes and regulations. Federal buildings have their own criteria, many of which are similar to the model codes. (See inset titled *Accessibility Requirements—ANSI, ADAAG, and UFAS*, on page 18.)

Second, the government can pass federal legislation creating a law that supersedes all other state and local codes and standards. Each is created by a specific federal agency. When passed as a law, the codes and standards become mandatory nationwide. This is typically done to create a uniform level of standard throughout the country. The *ADA* is one example. Although there is a wide variety of legislation covering everything from energy to transportation, only a few laws that pertain to the design of interiors are discussed below.

Americans with Disabilities Act

The *Americans with Disabilities Act (ADA)* is a four-part federal legislation that became law on 26 July, 1990 and became enforceable in 1992 and 1993. Prior to this, only federal buildings and federally funded projects had to comply with similar legislation under the *Uniform Federal Accessibility Standards (UFAS)*. Because of this legislation, many other types of projects are required to meet accessibility guidelines as outlined through the various titles of the law.

The *ADA* is a comprehensive civil rights law that protects individuals with disabilities in the area of employment (Title I), state and local government services and public transportation (Title II), public accommodations and commercial facilities (Title III), and telecommunication services (Title IV). The *ADA* was developed by the Department of Justice (DOJ) and the Department of Transportation (DOT).

The regulations that will apply most often to interior projects are found in Title III and Title IV. Title IV requires telephone companies to provide telecommunication relay services for the hearing and speech impaired. When you specify a public phone you must be familiar with the requirements. (See inset titled *Public Telephones* on page 211 in Chapter 8.)

Title III covers all public accommodations (any facility that offers food, merchandise, or services to the public) and commercial facilities (nonresidential buildings that do business but are not open to the general public). Title III's regulations have been incorporated into the *Americans with Disabilities Act Accessibility Guidelines (ADAAG)* as developed by the Architectural and Transportation Barriers Compliance Board (ATBCB or Access Board) and first published in 1991. The *ADAAG* deals with architectural concerns, such as accessible routes and restrooms, and communication concerns, such as visible alarm systems and signage. It is the *ADAAG* that is addressed throughout this book. (Other aspects of *ADA*, such as the varying levels of compliance and responsibility for compliance, are discussed further in Appendix E.)

Although *ADA* regulations are mandatory, they may not be the only guidelines for accessibility issues that you follow. Each of the building codes now references the ANSI standard. Depending on the edition, it could be referencing the 1992 or the 1998 *ANSI 117.1*, which are in some cases stricter that the *ADAAG*. Some states,

Note

The Access Board continues to initiate research and is responsible for updating and adding to the *ADAAG* when necessary. They also offer an 800 number, a web site (see Appendix D), and a variety of publications for guidance.

Note

The Appendix of the *ADAAG* provides additional guidelines that enhance and clarify the main text. Although they are helpful, they are not binding. The *ADAAG* text is law. The Appendix is not.

such as California and North Carolina, have also adopted their own accessibility requirements as well. You must research and follow the most stringent requirements for that jurisdiction while maintaining the minimum *ADAAG* requirements.

Fair Housing Act

The *Fair Housing Act (FHA)* is federal legislation enforced by the Department of Housing and Urban Development (HUD). Originally established in 1968, the *FHA* regulates fair housing and protects the consumer from discrimination in housing when buying or renting. In 1988, the *FHA* was expanded to include persons with disabilities. The *FHA* prohibits discrimination because of race, color, national origin, religion, sex, family status, or disability. The *FHA* regulations may apply to private housing, private housing that receives federal financial assistance, and state and local governmental housing.

Although the *FHA* is not specifically accessibility legislation, it does incorporate a number of provisions for people with disabil-

---

ACCESSIBILITY REQUIREMENTS—ANSI, ADAAG, AND UFAS

There are three accessibility documents that are used most frequently for interior projects. Although in many ways they are similar, none of them match exactly. It is important to know which document applies to your project.

ANSI A117.1 is developed by the American National Standard Institute (ANSI). It was one of the first accessibility guidelines used throughout the United States. It has served as the basis for other accessibility documents as well. The most current edition of the *ANSI A117.1/ICC* is the 1998 edition, which was developed in conjunction with the International Code Council and the Access Board. This edition has been changed to be more consistent with the *ADAAG* guidelines.

The Americans with Disabilities Act Accessibility Guidelines (ADAAG) was developed by the Architectural and Transportation Barriers Compliance Board (ATBCB or Access Board) as guidelines for the *ADA* legislation. It was based on 1986 *ANSI A117.1*, but added requirements that make it more strict than ANSI. The Access Board and the DOJ are currently working on updating the *ADAAG*.

The *Uniform Federal Accessibility Standards (UFAS)* applies mostly to government buildings and organizations that accept federal funding. These buildings are not currently required to conform to *ADA* regulations. Issued in 1989, the *UFAS* is based on the 1980 ANSI standard.

For most projects both the ANSI standard and the *ADAAG* must be reviewed for the strictest accessibility requirement. Remember, there may be additional and/or conflicting state or local accessibility codes that also need to be considered.

ities and families with children. It typically pertains to housing that has four or more dwelling units. As of March 1991 these buildings must have accessible public and common areas. Many of the interior aspects are regulated as well. These include location of thermostats, electrical outlets, light switches, and maneuvering areas in hallways, bathrooms, and kitchens. In addition, at least the ground floor units must be accessible and meet specific construction requirements.

The *FHA* can be considered the residential version of the *ADA*. (See Appendix E.) Both are based on the 1986 edition of the ANSI standards. However, the *FHA* does not require total compliance to the ANSI standards. It uses ANSI only as a reference.

Occupational Safety and Health Act

The *Occupational Safety and Health Act* is a set of laws passed in 1970 to protect the American employee in the work place. It also set up the Occupational Safety and Health Administration (OSHA) as a branch of the Department of Labor (DOL). OSHA sets new standards on an as-needed basis.

OSHA regulates the design of buildings and interior projects where people are employed. The regulations deal with occupational health and safety and are used in conjunction with codes and other standards. They impose a duty upon employers to furnish a safe place of employment for their employees. For example, electrical codes ensure safe design and building construction. OSHA sets additional regulations to cover those electrical parts that come into contact with the building occupants or employees. The OSHA standards are divided into subparts, each affecting a different part of a project.

OSHA regulations must be strictly observed by contractors and subcontractors. They stress the safe installation of materials and equipment to ensure a safe work environment for both the construction workers and the future occupants of the space. Although OSHA regulations are not covered in this book, as a designer you should be aware that these regulations exist and that they affect construction and installation.

STANDARDS ORGANIZATIONS

A standard is a definition, a recommended practice, a test method, a classification, or a required specification that must be met. Standards are developed by trade associations, government agencies, and standards-writing organizations where members are often

Note

Each of the model codes and the international code has a chapter listing the standards it requires.

Note

There are a number of smaller standards organizations that may be specific to an industry. For example, the Business and Institutional Furniture Manufacturers Association (BIFMA) and the Upholstered Furniture Action Council (UFAC) are two that are specific to the finish and furnishings industry. These and other organizations are listed in Appendix D in the back of this book.

allowed to vote on specific issues. The size of these groups can range from a worldwide organization to a small trade association that develops one or two industry-related standards.

By themselves standards have no legal standing; instead, they are referenced by the codes. The standards become law when the code is accepted by a jurisdiction. A standard can also be adopted individually by state, city, and municipal jurisdictions. When a standard is referenced, the acronym of the standard organization and a standard number is called out. For example, "*ASTM E-152*" is an American Society for Testing and Materials standard known as *E-152*. It is a standard method of fire testing for door assemblies. (The reference may also include the year of the latest revision of the standard.)

The most common standards organizations that pertain to interior projects are described below. Each develops a wide variety of standards. Some may need to be examined in detail prior to designing an interior project. Others may only need mentioning in the specifications of the project.

National Fire Protection Association

Note

The NFPA is sometimes referred to as NFiPA because there is another standards association with the same acronym: the National Forest Products Association, abbreviated as NFoPA. In this book NFPA is used to refer to the National Fire Protection Association.

The National Fire Protection Association (NFPA) was originally founded in 1896 to develop standards for the early use of sprinklers. Today it is one of the largest standards organizations. It develops and publishes approximately 250 different standards. Each document is available from NFPA in book or booklet form.

In addition to the *LSC* and the *NEC* discussed earlier in this chapter, the NFPA develops and publishes a wide variety of other standards for fire protection. NFPA committees establish standards designed to reduce the extent of injury, loss of life, and destruction of property during a fire. Their testing requirements cover everything from textiles to fire fighting equipment and means of egress design.

Note

The NFPA is currently developing a full set of codes, expected to be complete in 2003. In the future, jurisdictions will need to choose whether to enforce the international or the NFPA codes.

Many of these standards are referenced by the *LSC* and the *NEC*. Many are also used by the various code publications. This allows the codes to provide specific instructions without going into great detail. For example, instead of setting specific fire extinguisher requirements, the *Standard Building Code (SBC)* references the *NFPA 10: Portable Fire Extinguishers*. *NFPA 10* then becomes a part of the enforced building code.

American National Standards Institute

The American National Standards Institute publishes the *American National Standard*. Both are generally referred to as ANSI. ANSI

TESTING AGENCIES

Many standards affect the way building materials and other products are made. Manufacturers must know these standards and incorporate them into the manufacturing process. A number of finished building products must pass one or more specific tests before they can be sold and used.

These tests are developed by the standards organizations. Some of the organizations provide testing services, but many of them do not have the facilities. Instead, there are a number of independent testing laboratories and testing agencies throughout the country that are set up to perform these tests. These companies know the standards. A manufacturer will typically send them a finished product, which is then tested and evaluated. (See inset titled *UL Labels* on page 23.)

Tested products are given a permanent label or certificate to prove they pass a required standard. Depending on the test and the specific standard, the manufacturer will either attach a label to the product or keep a certificate on file. As the designer, you should be specifying tested products when required. The only way to know if they are required is to know the codes and standards and consult with local code officials.

is a private corporation that was originally founded in 1918 as the American Engineering Standards Committee. ANSI is a coordinator of voluntary standards development. Instead of developing standards, ANSI generally approves the standards developed by other organizations. It helps to establish priorities and avoid duplications between different standards.

ANSI undertakes the development of a standard only when commissioned by an industry group or government agency. Representing virtually every facet of trade, commerce, organized labor, and the consumer, ANSI's approval procedures ensure a consensus of interests. They are widely accepted on an international level, and local jurisdictions often require compliance with ANSI's standards.

The most common ANSI standard used by designers is *ANSI A117.1.* It concentrates on the accessibility features in the design of buildings and their interiors, allowing people with disabilities to achieve independence. It was the first standard written for accessibility and is the mostly widely known. The 1986 ANSI standard was used as the basis for the *ADAAG.* (See *Accessibility Requirements—ANSI, ADAAG, and UFAS* inset earlier in this chapter.) ANSI's standards are published annually, though the actual text is updated only on an as-needed basis.

The most current full edition of this ANSI standard is 1998 and is titled *ICC/ANSI A117.1: American National Standard/Accessible and Useable Building and Facilities.* It was developed in conjunction

Note

ICBO has developed its own *Book of Standards* for use in jurisdictions that have adopted the *UBC.* Many of these *UBC* standards and tests are similar to those of other standards organizations such as NFPA, ASTM, and the Underwriters Laboratories (UL).

Note

Each of the more current model and international building codes has a chapter dedicated to accessibility regulations. Basically they reiterate some of the ANSI standards. All four codes have adopted the ANSI standards and reference them for further information.

with the ICC and the Access Board. It has been revised to be more consistent with the requirements of the *ADAAG.*

American Society for Testing and Materials

The American Society for Testing and Materials (ASTM) is a standards-writing organization formed in 1898 as a nonprofit corporation. It does not perform testing or certify products. Instead, ASTM manages the development of standards and the promotion of related technical knowledge received from over 35,000 members around the world.

More than 10,000 ASTM standards are updated and/or published each year in the 72 volumes of the *ASTM Annual Book of Standards.* They are used to specify materials, assure quality, integrate production processes, promote trade, and enhance safety. Many are referenced in the codes and other reference materials. ASTM also publishes a special grouping of standards for the building construction industry.

American Society of Heating, Refrigeration, and Air-Conditioning Engineers

The American Society of Heating, Refrigeration, and Air-Conditioning Engineers (ASHRAE) came into existence in 1959 with the merger of two engineering groups. ASHRAE is a worldwide standards organization. It sponsors research projects and develops standards for performance levels of HVAC (heating, ventilating, and air conditioning) and refrigeration systems. ASHRAE standards include uniform testing methods, design requirements, and recommended standard practices. ASHRAE also distributes technological information to the public.

As a designer you will generally not refer to ASHRAE standards. They are typically used by mechanical engineers and refrigerant specialists and installers. One of ASHRAE's most widely used standards is *90A: Energy Conservation in New Building Design.* It is the basis for most of the energy building code provisions in the United States.

Underwriters Laboratories

Underwriters Laboratories (UL) is primarily a testing agency that approves products. It has a number of testing laboratories around the world. It tests various devices, systems, and materials to see if they meet specific requirements and to determine their relation to life, fire, casualty hazards, and crime prevention.

UL develops and performs tests in conjunction with other standards organizations. When testing new products, if a standard exists UL will use it. If no standard exists, UL will use its own existing standard or create a new one. All of the approximately 750 different UL safety standards are published in the UL *Catalog of Standards.*

UL's findings are recognized worldwide. When a product is approved it receives a permanent label or classification marking that identifies Underwriter Laboratories, the word "classified," a class rating, and a UL control number. (See example in Chapter 5, Figure 5.13, page 146.) UL also lists all approved products and assemblies in a number of product directories. The directories most likely to pertain to interior projects include *Building Materials, Fire Protection Equipment,* and *Fire Resistance.*

UL LABELS

Underwriters Laboratories (UL) tests a wide variety of products all over the world. The UL label is the most widely recognized mark of compliance with safety requirements. These safety requirements are based on UL standards as well as standards from other organizations. Most federal, state, and municipal authorities, as well as architects, designers, contractors, and building owners and users, accept and recognize the UL mark.

UL can test whole products, components, materials, and systems, depending on the standard required. The products tested include building materials, upholstered furniture, electrical products, HVAC equipment, fire fighting equipment, safety devices, and more. Once the initial product passes a test, it is retested at random to make sure it continues to function properly.

There are four types of labels or UL marks a product can receive. The UL brochure *Testing for Public Safety* (1992) describes them as follows:

LISTED MARK: The most popular, it indicates samples of the product have been tested and evaluated and comply with UL requirements. This mark generally includes the UL registered name or symbol, the product name, a control number, and the word "listed."

CLASSIFIED MARK: This label may list a product's properties, limited hazards, suitability for certain uses, and/or possible international standards. The label includes the UL name or symbol and a statement indicating the extent of the UL evaluation.

RECOGNIZED MARK: This covers the evaluation of a component only. The component is later factory-installed in a complete product or system. The label includes a manufacturer's identification and product model number.

CERTIFICATE: This is used when it is difficult to apply one label to a whole system. The certificate indicates the type of system and the extent of the evaluation. It accompanies the product and is issued to the end user upon installation.

Note

In addition to the standards organizations discussed in this chapter, there are two *national* organizations that can provide valuable information. Although they do not create codes or standards, they play a major role in supporting them. These organizations are the National Conference of States on Building Codes and Standards (NCSBCS) and the National Institute of Business Sciences (NIBS). Both supply a wide variety of helpful publications. (See Appendix D.)

LOCAL CODES

In addition to the codes, standards, and regulations mentioned above, there are also more specific codes within each jurisdiction. They can include, but are not limited to, local municipal ordinances, health codes, zoning regulations, historic preservation laws, and neighborhood conservation restrictions. For example, health codes must typically be followed when working on projects that involve food preparation, such as restaurants. In addition, other occupancies (i.e., hospitals) have regulations that must be incorporated into the design in order for the facility to obtain a license to operate. These regulations can control the size, location, and use of a building and are usually set and controlled at a local level.

This book does not cover these local codes, since they are specific to each jurisdiction. However, it is important to consult the jurisdiction of a project for these specific regulations so they can be appropriately researched and referenced.

INTERIOR CODES CHECKLIST

When working on a new project it can be difficult to remember all the applicable code sources that must be referenced. Depending on the type of interior project and the jurisdiction in which it is located, you could be using any number of the codes, regulations, and standards described in this chapter. Figure 1.2 is a checklist that provides a comprehensive list of these codes. Use this list, or develop your own, to be sure you reference the necessary codes and regulations.

Before starting an interior project refer to this checklist to determine which code publications must be referenced for your project. If you are uncertain, consult the code officials in the jurisdiction of the project. Check off the publications you will need in the "Required" column and enter the edition or year of the required publication in the next column. Remember that not every jurisdiction uses the most current edition of a code, and that a jurisdiction may have made amendments to an existing publication.

Do this for each code, regulation, and standard. A reminder for engineering involvement is given under each of the code headings. Blank spaces have been provided for specific state or local codes that must be consulted. Blank spaces have also been provided for you to fill in the specific standards to be used.

As you work on the project, continue to refer to the list to make sure each of the checked codes is being used. As the research

INTERIOR CODES CHECKLIST

PROJECT NAME: _____

PUBLICATION	YEAR OF EDITION	YEAR OF AMENDMENT (if required)	RESEARCH DATE
CODES AND REGULATIONS:			
BUILDING CODE - Circle One: NBC SBC UBC IBC OTHER	_____	_____	___/___/___
Structural Engineer Required? _____ YES _____ NO			
PLUMBING CODE - Circle One: NPC SPC UPC IPC OTHER	_____	_____	___/___/___
Plumbing Engineer Required? _____ YES _____ NO			
MECHANICAL CODE - Circle One: NMC SMC UMC IMC OTHER	_____	_____	___/___/___
Mechanical Engineer Required? _____ YES _____ NO			
ELECTRIC CODE - Circle One: NEC(NFPA 70) IEC OTHER	_____	_____	___/___/___
Electrical Engineer Required? _____ YES _____ NO			
LIFE SAFETY CODE (NFPA 101)	_____	_____	___/___/___
RESIDENTIAL CODE - Circle One: OTFDC IOTFDC IRC OTHER	_____	_____	___/___/___
ACCESSIBILITY REGULATIONS/STANDARDS			
Americans with Disability Act Accessibility Guidelines (ADAAG) *	_____	_____	___/___/___
ANSI A117.1 Accessible and Usable Buildings and Facilities	_____	_____	___/___/___
Other: _____	_____	_____	___/___/___
OTHER:** _____	_____	_____	___/___/___
_____	_____	_____	___/___/___
_____	_____	_____	___/___/___
_____	_____	_____	___/___/___
STANDARDS: * **			
NATIONAL FIRE PROTECTION ASSOCIATION (NFPA):			
NFPA ___: _____	_____	_____	___/___/___
NFPA ___: _____	_____	_____	___/___/___
NFPA ___: _____	_____	_____	___/___/___
NFPA ___: _____	_____	_____	___/___/___
AMERCIAN SOCIETY OF TESTING & MATERIALS (ASTM)			
ASTM ___: _____	_____	_____	___/___/___
ASTM ___: _____	_____	_____	___/___/___
UNDERWRITERS LABORATORIES (UL)			
UL ___: _____	_____	_____	___/___/___
UL ___: _____	_____	_____	___/___/___
AMERICAN SOCIETY OF HEATING, REFRIGERATION, AND AIR CONDITIONING ENGINEERS (ASHRAE)	_____	_____	___/___/___
OTHER: _____	_____	_____	___/___/___
_____	_____	_____	___/___/___
_____	_____	_____	___/___/___
_____	_____	_____	___/___/___

*   All projects should be reviewed for ADAAG compatibility with few exceptions (ie: federal buildings).

**   Be sure to check for state and local codes. Local codes can include special ordinances, health codes, zoning regulations, and historic preservation laws. List the specifc ones.

***   Refer to the codes as well as local requirements to determine which standards are required. List the specific publications.

Figure 1.2. Interior Codes Checklist.

is completed for each publication, enter the date in the "Research Date" column. You will find that as you do the code research additional standards may be required. Add these to the checklist in the spaces provided. When the project is complete, keep this form with the project's files for future reference and proof that each of the code sources was reviewed.

Remember, every jurisdiction does not require every code, regulation and standard. Some are nationally accepted and enforced, whereas others are regulated by the state. Still others are required on a local level as municipalities make amendments to the existing codes and create their own requirements. Once codes are accepted on either a federal, state, or local level, they become regulations enforceable by law. You should become familiar with the different code publications and find out from the code officials in the jurisdiction of your project which ones are required.

The specific codes that pertain to a particular project must be followed during both the design and the construction of an interior space. As you use this book and research the codes, remember the following about codes and standards:

1. They set minimum criteria. Stricter requirements can be followed at any time. (Some interior projects may require stricter guidelines to ensure better safety to the occupants of a building.)
2. They are not always perfectly clear. When two requirements are similar, typically the strictest *one* applies. Where codes are vague be sure to do additional research and consult the appropriate code official.
3. Not all of them will apply to every design situation, particularly when you are working in existing conditions. Work with the code official to resolve discrepancies.

When there is a question, it is the code officials in your jurisdiction who will make the final decision. Chapter 10 provides some additional guidance and explains the typical code procedure.

CHAPTER 2

OCCUPANCY CLASSIFICATIONS AND LOADS

The occupancy classification of a building or space is most often determined by how that building or space is to be used. However, the projected occupant load, or expected number of people, can also be an influential factor. Since occupancy classifications and occupant loads are, in a sense, dependent on each other, both should be considered at the beginning of a project. Also, establishing the occupancy classification and the occupancy load is important because these parameters are used to determine a number of other codes requirements. The first part of this chapter concentrates on occupancy classifications; occupancy loads are discussed in the second half of the chapter. A checklist for both is provided at the end.

DEFINITIONS

Before continuing, make sure you are familiar with the following terms. They are used throughout the chapter and this book.

BUILDING TYPE: A specific class or category within an occupancy. For example, a high school is a building type within the Educational occupancy.

OCCUPANT LOAD: The number of people or occupants for which the code will require you to provide means of egress, or exiting, in your design. The occupant load sets the minimum level of exiting that must be provided. See occupant content.

OCCUPANT CONTENT: The actual number of total occupants for which exiting has been provided. This is the maximum number of people that can occupy the space. Some of the building codes use the term "actual number" of occupants instead.

OCCUPANT: The person or people using the space, whether they are tenants, employees, customers, or whatever. For example, the occupants of a travel agency will include the travel agents as well as the clients who come for travel information.

USE GROUP OR TYPE: Depending on the code, use group or type can be defined in a number of ways. It can refer to a whole occupancy classification or it can represent a specific class or category within an occupancy. It can also be more specific; a single building type may have more than one type of use. For example, a library building type may have a stack area use and reading room use.

OCCUPANCY CLASSIFICATIONS

Note

The codes often reference the occupancy classifications by letters or a combination of letters and numbers. For example "A" represents Assembly occupancies and "R-2" represents a Residential occupancy category. (See Figure 2.2.)

For every interior project, an occupancy classification must be assigned to the building or space. Determining the occupancy classification of a building is one of the most important steps in the code process. It should be the first thing you determine when designing the interior of a building, since virtually every interior code and regulation is based on the building's occupancy. The occupancy of a space must be known to effectively use most of the remaining chapters in this book. Figure 2.1 lists the most common code requirements that are affected by an occupancy classification. Once you know the occupancy, it will guide you in your research.

OCCUPANCY LOADS	FIRE SUPPRESSION SYSTEMS
CONSTRUCTION TYPES	FIRE DETECTION SYSTEMS
BUILDING HEIGHTS	SMOKE DETECTION SYSTEMS
BUILDING AREAS	PLUMBING FIXTURES
MEANS OF EGRESS	VENTILATION SYSTEMS
EGRESS CAPACITIES	EMERGENCY LIGHTING
FIRE BARRIERS	FINISH SELECTION

Figure 2.1. Codes Affected by Occupancy.

In new buildings, the occupancy classification may have already been determined. But for a new or existing building that is intended to have different types of tenants, the occupancy classification for each tenant must be determined separately. These different tenants may in turn affect how the shared public spaces are classified. In existing buildings, determining the occupancy classification may be particularly important if the intended use of the building is changing significantly, such as if an old warehouse building is being renovated into apartments. Be sure to consult your code official early in a project whenever there is uncertainty. It is always a good idea to have a code official confirm your choice of occupancy. If you find out later that your choice is incorrect or is not approved by the code official, it could be a costly mistake.

Determining Classifications

Each code publication divides its occupancies into different categories. What they all have in common is that each classification is based on the activities occurring in the space, the associated level of hazards present and the number of people occupying the space at one given time. The 10 most common occupancy classifications used throughout the various building and life safety codes are listed below. Although some of the codes may combine or further divide these categories, they will all be represented.

Assembly occupancies
Business occupancies
Educational occupancies
Factory or Industrial occupancies
Hazardous occupancies
Institutional occupancies
Mercantile occupancies
Residential occupancies
Storage occupancies
Utility and Miscellaneous

Many of these classifications seem self-explanatory, especially if a building type is straightforward, but remember that you need to know two things before you can accurately determine the occupancy classification: (1) the expected number of occupants and (2) if any unusual hazards are present.

These two factors can affect the classification of a building type. Many of the classifications allow for a specific number of people. For example, even though another occupancy may seem

TYPES OF HAZARDS AND OCCUPANCIES

The type of hazards found in a building help to determine its occupancy classification. They can vary dramatically from one building type to the next. Each occupancy was created by the code organizations to handle different types of hazards. Jack Hageman, in his book *Contractor's Guide to the Building Code*, lists some of the most common hazards:

- ✦ Large groups of people
- ✦ Specific building types
- ✦ Night occupancies (where occupants sleep or rest)
- ✦ Spread of fire (due to air currents, dirt and lint, combustible finishes and decorations, and the structure itself)
- ✦ Toxic heat and gases
- ✦ Unprotected openings
- ✦ Lack of adequate separation between areas
- ✦ Exposure to adjacent buildings
- ✦ Height and size of a building

Some of the more current building codes, including the new *International Building Code*, provide lists of low and moderate hazard building types and products. Usually found in the Factory/Industrial or the Storage occupancy classifications, these lists help you to determine when an occupancy is considered hazardous.

more appropriate, if a particular building is planned to serve a large number of people, it may be classified as an Assembly. Unusual hazards can either change an occupancy to a stricter classification or simply require all or part of a building to be classified as a Hazardous occupancy subject to tougher codes.

Some other things to remember when selecting occupancies are the following.

MINOR OCCUPANCIES: When an occupancy classification is a minor part of another predominating occupancy, in most cases the codes will apply to the predominating occupancy. For example, a coffee shop in a book store would be classified as part of a Mercantile occupancy rather than a Business occupancy.

MIXED OCCUPANCIES: Many buildings today have more than one occupancy type under one roof. For example, each tenant may be a different occupancy with each being regulated separately under the corresponding occupancy classification. (See the section on Mixed Occupancies later in this chapter.)

UNUSUAL OCCUPANCIES: If a building type cannot be easily placed into one of the standard occupancies, be sure to consult the code officials in your jurisdiction in the early stages of a project.

You should also remember to reexamine an occupancy classification whenever changes are made to an existing occupancy. Some of these changes are obvious, such as a change in building type. Other changes are less noticeable. An occupancy classification can also change when the number of occupants increases or decreases.

List of Occupancies

Use the list of occupancies below to help you determine the occupancy classification of a building. The requirements of each occupancy are explained, and within each classification is a list of sample building types. A wide range of common building types have been provided to help you get started.

The list is not all-inclusive, and it does not replace the code books. You must refer to the building codes as well. Each code classifies its occupancies a little differently. In addition, an occupancy may be subdivided into smaller, more specific categories. For example, each code divides its Assembly occupancy into different subclassifications. See Figure 2.2 for a comparison of each occupancy in the model building codes, the *International Building Code (IBC)*, and the *Life Safety Code (LSC)*.

Assembly Occupancy: A building or part of a building where a specified number of people gather together for political, social, or religious functions, recreation, entertainment, eating, drinking, or awaiting transportation. In general, it holds a large number of people who are unfamiliar with the space. As the number of people occupying the space increases, the level of hazard is considered to increase. Because of this hazardous situation there are a number of additional codes that apply strictly to Assembly occupancies.

If there are less than the specified number of people in an Assembly occupancy, it may be classified under another more applicable occupancy that requires fewer occupants. Business is a common reclassification for building types such as small college classrooms, small office conference rooms, and small scale restaurants. For example, you may be using the *Standard Building Code (SBC)*, which requires 100 or more people in an Assembly occupancy. If a small lecture hall in a college is built to hold less than 100 people, it can be classified as a Business occupancy instead. (Other codes may use 50 people as the cut off point.) Each building code also has a chapter for special occupancy types that describes in more detail the requirements for unique circumstances such as malls, theaters with stages, and other building types that may seem to fit the Assembly use.

Note

Each code publication has its own minimum number of occupants required in an Assembly occupancy. 50 and 100 people are common denominators. (See Figure 2.2.) Any building type below this minimum number of people will usually be classified under another occupancy.

Sample Building Types

Amusement park buildings	Grandstands
Arenas	Gymnasiums
Armories	Health spas
Art galleries	Indoor skating rinks
Assembly halls	Indoor swimming pools
Auditoriums	Indoor tennis courts
Banquet halls	Lecture halls
Bars, Lounges	Libraries (can also be Business or Educational occupancy)
Bleachers	Locker rooms
Bowling lanes	Mortuary chapels
Churches and religious structures	Motion picture theaters
Club rooms	Museums
College classrooms	Night clubs
Community halls	Passenger stations, terminals, or depots (waiting areas)
Conference rooms	Pool rooms
Convention centers	Public assembly halls
Court rooms	Radio studios with audiences
Dance halls	Recreation halls and piers
Drinking establishments	Restaurants (can also be Business occupancy)
Exhibition halls	Stadiums and grandstands
Fair or carnival structures	Taverns (can also be Business occupancy)
Fellowship halls	Television studios with audiences
Funeral homes	Tents for assembly
Galleries	Theaters for stage production

Note

Depending on which building code you use, a restaurant can be classified as a Business occupancy (if the number of occupants is small enough), an Assembly, or as an incidental use to a larger adjacent occupancy.

Business Occupancy: A building or part of a building used for the transaction of business, such as accounting, record keeping, and other similar functions. It also includes the rendering of professional services. Limited areas that are a natural part of a business setting, such as small storage or supply areas and breakrooms, are included as well.

This classification can become very broad. For example, a smaller Assembly-type occupancy that has fewer number of occupants may be classified as a Business occupancy, such as a small restaurant. Conversely, when the function or size of any of the Business building types expands beyond a typical business, the occupancy needs to be reexamined. Examples might include city halls that include assembly areas or doctor's offices that are a part of a hospital. These types of buildings may be classified as an Assembly occupancy, an Institutional occupancy, or as a mixed occupancy. (See the section on Mixed Occupancies later in this chapter.)

Educational-type occupancies can also be confusing. Colleges and universities (educational facilities after the 12th grade) are considered Business occupancies. Yet, business and vocational schools are often considered as the same occupancy as the trade or vocation that is being taught, unless the occupant load requires it to be considered Assembly. For example, general classrooms for a college would be classified as Business, but the classrooms for instruction for automotive repair may be considered Factory/Industrial.

A good rule of thumb is that whenever a Business occupancy serves 50 or more people, you should research the requirements of an Assembly occupancy.

Sample Building Types

Airport traffic control towers

Animal hospitals, kennels, and pounds (part of building could be considered Storage)

Automobile and other motor vehicle showrooms

Automobile service stations (can also be considered Hazardous)

Banks

Barber shops

Beauty shops

Car washes

City halls

Civic administration buildings

College and university classrooms

Dentist's offices

Doctor's offices

Dry cleaning facilities (can also be considered Hazardous)

Educational facilities (above 12th grade)

Electronic data processing facilities

Fire stations

Florists and nurseries

Government offices

Greenhouses

Laboratories (nonhazardous)

Laundromats

Libraries (can also be considered Assembly or Business)

Medical offices (larger offices may be considered Institutional)

Office buildings

Outpatient clinics, ambulatory

Police stations

Post offices

Print shops

Professional offices

Radio and television stations

Repair garages (small, nonhazardous)

Telecommunication equipment buildings

Telephone exchanges

Travel agencies

> **Note**
>
> **A wide variety of building types can fall under the Business occupancy classification if the number of allowed occupants is small enough.**

Educational Occupancy: A building or part of a building used for educational purposes by a specified number of persons at any one time through the 12th grade. Usually the specified number of persons ranges from six to the minimum number of people required for the Assembly occupancy. (For colleges and universities see Assembly and Business occupancies.)

It is common for an Educational occupancy to be considered a Mixed occupancy due to the auditoriums and gymnasiums usu-

Note

Although it would seem normal for colleges and universities to fall under the Educational occupancy, these building types are typically classified as Business or Assembly occupancies.

ally built with them. In most cases, these additional uses will be classified separately under the Assembly occupancy. Vocational shops, laboratories, and similar areas within a school will usually be considered Educational, even though they may require additional fire protection. As mentioned in a previous section, some codes will require that vocational schools be considered as the trade or vocation being taught. In addition, a length of stay over 24 hours may require the reclassification of an Educational occupancy to Institutional, such as in a day care that provides extended care. You should verify the proper designation with the local code official.

Sample Building Types

Academies	Junior high schools
Day care centers	Kindergartens
Elementary schools	Nursery schools
High schools	Secondary schools

Factory or Industrial Occupancy: A building or part of a building used for assembling, disassembling, fabricating, finishing, manufacturing, packaging, processing, or repairing. It generally refers to a building in which a certain type of product is made. The product that is made or the materials used to make the product can be considered a low or moderate hazard. If it is a more hazardous material or product, the building or space where it is made can be considered a Hazardous occupancy. The sample product types below are typically considered low to moderate types of hazards by the building codes. However, each code groups them a little differently under the Industrial occupancy and there may be different code requirements, depending on which hazardous group it is in. Be sure to refer to the specific code to determine if a manufactured product is considered moderate or low hazard. If more hazardous materials are used or created in the space or building, see the Hazardous occupancy.

Sample Building Types

Assembly plants
Factories
Manufacturing plants
Mills
Processing plants

Low and Moderate Hazardous Products

Aircrafts

Appliances

Athletic equipment

Automobiles and other motor vehicles

Bakeries

Beverages (alcoholic)

Beverages (nonalcoholic)

Bicycles

Boats (building)

Boiler works

Brick and masonry

Brooms or brushes

Business machines

Cameras and photo equipment

Canneries

Canvas or similar fabric

Carpets and rugs, includes cleaning

Ceramic products

Clothing

Condensed powdered milk manufacturing

Construction and agricultural machinery

Creameries

Disinfectants

Dry cleaning and dyeing

Electric light plants and power houses

Electrolytic—reducing works

Electronics

Engines (includes rebuilding)

Film (photographic)

Food processing

Foundries

Furniture

Glass products

Gypsum products

Hemp products

Ice

Jute products

Laboratories (can also be considered Business)

Laundries

Leather products

Machinery

Metal products (fabrication and assembly)

Millwork (sash and door)

Motion pictures and television filming

Musical instruments

Optical goods

Paper mills or products

Plastic products

Printing or publishing

Recreational vehicles

Refineries

Refuse incineration

Sawmills

Shoes

Smoke houses

Soaps and detergents

Sugar refineries

Textiles

Tobacco

Trailers

Upholstering

Water pumping plants

Wood (distillation of)

Woodworking (cabinetry)

Hazardous Occupancy: A building or part of a building that involves the generation, manufacturing, processing, storage, or other use of hazardous materials. These materials can include flammable dust, fibers, or liquids, combustible liquids, poisonous gases, explosive agents, corrosive liquids, oxidizing materials, radioactive materials, and carcinogens, among others. In general, this classification is categorized by an unusually high degree of explosive, fire, physical, and/or health hazards.

Hazardous building types require additional precautions. Each of the code publications sets different standards and has special sections dedicated to hazardous uses, which list very specific materials. In most cases, a Hazardous occupancy can be subclassified into either a low, medium, or high hazard. Each building code categories them a little differently. Often the lower hazards are made part of the Factory/Industrial or Storage occupancy classification. Each code also has a different number of subclassifications. (See Figure 2.2.)

Another factor to consider is the amount of hazardous materials. If the amount of hazardous materials is small enough, the space or building may not be considered Hazardous by the codes. A common example is a chemistry lab in a high school. As more performance-type requirements are introduced into code publications, more emphasis will be placed on the types of products or materials used in a space rather than concentrating on the type of building.

If you are designing the interior of a building that you believe to be hazardous, be sure to consult the specific codes and work closely with the local code officials. Some buildings may require only part of the building to be classified as Hazardous. (Hazardous buildings and materials are beyond the scope of this book.)

Sample Building Types

Airport hangers or airport repair hangers	Paint and solvent manufacturers
Dry cleaning plants	Paint shops and spray painting rooms
Explosives manufacturers	Pesticide warehouses
Film storage, combustible	Power plants
Firearm/ammunition warehouses	Pumping/service stations
Gas plants	Tank farms
Laboratories with hazardous chemicals	Warehouses with hazardous materials

Institutional Occupancy: This broad category is subdivided by some of the codes into Detentional/Correctional facilities and Health Care facilities (otherwise known as restrained care institutions and unrestrained care institutions, respectively). The primary distinction of this classification is that the occupants lack free mobility; they must depend on others to help them evacuate the building in case of an emergency. See the subclassifications below.

DETENTIONAL/CORRECTIONAL OR RESTRAINED: A building or part of a building used to house individuals under varied degrees of

Note

Sometimes two different buildings with the same building type may have different occupancy classifications if hazardous materials are present in one but not the other. For example, some auto repair shops are considered a Hazardous occupancy. Others are considered a Business occupancy.

restraint or security consisting of a specified number of adults or juveniles. The occupants are incapable of self-preservation because security measures are not under the occupants' control.

Sample Building Types

Correctional institutions	Prerelease centers
Detention centers	Prisons
Jails	Reformatories
Penal institutions	Work camps

HEALTH CARE OR UNRESTRAINED: A building or part of a building used for medical, nursing, psychiatric, surgical, or custodial care on a 24-hour basis. Subclassifications may be based on the number of people for whom care is being given. For most codes, care being given to six or more people will require that the building be considered Institutional instead of Educational or Residential. These persons are mostly incapable of self-preservation because of age, physical, or mental disability.

Sample Building Types

Ambulatory health care facilities	Nurseries, full-time care
Board and care facilities	Nursing homes (intermediate care and skilled nursing)
Care institutions for the mentally retarded	Retirement centers
Hospitals	Sanitariums
Infirmaries	Treatment or rehabilitation centers
Limited care facilities	Day cares (on a 24-hour basis)
Mental hospitals	

Note

First introduced in its 1997 edition, the *LSC* now has an occupancy classification specifically for day care facilities.

In addition, certain types of care facilities can be considered a Residential occupancy in most codes if the number of people receiving care is between 5 and 16. The *NFPA 101* determines the difference based on the kind of care being provided, whether medical or personal care. The list below is a sample list of the types of facilities that could be considered Institutional or Residential. You should discuss this with a code official to confirm whether the jurisdiction will consider your facility Institutional or Residential. The requirements can vary significantly.

Alcohol and drug centers	Detoxification facilities
Assisted living facilities	Group homes
Congregate care facilities	Halfway houses
Convalescent facilities	Social rehabilitation facilities

Mercantile Occupancy: A building or part of a building that is open to the public and used for the display, sale, or rental of merchandise. It is not uncommon for a Mercantile occupancy to be considered a minor occupancy where it is subject to the predominant occupancy. For example, a newsstand (which normally would be classified as Mercantile) located in an office building would be classified within the Business occupancy, and a small gift shop in a sports arena would be classified within the Assembly occupancy.

Sample Building Types

Auction rooms	Retail stores
Automotive service stations	Salesrooms
Bakeries	Shopping centers
Department stores	Shops
Drug stores	Show rooms
Grocery stores	Specialty stores
Markets	Supermarkets
Paint stores (without bulk handling)	Wholesale stores (other than warehouses)
Rental stores	

Residential Occupancy: A building or part of a building that acts as a dwelling and provides sleeping accommodations for normal residential purposes. Most of the codes further categorize this classification based on the probable number of occupants and how familiar they are with their surroundings. For example, a person in a hotel would probably not be familiar with the escape routes, making it more hazardous. Such an occupancy will need stricter codes than an apartment complex where a tenant should be more familiar with his/her surroundings. (For other occupancies that provide sleeping accommodations but with additional care, see Institutional occupancy.)

Note that each code has a subclassification specifically for residential buildings that are single or duplex units. (See Figure 2.2.) Although each of the building codes will typically include requirements for these types of buildings, single family residences and duplexes are most often covered in the *International Residential Code (IRC)*, as described in Chapter 1. The *IRC* is a code specifically developed for one- and two-family homes. (See Appendix A for more information.) Verify with your code official which code is applicable to your residential project.

Sample Building Types

Apartments

Boarding houses

Child care facilities (can also be classified as
    Educational or Institutional—unrestrained)

Condominiums

Congregate care facilities (can also be classified
    as Institutional—unrestrained)

Convents

Dormitories

Dwelling units

Fraternities/sororities

Hotels

Inns

Lodging and rooming houses

Monasteries

Motels

Multiple family dwellings

Multiple single family dwellings

One-family dwellings

Rectories and parsonages

Residential care facilities (can also be classified
    as Institutional—unrestrained)

Rooming houses

Townhouses

Two-family dwellings

Storage Occupancy: A building or a predominant part of a building used for storing or sheltering products, merchandise, vehicles,
and animals. Minor storage uses, such as smaller storage rooms
and supply closets, are typically treated as part of the predominant occupancy.

Similar to the Factory/Industrial occupancies, low or moderate hazard contents are typically allowed in the Storage occupancy, while high hazard contents are classified under Hazardous.
The classification depends on the type of hazard and the quantity
being stored. It is important to check the code to determine the
level of hazard of the material being stored. A list of low and moderate hazardous items are listed below, but remember that each
code groups them differently and each level will have slightly different requirements. If you are unsure about the type of hazardous
materials being stored, check with the code official in your jurisdiction.

In addition, within Storage building types it is generally
understood that relatively few people will occupy the space. If the
number of occupants is large or increases substantially in the
future, the building occupancy may need to be reclassified.

Sample Building Types

Aircraft hangers (nonhazardous)

Barns

Creameries

Cold storage facilities

Freight terminals and depots

Grain elevators

Repair garages (nonhazardous)

Stables

Truck and marine terminals

Warehouses (nonhazardous)

Sample Low and Moderate Hazard Storage Contents

Asbestos

Beer or wine up to 12% alcohol in metal, glass, or ceramic containers

Cement in bags

Chalk and crayons

Cold storage

Creameries

Dairy products in non-wax-coated paper containers

Dry cell batteries

Dry insecticides

Electrical coils

Electrical insulation

Electrical motors

Empty cans

Food products

Foods in noncombustible containers

Fresh fruits and vegetables in nonplastic trays or containers

Frozen foods

Glass

Glass bottles, empty or filled with noncombustible liquids

Gypsum board

Inert pigments

Ivory

Meats

Metal cabinets

Metal desks with plastic tops and trim

Metal parts

Metals

Mirrors

New empty cans

Oil-filled and other types of distribution transformers

Open parking structures

Porcelain and pottery

Stoves

Talc and soapstone

Washers and dryers

Utility or Miscellaneous Occupancies: A building or part of a building that is not typical and/or cannot be properly classified in any of the other occupancy groups. Each of the building codes and *LSC* lists different items in this category and they are usually covered in a separate chapter by each of the codes.

If any of the other occupancies are being housed in an unusual structure, additional codes are usually required. The size of the space or building should be a consideration as well. If you are unsure if a building would be considered a utility or miscellaneous occupancy, check with the code official in the building's jurisdiction in the early stages of a project. (Unusual structures are beyond the scope of this book.)

Sample Building Types

Agricultural buildings, including barns, stables, livestock shelters

Carports

Grain silos

Greenhouses

High-rise buildings

Mobile homes

Open structures

Parking garages

Private garages

Retaining walls

Sheds

Tall fences

Tanks

Temporary structures

Towers

Underground structures

Walkways and tunnels, enclosed

Water-surrounded structures

Windowless buildings

Comparing the Codes

As mentioned earlier the *BOCA National Building Code (NBC)*, the *Standard Building Code (SBC)*, the *Uniform Building Code (UBC)*, the *International Building Code (UBC)*, and the *Life Safety Code (LSC)* each classifies its occupancies a little differently. A comparison of each code is provided in Figure 2.2.

Notice that some classifications have more subcategories than others. Like the occupancy classifications, these subclassifications are divided into groups based on the amount of hazard to the occupants. In some cases the hazard is the number of occupants, since the more people there are in a building the more dangerous it can become in an emergency.

Some of the codes have combined the occupancies. For example, the *LSC* has a Health Care and a Correctional/Detentional occupancy, whereas the building codes combine these under the Institutional occupancy with different subclassifications. On the other hand, the *LSC* combines the Hazardous and Industrial occupancies.

It is important to refer to the codes in your jurisdiction to get the exact occupancy classification. Each code also has its own set of special requirements or restrictions for each occupancy classification. Therefore, once you know the occupancy of your project, pay particular attention to special occupancy requirements throughout the codes as you continue your research. Be sure to refer to the *ADA Accessibility Guidelines (ADAAG)* as well. The *ADAAG* has additional requirements that must be met for certain occupancies. (See the section on *ADA* regulations later in this chapter and Appendix E for more information.)

New Versus Existing

Whether an occupancy is new or existing becomes important when using the *LSC*, because the *LSC* separates its regulations into these two different categories for each occupancy classification. An occupancy is considered *new* if it falls into one of the following categories.

1. The occupancy is in a newly constructed building.
2. The occupancy is relocated to an existing building.
3. The occupancy is in a new addition to an existing building.
4. The occupancy is remaining in the same building, but changing its size or use to a different subclassification.

This last category is important to remember since it is the least obvious. A change in occupancy classification can affect a

Note

When using the *LSC*, it makes a difference if the project is in a new building or an existing building.

COMPARISON OF OCCUPANCY CLASSIFICATIONS

I.C.C. INTERNATIONAL BUILDING CODE	B.O.C.A. NATIONAL BUILDING CODE	S.B.C.C. STANDARD BUILDING CODE	I.C.B.O. UNIFORM BUILDING CODE	N.F.P.A. LIFE SAFETY CODE
A-1 Assembly, Theaters (Fixed Seats)	A-1 Assembly, Theaters, etc. with stage	A-1 Assembly, Large with working stage, O.L. ≥700	A-1 Assembly, with stage, O.L. ≥ 1000	A-A Assembly, O.L. > 1000
A-2 Assembly, Food and/or Drink Consumption	A-2 Assembly, Public Assembly without stage	A-1 Assembly, Large without working stage, O.L. ≥1000	A-2 Assembly, with stage, O.L. < 1000	A-B Assembly, O.L. > 300 ≤ 1000
A-3 Assembly, Worship, Recreation, Amusement	A-3 Assembly, Amusement, Entertainment, Recreation	A-2 Assembly, Small with working stage, O.L. ≥100 < 700	A-2.1 Assembly, without stage, O.L. ≥ 300	A-C Assembly, O.L. ≥50 ≤ 300
A-4 Assembly, Indoor Sporting Events	A-4 Assembly, Place of Worship	A-2 Assembly, Small without working stage, O.L. ≥100 < 1000	A-3 Assembly, without stage, O.L. < 300	
A-5 Assembly, Outdoor Activities	A-5 Assembly, Outdoor		A-4 Assembly, Stadiums, Reviewing Stands, Amusement Parks	
B Business	B Business	B Business	B Business	B Business
E Educational (includes some Day Care)	E Educational	E Educational	E-1 Educational, O.L. ≥50	E Educational
			E-2 Educational, O.L. < 50	
			E-3 Educational, Day Care	
F-1 Factory Industrial, Moderate Hazard	F-1 Factory and Industrial, Moderate Hazard	F Factory-Industrial	F-1 Factory and Industrial, Moderate Hazard	I-A Industrial, General
F-2 Factory Industrial, Low Hazard	F-2 Factory and Industrial, Low Hazard		F-2 Factory and Industrial, Low Hazard	I-B Industrial, Special Purpose
				I-C Industrial, High Hazard
H-1 Hazardous, Detonation Hazard	H-1 High Hazard, Detonation Hazard	H-1 Hazardous, Detonation Hazard	H-1 Hazardous, High Explosives	(included in Group I)
H-2 Hazardous, Deflagration Hazard or Accelerated Burning	H-2 High Hazard, Deflagration Hazard or Accelerated Burning	H-2 Hazardous, Deflagration Hazard or Accelerated Burning	H-2 Hazardous, Accelerated Burning or Moderate Explosives	
H-3 Hazardous, Physical or Combustible Hazard	H-3 High Hazard, Physical or Combustible Hazard	H-3 Hazardous, Physical or Combustible Hazard	H-3 Hazardous, High Fire or Physical Hazard	
H-4 Hazardous, Health Hazard	H-4 High Hazard, Health Hazard	H-4 Hazardous, Health Hazard	H-4 Hazardous, Repair Garages	
H-5 Hazardous, Hazardous Production Materials (HPM)			H-5 Hazardous, Aircraft Repair Hangers	
			H-6 Hazardous, Hazardous Production Materials (HPM)	
			H-7 Hazardous, Health Hazards	

Figure 2.2. This chart is a summary of information contained in the *International Building Code (IBC)*, the *BOCA National Building Code (NBC)*, the *Standard Building Code (SBC)*, the *Uniform Building Code (UBC)*, and the *Life Safety Code (LSC)*. (The ICC, BOCA, SBCCI, ICBO, and NFPA do not assume responsibility for the accuracy or the completeness of this chart.)

I.C.C. INTERNATIONAL BUILDING CODE		B.O.C.A. NATIONAL BUILDING CODE		S.B.C.C. STANDARD BUILDING CODE		I.C.B.O. UNIFORM BUILDING CODE		N.F.P.A. LIFE SAFETY CODE	
I-1	Institutional, Supervised Personal Care, O.L. > 16	I-1	Institutional, Residential Care and Group Homes	I-U	Institutional, Unrestrained	I-1.1	Institutional, Health Care, Nonambulatory	D-I	Detentional/ Correctional Free Egress
I-2	Institutional, Health Care	I-2	Institutional, Health Care	I-R	Institutional, Restrained	I-1.2	Institutional, Health Care, Ambulatory	D-II	Detentional/ Correctional Zoned Egress
I-3	Institutional, Restrained	I-3	Institutional, Restrained			I-2	Institutional, Residential Care and Group Homes	D-III	Detentional/ Correctional Zoned Impeded Egress
I-4	Institutional, Day Care Facilities					I-3	Institutional, Restrained	D-IV	Detentional/ Correctional Impeded Egress
								D-V	Detentional/ Correctional Contained
								H	Health Care
								DC	Day Care
M	Mercantile	M	Mercantile	M	Mercantile	M	Mercantile	M-A	Mercantile, > 3 levels or >30,000 sq.ft.
								M-B	Mercantile, floor above or below grade level, or >3000 ≤ 30,000 sq.ft.
								M-C	Mercantile, one story and ≤3000
R-1	Residential, Transient	R-1	Residential, Hotels, Motels, Boarding Houses	R-1	Residential, Multiple Dwelling, Transient	R-1	Residential, Hotels Apartments, etc, O.L. > 10	R-A	Residential, Hotels, Motels, Dormitories
R-2	Residential, Multi-Dwelling Unit	R-2	Residential, Multi-Family Dwelling Units	R-2	Residential, Multiple Dwelling, Permanent	R-2	NOT USED	R-B	Residential, Apartments
R-3	Residential, One and Two Dwellings Units	R-3	Residential, Multiple One or Two Family Dwellings Units	R-3	Residential, Child Care Facilities, One and Two Family Dwellings	R-3	Residential, Dwellings, Lodging Houses, etc., O.L. ≤ 10	R-C	Residential, Lodging or Rooming Houses
R-4	Residential, Care and Assisted Living Facilities O.L. > 5 ≤ 16	R-4	Residential, Individual One and Two Family Dwellings	R-4	Residential, Care and Assisted Living Facilities			R-D	Residential, One and Two Family Dwellings
								R-E	Residential, Board and Care Facilities
S-1	Storage, Moderate Hazard	S-1	Storage, Moderate Hazard	S-1	Storage, Moderate Hazard	S-1	Storage, Moderate Hazard	S	Storage
S-2	Storage, Low Hazard	S-2	Storage, Low Hazard	S-2	Storage, Low Hazard	S-2	Storage, Low Hazard		
						S-3	Storage, Repair Garages		
U	Utility and Miscellaneous	U	Utility and Miscellaneous		Special Occupancies	U-1	Utility, Private Garages, Carports, Sheds, etc.		Special Structures and High Rise Buildings
						U-2	Utility, Fences over 6'-0", Tanks, Towers, etc.		

Figure 2.2. Continued.

number of other code regulations. It affects both the building codes and the *LSC*. (See Appendix B for more information about existing buildings.)

Mixed Occupancies

Two or more occupancies can occur in the same building. A mixed occupancy occurs when more than one use is located in the same building and each is a different occupancy. A common example is a large hotel. Many larger hotels have restaurants and indoor pools with exercise rooms. The hotel itself would be classified as Residential, and the restaurant and pool would be classified as an Assembly occupancy. This combination of building types is common today and seems to be the trend for the future.

Some common examples are indicated below to help you to begin analyzing different building types and distinguishing between various uses. (There are many other possibilities.) Notice how often the Assembly and the Business occupancies occur together. These are occupancies you especially want to look for in mixed building types.

- ✦ Hotels (Residential) with restaurants, ballrooms, or work-out rooms (Assembly or Business)
- ✦ Grammar and high schools (Educational) with gymnasiums, auditoriums, and cafeterias (Assembly)
- ✦ Office buildings (Business) with day care centers (Educational)
- ✦ Hospitals (Institutional) with cafeterias (Assembly)
- ✦ Reformatories (Detentional/Correctional) with recreational rooms (Assembly) and offices (Business)
- ✦ Factories (Industrial) combined with the office headquarters (Business)
- ✦ Malls (Mercantile) with small restaurants (Business) or large food courts (Assembly)

It is important to determine up front if more than one occupancy is occurring in the same building because different codes will apply to each. In most cases the different occupancies must be separated by fire-rated partitions or fire walls so that each occupancy is contained and kept separate. (See Chapter 5.) Each occupancy will then be treated as its own entity.

When fire-rated partitions between the occupancies are not possible, the requirements of the most restrictive occupancy will usually apply to all occupancies in the building. In this case the means of egress becomes an important factor and requires close examination. (See Chapter 4.) The ultimate goal is to provide the safest building possible.

ADA Regulations

Certain occupancy classifications are also affected by the *Americans with Disabilities Act (ADA)*. The *ADA Accessibility Guidelines (ADAAG)* generally regulates all buildings with public accommodations; however, there are building types within some occupancies that have specific requirements. Currently, the building types that require special regulations include restaurants and cafeterias (Assembly), libraries (Business or Educational), many businesses and mercantile establishments, medical facilities (Health Care), and transient lodging (Residential and Correctional/Detentional). The other categories as listed below are pending and waiting for an official ruling. In addition, the Access Board has recently issued proposed *ADAAG* regulations with dimensions that are more appropriate for children, although these regulations have not yet been officially incorporated into the law by the Department of Justice (DOJ). In the future, when these *ADAAG* regulations become law, they could affect all building types where children are the primary occupants. It is important to keep abreast of the new *ADAAG* requirements as they are issued. Additional regulations for special occupancies will be added in the future.

Below is a general list of the special accessibility requirements for each of these building types. In addition, there are specific storage requirements for any occupancy that requires accessible storage. When working within these occupancies your research should include reviewing current *ADAAG* requirements as well as comparing them to other codes enforced in your area to see if there are contradictory or stricter codes. When necessary, consult your local code official or the ADA Access Board for clarification. (See resources in Appendix D.)

Assembly Areas

Percentage of accessible wheelchair locations
Location/size of wheelchair areas in relation to fixed seats
Access to performance areas
Types of floor surfaces
Possible assistive listening systems
Types and placement of listening systems

Businesses and Mercantile

Size of service and checkout counters

> **Note**
>
> Revisions to the *ADAAG* made by the Access Board are enforceable only when voted into law by the Department of Justice (DOJ).

Clearance and height of self-service shelves/display units
Size of teller windows and information counters
Width and quantity of checkout aisles
Clearance at security elements
Quantity, size, and types of dressing/fitting rooms
Type and clearance of automatic teller machines

Libraries

Percentage of accessible fixed seating, tables, and study carrels
Width of access aisles
Number and size of accessible checkout areas
Clearance at security elements
Height of card catalogs and magazine displays
Systems for book retrieval

Medical Facilities

Size of covered entrances for unloading patients
Percentage of accessible toilets
Percentage of accessible patient bedrooms
Size of maneuvering spaces in patient rooms
Clearance area at patient beds
Width of accessible doors and aisles

Restaurants and Cafeterias

Percentage of accessible fixed tables
Access to sunken and raised platforms
Width of food service lines
Height of counters and self-service shelves
Access to controls of vending machines
Width of access aisles

Transient Lodgings

Percentage of accessible sleeping rooms
Specific requirements within accessible rooms
Number of hearing impaired rooms
Access to rooms, public, and common areas
Width of door openings
Size of maneuvering spaces
Percentage of accessible amenities (ice machines, washers
    and dryers, etc.)
Clearance, height, and hardware of storage units

Judicial, Legislative, and Regulatory Facilities
    (pending incorporation by the DOJ)

Access to secured entrances (including accessible security
    system)
Access to courtroom elements (judges bench, jury assembly
    and deliberation areas, etc.)
Access to holding cells (and amenities)
Accessible security systems
Percentage of assisted listening systems

Detention and Correctional Facilities
    (pending incorporation by the DOJ)

Access to cells and visiting areas
Percentage of holding and housing cells or rooms
    (and amenities)

DESIGN LOADS

Occupant loads as described in this chapter are not to be confused with two other types of design loads required by the codes—dead loads and live loads. *Dead loads* include all permanent components of a building's structure, such as the walls, floors, and roof. *Live loads,* on the other hand, include any loads that are not the actual weight of the structure itself. They include interior elements such as people, furniture, equipment, appliances, and books. Other loads that are sometimes considered live loads but are separate exterior elements include wind loads, snow loads, and earthquake loads.

Specific calculations must be made to determine each type of load. These calculations are typically done by engineers during the initial design and construction of a building. Most of the calculations take into consideration that some of the loads will change during the normal use of a building. For example, in office buildings it is common for interior walls to change and be relocated as tenants move. The number of people will vary as well.

Some interior projects may require you to research additional loads. The most common situations include (1) adding a wall, such as brick or concrete, that is substantially heavier than a standard wall; (2) creating a filing or library area that concentrates the weight at one point; (3) adding a heavy piece of equipment; and (4) adding an assembly seating area in an existing room.

In most cases you will need to work with a structural engineer to determine if the existing structure will hold the added load/weight. If not, the engineer will need to determine how to add additional support.

OCCUPANT LOADS

An occupant load is the second thing you need to determine at the beginning of a project. Most of the codes discuss occupant load requirements within the means of egress chapters. Remember, however, that you may have made some decisions about the occupancy classification based on a projected occupant load. If this changes, then you may have to reconsider the occupancy classification. For example, if you are designing a restaurant that is intended to serve less than 50 people, the building codes would typically allow you to classify the restaurant as a Business occupancy. When you are determining the occupant load for the space in the building that has been assigned for the restaurant, and you discover that the occupant load has increased to over 100 people, the building codes will typically require the project to be classified as an Assembly. In this case, you would need to decide either to limit the area of the restaurant (and thus reduce the occupant load) or to change the occupancy classification of the space to Assembly. Many of the occupancy subclassifications, as well, are based on the load of an occupancy load.

The codes provide information as to how to design a safe area or building. They set minimum requirements for safety. The occupant load sets a minimum number of occupants for which you must design the means of egress from a building or specific area. Each code publication assigns a predetermined amount of space or square feet required for each occupant within specific occupancies and building uses. This specific figure is called the *load factor*. The load factor is used to help you determine the required occupant load of a space or building. In other words, you can determine the number of people that you must assume will be using the corridors, stairs, and exits in the event of a fire.

An occupant load is important to determine. Not only will it guide you in the correct selection of a building's occupancy, but it is also needed to figure means of egress codes (see the Means of Egress section later in this chapter and Chapter 4). The remainder of this chapter deals with occupant loads.

Note

The terms "occupancy load" and "occupant load" are often used interchangeably and mean the same thing. However, do not confuse them with occupancy classifications.

The Table

Figure 2.3 is the load factor Table 1003.1, titled "Minimum Occupant Load," and is taken from the *SBC*. Each building code has a similar table or chart. The *NBC* uses Table 1008.1.2, "Maximum Floor Area Allowances per Occupant," the *UBC* uses Table 33A, "Minimum Egress Requirements," and the *IBC* uses Table 1003.2.2.2,

TABLE 1003.1
MINIMUM OCCUPANT LOAD

USE	AREA PER OCCUPANT[2,3] (sq ft)
Assembly without fixed seats	
Concentrated (includes among others, auditoriums, churches, dance floors, lodge rooms, reviewing stands, stadiums)	7 net
Waiting Space	3 net
Unconcentrated (includes among others conference rooms, exhibit rooms, gymnasiums, lounges, skating rinks, stages, platforms)	15 net
Assembly with fixed seats	Note 1
Bowling alleys, allow 5 persons for each alley, including 15 ft of runway, and other spaces in accordance with the appropriate listing herein	7 net
Business areas	100 gross
Courtrooms without fixed seats	40 net
Courtrooms with fixed seats	Note 1
Educational (including Educational Uses Above the 12th Grade)	
Classroom areas	20 net
Shops and other vocational areas	50 net
Industrial areas	100 gross
Institutional	
Sleeping areas	120 gross
Inpatient treatment and ancillary areas	240 gross
Outpatient area	100 gross
Resident housing areas	120 gross
Library	
Reading rooms	50 net
Stack area	100 gross
Malls	Section 413
Mercantile	
Basement and grade floor areas open to public	30 gross
Areas on other floors open to public	60 gross
Storage, stock, shipping area not open to public	300 gross
Parking garage	200 gross
Residential	200 gross
Restaurants (without fixed seats)	15 net
Restaurants (with fixed seats)	Note 1
Storage area, mechanical	300 gross

For **SI:** 1 sq ft = 0.0929 m².

Notes:

1. The occupant load for an area having fixed seats installed shall be determined by the number of fixed seats. Capacity of seats without dividing arms shall equal one person per 18 inches (457 mm). For booths, one person per 24 inches (610 mm).

2. See 202 for definitions of gross and net floor areas.

3. The occupant load of floor areas of the building shall be computed on the basis of the specific occupancy classification of the building. Where mixed occupancies occur, the occupant load of each occupancy area shall be computed on the basis of that specific occupancy.

Figure 2.3. *Standard Building Code (SBC) Table 1003.1 Minimum Occupant Load (Reproduced from the 1999 SBC with permission of the copyright holder, Southern Building Code Congress International, Inc., all rights reserved.)*

"Maximum Floor Area Allowances per Occupant." The *LSC* specifies the load factors within each occupancy chapter. The *LSC* also lists them in the "Occupancy Load Factors" in its Appendix.

Notice that the first column in Figure 2.3 is titled "Use." This column lists the different occupancy classifications and use groups. The load factors listed under "Area per Occupant" column are given for each of the specific uses or building types. The load factor indicates the amount of space or area it is assumed each person present will require. Although the square foot figures may seem high for one person, they allow for furniture and equipment and, in some cases, corridors, closets, and other miscellaneous areas.

The table records the area per occupant in square feet. The area in this case refers to the floor area of a building, the area *within* the exterior walls. Notice that some of the load factors are listed in gross square feet and others in net square feet. The *gross* area refers to the building as a whole and includes all miscellaneous spaces within the exterior walls. The *net* area refers to actual occupied spaces and does not include accessory spaces such as corridors, restrooms, utility closets, or other unoccupied areas. (The *UBC* does not distinguish between net and gross areas.)

When net figures are required, it is assumed that the occupants who are using an accessory area would have left the occupied space to do so and, therefore, would already be taken into account. For example, a person in the corridor of a school would most likely be a student or teacher already accounted for in a classroom. Usually, deductions are also made for fixed items that take up space, such as interior walls, columns, and built-in counters and shelving (areas that are not habitable).

Note

The load factor does not mean that each person is required to receive a particular amount of square feet when space planning a project. The figure is used only to determine an occupant load. The placement of furniture, equipment, and walls will greatly affect the final space.

The Formula

The formula that is used with the load factor tables is

Occupancy Load = Floor Area (sq ft) ÷ Occupant Factor

Using the table in Figure 2.3 and the formula above, load factors can be used in two different ways. First, they can help the person building a new structure to *determine the required area, in square feet,* for a particular occupancy. Generally, you need to know how many people will occupy the building and the occupancy classification or use of the building. Use the table to look up the occupant load factor for the planned occupancy and multiply it by the number of people you want to occupy the space to determine how large to make the building.

Since we are discussing building interiors, we will concentrate on the second way to use the load factor table, which is to *determine the occupancy size* allowed in a building. Assume you are working in an existing building. You will need to know if the square footage is enough to hold the building type you are designing. Take the square footage of the existing interior space and divide it by the load factor for your occupancy use to find out how many occupants are allowed. See the example below.

Example

To help you further understand the difference between gross and net area and how to use the load factor table, refer to the example floor plan for a library in Figure 2.4.

If you are using the *SBC*, a library is considered a Business occupancy. However, if you look at the *SBC* table in Figure 2.3 you will see that libraries have been listed separately and divided into two separate uses: *reading rooms* and *stack areas*. The occupant load for each must be determined separately.

The occupant load factor for the reading rooms is set at "50 *net*," meaning the area or square footage should not include accessory spaces. Therefore, the corridor or the utility closet adjacent to the reading rooms on the floor plan should not be included when determining the square footage of the reading rooms. The load

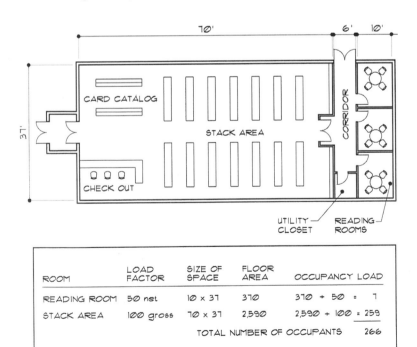

ROOM	LOAD FACTOR	SIZE OF SPACE	FLOOR AREA	OCCUPANCY LOAD	
READING ROOM	50 net	10 x 37	370	370 ÷ 50 =	7
STACK AREA	100 gross	70 x 37	2,590	2,590 ÷ 100 =	259
				TOTAL NUMBER OF OCCUPANTS	266

Figure 2.4. Example: Library.

Note

Even if the number of occupants you are planning for in your design is less than the determined occupant load, you must use the determined load figure as required by the codes.

factor, however, for the stack area of the library is set at "100 *gross*," so the square foot measurement should include the entire stack area with aisles, checkout counter, and so on. (Do not include the corridor since it is enclosed with the reading room area.)

Using the dimensions of the floor plan and the occupant load formula to determine the area for each space, Figure 2.4 shows you how to determine the occupant load for the entire library. The total occupant load is 266 people. Note that in other codes, a library may be considered an Assembly occupancy or an Educational occupancy if the library is used exclusively by a school. This can affect the load factor and in turn affect the total occupant load.

Mixed Uses or Occupancies

When there is more than one building use or occupancy in the same building, each occupant load must be measured and calculated separately. For example, a multistory building may have a mixture of Mercantile and Business spaces on the first floor and multiple Business spaces on the remaining floors. To figure the occupant load for a floor, each space must be figured separately. Be sure to note whether each area needs to be measured as net or gross square feet. Once you have the occupant load for each space, add them together to get the total occupant load for the whole floor.

Sometimes a different minor occupancy should be considered separately from the occupancy type of the larger space. For example, the occupancy load for a large conference room in a Business occupancy might need to be calculated using an Assembly factor. This would provide an occupant load that more accurately addresses the use of the space.

Multiple Uses or Occupancies

Note

When reading code tables it is important to read all the footnotes at the bottom of the tables for additional information and possible exceptions.

Some buildings or building areas provide more than one use. For example, a church fellowship hall might be used for a large assembly one night and as a cafeteria the next. The following weekend it might be used as a gymnasium or exercise room. In other words, any area of a building that has more than one type of function is considered to have multiple uses. The occupant load is determined by the use that indicates the largest concentration of people.

Fixed Seats

Fixed seating arrangements are common in some building types, especially in Assembly occupancies. The seats are considered fixed if they are not easily moved and/or if they are used on a more permanent basis. Instead of using the standard formula for calculating the occupant load, when fixed seats are present the actual seats are counted.

In the table in Figure 2.3, the *SBC* allows for both the Assembly and the Business use to contain fixed seats. In both cases it refers to "Note 1," which simply states: count the number of fixed seats to obtain the occupant load. The *SBC* table also provides a variable to be used with continuous seating such as benches, bleachers, and pews. It allows 18 inches of seating for each occupant. Booth seating has a separate variable.

Counting seats with arms is self-explanatory. Continuous seating gets somewhat more complicated. If, for example, you are working on a church that has 45 pews and each pew is 12 feet long, you would use the 18-inch variable given in "Note 1" in the load factor table in Figure 2.3. A 12-foot pew equals 144 inches. Divide the 144 by the 18-inch variable to get 8 people per pew. Since there are a total of 45 pews, this church has an occupant load of 360 people (45 pews × 8 people/pew).

Means of Egress

The occupant loads you determine in the beginning of a project will be used again later in your code research to determine the means of egress, such as the number of exits and the width of the exits. (See Chapter 4.)   Now is the time to find out if your proposed space and occupancy class will allow the occupant load you need. If after figuring the occupant load, you find that the code will not allow the number of occupants you are planning for in your design, you may have to increase the size of the space. (This in turn may change the occupancy classification.) In some cases, the codes may allow you to plan your design based on the "actual number" of people that would occupy the space. This would be designing for the occupant content or "actual number" and would require that you provide an adequate number of exits to allow for the increase in occupants.

On the other hand, you may be working in a building with large existing corridors and more exits than required by the occupant load. In this case you may also plan for an increased number of occupants, which would be using the occupant content in your calculations. Remember, that the "occupant load" is the minimum number of people that you must assume will be using your space, but the occupant content is the "actual number" of people that your design has provided means of egress for.

Note

Every assembly room or Assembly occupancy usually requires the approved occupant load to be permanently posted near the main exit from the space. A typical sign might read: "Occupancy by more than 100 persons is dangerous and unlawful."

There may also be occasions when your building type is not typical and the occupant load factor may not be appropriate, or a specific occupancy use may not be listed on the table. On other occasions you may have a space that does not clearly fit one of the use categories. When this occurs you should meet with the code official in your jurisdiction for guidance. Only the code official can make the final decision. (Another option is to obtain an appeal. See Chapter 9). It is important for this decision to be made at the beginning of a project, because occupancy classifications and many of the codes depend on the determined occupant load.

CHECKLIST

Figure 2.5 is designed to help you determine occupancy classifications and occupant loads. It is a basic checklist that is set up to make sure you address the same typical occupancy questions for each project.

The first half of the checklist is used to determine occupancy classification. The first space is the building type. Use the multiple lists in this chapter in conjunction with the building code to help you determine the use of your building or space. If there is more than one building type, use a separate checklist for each. Whether the space is new or existing becomes important later when using the *LSC*.

The number of occupants in the second space can be an estimated range of people in a preliminary design, although an actual occupant load figure determined from a code table would be more accurate. (Use the second half of the checklist to help you do this.) If hazards are present, note them in the next space. Each of the code publications list the types of hazards to look for and whether they are explosive, fire, physical, or health hazards.

To determine the occupancy and its subclassification in the next spaces, compare the occupancy types, the number of occupants, and the types of hazards in your building or space to what is specified by the codes. When you do this, you will probably find some special occupancy requirements within the codes. List them in the last space as a reminder when designing your project. Be sure to check the *ADAAG* and other required standards when necessary.

Note

Not only can a building have more than one occupancy, but each occupancy can have more than one use for the purpose of determining the occupant load. Therefore, one building can have a number of calculations.

The second half of the checklist is to help you determine the occupant load for the building type or occupancy you have listed in the first half of the checklist. Remember that each occupancy can have more than one use. These uses are listed in the code

OCCUPANCY CHECKLIST

PROJECT NAME: _____

OCCUPANCY CLASSIFICATIONS

BUILDING TYPE/USE: _____
___ NEW ___ EXISTING

NUMBER OF OCCUPANTS: _____
___ ESTIMATED ___ ACTUAL OCCUPANCY LOAD (see below)

TYPE OF HAZARDS: _____
___ EXPLOSIVE ___ FIRE ___ PHYSICAL ___ HEALTH ___ OTHER _____

OCCUPANCY CLASSIFICATION: _____
CODE SOURCE: ___ NBC ___ SBC ___ UBC ___ IBC ___ LSC ___ OTHER:_____

OCCUPANCY SUBCLASSIFICATION: _____
CODE SOURCE: ___ NBC ___ SBC ___ UBC ___ IBC ___ LSC ___ OTHER:_____

SPECIAL OCCUPANCY REQUIREMENTS: _____
CODE SOURCE: ___ NBC ___ SBC ___ UBC ___ IBC ___ LSC ___ OTHER:_____

OCCUPANCY LOADS

OCCUPANCY USE AND LOAD FACTOR:
Use 1: _____Load Factor: _____ ( ) Gross ( ) Net
Use 2: _____Load Factor: _____ ( ) Gross ( ) Net
Use 3: _____Load Factor: _____ ( ) Gross ( ) Net
Use 4: _____Load Factor: _____ ( ) Gross ( ) Net
CODE SOURCE: ___ NBC ___ SBC ___ UBC ___ IBC ___ LSC ___ OTHER:_____

TOTAL FLOOR AREA: (SF = Square Feet)
Use 1: _____ ( ) Net SF ( ) Gross SF ( ) Other: _____
Use 2: _____ ( ) Net SF ( ) Gross SF ( ) Other: _____
Use 3: _____ ( ) Net SF ( ) Gross SF ( ) Other: _____
Use 4: _____ ( ) Net SF ( ) Gross SF ( ) Other: _____

OCCUPANCY LOAD: (FORMULA: Load = Area (Sq. Ft.) / Load Factor
Use 1: _____ ( ) Using Formula ( ) Fixed Seat Variable _____
Use 2: _____ ( ) Using Formula ( ) Fixed Seat Variable _____
Use 3: _____ ( ) Using Formula ( ) Fixed Seat Variable _____
Use 4: _____ ( ) Using Formula ( ) Fixed Seat Variable _____

TOTAL OCCUPANCY LOAD: _____

LOCAL CODE APPROVAL REQUIRED
___ NO ___ YES: NAME:_____DATE:_____

NOTE: If there is more than one building type in the project, use a separate checklist for each.

Figure 2.5. Occupancy Checklist.

books in the occupant load tables. (See the example in Figure 2.3.) Record the use(s) in the first space. In the adjacent space record the corresponding occupant load factor for that use. Note whether they are net or gross figures, and check which code source you have obtained them from.

The second space is used to record the actual square foot measurement of your building or space. Measure each use separately and note whether you measured net or gross square feet. Using the code load factor and the measured floor area, determine the occupant load in the next space for each use you have listed and note how each was determined. After you have calculated each use, add them to get the total occupant load.

A code approval section has been included at the bottom of the chart. It may not always be necessary to get approval from your code official at this point in a project, but each situation is different. (See the section on Preliminary Approval in Chapter 10.) If you have a large or unusual project, or if you just want to confirm your own findings, you may want to discuss the results with a code official. Record the date of your discussion and to whom you spoke.

Remember, it is important to accurately determine both the occupancy classification and occupant load in the beginning of a project, since a number of the other codes depend on them.

CHAPTER 3

CONSTRUCTION TYPES AND BUILDING SIZES

Construction types are very important at the time a building is being constructed. Structural engineers and architects must be thoroughly familiar with them to determine the type of construction materials that can be used throughout a building—both exterior and interior.

Construction types become a factor on interior projects as well. When working on an interior project that requires the reconfiguring of building elements, such as relocating walls or adding a stairway, you must be familiar with the different types of construction to determine if and when specific regulations must be followed. Some construction types are stricter than others. Each code will also list minimum construction type requirements for specific types of occupancy classifications.

In addition, construction types are used in conjunction with occupancy classifications to determine the building's maximum height and floor area. You should be aware of the codes that apply to a building's size and when they would affect a project. For example, you may need to research the size of a building for a specific occupancy.

This chapter familiarizes you with construction types, building heights, and floor areas. It includes how they are typically used for new construction and when they are necessary for an interior project. The first part of this chapter concentrates on construction types. The second half discusses how they relate to occupancy classifications and building sizes.

DEFINITIONS

When discussing construction types and building sizes there are a number of recurring terms you should be familiar with. The most common ones are listed below.

COMBUSTIBLE: A material that is capable of being ignited or affected by excessive heat or gas in a relatively short amount of time.

FIRE RESISTIVE: A material that *prevents or retards* the passage of excessive heat, hot gases, or flames.

FLOOR AREA: The amount of floor surface included within the exterior walls.

HEIGHT: Vertical distance. *Building height* is from the grade plane to the average height of the highest roof surface. *Story height* is measured from finished floor to finished floor or finished floor to roof. (Note that each building code calculates these heights slightly differently.)

LIMITED COMBUSTIBLE: A material that is not considered noncombustible but that still has some fire resistive qualities. (A term used by the National Fire Protection Association's *Life Safety Code (LSC)*.)

NONCOMBUSTIBLE: A material that will not ignite, burn, support combustion, or release flammable vapors when subject to fire or heat.

PROTECTED: A material that has been chemically treated or covered so that it obtains a fire resistance rating. For example, a nonrated material could gain a fire rating of one or more hours after protection has been added.

UNPROTECTED: A material in its natural state that has not been specially treated. Some materials will be naturally noncombustible, but most unprotected materials will range from combustible to limited combustible.

Note

On interior projects you must make sure you do not affect the fire rating of existing structure elements. For example, removing the gypsum board from a structural column can reduce the rating of the column.

CONSTRUCTION TYPES

Every building is made up of a variety of what the codes define as *building elements*. (The *NBC* and *UBC* sometimes refer to them as *structure elements*.) They could be as simple as four exterior walls and a roof or as complicated as the many parts that make up a high-rise building. The various construction types found in the code govern the type of materials allowed to construct each of the structure elements in a building. These building elements can include most or all of the following, depending on the type of building:

Structural frames
Fire walls and party walls ·
Exterior load-bearing walls
Exterior non-load-bearing walls
Exterior doors and windows
Interior load-bearing walls
Interior non-load-bearing walls
Fire-rated partitions
Shaft enclosures
Smoke barriers
Columns
Beams, girders, trusses, arches
Floors and ceilings
Roofs and ceilings

Each construction type assigns the above structure or building elements a minimum fire protection rating. These ratings are based on the number of hours the building element must be fire resistant, meaning it will not be adversely affected by flame, heat, or hot gases. Note, though, that fire resistant does not mean fireproof. Instead, it is an hourly *fire endurance rating*. By controlling each element, the codes are able to regulate the fire resistance of a whole building. On an interior project, the most critical building element will be interior walls, but you could be working with a number of the other elements as well.

The Table

Each building code and the *LSC* has a similar table that lists the requirements for each type of construction. Figure 3.1 is the *BOCA National Building Code (NBC)* construction type table, Table 602, "Fireresistance Ratings of Structure Elements." The *Standard Building Code (SBC)* uses Table 600, "Fire Resistance Ratings/ Required Fire Resistance in Hours," and the *Uniform Building Code (UBC)* has Table 6-A, "Types of Construction—Fire-Resistive Requirements (In Hours)." The *International Building Code (IBC)* uses Table 601, "Fire Resistance Rating Requirements for Building Elements." The *LSC* table is found in the Appendix of the *LSC.* It is titled "Fire Resistive Requirements for Type I Through Type V Construction."

In the *NBC* table in Figure 3.1 the construction types are listed across the top of the table in descending order from the most fire resistive (Type 1) to the least fire resistive (Type 5). Each of the

Table 602
FIRERESISTANCE RATINGS OF STRUCTURE ELEMENTS[k]

Structure element Note a		Type 1 Section 603.0 Protected 1A	1B	Type 2 Section 603.0 Protected 2A	2B	Unprotected 2C	Type 3 Section 604.0 Protected 3A	Unprotected 3B	Type 4 Section 605.0 Heavy timber Note c 4	Type 5 Section 606.0 Protected 5A	Unprotected 5B
1 Exterior walls	Loadbearing	4	3	2	1	0	2	2	2	1	0
		Not less than the fireresistance rating based on fire separation distance (see Section 705.2)									
	Nonloadbearing	*Not less than the fireresistance rating based on fire separation distance (see Section 705.2)*									
2 Fire walls and party walls (Section 707.0)		4	3	2	2	2	2	2	2	2	2
		Not less than the fireresistance rating required by Table 707.1									
3 Fire separation assemblies (Section 709.0)	Fire enclosure of exits (Sections 1014.11, 709.0 and Note b)	2	2	2	2	2	2	2	2	2	2
	Shafts (other than exits) and elevator hoistways (Sections 709.0, 710.0 and Note b)	2	2	2	2	2	2	2	2	1	1
	Mixed use and fire area separations (Section 313.0)	*Not less than the fireresistance rating required by Table 313.1.2*									
	Other separation assemblies (Note i)	1	1	1 Note d	1	1	1	1	1	1	1
4 Fire partitions (Section 711.0)	Exit access corridors (Note g)	*Not less than the fireresistance rating required by Section 1011.4* Note d									
	Tenant spaces separations (Note f)	1	1	1 Note d	1	0	1	0	1	1	0
5 Dwelling unit and guestroom separations (Sections 711.0, 713.0 and Notes f and j)		1	1	1 Note d	1	1	1	1	1	1	1
6 Smoke barriers (Section 712.0 and Note g)		1	1	1	1	1	1	1	1	1	1
7 Other nonloadbearing partitions		0	0	0 Note d	0	0	0	0	0	0	0
8 Interior loadbearing walls, loadbearing partitions, columns, girders, trusses (other than roof trusses) and framing (Section 716.0)	Supporting more than one floor	4	3	2	1	0	1	0	see Sec. 605.0	1	0
	Supporting one floor only or a roof only	3	2	1½	1	0	1	0	see Sec. 605.0	1	0
9 Structural members supporting wall (Section 716.0 and Note g)		3	2	1½	1	0	1	0	1	1	0
		Not less than fireresistance rating of wall supported									
10 Floor construction including beams (Section 713.0 and Note h)		3	2	1½ Note l	1	0	1	0	see Sec. 605.0 Note c	1	0
11 Roof construction, including beams, trusses and framing, arches and roof deck (Section 715.0 and Notes e, m)	15' or less in height to lowest member	2	1½	1	1	0 Note d	1	0	see Sec. 605.0 Note c	1	0
	More than 15' but less than 20' in height to lowest member	1	1	1	0	0 Note d	0	0	see Sec. 605.0	1	0
	20' or more in height to lowest member	0	0	0	0	0 Note d	0	0	see Sec. 605.0	0	0

Note a. For fireresistance rating requirements for structural members and assemblies which support other fireresistance rated members or assemblies, see Section 716.1.

Note b. For reductions in the required fireresistance rating of exit and shaft enclosures, see Sections 1014.11 and 710.3.

Note c. For substitution of other structural materials for timber in Type 4 construction, see Section 2304.2.

Note d. For fireretardant-treated wood permitted in roof construction and nonloadbearing walls where the required fireresistance rating is 1 hour or less, see Sections 603.2 and 2310.0.

Note e. For permitted uses of heavy timber in roof construction in buildings of Types 1 and 2 construction, see Section 715.4.

Note f. For reductions in required fireresistance ratings of tenant separations and dwelling unit separations, see Sections 1011.4 and 1011.4.1.

Note g. For exceptions to the required fireresistance rating of construction supporting exit access corridor walls, tenant separation walls in covered mall buildings, and smoke barriers, see Sections 711.4 and 712.2.

Note h. For buildings having habitable or occupiable stories or basements below grade, see Section 1006.3.1.

Note i. Not less than the rating required by this code.

Note j. For Use Group R-3, see Section 310.5.

Note k. Fireresistance ratings are expressed in hours.

Note l. In buildings which are required to comply with the provisions of Section 403.3, the required fireresistance rating for floor construction, including beams, shall be 2 hours (see Section 403.3.3.1).

Note m. 1 foot = 304.8 mm.

Figure 3.1. *BOCA National Building Code (NBC)* Table 602, "Fireresistance Ratings of Structure Elements." (Copyright 1999, Building Officials and Code Administrators International, Inc., Country Club Hills, Illinois, *BOCA National Building Code/1999*. Reproduced with permission. All rights reserved.)

structure elements are listed down the side to the left. The hourly fire endurance ratings are listed under the construction types for each structure element in the body of the table.

Some of the construction types are further divided into subcategories. In addition, the *NBC* uses the words "protected" and "unprotected" to highlight some of the differences. Construction Type 2 has as many as three different classifications: 2A, 2B, 2C. This allows for a wide variety of construction types.

Every building, whether it is new or existing, must fall under one of the construction types. To be classified it must meet the minimum requirements for every structure or building element in that type. If it fails to meet even one of the criteria, it will be classified in the next less restrictive type of construction. For example, if a building meets all the requirements of a construction Type 1 in Figure 3.1 except that the floor construction is rated only one hour, the whole building will be classified as a Type 2.

This becomes important on interior projects. When adding new or modifying existing interior building elements you need to know the construction type of the building. You need to be consistent with the existing building materials. If you do not use the rated materials or assemblies required by the building's construction type, you could reduce the whole building's classification. Not only would you be ignoring the building codes, but you would be reducing the safety of the building and affecting such things as building insurance and liability.

Comparing the Codes

A comparison of the construction types in the various codes can be seen in Figure 3.2. Although each code classifies the construction types a little differently, when compared, each basically covers the same fire rating situations. Even the headings are different, though similar in meaning. They include protected, fire resistive, one hour, heavy timber, unprotected, and no resistance.

The *SBC* is the only code that has more than five types of construction. However, the *SBC* is similar to some of the other building codes in that it covers interior non-load-bearing walls in other sections of the code. The *SBC* uses four additional tables: Table 609.2, Table 704.1, Table 704.2, and Table 705.2. Other building codes include some or all of these requirements in the construction type tables. If you refer to Figure 3.1, you will see that the *NBC* lists such walls as fire partitions, dwelling separation, smoke bar-

COMPARISON OF CONSTRUCTION TYPES

B.O.C.A. NATIONAL BUILDING CODE	S.B.C.C.I. STANDARD BUILDING CODE	I.C.B.O. UNIFORM BUILDING CODE	I.C.C. INTERNATIONAL BUILDING CODE	N.F.P.A. NFPA 220 STANDARD
TYPE 1A Protected	TYPE I	TYPE I Fire Resistive	TYPE IA Protected	I (443)
TYPE 1B	TYPE II		TYPE IB Unprotected	I (332)
TYPE 2A Protected	TYPE IV One-hour Protected	TYPE II Fire Resistive	TYPE IIA Protected	II (222)
TYPE 2B	TYPE IV Unprotected	TYPE II One-hour	TYPE IIB Unprotected	II (111)
TYPE 2C Unprotected		TYPE II No Resistance		II (000)
TYPE 3A Protected	TYPE V One-hour Protected	TYPE III One-hour	TYPE IIIA Protected	III (211)
TYPE 3B Unprotected	TYPE V Unprotected	TYPE III No Resistance	TYPE IIIB Unprotected	III (200)
TYPE 4 Heavy Timber	TYPE III Heavy Timber	TYPE IV Heavy Timber	TYPE IV Heavy Timber	IV (2HH) Heavy Timber
TYPE 5A Protected	TYPE VI One-hour Protected	TYPE V One-hour	TYPE VA Protected	V (111)
TYPE 5B Unprotected	TYPE VI Unprotected	TYPE V No Resistance	TYPE VB Unprotected	V (000)

Figure 3.2. Comparison of Construction Types. (This chart is a summary of information contained in the *International Building Code (IBC)*, the *BOCA National Building Code (NBC)*, the *Standard Building Code (SBC)*, the *Uniform Building Code (UBC)*, and the *Life Safety Code (LSC)*. The ICC, BOCA, SBCCI, ICBO, or NFPA do not assume responsibility for the accuracy or the completeness of this chart.)

riers, and other non-load-bearing partitions. (See Chapter 5 for more information on fire-rated interior structure elements.)

The *LSC* is different than the building codes. Since it is not considered a building code it does not go into great detail on construction types. Instead, it refers you to the table and descriptions found in the *NFPA 220: Standard on Types of Building Construction*. The *LSC* will refer to a construction type within its text. For each occupancy it will list the "minimum construction requirements" indicating which construction types are allowed, but you must reference the *NFPA 220* to get the specifics. Note the construction type table found in the *NFPA 220* is repeated in the Appendix of the *LSC* for easy reference.

The *NFPA 220* differs from the building codes in that it does not specify interior non-load-bearing walls. For those you need to refer to the building codes. However, *NFPA 220* does establish minimum construction requirements for most of the other structure elements. If both a building code and the *LSC* are required in your jurisdiction, you will need to compare the fire endurance ratings of both and use the strictest requirements.

In addition, the *NFPA 220* assigns a three-digit code to describe each construction type instead of using words such as protected, fire resistance, and one-hour. For example, if you refer to Figure 3.2 under the NFPA column, the second item in the chart is Type 1 (332). The three digits in the parentheses represent the hourly fire ratings for three structure elements: three-hour, three-hour, and two-hour ratings. As a standard the first digit pertains to exterior load bearing walls, the second digit includes the frame, columns, and girders, and the third digit represents floor construction. These three digits are a helpful quick reference, but they do not provide all the necessary information. You must refer to the rest of the *NFPA 220* table to obtain the ratings for the remaining structure elements.

> **Note**
>
> **Nearly all materials are eventually affected by flame and heat. Even materials that have been treated to become fire retardant will still burn or char when exposed to a continuous flame.**

Combustible Versus Noncombustible

The hourly ratings on a construction type table such as the *NBC* table in Figure 3.1 indicate how fire resistant a material must be. The ratings represent the length of time a material must resist fire. The resistance of these materials is based on how easily they ignite, how long they burn once ignited, how quickly the flames spread, and how much heat the material generates. Most products are differentiated as either noncombustible, fire resistant, or combustible. The higher hourly fire ratings typically tell you noncombustible materials are required, and the lower ratings indicate that fire resistant materials or limited combustible materials are allowed. Combustible materials are usually allowed by the codes when no ratings are specified.

Noncombustible materials are defined as materials that will not ignite and burn when subject to fire. They are used to prevent substantial fire spread since they do not contribute fuel to a fire. (See inset titled *High-Rise Buildings* on page 72.) Four basic materials are generally considered noncombustible: steel, iron, concrete, and masonry. Their actual performance in the event of a fire, however, depends on how they are used. Occasionally they may require additional fire treatment or protection for extra strength and stability. For example, steel has a rapid loss of strength at high tem-

> **Note**
>
> **After a fire occurs in a building the exposed structure elements may be altered. Many noncombustible materials may appear to have endured the fire unchanged, but flame and heat can change the strength and structural makeup of noncombustible materials. Unseen damage can occur.**

Note

According to Joseph T. Holland III in his article "Fire Retardant Treated Wood" in the September/ October 1993 issue of *Southern Building*, some fire retardant chemicals can cause wood to absorb more moisture. This can cause loss of strength, rot, decay, corrosion of fasteners, poor paint adhesion, staining, and even loss of the fire retardant chemical. Therefore, in high moisture areas be sure to specify the correct type of fire-treated wood.

peratures and must be given extra protection if used on its own. To avoid this, steel is often encased in concrete or covered in a protective coating.

On the other side of the spectrum are *combustible materials*. These are materials that will ignite and continue to burn when the flame source is removed. Wood is a common combustible item, yet it can be chemically treated to gain some amount of fire resistance. Chemically treated wood is called fire retardant treated wood (also commonly known as FRTW). Like other *fire resistant materials*, once treated it will delay the spread of a fire by a designated time period. It will prevent or retard the passage of heat, hot gases, and flames. The fire retardant treatment allows wood to be used in more places throughout a building. In some cases it can even be substituted for materials required to be noncombustible.

Wood can also be considered fire resistant if it is large enough in diameter. *Heavy timber* is considered to be fairly fire resistant because of its size. Typically, columns are required to be at least 8 × 8 inches and beams a minimum of 6 × 10 inches. The bigger the timber, the longer it takes to burn. Heavy timber builds up a layer of char during a fire that helps to protect the rest of the timber.

Like wood, most construction materials that are usually considered combustible can be treated to gain some amount of fire resistance. Plus, these fire resistant and limited combustible materials can be used in conjunction with other materials to create rated assemblies. The materials work together as an assembly to create a higher fire resistance. (See Chapter 5.) For example, wood studs used with gypsum board on both sides can create a one-hour-rated wall. Other common fire resistant materials include gypsum concrete, gypsum board, plaster, and mineral fiber products.

When the construction type tables specify a rated structure or building element, it means the element must be composed of a rated building material. You must be sure you are specifying fire-rated products or fire-rated assemblies when required. All fire-rated products are tested to obtain an hourly fire rating. Manufacturers must label their tested products to ensure that they have passed the tests. Chapter 5 elaborates on fire ratings and how to specify rated materials and assemblies.

Using the Table

Each building code and the *NFPA 220* gives a detailed description of the listed construction types. The construction type tables, such as the one shown in Figure 3.1, need to be used in conjunction with these descriptions. Since each code is slightly different, it is difficult to specifically summarize all the construction types. Instead, some generalities have been made below. Generally, the easiest way to determine the construction type of an existing building is by process of elimination. You need to determine what materials have been used to construct the building as well as what materials have not been used.

The strictest construction types, such as *Types I and II*, are typically constructed with steel and concrete and are considered noncombustible buildings. Wood is very rarely used, and is highly fire retardant if used at all. High-rise buildings and many large buildings fall into this category. On the other hand, the most combustible structures, such as *Types V and VI*, are basically all wood structures. These buildings are usually characterized by wood exterior walls and are small in size. A common example is a residential house. When large size timber is used for the main structure elements or frame of the building, the building becomes a *Heavy Timber* construction type. Although these buildings are still predominantly wood, the larger timber makes these buildings relatively easy to identify.

The remaining construction types fall in the middle range. They are a combination of noncombustible materials, fire resistive materials, and wood. Usually the exterior walls are made of masonry and the interior structure elements are wholly or partially constructed with wood. If the building is a class higher, some of the interior structural members are of noncombustible materials. For these types of buildings you need to examine almost every structure element using the process of elimination.

Example

When working on interior projects where reconfiguration or addition of structure elements is required, you will need to determine the construction type(s) of the building. Although you will be dealing mostly with non-load-bearing walls, which are described in other parts of the code (see Chapter 5 in this book), the ratings of some *interior* structure elements will be found in the construction type table, such as the one in Figure 3.1. These structure elements include load-bearing walls, party walls, and demising walls, as well as shaft enclosures and other structure elements.

As you will see in Chapter 5 these elements become important when you are adding such things as walls, ceilings, doors, and windows. They will also be a factor when you are penetrating them with items such as sprinkler pipes and ducts. Remember, it is important to specify the correct building material for interior partitions, because if the rating is too low, a whole building might be reclassified into a lower category.

Let's say, for example, that you are asked to design office spaces on the first floor of an existing three-story building. Before you can specify the correct rating and materials for the interior walls and ceilings, you need to determine the building's type of construction. To do this you need to know what materials were used to construct the building's existing structure. Ask yourself: Is the frame wood, steel, concrete block, or other masonry? What are the exterior walls? Are the floors wood or concrete? And go through the process of elimination described in the section above.

As you examine the building and answer these questions, you will be able to pinpoint the materials used and determine which construction type fits the structure of the building. When necessary, try to obtain the original construction documents, consult the original building architect, or review the building with a

ATRIUMS AND MEZZANINES

Atriums and mezzanines are common design elements used on the interior of a building. The codes set a number of additional requirements for them, some of which are described below. However, be sure to check the codes for the specifics and work closely with the local code officials. (Typically, engineers are required as well.)

ATRIUMS: An atrium is commonly found in lobbies and shopping malls. It is basically a multistory space contained within a building. A common atrium design has a glass enclosure and surrounding balconies. It should be noted that these glass walls are often restricted by the codes, since most atriums must be enclosed in a one-hour fire-rated wall. (Some of the newer fire-rated glazing products allow more options.) The codes also usually allow at least three floors of a building to be directly open to the atrium. Atriums are only allowed in fully sprinklered buildings. In addition, a mechanical smoke exhaust system must usually be provided at the ceiling. It must be tied into other fire protection systems that would activate the exhaust system should a fire occur.

MEZZANINES: A mezzanine is an intermediate floor level placed between the floor and the ceiling of a room or space. It is usually allowed only if it does not exceed more than one-third of the room or area in which it is located. There could be more than one mezzanine in a space and even some at different levels, but the one-third rule would still apply. The appropriate headroom must also be provided at each level. The construction of a mezzanine must be the same as the construction type of the building in which it is located, and it usually is not counted as a story when determining the building height. Typically the mezzanine must be open to the room in which it is located and requires one to two exits to the room or space below.

structural engineer. Once you know the construction type, you will use the construction type table and other information in the codes to design the interior elements of a space such as walls, ceilings and column wraps. Other examples are given in Chapter 5.

Mixed Construction Types

One building can be divided into more than one construction type. For a section to be considered as a separate construction type, however, that portion must be separated from the rest of the building by a separation wall. This separation wall is called a *fire wall* or *party wall*. It creates, in effect, two or more separate buildings.

A fire wall must typically extend from the foundation of a building through the roof to a parapet wall and must be constructed so that it will remain stable even if one side of the wall or building collapses during a fire. A fire wall is considered a structure element and its rating is specified by the codes in the construction type tables such as the one in Figure 3.1. (See Chapter 5 for additional information on fire walls.)

Note

It could become a costly endeavor if you were to try to section off a part of an existing building by using a fire wall. The wall must be continuous and would have to cut through vertical and horizontal elements. Be sure to consult an engineer.

Occupancy Requirements

Construction types set minimum building requirements. These requirements determine the structural integrity of a building for a required time period in case there is a fire. For example, Type I is the strictest and will result in the most fire resistant building and allow the most evacuation time. This evacuation time is critical for each occupancy classification.

Since some occupancies will require more evacuation time than others, they will require a stricter construction type. Assembly and Institutional occupancies are two of the strictest. They are usually allowed in only the most noncombustible buildings—Type I and possibly Type II—because of the number of occupants and the restricted mobility of the occupants. Other occupancies may allow more construction type options.

Specific sections of each building code and each occupancy chapter in the *LSC* will specify the minimum construction requirements for each occupancy. This becomes important especially when the occupancy classification of an existing building is being changed. Since many jurisdictions use both a building code and the *LSC*, it is important to consult both codes and use the strictest construction type requirements. When there are discrepancies, consult the code official in your jurisdiction for clarification. (Additional fire restrictive requirements are described in Chapter 5 and Chapter 6.)

PROTECTED OR UNPROTECTED

When discussing building limitations in the building code, the issue of protected and unprotected is often a source of confusion. Whether the construction of a building is considered protected or unprotected does not have anything to do with the use of an automatic sprinkler system. Instead, *unprotected* indicates that the structure or building elements of a building have not been treated in any additional way to increase their fire resistance beyond the natural characteristics of the materials. *Protected* indicates that the structure elements of a building have been treated to increase their fire resistance. This may include the use of noncombustible or chemically treated materials or the covering of elements by fire proofing materials.

In the most fire resistant construction types, such as Type I and Type II, the structure elements are considered to be protected. However, other construction types allow less fire resistant materials to be used, and therefore allow for protected or unprotected systems to be used. This recognizes that if additional methods of protecting the structure are included in the construction, the structure is safer. For example, a building with Type V-protected construction allows a greater building area than a Type V-unprotected building. (See Figure 3.3.)

Note, however, that the inclusion of a sprinkler system within a building does affect the building limitations in a similar way. A building that has a sprinkler system is allowed greater area and often additional stories than the same construction type that is not sprinklered. Sprinklering a building will often double the allowable area for a particular construction type. (See Chapter 6 for additional sprinkler trade-offs.)

BUILDING HEIGHT AND AREA

Note

If your project entails enlarging a building either horizontally or vertically, be sure to consult the codes as well as the appropriate experts—engineers, architects, contractors, and local code officials. Such a project is beyond the scope of this book.

Building height and area are directly related to construction types. Building height and floor area control the overall size of a building. Similar to construction types, a building's size is usually determined at the time the building is originally constructed.

Although code limitations on building size will not play a major role on interior projects, it is important to be aware of them and know when they are necessary. Many interior projects will not require you to analyze the size requirements. In most instances the height and area of a building will be predetermined and will not need to be considered. In other situations it will be your responsibility to make sure an occupancy is appropriate for the selected building. (See the example on page 70.)

The Table

The building codes control a building's height and area and each has a chart that sets specific parameters. Figure 3.3 is a table taken

Table 503
HEIGHT AND AREA LIMITATIONS OF BUILDINGS
Height limitations of buildings (shown in upper figure as stories and feet above grade plane)^m, and area limitations of one- or two-story buildings facing on one street or public space not less than 30 feet wide (shown in lower figure as area in square feet per floor^m). See Note a.

Use Group			Type 1 Protected Note b — 1A	Type 1 1B	Type 2 Protected — 2A	Type 2 2B	Type 2 Unprotected — 2C	Type 3 Protected — 3A	Type 3 Unprotected — 3B	Type 4 Heavy timber — 4	Type 5 Protected — 5A	Type 5 Unprotected — 5B
A-1	Assembly, theaters		Not limited	Not limited	5 St. 65' 19,950	3 St. 40' 13,125	2 St. 30' 8,400	3 St. 40' 11,550	2 St. 30' 8,400	3 St. 40' 12,600	1 St. 20' 8,925	1 St. 20' 4,200
A-2	Assembly, nightclubs and similar uses		Not limited	Not limited 7,200	3 St. 40' 5,700	2 St. 30' 3,750	1 St. 20' 2,400	2 St. 30' 3,300	1 St. 20' 2,400	2 St. 30' 3,600	1 St. 20' 2,550	1 St. 20' 1,200
A-3	Assembly	Lecture halls, recreation centers, terminals, restaurants other than nightclubs	Not limited	Not limited	5 St. 65' 19,950	3 St. 40' 13,125	2 St. 30' 8,400	3 St. 40' 11,550	2 St. 30' 8,400	3 St. 40' 12,600	1 St. 20' 8,925	1 St. 20' 4,200
A-4	Assembly, churches	Note c	Not limited	Not limited	5 St. 65' 34,200	3 St. 40' 22,500	2 St. 30' 14,400	3 St. 40' 19,800	2 St. 30' 14,400	3 St. 40' 21,600	1 St. 20' 15,300	1 St. 20' 7,200
B	Business		Not limited	Not limited	7 St. 85' 34,200	5 St. 65' 22,500	3 St. 40' 14,400	4 St. 50' 19,800	3 St. 40' 14,400	5 St. 65' 21,600	3 St. 40' 15,300	2 St. 30' 7,200
E	Educational	Note c	Not limited	Not limited	5 St. 65' 34,200	3 St. 40' 22,500	2 St. 30' 14,400	3 St. 40' 19,800	2 St. 30' 14,400	3 St. 40' 21,600	1 St. 20' 15,300 Note d	1 St. 20' 7,200 Note d
F-1	Factory and industrial, moderate		Not limited	Not limited	6 St. 75' 22,800	4 St. 50' 15,000	2 St. 30' 9,600	3 St. 40' 13,200	2 St. 30' 9,600	4 St. 50' 14,400	2 St. 30' 10,200	1 St. 20' 4,800
F-2	Factory and industrial, low	Note h	Not limited	Not limited	7 St. 85' 34,200	5 St. 65' 22,500	3 St. 40' 14,400	4 St. 50' 19,800	3 St. 40' 14,400	5 St. 65' 21,600	3 St. 40' 15,300	2 St. 30' 7,200
H-1	High hazard, detonation hazards	Notes e, i, k, l	1 St. 20' 10,000	1 St. 20' 14,400	1 St. 20' 11,400	1 St. 20' 7,500	1 St. 20' 4,800	1 St. 20' 6,600	1 St. 20' 4,800	1 St. 20' 7,200	1 St. 20' 5,100	Not permitted
H-2	High hazard, deflagration hazards	Notes e, i, j, l	5 St. 65' 16,800	3 St. 40' 14,400	3 St. 40' 11,400	2 St. 30' 7,500	1 St. 20' 4,800	2 St. 30' 6,600	1 St. 20' 4,800	2 St. 30' 7,200	1 St. 20' 5,100	Not permitted
H-3	High hazard, physical hazards	Notes e, l	7 St. 85' 33,600	7 St. 85' 28,800	6 St. 75' 22,800	4 St. 50' 15,000	2 St. 30' 9,600	3 St. 40' 13,200	2 St. 30' 9,600	4 St. 50' 14,400	2 St. 30' 10,200	1 St 20' 4,800
H-4	High hazard, health hazards	Notes e, l	7 St. 85' Not limited	7 St. 85' Not limited	7 St. 85' 34,200	5 St. 65' 22,500	3 St. 40' 14,400	4 St. 50' 19,800	3 St. 40' 14,400	5 St. 65' 21,600	3 St. 40' 15,300	2 St. 30' 7,200
I-1	Institutional, residential care		Not limited	Not limited	9 St. 100' 19,950	4 St. 50' 13,125	3 St. 40' 8,400	4 St. 50' 11,550	3 St. 40' 8,400	4 St. 50' 12,600	3 St. 40' 8,925	2 St. 35' 4,200
I-2	Institutional, incapacitated		Not limited	Not limited	4 St. 50' 17,100	2 St. 30' 11,250	1 St. 20' 7,200	1 St. 20' 9,900	Not permitted	1 St. 20' 10,800	1 St. 20' 7,650	Not permitted
I-3	Institutional, restrained		Not limited	Not limited	4 St. 50' 14,250	2 St. 30' 9,375	1 St. 20' 6,000	2 St. 30' 8,250	1 St. 20' 6,000	2 St. 30' 9,000	1 St. 20' 6,375	Not permitted
M	Mercantile		Not limited	Not limited	6 St. 75' 22,800	4 St. 50' 15,000	2 St. 30' 9,600	3 St. 40' 13,200	2 St. 30' 9,600	4 St. 50' 14,400	2 St. 30' 10,200	1 St. 20' 4,800
R-1	Residential, hotels		Not limited	Not limited	9 St. 100' 22,800	4 St. 50' 15,000	3 St. 40' 9,600	4 St. 50' 13,200	3 St. 40' 9,600	4 St. 50' 14,400	3 St. 40' 10,200	2 St. 35' 4,800
R-2	Residential, multiple-family		Not limited	Not limited	9 St. 100' 22,800	4 St. 50' 15,000 Note f	3 St. 40' 9,600	4 St. 50' 13,200 Note f	3 St. 40' 9,600	4 St. 50' 14,400	3 St. 40' 10,200	2 St. 35' 4,800
R-3	Residential, one- and two-family and multiple single-family		Not limited	Not limited	4 St. 50' 22,800	4 St. 50' 15,000	3 St. 40' 9,600	3 St. 40' 13,200	3 St. 40' 9,600	3 St. 40' 14,400	3 St. 40' 10,200	2 St. 35' 4,800
S-1	Storage, moderate		Not limited	Not limited	5 St. 65' 19,950	3 St. 40' 13,125	2 St. 30' 8,400	3 St. 40' 11,550	2 St. 30' 8,400	4 St. 50' 12,600	2 St. 30' 8,925	1 St. 30' 4,200
S-2	Storage, low	Note g	Not limited	Not limited	7 St. 85' 34,200	5 St. 65' 22,500	3 St. 40' 14,400	4 St. 50' 19,800	3 St. 40' 14,400	5 St. 65' 21,600	3 St. 40' 15,300	2 St. 30' 7,200
U	Utility, miscellaneous		Not limited	Not limited	5 St. 65' 19,950	4 St. 50' 13,125	2 St. 30' 8,400	3 St. 40' 11,550	2 St. 30' 8,400	4 St. 50' 12,600	2 St. 30' 8,925	1 St. 20' 4,200

Note a. See the following sections for general exceptions to Table 503:
    Section 504.2 Allowable height increase due to automatic sprinkler system installation.
    Section 506.2 Allowable area increase due to street frontage.
    Section 506.3 Allowable area increase due to automatic sprinkler system installation.
    Section 506.4 Allowable area reduction for multistory buildings.
    Section 507.0 Unlimited area one-story buildings.
Note b. Buildings of Type 1 construction permitted to be of unlimited tabular heights and areas are not subject to special requirements that allow increased heights and areas for other types of construction (see Section 503.1.3).
Note c. For height exceptions for auditoriums in occupancies in Use Groups A-4 and E, see Section 504.3.
Note d. For height exceptions for day care centers in buildings of Type 5 construction, see Section 504.4.
Note e. For exceptions to height and area limitations for buildings with occupancies in Use Group H, see Chapter 4 governing the specific use groups.
Note f. For exceptions to height of buildings with occupancies in Use Group R-2 of Types 2B and 3A construction, see Sections 504.6 and 504.7.
Note g. For height and area exceptions for open parking structures, see Section 406.0.
Note h. For exceptions to height and area limitations for special industrial occupancies, see Section 507.1.
Note i. Occupancies in Use Groups H-1 and H-2 shall not be permitted below grade.
Note j. Rooms and areas of Use Group H-2 containing pyrophoric materials shall not be permitted in buildings of Type 3, 4 or 5 construction.
Note k. Occupancies in Use Group H-1 are required to be detached one-story buildings (see Section 707.1.1).
Note l. For exceptions to height for buildings with occupancies in Use Group H, see Section 504.5.
Note m. 1 foot = 304.8 mm; 1 square foot = 0.093 m^2.

Figure 3.3. *BOCA National Building Code (NBC)* Table 503, "Height and Area Limitations of Buildings." (Copyright 1999, Building Officials and Code Administrators International, Inc., Country Club Hills, Illinois, *BOCA National Building Code/1999.* Reproduced with permission. All rights reserved.)

from the *NBC*, titled Table 503, "Height and Area Limitations of Buildings." It is similar to Table 500, "Allowable Heights and Building Areas" found in the *SBC*, Table 5-B, "Basic Allowable Building Heights and Basic Allowable Floor Area for Buildings One Story in Height," found in the *UBC*, and Table 503 "Allowable Height and Building Areas" in the *IBC*. (Note that the *LSC* does not regulate a building's size.)

These tables govern the size of a building by setting height and floor area limits by occupancy classification within each type of construction. In Figure 3.3 each of the occupancy classifications or use groups used by the *NBC* is listed down the left side of the table. Along the top is each of the construction types as they were defined by the *NBC* table shown in Figure 3.1. The remainder of the table provides the height and area limitations for these categories.

When the type of construction is cross-referenced with the occupancy classification, the table will indicate two figures. The top figure indicates the maximum number of stories and the total feet above grade allowed. The bottom figure in the corresponding box indicates the maximum allowed area or square feet per floor.

Example

If you are hired to do a design for a particular occupancy that is moving into a new building not originally built for that occupancy classification, you may be required to determine if it is allowed by codes. It is important to determine this early in the design. Since each code places restrictions by limiting the type of construction in certain occupancy classifications, you may find that a project is not feasible.

You may be helping a client select a space or building or helping a client who owns a building look for a particular tenant. If you are doing the former, you will need to determine the occupancy of the client, calculate the approximate number of occupants, and determine the construction type restrictions for that occupancy. The code will either (1) give you restrictions for a specific occupancy to help limit the choice of buildings to the stricter construction types or (2) give you no restriction so you know any type of building is allowed.

For example, a restaurant owner may hire you to design a new interior. However, he or she may still be in the process of deciding on the final location. If you are asked to help make the final decision, the first step is to determine the expected occupancy of the restaurant. By asking the owner how many people the restaurant will serve, you will be able to determine if the occupancy classification is Business or Assembly. The *NBC* draws the cutoff point at 50 people. (See Chapter 2.) In this case, if the owner plans to open a restaurant that seats no more than 40 people, it would be classified as a Business occupancy or use group.

Next, you need to use the occupant load table and formula found in Chapter 2 to determine how much square footage is required for a 40 seat, or 40-person, restaurant. The *NBC* occupant load Table 1008.1.2 (similar to the one in Figure 2.2 in Chapter 2) requires an occupant load factor of 100 gross square feet (GSF) per occupant. By adjusting the formula Occupant Load = Floor Area/Load Factor, to Floor Area Required = Load Factor × Occupant Load, the total would be 40 people × 100 GSF = 4000 square feet or floor area.

With this minimum square foot figure of 4000 go back to the building size table in Figure 3.3. Even if you were to add an additional 1000 square feet to the restaurant to account for additional personnel, storage, kitchen, and other areas, as you look along the table, all the square footage listed across the Business occupancy is well over that amount. Therefore, this restaurant can occupy a building with any construction type as long as it falls within the height limitations. Unless the owner occupies a fully noncombustible building, most of the other types of construction will limit the building to one to three stories.

What if the owner plans instead to open an 800-person nightclub? In that case it would be classified by the *NBC* as an A-2 Assembly occupancy. You would use the same tables and method to determine the total required square footage. The *NBC* occupancy load table requires 7 net square feet (NSF) per person with concentrated seating. Therefore, 800 people × 7 NSF = 5600 square feet. Looking at the table in Figure 3.3 you would find that only three construction types under the A-2 Assembly category are satisfactory: Types 1A, 1B, and 2A.

Height and Area Limitations

As you can see from the many notes listed at the bottom of the table in Figure 3.3, there are a number of exceptions to the table. A building's maximum size is limited by many factors, such as construction type, occupancy classification, and location. In other cases the regulated size may be exceeded if the building is equipped with features such as automatic sprinklers and fire walls.

Below are some of the typical rules and most common exceptions when evaluating allowable building heights and floor areas.

HIGH-RISE BUILDINGS

The most common definition of a high-rise building is any building that exceeds 75 feet (23 m) in height. This dimension is based on the fact that the ladders on fire department vehicles do not reach past this point. Therefore, the building height is typically measured from the lowest ground level a fire truck can access outside the building to the floor of the highest occupiable story.

The codes apply stricter requirements to high-rise buildings because it is assumed that they will not be totally evacuated in an emergency. Wall and floor assemblies are used to create separate compartments within the building. This is called *compartmentation* and is very important to restrict the spread of fire and smoke and to provide safe *areas of refuge* to the occupants during a fire. (See Chapter 5.) Only noncombustible building materials and assemblies with fire ratings are allowed. Additional safeguards include the mandatory use of automatic sprinkler systems and an overlapping of detection and suppression systems. (See Chapter 6.)

NOTE: Some local jurisdictions may use a shorter dimension to define the height of a high-rise building, based on the local conditions and fire department equipment.

They are listed as reference points to help guide you in your research. If you ever need to determine or analyze a building's allowed height and area, be sure to consult the building code in the jurisdiction of your project and reference the correct tables. Each building code will vary slightly.

1. **Construction Type:** Generally, the stricter the construction type, and the more noncombustible a building, the larger the allowed building. For example, Type I construction, which is the most noncombustible, usually has no height limitations and few area limitations.
2. **Occupancy Classification:** Certain occupancy classifications will restrict the size of a building as well as the type of construction. Other occupancies need to meet specific requirements to allow an increase in area and/or height. These requirements are stated in other sections of the code, usually by occupancy. For example, an educational building that has at least two exits per classroom with one opening directly outdoors can increase in size.
3. **Number of Occupants:** As the number of occupants increases and the occupants become more immobile, there will be more restrictions on the height and area. Assembly and Institutional occupancies are especially affected. (See Chapter 2 for occupant loads.)

4. **Location:** The location or distance of adjacent buildings as well as the amount of street frontage can affect the allowed area. For example, buildings with permanent surrounding open spaces can increase the amount of floor area. This exterior space prevents fire spread to or from adjacent buildings.

5. **Sprinklers:** The use of approved automatic sprinklers can increase the number of stories or the floor area allowed. Some occupancies require sprinklers in buildings of every size. Other occupancies may limit this option. (See Chapter 6 for additional sprinkler trade-offs.)

6. **Fire Walls:** Fire walls can subdivide a building so that each created space is treated as a separate entity. Each created fire area or compartment must stay within its own size limitation, allowing the overall building to become larger. (See Chapter 5 for more information.)

7. **Hazardous:** Hazardous occupancies have a number of specific requirements. Refer to the codes.

8. **Single Stories:** Single-story buildings are usually allowed greater flexibility in size of floor area. Each code sets a limit on the height of the story.

9. **Mezzanines:** Each code treats mezzanines differently. They can be considered part of the story in which they are located or they can be treated as a separate story. There are a number of other limitations as well. (See inset titled *Atriums and Mezzanines* on page 66.)

10. **Basements:** Area and height requirements for basements are specific to each code. Whether a basement is counted as a story depends on how much of it is above ground level and the occupancy of the building.

Determining construction types and building sizes may not be a part of every interior project. These variables are usually determined at the initial construction of the building. However, if the occupancy of a building changes, it will be important to be able to analyze an existing building and determine its construction type and building size. You need to do this in the early stages of the design. You may determine the project is not feasible, or you may need to include certain things (i.e., sprinklers) in your design to make it comply with the codes. Be sure to work closely with the appropriate professionals when necessary. These include architects, engineers, contractors, and code officials.

Construction types are discussed again in Chapter 5 in the topic of fire separation. Construction types are used in conjunction with other table and code information to determine the required fire ratings of interior construction such as walls and ceilings. Compartmentation and fire walls become an important means of controlling potential fires as well. Chapter 5 and Chapter 6 continue the discussion and concentrate on the control of fire and smoke in the interior of a building.

CHAPTER 4

MEANS OF EGRESS

A means of egress is most commonly described as a continuous and unobstructed path of travel from any point in a building to its exterior or public way. It can also be the path of travel an occupant uses to obtain a safe area of refuge within a building. A means of egress comprises both vertical and horizontal passageways, including such components as doorways, corridors, stairs, ramps, enclosures, and intervening rooms. The design of these components is crucial to the safety of the building occupants in normal use of a building and especially during emergencies.

This chapter explains the various means of egress. The first half of the chapter concentrates on the different types and components of the egresses. The rest of the chapter discusses how to determine means of egress—their required quantities, sizes, and locations. Accessibility requirements are also discussed. Although the codes usually separate means of egress codes and accessibility requirements, they should be considered together. Many of the requirements overlap, so you must compare them to make sure you are using the strictest ones. This chapter has combined the discussion of these topics wherever possible.

Remember that not every means of egress mentioned in this chapter will be used in every interior project. In addition, many existing buildings will already have the required number of exits. You may be working with just one occupant or tenant in the building and will need to consider only the exiting within and from that tenant space. Some projects may require you to reevaluate the existing exit requirements and make alterations. Other

> **Note**
>
> **Elevators, escalators, and moving walks are typically *not* considered a means of egress, since the codes do not usually allow them to be used as an exit during an emergency. In rare cases they are required as an accessible means of egress. (See *Elevators*, p. 85.)**

projects will require new calculations. Either way, every interior project must meet specific means of egress requirements.

In this chapter you will learn how and when to use a wide variety of codes, standards, and federal regulations that pertain to the various means of egress. Some of the requirements are based on occupant loads that have been discussed in Chapter 2. Specific fire ratings are also required for each means of egress. These are further explained in Chapter 5. Chapter 9 explains the different types of finishes allowed in each area of a means of egress.

DEFINITIONS

Before continuing be sure you are familiar with some of the common means of egress terms described below.

AREA OF REFUGE: A protected area where persons unable to use stairways can remain temporarily to await instructions or assistance during emergency evacuation. An area of refuge is most often located with a direct access to an exit.

BUILDING CORE: A building element that is vertically continuous through one or more floors of a building for the vertical distribution of mechanical, electrical, plumbing, and other services. Elevators are also typically located in the building core.

COMMON PATH OF TRAVEL: That portion of an exit access that leads to two separate and distinct paths of egress travel or two separate exits. Paths that merge are also considered common paths of travel.

CORRIDOR: An enclosed passageway that provides a path of egress to an exit. A corridor is typically considered an exit access component of the means of egress.

HORIZONTAL PASSAGE: Allows movement between rooms or areas on the same floor or story such as a corridor or a door.

NATURAL PATH OF TRAVEL: The most direct route a person can take while following an imaginary line on the floor, avoiding obstacles such as walls, equipment, and furniture, to arrive at the final destination.

OCCUPANT LOAD: The (minimum) number of people or occupants for which the code will require you to provide means of egress or exiting in your design. (See occupant content.)

OCCUPANT CONTENT: The actual number of total occupants for which exiting has been provided. This is the maximum number of people that can occupy the space. Note that the *IBC* uses the term *actual occupant load*, instead.

PASSAGEWAY: An enclosed pathway or corridor.

STAIRWAY: One or more flights of stairs with the required land-ings and platforms necessary to form a continuous and unin-terrupted vertical passage.

STORY: The portion of a building from the finished floor to the fin-ished floor or roof structure above.

TENANT: A person or group of people (i.e., a company) who use or occupy a portion of a building through a lease and/or payment of rent.

VERTICAL PASSAGE: A passage, such as a stairway or an elevator, that allows movement from floor to floor.

COMPARING THE CODES

As the different types of means of egress are described in this chapter, a number of codes, standards, and regulations are men-tioned. The building codes and the *Life Safety Code (LSC)* set most of the requirements for each of the means of egress types. Each of these code publications has a whole chapter dedicated to "means of egress."

Each code sets similar requirements. Some of the require-ments are listed in a table such as the *Standard Building Code* (*SBC*) table in Figure 4.1. Table 1004, "Travel Distance, Deadend Length, Exit, and Means of Egress Width," lists a number of the variables and dimensions discussed throughout this chapter. The other codes either use more than one table to list the same information, such as the ones shown in Figures 4.9 and 4.14, or give the require-ments within their text.

These codes must be reviewed in conjunction with the federal *Americans with Disabilities Act Accessibility Guidelines (ADAAG)*. The *ADAAG* sets minimum requirements that are in many cases stricter than the codes. Some of these code differences are explained in this chapter. You will find others as you do your research for particular projects. If your jurisdiction requires a building code as well as the *LSC*, be sure to compare them to each other in addition to the *ADAAG*. In most instances, following the strictest regulation is the solution. If in doubt, be sure to discuss it with the code officials in the jurisdiction of the project.

In addition, be sure to review the particular occupancy classi-fication(s) of your project. Although most of the regulations are fairly consistent, some occupancies allow certain exceptions or have additional requirements. Some of the exceptions are given within the means of egress chapters, and others are grouped by

Note

The *ADAAG* is used as the main accessibility source in this chapter since it is required country wide. However, if a jurisdiction requires you to use the ANSI standards, you should check both the *ADAAG* and ANSI to make sure you are using the most stringent requirement.

TABLE 1004
TRAVEL DISTANCE, DEAD-END LENGTH, EXIT AND MEANS OF EGRESS WIDTH

OCCUPANCY CLASSIFICATION	MAXIMUM TRAVEL DIST. TO EXIT (FT)		MAXIMUM DEAD END CORRIDOR LENGTH (FT)	EGRESS WIDTH PER PERSON SERVED (IN)		MINIMUM CORRIDOR/ AISLE WIDTH (IN)	MINIMUM CLEAR OP'G OF EXIT DOORS (IN)	MINIMUM STAIR WIDTH[10] (IN)
	UNSPRK.	SPRK.		LEVEL[12]	STAIRS			
Group A	200	250	20	0.2	0.37^{14}	$44^{1,10}$	32	44
Group B	200	250	20	0.2	0.37^{14}	44^{10}	32	44
Group E	200	250	20	0.2	0.37^{14}	72^{2}	32	44
Group F	200	250^{7}	20	0.2	0.37^{14}	44^{10}	32	44
Group H	NP	100^{13}	20	0.4	0.7	44^{10}	32	44
Group I Restrained	$Varies^{11}$	$Varies^{11}$	20	0.2	0.37^{14}	48	32	44
Group I Unrestrained	150	200	20	0.2	0.37^{14}	44^{3}	36^{9}	44
Group M	200	250	20	0.2	0.37^{14}	$44^{4,10}$	32	44
Group R	200	250	20^{8}	0.2	0.37^{14}	$44^{5,10}$	32	44
Group S	200^{6}	$250^{6,7}$	20	0.2	0.37^{14}	44^{10}	32	44

For SI: 1 in = 25.4 mm, 1 ft = 0.305 m.
Notes:
1. See 1019.10.2.
2. For occupant loads less than 100 persons, 44 inches may be used.
3. 96 inches shall be provided in areas requiring the movement of beds.
4. See 413 for covered mall buildings.
5. 36 inches shall be permitted within dwelling units.
6. Maximum travel distance shall be increased to 300 ft if unsprinklered and 400 ft if sprinklered for Group S2 occupancies and open parking structures constructed per 411.
7. See 1004.1.6 for exceptions.
8. See 1026.1.1 for exceptions.
9. 44 inches required in areas requiring movement of beds.
10. 36 inches acceptable if stair or corridor serves occupant load of less than 50.
11. See 1024.2.6.
12. Applies to ramps, doors and corridors.
13. For HPM facilities, as defined in 408, the maximum travel distance shall be 100 ft.
14. Use 0.3 for stairs having tread depths 11 inches or greater and riser heights between 4 inches minimum and 7 inches maximum.

Figure 4.1. *Standard Building Code (SBC)* Table 1004, "Travel Distance, Dead-end Length, Exit and Means of Egress Width." (Reproduced from the 1999 *SBC* with permission of the copyright holder, Southern Building Code Congress International, Inc., all rights reserved.)

occupancy classification in different sections of the codes. Assembly occupancies especially must be reviewed, since the use of fixed seats can create unusual egress paths. (See the section on Aisles later in this chapter.)

TYPES OF MEANS OF EGRESS

A means of egress is a broad term that covers a variety of building components. Each of the codes divides a means of egress into three main categories: exit access, exit, and exit discharge. A public way is the final destination of a means of egress. All four means of egress are defined below. The first three deal with the interior of a building and are described in the first half of this chapter.

EXIT ACCESS: The portion of a means of egress that leads to the entrance of an exit. It includes any room or space occupied by a person and any doorway, aisle, corridor, stair, or ramp traveled on the way to the exit.

EXIT: The portion of a means of egress that is protected and fully enclosed and is between the exit access and the exit discharge or public way. It can be as basic as the exterior exit door or it can include enclosed stairwells and ramps. In some special cases, it can include certain corridors or passageways. The components of an exit are distinguished from the exit accesses by higher fire ratings.

EXIT DISCHARGE: The portion of a means of egress between the termination of an exit and the public way. It can be inside a building such as the main lobby, or outside a building such as an exterior vestibule, courtyard, patio, small alley, or other safe passageway.

PUBLIC WAY: The area outside a building between the exit discharge and a public street. Examples would include an alley or a sidewalk. The area must have a minimum clear width and height of not less than 10 feet (3048 mm) to be considered a public way.

A diagram has been provided in Figure 4.2 to help clarify some of the differences between each of these areas. As indicated in the diagram, certain parts of a building can be defined as a specific type of egress, but this is not always the case. For example, the *IBC*, *UBC*, and *LSC* consider an exit passageway as part of the exit component of the means of egress, while the *SBC* and the *NBC* consider it part of the exit discharge. The location of an occupant can also define a means of egress. For example, if a person were standing in the lobby of this diagram, the distance from the person to the exit door would be the exit access and the exit door would be the exit.

Although the parts of an exit can be defined differently among the various codes, they all assume that a means of egress will be continuous. This path provides protection to the occupant from the floor of origin to the ground level and public way. And, because an exit has a higher fire rating and provides a better level of protection, the codes also assume that an occupant is relatively

> **Note**
>
> **What distinguishes a public way from an exit discharge is its size. For example, any alley can be an exit discharge, but if it is over 10 feet wide and 10 feet high it is a public way.**

> **Note**
>
> **Depending on which code you are using, an exit passageway can be considered an exit or an exit discharge.**

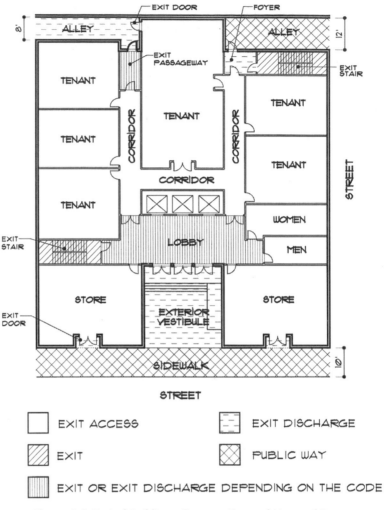

Figure 4.2. Typical Building—Common Types of Means of Egress.

safe once he or she reaches an exit. The requirements for the types of means of egress and its components are to assure that the level of protection is maintained until the occupant is in the public way.

What follows is a description of the types of means of egress and the various components of each. Exit accesses are described first. These components are elaborated in more detail, since similar components in the other means of egress categories have many of the same requirements. For example, *exit access* stairs and *exit* stairs are used for different purposes and require different fire protection, but they both use the same tread and riser dimensions, landing widths, handrail requirements, and so on.

Exit Accesses

An exit access is that portion of a means of egress that leads to an exit. It leads an occupant from a room or space to an exit and can include doors, stairs, ramps, corridors, aisles, and intervening rooms. Exit accesses do not necessarily require a fire rating or need to be fully enclosed. For example, a corridor in a tenant space usually does not need to be rated; however, a main building corridor connecting the tenants and the public spaces may be required to be rated. (See Chapter 5 for information on fire ratings.)

The type and location of an exit access depends on the layout of the building or space and the location of the occupants in the area. For example, in a large open space or room that has a door as the exit, the exit access is the path of travel to that exit door. In a multistory building where an enclosed stair is the exit, the exit access can include the enclosed corridor leading to the exit and the rooms and doors leading into the corridor. (See Figure 4.1.)

Each component of an exit access is described below. The descriptions include a discussion of the basic code requirements as well as some of the necessary accessibility standards. The second half of this chapter discusses how to determine the quantity, width, and location of an exit access.

Doors: The codes regulate each component of a doorway. First, the door itself must be of a particular type, size, and swing, depending on where it is located. The most common exit access door is used along a corridor and connects the adjacent rooms or spaces to the exit access corridor. Since these corridors often have a one-hour fire rating, the doors must be rated as well. (See the section on Fire Doors, page 134.) Other exit access doors, such as within a tenant space, are not typically required to be rated.

Determining the required number of doors and the required width of each is described in the section on Exit Width later in this chapter, but the codes set minimum dimensions and other requirements that must be followed as well. Most doors in the means of egress cannot be less than 6 feet 8 inches high. Each of the building codes and the *ADAAG* specify that when in an open position a door must provide 32 inches of clear width. Since this must be the clear inside dimension, as shown in Figure 4.3, typically, a door that is at least 36 inches in width must be used. Other clearance dimensions are required by both the codes and the *ADAAG*, depending on the type of door, its location within the space, and the occupancy classification. This includes minimum clearances on the jamb side of the door and allowable projections (including hardware). (See Figure 4.4. for typical clearances at doorways.)

> **Note**
>
> When determining the location of means of egress remember that, except for doors, the typical headroom required from floor to ceiling or tread to ceiling is 80 inches.

> **Note**
>
> Exit access doors typically have a lower rating than exit doors.

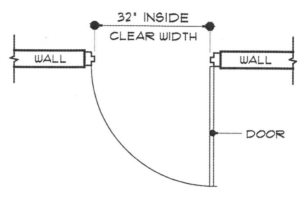

Figure 4.3. Accessible Door, Clear Door Width.

Usually, an egress door must be side-hinged, swinging doors. The direction of the swing depends on its location. In most cases, means of egress doors must swing in the direction of exit travel. However, the door cannot reduce any required stair landing dimensions by more than 7 inches when the door is fully open and not more than half of the required corridor width at any open position. The *ADAAG* lists additional maneuvering clearances as well. Depending on whether the approach to the door is from the push or pull side and hinge or latch side, the *ADAAG* will require 12, 18, or 24 inch minimum clearances. (See Figure 4.4.)

To avoid obstructing the required widths, the codes allow some smaller occupancies or rooms to have doors that swing into a space. An example would be an office or small conference room. (Usually the cutoff is 50 occupants.) On the other hand, if an interior project requires a door to swing out toward the path of exit travel, there are several options that can be used to meet the minimum code requirements. The most common are listed below. Figure 4.4 indicates these options and highlights the critical dimensions required by codes, *ADAAG*, and ANSI.

1. Use a 180-degree swing door instead of a 90-degree door to allow it to fully open against the wall. (This can be done only if a corridor is wide enough.)
2. Recess the door into the room so that the walls create an alcove that the door can swing into. (The alcove must allow maneuvering room.)
3. Enlarge the landing at the door, such as widening a corridor or lengthening a vestibule, to allow enough maneuvering space.
4. Use a sliding door in low traffic areas and when allowed by the codes.

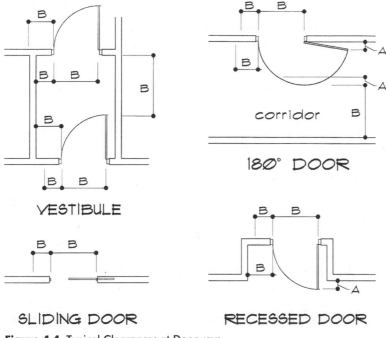

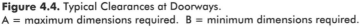

Figure 4.4. Typical Clearances at Doorways.
A = maximum dimensions required. B = minimum dimensions required.

Other door types are allowed to be used as part of the means of egress in certain situations. These types include revolving doors, power-operated swinging doors, and power-operated horizontal sliding doors. Because they work differently than swinging door types, the codes impose additional requirements for their use in the case of an emergency. Revolving doors are required to collapse to provide the minimum clear width, and power-operated doors are required to be capable of opening manually in case of an emergency or loss of electricity. In addition, the codes often limit the number of these special door types, which can be used as part of the exits in a project. The occupancy type can also determine if these door types can be used for a project. For example, many of these special doors are limited to use in occupancies such as Institutional and Mercantile.

The threshold is another part of a doorway regulated by the codes. Each code states that the finished floor surface or landing on either side of an interior door must be at the same elevation as the threshold or within ½ inch of the threshold. In addition, if the transition is greater than ¼ inch, the *ADAAG* requires both sides of the threshold be beveled at a specific slope.

Hardware on means of egress doors is also regulated. The *ADAAG* requires that all door pulls be accessible operating

Note

Where doors are subject to two-way travel it is suggested that a vision panel be used in the door to avoid collisions.

devices. They must be a certain shape and be installed at a specific height. Any operating device must be capable of operation with one hand and without much effort. For example, lever, push-type, and **U**-shaped pulls are accessible. In most cases, locks that would hinder an egress are not allowed. (See codes for exceptions.) Both the codes and the *ADAAG* set other requirements, such as door opening forces, the use of self-closing doors, and clearances at doors. (For additional information, see section on Security in Chapter 8.)

Elevators: There are two main types of elevators—freight and passenger elevators. In most cases, the elevator will not be considered as part of the means of egress required for a space or building. That means that *they will not be counted* when determining the total exits needed. Instead, elevators are usually linked to a building's smoke alarm system. (See Chapter 6 for more information.) When a smoke detector is activated during an emergency, the elevators are automatically recalled to an approved location (usually the ground floor) that, when necessary, can be activated manually with a key by the fire fighters. If the elevator is not being used for part of the means of egress, you must have directional signage and diagrams that identify the direction to the nearest exit.

On the other hand, there are certain situations that require an elevator to be a mean of egress. Since both the codes and *ADAAG* require that an accessible means of egress be provided, you may need to determine if you must include the elevator as part of the means of egress. For example, if an area of refuge is not provided at the stairways, it may be necessary to include the elevator as part of the accessible means of egress The number of stories in a building may also dictate whether an accessible elevator is required.

Note

Platform lifts are a form of an elevator. They are usually used in existing buildings when short vertical distances must be covered for accessibility reasons. Most are not allowed as a means of egress, but the *ADAAG* does provide exceptions.

For an elevator to be considered part of the means of egress, additional provisions must be met. The elevator itself must comply with emergency operation and signaling device requirements as specified in ANSI/ASME A17.1 and be provided with standby power. It must also be located adjacent to an area of refuge or be separated from the fire area by a horizontal exit. (See inset titled *Area of Refuge*, page 94, and the discussion on horizontal exits, page 92.) Complying with these requirements provides for an accessible means of egress for persons with disabilities. (See the inset on the facing page for additional accessibility information.)

Stairs: Exit access stairs are not as common as exit stairs. They are typically found within a space when one tenant occupies more than one floor of a building or where there is a mezzanine within a

ELEVATORS

Elevators are not typically considered a means of egress, especially during an emergency. However, since they are used on a daily basis during normal operation, elevators must meet specific accessibility requirements as defined in the codes, the *ADAAG*, and the ANSI standards. Below is a list of the main requirements to consider. (Diagrams are available in the *ADAAG* and the ANSI standards.)

1. Automatic operation with self-leveling within a certain range.
2. Power-operated sliding doors that open to a minimum width.
3. Door delay and automatic reopening device effective for a specific time period.
4. Standard size car, depending on the type of sliding door.
5. Hall call buttons and car controls with specific arrangement, location, and height (including Braille and raised lettering).
6. Minimum distances from hall call button to elevator door.
7. Hall lanterns and car position indicators that are visual and audible.
8. Specific two-way emergency communication system.
9. Handrail on at least one wall of the car.
10. Floor surfaces that are firm, stable, and slip resistant.
11. Minimum lighting levels.
12. Specific door jamb signage at hoistway entrance on each floor.
13. Emergency exit signs located near elevator doors.

Buildings with at least one elevator must have a minimum of one accessible elevator, with the exception of some two-story buildings. Many new buildings are required to make all passenger elevators accessible. If you are working with existing elevators you must make them as accessible as possible. New elevators are usually designed in conjunction with an engineer or an elevator consultant.

space. For example, a flight of stairs between the 16th and 17th floors within a tenant space will allow the occupant to move between the two floors without leaving the tenant space. Usually these exit access stairs do not need to be enclosed within fire-rated walls unless the same stair connects more than two floors.

There are a number of different stair types in addition to the straight run stair. These include curved, winder, spiral, scissor, switchback, and alternating tread stairs. Most of these are allowed by the codes on a limited basis, depending on the occupancy classification, the number of occupants, the use of the stair, and the dimension of the treads. In addition, the materials used to

Note

The *LSC* permits new stairs in existing buildings to comply with previous stair requirements when alterations are made. However, depending on the location of the stairs, be sure you follow any necessary *ADA* regulations.

Note

When determining stair dimensions you should know what floor covering will ultimately cover the construction. Some floor coverings may change the final dimension of the treads or risers and, therefore, the effectiveness of the stair. The required dimensions are based on much research and are critical for ease of use.

build the stairway must be consistent with the construction type of the building. (See Chapter 3.)

All stairs are required to meet specific code and accessibility requirements. The most important are the tread and riser dimensions. The most common dimensions are shown in Figure 4.5, with a minimum tread depth of 11 inches and a range of 4 to 7 inches for riser height. The actual size of the riser will be determined by the overall vertical height of the stairway. Once the riser size is determined it is not allowed to fluctuate more than a small fraction from step to step. The shape and the size of the nosings are defined as well.

Each run of stairs must have a landing at the top and the bottom. In addition, the codes do not usually allow a stairway to rise more than 12 feet without an intermediate platform or landing. The width of the stair (as determined later in this chapter) determines the minimum dimensions of these required landings or platforms. Other variables may also increase the size of the landing. For example, if a door swings into the stairway, the location of the door may increase the size of the landing. The required areas of refuge may also increase the size of a landing. (See inset titled *Areas of Refuge* on page 94.)

Handrails and guardrails are regulated as well. Most stairs require a handrail on both sides. (See the codes for exceptions.)

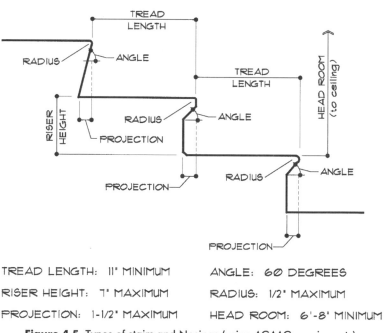

TREAD LENGTH: 11" MINIMUM   ANGLE: 60 DEGREES

RISER HEIGHT: 7" MAXIMUM   RADIUS: 1/2" MAXIMUM

PROJECTION: 1-1/2" MAXIMUM   HEAD ROOM: 6'-8" MINIMUM

Figure 4.5. Types of stairs and Nosings (using AGAAG requirments).

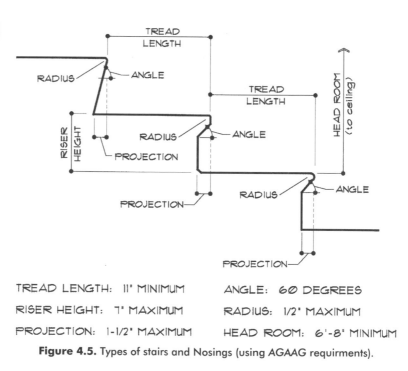

When wide stairs are used, additional intermediate handrails may be required. Building codes and accessibility codes require handrails to be certain styles and sizes, to be installed at specific heights and distances from the wall, and to be continuous wherever possible. Figure 4.6 indicates some of these typical handrail dimensions and locations. Note that the handrail must extend a certain distance beyond the top and bottom of the stairway and have an uninterrupted grip. In addition, when open on both sides, the handrail must be constructed so that nothing with a 4-inch diameter can pass through any opening created by the rail config-

Note

Handrails are critical during an emergency. When stairs are full of smoke, handrails often are the only guide to an exit.

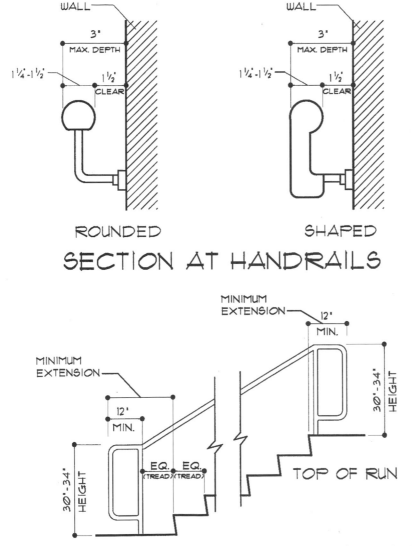

Figure 4.6. Extension of Handrails (using AGAAG requirments).

uration. (Note that some handrails may be recessed if the recess is in compliance with the *ADAAG*.)

Guardrails (or guards as they are now called by the *IBC*) are typically necessary whenever there is a change in elevation over 30 inches where occupants are walking. The most common example of this is at a stair when any side of the stair is exposed and not enclosed by a wall. In most instances, the guardrail must be at least 42 inches high and be constructed with the same 4-inch rule as the handrail. The guardrail does not take the place of a handrail as required for accessibility. Rather, the *ADAAG* requires a handrail to be located within the 34- to 38-inch height in addition to the guardrail. These requirements must be met whether you are specifying a prefabricated rail system or designing your own.

Escalators and Moving Walks: Like elevators, escalators and moving walks are not typically allowed as a *means* of egress. However, there are some exceptions in existing buildings. Existing escalators are allowed only if they are fully enclosed within fire-rated walls and doors. Some may also require specific sprinkler requirements.

Newer escalators and moving walks are usually installed as an additional path of travel or as a convenience to the occupants of a building. Some of the more common occupancy classifications that use escalators and moving walks are Assemblies and large Mercantile and Residential occupancies. When the escalators or moving walks are used they are *not counted as a means of egress*. Each space or building must still have the required number of enclosed stairs as specified by the codes.

Ramps: In general, ramps are used anywhere there is a change in elevation and accessibility is required. You should try to avoid changes in elevation on a single floor. If steps are required, such as in a corridor, then a ramp must be provided as well. The most important requirement of a ramp is the slope ratio. Most codes and accessibility standards set the *maximum* ratio at 1 to 12. That means for every vertical rise of 1 inch, the horizontal run of the ramp must extend 12 inches. This is shown in Figure 4.7.

The other important requirement is the use of landings. Both the codes and the *ADAAG* require landings at certain intervals and of certain dimensions. The exact requirements depend on the length of the ramp and any changes in direction. Landings are also required at the top and bottom of every ramp and must take into

---

Note

The *IBC* uses the term guard instead of guardrail.

Note

A ramp with a lower slope ratio should be used whenever possible. For example, a 1 to 16 ratio is more manageable and safer for persons with disabilities.

Note

Ramps not specifically designed or intended for the disabled can usually have a slightly steeper slope as allowed by the codes. (Verify this with your code official.) However, it is advisable to use an accessible slope whenever possible.

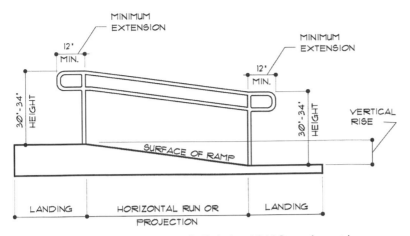

Figure 4.7. Typical Ramp with Handrails (using AGAAG requirments).

account any adjacent doors. Both the landings and the ramps require specific edge details and a rough type of nonslip surface.

The construction of the ramp and its handrails is similar to that of stairs. Handrails are typically required when the ramps exceed a certain length or rise. Similar to stairs, the handrails are required to extend a certain distance beyond the landing. Guardrails may also be required. Width and clearance requirements for ramps are similar to those for corridors.

Corridors: A corridor consists of the surrounding walls and the ceiling above. An exit access corridor is any corridor leading to the exit in a building. Typically, these corridors are either nonrated or have a one-hour fire-rating, depending on their location, the occupant load that they are serving, and if the building is sprinklered. For example, corridors in a small tenant space or an apartment unit leading to a door entering the exit access corridor for the building typically do not need to be rated. On the other hand, the corridor that connects each of these tenant spaces or apartment units and leads to the exit stairs will typically be required to be rated one hour. (In some jurisdictions, if sprinklers are used, a rating may not be required.) This rating also determines the fire rating of the doors entering the exit access corridor. (See section on Corridor Walls in Chapter 5, page 128.)

Both the width and the length (travel distance) of a corridor are limited by the codes. (This is described later in this chapter.) In addition, there are specific accessibility clearances that must be met. These include (1) minimum clearances for corridors that change direction, (2) passing spaces in extra long corridors, and

Note

There is a distinction between ramps and curb ramps. Curb ramps are typically exterior ramps cut through or leading to a curb. Other ramps can be interior or exterior.

Note

Movable walls, panel systems, counters, and similar space dividers can sometimes be considered a corridor, depending on the jurisdiction. (See the discussion of Aisles on page 90.)

Note

The required dimensions for stairs and ramps used in Assembly aisleways are different than those for other standard ramps and stairs. Typically, the riser of the stair is shorter and the slope of the ramp is smaller to accommodate the large number of people.

(3) maximum depth of objects protruding into the corridor. When doors are recessed or used at the end of a corridor, additional clearances must be added to the width of the corridor to make sure the access to the door is wide enough. (See clearances in Figure 4.4 and the example given in the section on Exit Width, page 103.)

Aisles: An exit access aisle is similar to a corridor in that it is a passageway required to reach an exit. The difference is that a corridor is enclosed by full height walls, while an aisle is a pathway created by furniture or equipment. The codes and *ADAAG* set minimum widths for different situations. Some of the requirements are similar to those for corridors, ramps, and stairs. Other specific requirements must be met as well. Since there are a variety of requirements, it is important to consider and compare each.

The necessary requirements depend on whether the aisle is created with fixed seats or without fixed seats. When there are *no fixed seats*, aisles can be created by tables, counters, furnishings, equipment, merchandise, and other similar obstructions. For example, aisles are created between movable panel systems in offices, between tables and chairs in restaurants, and between display racks in retail stores. The codes and the *ADAAG* give specific width requirements in these situations.

Aisles created by *fixed seats* are typically found in Assembly occupancies. Because of the large number of occupants, the codes set strict requirements on the width of these aisles, depending on the size of the occupancy, the number of seats each aisle is serving, and whether the aisle is a ramp or a stair. The minimum distances between the seats and where the aisles terminate is also regulated. (Refer to Assembly occupancies in the codes.)

Adjoining or Intervening Rooms: Although an exit access should be as direct as possible, some projects may require an access path to pass through an adjoining room or space before reaching a corridor or exit. Most of the codes will allow this as long as the path provides a direct, unobstructed, and obvious means of travel toward an exit. Such a path may be as simple as a route from a doctor's office that requires passing through the waiting room to reach the corridor.

It is this requirement that allows smaller rooms adjoining larger spaces to exit through the large room to access a corridor. For example, a number of private offices might surround an open office space. Some other common adjoining or intervening rooms that are not restricted by the codes include reception areas, lobbies, and foyers. Exit accessways are allowed to pass through these rooms as long as they meet the specified code requirements.

The codes do place some restrictions on this rule, especially on rooms that tend to be locked some or all of the time. Kitchens, storerooms, restrooms, closets, bedrooms, and other similar spaces subject to locking are not allowed to be a part of an exit access unless the occupancy is a dwelling unit or has a minimum number of occupants. Rooms that are more susceptible to fire hazards are also restricted. (Refer to the building codes and the *LSC* in your jurisdiction for additional requirements.)

Exits

An exit is the portion of the means of egress that is separated from all other spaces of the building. Unlike an exit access, exits must be *fully enclosed* and *fire rated* with minimal penetrations. A typical example of an enclosed and rated exit is a stairway. Fire-rated walls, rated doors, and other rated through-penetrations are used to make an exit a *protected way of travel* from the exit access to the exit discharge. The typical fire rating for an exit is one or two hours. (See Chapter 5 for additional fire rating information.)

There are four main types of exits: exterior exit doors, enclosed exit stairways, horizontal exits, and exit passageways. These are explained below. They must exit into another exit type, into an exit discharge, or directly onto a public way. Keep in mind that the codes have specific quantity, location, and size requirements for all exits. These are explained later in this chapter. Everything that composes the exit must have the same hourly rating. For example, if an exit stair that has a 2-hour rating empties into an exit passageway, the exit passageway would be rated 2 hours as well. Other basic code requirements and accessibility standards are similar to those for exit accesses as described in the previous section.

Exterior Exit Doors: An exterior exit door is an exit that simply consists of a doorway. It is located in the exterior wall of the building and typically leads from the ground floor of the building to the open air of an exit discharge or a public way. In older buildings there may be an exterior door on each floor that leads to a fire escape attached to the exterior of the building. An exterior door is not typically required to be rated unless the exterior wall is rated because of the potential exposure to fire from an adjacent building.

Exit Stairs: An exit stair is the most common type of exit, which is composed of a protected enclosure. It includes the stair enclo-

> **Note**
>
> The main difference between an exit discharge and an exit, such as an exit passageway, is the hourly fire rating required by the codes. Exits are typically required to have a two-hour fire separation, while exit access and exit discharges require up to a one-hour fire rating.

> **Note**
>
> The exterior exit door is the only type of exit door that consists of the doorway alone. Other exit doors are found in exit stairs, exit passageways, and horizontal exits, but they are a part of the whole exit enclosure. (See the section on Fire Doors in Chapter 5 for additional door requirements.)

Note

When exit stairs continue past the exit discharge at grade level, an approved barrier must be used. Typically a gate (i.e., metal gate) is installed at the grade level landing of the stair to prevent occupants from continuing to the basement or sublevels during an emergency.

sure, any doors opening into or exiting out of the stairway enclosure, and the stairs and landings inside the enclosure. What makes an exit stair different from other stairs is that its enclosure must be fire-rated. (See Chapter 5.)

Exit stair widths are determined in the same manner as the widths of other exits as explained later in this chapter. The doors of an exit stair must swing in the direction of the exit discharge. In other words, all the doors swing into the stairway except at the ground level, where they swing toward the exit discharge or public way. (The basic stair requirements are described above under Stairs in the section on Exit Accesses.)

Horizontal Exits: A horizontal exit is different from the other exits because it does not lead a person to the exterior of a building. Instead it provides a protected exit to a safe area of refuge. (See inset titled *Areas of Refuge* on page 94.) This area of refuge may be another part of the same building or an adjoining building. As the name implies, there is no change in level. This allows the occupants to move into a safe zone where they can either wait for help or use another exit to safely leave the building.

Note

The codes place certain limitations on a horizontal exit, such as the size and the number of occupants it can serve. Some are mentioned later in this chapter. Refer to the codes for the specific limitations.

Horizontal exits can be used in any occupancy classification. The most common use is in Institutional occupancies. Hospitals use horizontal exits to divide a floor into two or more areas of refuge. This allows the employees to roll a patient's bed into safe areas protected by a rated fire wall should a fire occur. Prisons also use horizontal exits so that a fire can be contained and the entire prison will not have to be evacuated in an emergency. Other common types of buildings that use horizontal exits are large factories, storage facilities, and high-rise buildings.

The components of a horizontal exit consist of the walls that create the enclosure around the areas of refuge and the doors through these walls. The top of Figure 4.8 indicates the horizontal exits between the rated walls of the building core and the exterior walls. When the horizontal exit leads to another building, such as in the bottom of Figure 4.8, structural features such as balconies and bridges can also be used.

Note

When determining the width for the doors as described later in this chapter, only the doors swinging in the direction of egress may be counted. (See top of Figure 4.8.)

The codes place strict requirements on these horizontal exit components. Since they are part of an exit, the walls and doors used to make the enclosures must be fire rated. The walls must either be continuous through every floor to the ground or be surrounded by a floor and ceiling that is equally rated. This rated wall becomes a separation wall. The doors must also be fire rated and swing in the direction of an exit. If the horizontal exit has an area of refuge on either side, two doors must be used together, each

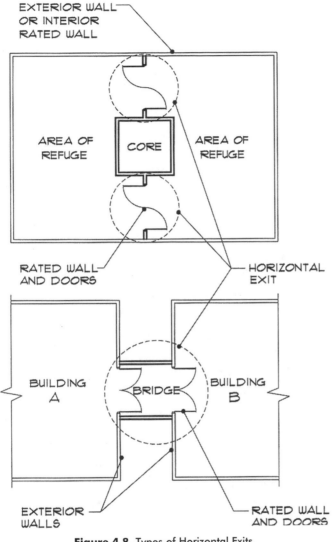

EXTERIOR WALL
OR INTERIOR
RATED WALL

AREA OF
REFUGE

CORE

AREA OF
REFUGE

RATED WALL
AND DOORS

HORIZONTAL
EXIT

BUILDING
A

BRIDGE

BUILDING
B

EXTERIOR
WALLS

RATED WALL
AND DOORS

Figure 4.8. Types of Horizontal Exits.

swinging in the opposite direction, to serve the occupants on either side. (See Figure 4.8.) In most cases, horizontal exits can be used for only a portion of the total number of required exits. The number allowed varies according to occupancy type. A horizontal exit cannot serve as the only exit in any case.

Exit Passageway: An exit passageway is a type of horizontal passage that provides the same level of protection as an exit stair. Depending on the code you are using, the exit passageway may be considered part of the exit or part of the exit discharge. In either case, it is a fully enclosed, fire-rated corridor or hallway that con-

Note

If you are using the *SBC* or *NBC,* an exit passageway is considered an exit discharge.

AREAS OF REFUGE

An area of refuge is an area where one or more people can wait safely for assistance during an emergency. While the codes typically use the term "area of refuge," the *ADAAG* and accessibility standards use the term "area of rescue assistance." Such areas provide safety since they are enclosed in fire and/or smoke partitions. In addition, specific accessibility requirements must be met. These include minimum space dimensions, specific two-way emergency communication systems, and required identification. (The typical wheelchair size is 30 inches wide by 48 inches long.) In most cases, the area must be protected by rated walls.

Whether you are referring to the codes, standards, or the *ADAAG* requirements, an area of refuge can be used in a number of different locations:

1. At a horizontal exit, when you pass through the door the whole space beyond the door becomes an area of refuge. (See the section on Horizontal Exits in this chapter.) You can either wait for assistance or use the available exit stairs.
2. In an exit stairwell, the landings at the doors entering the stair can be enlarged so that one or more wheelchairs can comfortably wait for assistance without blocking the means of egress.
3. A portion of an exit access corridor located immediately adjacent to an exit enclosure can have an alcove created for one or more wheelchairs to wait.
4. Within an enclosed exit discharge, such as a vestibule or foyer, a space immediately adjacent to an exit enclosure can be created for an area of refuge.
5. If an elevator is serving as part of the means of egress, an area of refuge must be located adjacent to the elevator.

sists of the surrounding walls, the ceiling, and the doors leading into the passageway. It is most commonly used to extend an exit. For example, if an enclosed exit stairway is not located at an exterior wall, an exit passageway can be used to connect the bottom of the exit stair to the exterior exit door. This allows the occupants a continuous level of protection without having to leave the fire-rated means of egress.

An exit access such as a corridor can also exit into an exit passageway. This typically occurs on the ground floor of a building when secondary exits are required. When the tenants occupy the perimeter of the building, an exit passageway is created between two of the tenants so that an exterior door can be reached off the common corridor. This is often seen in malls and office buildings with center building cores.

Another way to use an exit passageway is to bring an exit closer. This is especially useful when you need to shorten a travel

Note

The length of an exit passageway cannot exceed the maximum dead end corridor length specified by the code. (See the section on Dead End Corridors later in this chapter.)

distance. (Travel distance is explained later in this chapter.) For example, if the travel distance to the door of an exit stair is 10 feet longer than allowed, instead of relocating the exit stair you can add a 10-foot enclosed, fire-rated corridor leading to the door of the exit stair. This corridor becomes an exit passageway once it has the same rating as the exit stair. The door of this newly created exit passageway is now the end point for measuring the travel distance. (See the example in Figure 4.15.)

Note

In some instances, an exit passageway can have an occupied room or rooms enter directly into it; however, since it is a rated corridor, the codes limit the type of rooms and require rated doors into the rooms. Be sure to refer to the codes for specific requirements.

Exit Discharges

An exit discharge is that part of a means of egress that connects an exit with a public way. It is typically found on the ground floor of a building; however, in older buildings a fire escape is sometimes described as an exit discharge—connecting the exterior exit door(s) on each level to the sidewalk or alley. The required fire rating of an exit discharge will vary, depending on the type and where it is located. In some types of exit discharge, the enclosure may be allowed to have a lower rating than the exit it serves.

Following are descriptions of some of the more typical exit discharges. The first three are interior exit discharges, and the last two are exterior exit discharges. The width of an exit discharge is typically dictated by the width of the exit it is supporting, but accessibility requirements must be taken into consideration as well. Usually, when more than one exit leads into the exit discharge, the width of the exit discharge is a sum of these exit widths. In existing buildings an existing exit discharge may dictate the maximum size of an interior means of egress. The typical minimum ceiling height of an exit discharge is 8 feet.

Note

The lobby or main entrance of a building often varies as a means of egress. It might act as the exit if it is fully enclosed and has the appropriate fire rating. If it is an extension of the corridors on that floor it can be considered an exit access with the exterior door(s) acting as the exit. The lobby can also be an exit discharge if an exit stair empties into the space. (See Figure 4.2.)

Main Lobby: One of the most common interior exit discharges is the ground floor lobby of a building. For example, an exit stair may empty out into the lobby. The distance between the door of the exit stair and the exterior exit door is the exit discharge.

Foyer or Vestibule: An exit discharge can include an enclosed foyer or vestibule. These are small enclosures on the ground floor of a building between the end of a corridor and an exterior exit door. If the size of the enclosure is kept to a minimum, the codes may not require it to have a high fire rating. Therefore, it would be considered an exit discharge instead of an exit passageway. Remember that the *ADAAG* requires the size to be large enough to allow adequate maneuvering clearance within the vestibule or foyer and the swing of the doors. (See Figure 4.4.)

Note

The codes allow some of the occupancy classifications additional exceptions on interior exit discharges, especially Detentional/Correctional occupancies. Check the specific occupancies in the codes for details.

Discharge Corridor: Occasionally, a corridor is considered an exit discharge. Usually this occurs in older buildings where an exit stair empties into a ground floor corridor. If there is not a fire-rated exit passageway connecting the exit stairs to the exterior exit door, the corridor becomes an exit discharge. Usually this is not recommended and is allowed only if the entire corridor is protected by automatic sprinklers. (See the *LSC* for specifics.)

Exit Court: An exit court is an exterior exit discharge. It can be in the form of a courtyard, patio, or exterior vestibule. It is the portion of the exit that connects the exterior exit door to the public way.

Small Alley or Sidewalk: If the width of an alley or sidewalk is less than 10 feet, it is no longer considered a public way. Instead it becomes an exterior exit discharge that connects the exterior exit door to a larger alley, sidewalk, or street.

MEANS OF EGRESS CAPACITY

This section of the chapter concentrates on determining means of egress capacities. It answers the questions: How many? How large? and What locations? There are four specifics to be determined: number of exits, exit width, arrangement of exits, and travel distance. These must be determined on any interior project, whether you are changing a room, a tenant space, one floor, or an entire building.

In most cases you will not need to change the exiting capacity of the building itself. Exits for an entire building are determined during the initial building design and they usually allow for future changes within the building. However, there may be instances in which you are redesigning an entire floor and need to add or enlarge an exit. For example, a new occupant may require the exits to be updated to meet a more current code, or a different occupant type or greater occupancy load may require additional exits. Since adding an exit or increasing the size of an exit above the ground floor in a building is not typically feasible, you may need to change the scope of the project to make the project work in a particular building.

It does not matter which aspect of exit capacity is considered first. None can be finally determined until all have been calculated, since each is dependent on the others. For example, exit widths cannot be determined unless you know the required number of exits. And you cannot properly arrange the exits unless you know the maximum travel distances allowed. Another point to remem-

Note

When an interior project involves only part of a building or floor, you need to determine the exit capacity for this new area. However, it is also your responsibility to make sure the other existing building exits can accommodate this new area. In some cases you may need to increase the existing exits or decrease the size of the new space or occupancy load.

ber as you are determining exit capacities is that the requirements must be determined using the building codes and the *LSC* as well as any accessibility requirements, such as those found in the *ADAAG* or ANSI standards. When necessary, have a code official review and approve your calculations during the schematic phase of your project. (See Chapter 10.)

Number of Exits

You should determine the number of exits required by the codes before determining the total width required for each exit. Most of the codes require a minimum of two exits, whether they are for an entire building or a space within the building. However, in each occupancy a single exit from a space or building is sometimes allowed when specific requirements are met.

The number of exits is based on the occupancy load of the space or building. Use the occupant load tables in the codes (such as the one shown in Figure 2.2 in Chapter 2) to determine the occupant load of the area requiring exits. If you are determining the required number of exits for an entire building, you must calculate the occupant load of each floor or story. Each floor is considered separately.

When a floor has mixed occupancies or more than one tenant you must calculate the occupant load of each occupancy or tenant and add them together to get the total occupancy for the floor. If you are determining the number of exits for a particular room, space, or tenant within the building, you only need to figure the occupant load for that area. (Refer to Chapter 2 for a more detailed explanation of occupant loads and how to calculate them.)

Once you know the occupant load for the space or entire floor, refer to the building codes and/or the *LSC* to calculate the required number of exit locations. Each code has the same basic breakdown, as shown below. Although some of the codes go into more detail by occupancy, we will use these quantities to determine the number of exits for the purpose of this book. (See the Example on page 98.)

> **Note**
>
> None of the codes specifically requires more than four exits in a building, yet additional exits are typically required to satisfy the travel distance limits.

Occupant Load per Story or Area	Minimum Number of Exits
1–500	2
500–1000	3
over 1000	4

The important factor to remember when confirming the required exits for a multistory building is that the number of exits cannot decrease as one proceeds along the egress path toward the

Note

In some projects you may be able to increase the occupant load or occupant content from that required in the code by providing extra exits. This usually means increasing the provisions of every exit requirement, but remember that any such increase must be approved by the code officials in that jurisdiction.

Note

The occupant load, travel distance, and exit width can all affect the required number of exits.

Note

If a lower floor requires fewer exit stairs than the floor above, you may be able to leave one of the stairs inaccessible or blocked off on that lower floor. Although it is not recommended, check with your local code officials if it becomes necessary.

Note

It is not uncommon for a multistory building to have a large Assembly occupancy on the top floor. If it has the largest occupant load it could dictate the exit requirements for the whole building.

public way. Therefore, the floor with the largest occupant load determines the number of required exits for all lower floors. For example, if the floor with the highest occupant load is in the middle of the building, all the floors below it must have the same number of exits. This is easily accomplished by one continuous exit stairwell that counts as an exit on each floor that opens into it. (See the Example below.)

Each of the codes allows exceptions to the total number of exits. The most typical exception allows only one exit in smaller buildings or spaces. This is generally allowed in an occupancy that has a minimum number of occupants and a minimum travel distance to the exit. Figure 4.9 shows two tables from the *International Building Code (IBC)*. Table 1005.2.2, titled "Buildings with One Exit," lists the one-exit requirements for entire buildings, and Table 1004.2.1, titled "Spaces with One Exit," lists the one-exit requirements for separate tenant spaces or areas. In both tables the information is listed by occupancy classification (or use group). The *SBC*, the *UBC*, and the *LSC* give similar information within their texts.

Each code has additional exceptions as well. You must check the specific occupancy section of the required code publications to determine the exceptions, since each occupancy type addresses unique means of egress issues. Some occupancies may require additional exits, while others may reduce the number of exits, depending on the situation. The occupancy classifications with the most exceptions and special requirements are the Assembly, Institutional, and Residential occupancies. The following example, which describes how to determine exits for an entire building, provides you with an overall concept for determining exit quantities. (See the next section for additional examples.)

Example: Figure 4.10 indicates the outlined section of a multistory building. It calls out the occupant load for each floor and the number of exits based on these occupant loads. As you can see, the fourth floor has the largest occupant load, with a total of 1020, and, therefore, requires the largest number of exits. The code specifies four exits for any occupant load over 1000. As a result, every floor below it must also have four exits, even though their occupant loads specify fewer exits. Four separate exit stairs that are continuous from the fourth to the first floor would meet the requirement. The first floor would require the exit doors to be located in four separate locations.

Notice the floors above the fourth floor. Each of these floors has lower occupant loads than the fourth floor and requires only two to three exits. Since these floors are above the fourth floor, fewer exits can be used. The seventh floor has the largest occupant

TABLE 1005.2.2
BUILDINGS WITH ONE EXIT

OCCUPANCY	MAXIMUM HEIGHT OF BUILDING ABOVE GRADE PLANE	MAXIMUM OCCUPANTS (OR DWELLING UNITS) PER FLOOR AND TRAVEL DISTANCE
A, B[d], E, F, M, U	1 Story	50 occupants and 75 feet travel distance
H-2, H-3	1 Story	3 occupants and 25 feet travel distance
H-4, H-5, I, R	1 Story	10 occupants and 75 feet travel distance
S[a]	1 Story	30 occupants and 100 feet travel distance
B[b], F, M, S[a]	2 Stories	30 occupants and 75 feet travel distance
R-2	2 Stories[c]	4 dwelling units and 50 feet travel distance

For SI: 1 foot = 304.8 mm.

a. For the required number of exits for open parking structures, see Section 1005.2.1.1.

b. For the required number of exits for air traffic control towers, see Section 412.1.

c. Buildings classified as Group R-2 equipped throughout with an automatic sprinkler system in accordance with Section 903.3.1.1 or 903.3.1.2 and provided with emergency escape and rescue openings in accordance with Section 1009 shall have a maximum height of three stories above grade.

d. Buildings equipped throughout with an automatic sprinkler system in accordance with Section 903.3.1.1 with an occupancy in Group B shall have a maximum travel distance of 100 feet.

Figure 4.9. *International Building Code (IBC) Table 1005.2.2, "Buildings with One Exit" and Table 1004.2.1, "Spaces with One Means of Egress."* (Written permission to reproduce this material was granted by the copyright holder, International Code Council, Inc., 5203 Leesburg Pike, Suite 708, Falls Church, VA 22041.)

TABLE 1004.2.1
SPACES WITH ONE MEANS OF EGRESS

OCCUPANCY	MAXIMUM OCCUPANT LOAD
A, B, E, F, M, U	50
H-1[a], H-2, H-3	3
H-4, H-5, I-1, I-3, R	10
S	30

Note a. For requirements for areas and spaces in Group H-1, see Section 415.

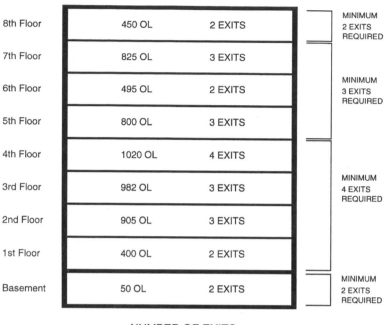

8th Floor	450 OL	2 EXITS
7th Floor	825 OL	3 EXITS
6th Floor	495 OL	2 EXITS
5th Floor	800 OL	3 EXITS
4th Floor	1020 OL	4 EXITS
3rd Floor	982 OL	3 EXITS
2nd Floor	905 OL	3 EXITS
1st Floor	400 OL	2 EXITS
Basement	50 OL	2 EXITS

MINIMUM 2 EXITS REQUIRED

MINIMUM 3 EXITS REQUIRED

MINIMUM 4 EXITS REQUIRED

MINIMUM 2 EXITS REQUIRED

NUMBER OF EXITS
OL = Occupancy Load per Floor

Figure 4.10. Example: Multistory Building.

load, so it controls the exit quantity. Three exits must be used on the fifth, sixth, and seventh floors. Two exits are allowed on the top floor because its occupant load is even lower.

Exit Widths

Each of the building codes and the *LSC* calculate exit widths the same way. The calculated exit widths determine the size of the exit enclosures, the exit doors, and the exit access corridors and doors leading up to the exits. Different components will require different exit widths. Remember, this minimum width must be maintained throughout the means of egress. It cannot be reduced anywhere along the path of travel as it moves toward the exit discharge and/or public way. It is important to determine the exit width of each exit component in question so that the minimum exit width can be obtained.

Like the number of exits, exit widths are based on the occupant load of an area or floor. Each is calculated separately to accommodate a specific area. If you are determining the exit widths for a multistory building, the exit sizes are determined by the floor with the largest occupant load. Usually that means figuring the occupant load of every floor to find the one with the largest occupant load. That floor will require the largest exit widths and

Note

Many smaller enclosed rooms, such as offices and dwelling units, are small enough that they will not require calculating the exit width. The calculation will be required on larger rooms, such as the ones found in open office spaces, factories, malls, and assembly buildings.

dictate the exit widths of every floor below it. For example, in Figure 4.10, the fourth floor would determine the width of the exit stairs from the fourth floor down to the first floor.

Exit widths must also be determined for every enclosed area and separate tenant space. The same basic principles apply. Instead of using the occupant load of the entire floor, use the occupant load for that particular space. If it is a room, the calculation will determine the width of the door. If it is a tenant space, the exit door(s) and any corridor(s) leading up to the door(s) will be determined. On the other hand, the width of the exit access corridor leading from each tenant space to the exit stairs is based on the total occupant load for that floor. If there is more than one tenant on a floor, the occupant loads of each must be added together to determine the required exit width for that floor.

Once you know the occupant load for the floor or space, it is multiplied by specific width variables supplied by the codes. The most common variables are

0.3   for exit stairs
0.2   for level exits

The difference in these width variables is based on the fact that stairs cause a person to decrease speed and, therefore, could result in more people using the stairwell at one time during an emergency. The larger stair variable allows for stairs to be wider than level exits such as corridors and ramps. Therefore, if you are calculating exits widths for an exit stair and the exit passageway or corridors leading from the stairs, you should calculate the stairs first. Stairs require a larger width and will end up dictating the width of the passageway, since an exit width must be maintained as it moves toward the public way.

These width variables vary slightly from code to code. Some codes provide separate width variables by occupancy for sprinklered and nonsprinklered buildings. The codes supply other variables as well—usually under special occupancy sections. These additional variables in each code allow for the difference in occupancy classifications where wider exit widths are needed for faster egress times in more hazardous occupancies.

After determining the total exit width required by the code, it must be compared to the total number of exits already determined for that space or floor. (See previous section.) The total width must be equally distributed between the total number of exits serving the area. For example, if you are calculating the width for an entire floor, the determined width must be divided among all exits leaving the floor. If the determined width is for a room or tenant space, it is divided among the exits leaving the calculated area. (See the Exam-

Note

Aisle accessways and horizontal exits have additional variables and specific requirements that must be met. Refer to the codes.

ple that follows.) The main exception to this is in an Assembly occupancy, which allows for a higher percentage of the occupant load to be accommodated at the main entrance or exit. This percentage varies in each building code and the *LSC*. If you are designing an Assembly occupancy, you need to refer to the specific code.

As you are determining exit widths make note of the following additional requirements. All of them can affect the final width. (Additional ones may be required for specific occupancies.)

1. Building codes and accessibility standards require all means of egress doors to provide a *minimum* clear width of 32 inches. In practical terms, a standard 36-inch-wide door when open will provide 32 inches of clear width. (See Figure 4.3 for a diagram for clear width dimension.) Therefore, if you calculate a 30-inch exit width you will still need to specify a 36-inch door.

2. The building codes do not allow any leaf of a door used as part of the means of egress to be more than 4 feet wide. Therefore, if you need 60 inches of exit width, you will need to provide more than one door. If two separate 36-inch doors are used, this will provide 64 inches of clear width. This exceeds the required width but is the closest increment. (Remember, each single 36-inch-wide door must be considered in increments of 32 inches of clear width, which is the minimum for the codes and the *ADAAG*.) If 40 inches of exit width is required, a 48-inch door would provide adequate width where a 36-inch door would not and two 36-inch doors might seem excessive.

3. The required width of an exit access (i.e., corridor) can be affected if it leads to more than one exit on the floor that it serves. In that case, you may be able to reduce its width. This is determined by dividing the total occupant load of the floor by the number of exits to which the exit access connects. This is done before making any calculations. (See the Example on the facing page.)

4. When an exit discharge, such as a corridor, leads from an exit enclosure, its width cannot be less than that of the exit.

5. In no case can a corridor width or stair width be less than 36 inches; however, the typical accessible minimum is 44 inches and some codes require accessible stairs to be a minimum of 48 inches wide. The building codes set additional minimums for most occupancy classifications. The *ADAAG* also specifies certain accessibility and clearance requirements that may affect the width of a means of egress. (See Figure 4.4 and the Example on the facing page.)

6. If a building has a basement that is occupied, some codes require the occupant load to be increased. The exit discharge on the ground floor would need to allow for the exiting of the basement level(s) in addition to the upper floors. (Not all of the codes require this cumulative effect.)

7. Horizontal exits are allowed only if the area of refuge created is large enough to accommodate its own occupants and those from the "fire side." For most occupancies the codes allow 3 square feet (0.28 square meter) of floor space per occupant. Increased area for the area of refuge is required for Institutional occupancies.

8. The exit path must be clear and unobstructed. Unless the codes or accessibility requirements specifically state that a projection is permitted, nothing may reduce the determined exit width. The most common exceptions include handrails that meet *ADAAG* requirements, nonstructural trim or wall application less than ½ inch thick, wall sconces not deeper than 4 inches, and doors that do not project more than 7 inches when open.

9. In jurisdictions that enforce the *UBC* and the *IBC*, the codes require that the loss of any one exit location cannot reduce the total capacity of *exit width* by more than 50 percent. For example, in an Assembly occupancy, if multiple exit doors are required at the main entrance/exit, and that location becomes blocked by fire, the total exit width may be reduced significantly. If additional exit locations do not provide for at least 50 percent of the total exit width required, additional exit locations or additional doors at the other exits must be added.

> **Note**
>
> **The total width of the exits will usually be more than that required by the codes, because of all the additional code and accessibility requirements.**

The goal of these and other exit requirements is to balance the flow of the occupants during an emergency. You want to make sure an occupant can reach an exit and then get through it without any delay.

Example: Figure 4.11 is the floor plan of the second floor in a two-story, mixed use building. Imagine that this floor is vacant and you are asked to lay out three tenant spaces. As you are laying it out, you need to make sure you have the correct number and width of exits. Spaces A and C (Business occupancies) are typical tenant office spaces and Space B is a wholesale retail store (Mercantile occupancy). If this building is located in a jurisdiction using the *SBC*, the exit widths for the spaces and the floor must be determined using the *SBC* table in Figure 4.1.

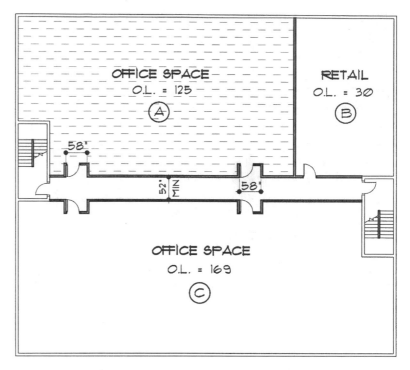

TOTAL OCCUPANCY LOAD (O.L.) = 125 + 30 + 169 = 324

Figure 4.11. Example: Mixed-Occupancy Building.

SPACE A: From the occupant load, you have already determined that two means of egress leading out of the Space A are required. (Referring to the chart shown earlier in the chapter, the occupant load of 125 is under 500.) You now need to determine the required width of the exits for Space A to make sure two 36-inch doors are enough.

This space is considered a Business occupancy. For Group B on the *SBC* table, the exit width variable for level exits is 0.2. To determine the width of the exit doors, take the occupant load of 125 and multiply it by the level exit variable of 0.2. This equals 25 inches. This is the total required width that must be divided between the two doors. Hence each door must be at least 12.5 inches wide. However, since the code requires all means of egress doors to provide a minimum clear width of 32 inches, each door must be specified as a 36-inch-wide door. (Note that the 25 inches seems to indicate that only one door or exit is required instead of two. That is why the number of exits required should be determined first.)

The size of the doors will also determine the minimum door alcove into the space and corridor width within the tenant space. In this case, the corridors must work with a 36-inch door.

However, the *SBC* table in Figure 4.1 also specifies that a corridor cannot be less than 44 inches. Additional accessibility standards require at least 18 inches to be clear on the latch and pull side of the door. (Refer to Figure 4.4 and the *ADAAG*.) Therefore, you will need a minimum of 54 inches (36 + 18) for the door and pull clearance. On the hinge side of the door you will also need a minimum of 4 inches to allow for a hollow metal door frame and the framing around the door. Adding these together, you will require a minimum 58-inch-wide alcove on the pull side of the door.

Inside the tenant space on the push side of the door, accessibility standards require a clearance of 12 inches (instead of 18 inches). Therefore, you can reduce the required width on the tenant side to 52 inches. (See note at side.)

FLOOR: This is a mixed occupancy floor. That means that before you determine the exit widths for the entire floor you must first make sure the egress width variables are the same for both Group B and Group M occupancies. From the *SBC* table in Figure 4.1 both require 0.37 for stairs and 0.2 for level exits. (If they were different, you would use the higher of the two variables.) You must also add up the occupant loads for each tenant to obtain the total for the floor. This total is 324 occupants.

Since the width variable for the stairs will result in a larger width, it should be determined first. The occupant load of 324 multiplied by the 0.37 *stair variable* equals 199.9 or 120 inches. This total is divided between the two exit stairs, leaving 60 inches. Therefore, each run of both stairs must be at least 60 inches wide to meet the code requirements. (Note that this 60 inch width cannot be reduced as the exit moves toward the public way. If the exit stairs empty into a corridor or exit passageway at the ground level, it must be at least 60 inches wide as well.)

To figure the width of the corridor leading to the exit stairs, you must first examine the layout of the floor plan. Since there are two exit stairs, each stair needs to serve only one-half of the total occupant load for the floor. Therefore, the corridor width can be reduced as well. Take the total occupant load of 324 and divided it in half to obtain 162 occupants. When you multiply 162 by the level variable of 0.2, you obtain a minimum corridor width of 32.4 or 33 inches. That means that the doors entering the exit stairs can each be the minimum 36-inch width. However, the *SBC* table specifies a 44-inch minimum for the corridor. If you use the same 36 inch door, allow 4 inches on the hinge side of the door and the 12-inch *ADA* requirement on the push side of the door. The total exit width of the corridor for the floor is 52 inches. (See note above.) An additional consideration is that it takes 60 inches for a person in a wheelchair

Note

The accessibility clearance (12", 18", or 24") at the latch side of the door starts at the door latch and can include the width of the door frame adjacent to the latch.

Note

As you can see from these examples, all the means of egress requirements must be determined and compared together. Each affects the other.

to turn around. If the corridor is not 60 inches wide, people using wheelchairs will have to use the alcoves to change directions.

Arrangement of Exits

The arrangement of exits is also specified by the codes. Each of the building codes and the *LSC* requires exits to be located as remotely from each other as possible so that if one becomes blocked during an emergency the other(s) may still be reached. When two or more exits are required at least two of the exits must be a certain distance apart. This is referred to as the *half-diagonal rule.*

The half-diagonal rule requires that the distance between two exits be at least one-half of the longest diagonal distance within the building or building area the exits are serving. The easiest way to understand this rule is to review Figure 4.12. These diagrams

Note

In some jurisdictions either type of measurement can be used when arranging exits. Either way, keep in mind that the codes also place a maximum travel distance on the length of an exit access. See the following section on Travel Distance.

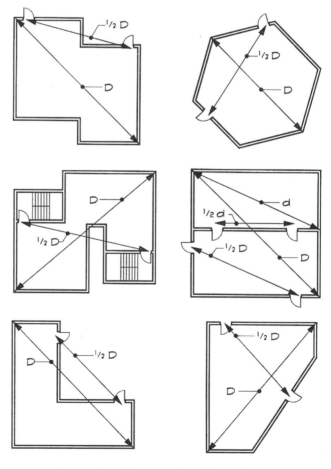

D = DIAGONAL OR MAXIMUM DISTANCE
¹/₂D = HALF OF DIAGONAL OR MINIMUM DISTANCE

Figure 4.12. Half Diagonal Rule.

are representative of open building plans or separate tenant spaces within a building. In a tenant space, the measurement is unaffected by the presence of other surrounding spaces.

Notice that the shape or size of the area or the building does not matter. You must find the longest possible diagonal in that space. Measure the length of that diagonal in a straight line from one corner of the floor plan to the other corner. Then take one-half of that length. The result indicates how far apart the exits must be. This is the *minimum* distance allowed between the two exits.

When a building has exit enclosures, such as exit stairs, that are interconnected by a fire rated corridor, some of the codes require the exit distance to be measured differently. Figure 4.13 illustrates this point for both a tenant space and an entire floor. Notice that the overall diagonal length is measured the same in a straight line across the top of the floor plan. On the other hand, when you are placing the two exits, the half-diagonal distance between the exits is measured along the path of travel within the rated corridor.

When more than two exits are required, at least two of the exits must be placed using the half-diagonal rule. The remaining exits should be placed as remotely as possible so that if one exit becomes blocked in an emergency the others would be accessible. Most of the codes also allow an exception to the half-diagonal rule if the entire building is equipped with an automatic sprinkler system. Usually the one-half measurement can be reduced to one-third or even one-fourth. (Refer to the codes.)

Note

The *UBC* and the *IBC* take the arrangement of exits one step further. In addition to the half-diagonal rule, they require any two enclosed exits to be a minimum of 30 feet apart to assure that the exits are not too close together.

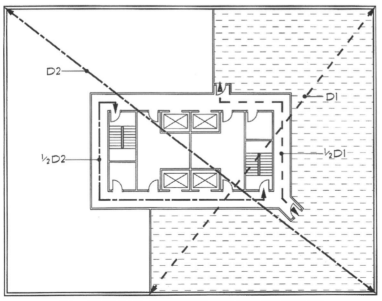

DI = DIAGONAL DISTANCE FOR TENANT SPACE
D2 = DIAGONAL DISTANCE FOR ENTIRE FLOOR

Figure 4.13. Exit Arrangement.

The overall objective of each of the codes is to make the exits as far apart as possible, for example, at opposite ends of a corridor or tenant space. The best scenario is to allow every occupant the choice of two exit paths no matter where he or she is located. Although this may not always be possible, especially in older buildings, as the designer you need to use your space planning skills as well as your common sense to arrive at the best solution.

Travel Distance

In general, travel distance is the measurement of an exit access. It is the measurement of the distance between the most remote, occupiable point of an area, room, or space to the exit that serves it. Two types of travel distance are regulated by the codes. The codes limit the length of travel distance from within a single space to the exit access corridor. This is known as a common path of travel, because all the occupants of that space will have to travel approximately the same direction before they come to two options for exiting. (See the section on Common Path of Travel on page 114.) The codes also regulate the length of travel distance from anywhere in a building to the exit of the building or floor. These are separate travel distance calculations and the information is located in different areas of the codes.

Travel distance from within a *single space* is basically determined the same way by each of the building codes and the *LSC*. Travel distance within a single space is important when the occupant load requires only one exit. Typically, if the travel distance within a tenant space exceeds 75 feet, then an additional exit is required even if it is not required by the occupant load. The *NBC* uses Table 1010.3, "Buildings with One Exit," as shown in Figure 4.14. The *SBC*, *UBC* and the *IBC* include the regulation within their text. The *LSC* includes the regulations in each occupancy chapter. There are exceptions to this code. The most obvious is the addition of an automatic sprinkler system. For example, if there is an automatic sprinkler system within the building, the travel distance usually can be increased to 100 feet. Other exceptions may require shorter travel distances, such as in some Hazardous occupancies. (Refer to the specific codes for more information.)

Likewise, travel distance to the *exit for the entire building* or *individual floor* is basically determined the same way by each of the building codes and the *LSC*. The difference in each code is the standard distance allowed and the format of the information. Each code has its own version of a travel distance table. For example, the *SBC* includes it with other egress information in Table 1103,

Note

If an occupancy has an open stairway within its space that is part of an exit access, it must be included in the travel distance. You measure up to the nosing of the top tread. Then the measurement of the stair is taken on the angle of the stairway in the plain of the tread nosing. You measure from the top tread nosing to the bottom tread nosing to get the stair travel length. To continue the overall travel distance start at the bottom edge of the last riser to the exit.

Table 1010.3
BUILDINGS WITH ONE EXIT

Use Group	Maximum number of stories above grade	Maximum per floor occupants, travel distance[e] dwelling units
A, B[a], E, F, M	1 Story	50 occupants and 75 feet travel
H-2, H-3	1 Story	3 occupants and 25 feet travel
H-4, I, R	1 Story	10 occupants and 75 feet travel
S[b]	1 Story	30 occupants and 100 feet travel
B[a,c], F, M, S[b], U	2 Stories	30 occupants and 75 feet travel
R-2	2 Stories[d]	4 dwelling units

Note a. Buildings equipped throughout with an automatic sprinkler system in accordance with Section 906.2.1 with an occupancy in Use Group B shall have a maximum travel distance of 100 feet.

Note b. For the required number of exits for open parking structures, see Section 1010.5.

Note c. For the required number of exits for air traffic control towers, see Section 414.0.

Note d. Buildings equipped throughout with an automatic sprinkler system in accordance with Section 906.2.1 or 906.2.2 with an occupancy in Use Group R-2 shall have a maximum height of three stories above grade.

Note e. 1 foot = 304.8 mm.

Figure 4.14. BOCA *National Building Code* (*NBC*) Table 1010.3, "Buildings with One Exit." (Copyright 1999, Building Officials and Code Administrators International, Inc., Country Club Hills, Illinois, *BOCA National Building Code*/1999. Reproduced with permission. All rights reserved.)

"Travel Distance, Dead End Length, Exit, and Means of Egress Width," as shown in Figure 4.1. The *NBC* uses Table 1006.5, "Length of Exit Access Travel." The *IBC* uses Table 1004.2.6, "Exit Access Travel Distance," and the *LSC* has Table A-5-6. 1, "Common Path, Dead End, and Travel Distance Limits (by Occupancy)." The *UBC* does not use a table, but it lists the information within its text.

Travel distance is *not* measured in a straight line; instead it is measured on the floor along the centerline of the natural path of travel. You start one foot from the wall at the most remote point (usually the corner of a room) and move in a direct path toward the nearest exit, curving around any obstructions such as walls, furniture and equipment, or corners with a clearance of one foot. The measurement ends where the exit begins.

Ending the travel distance at an exit means the center of the doorway leading to the exit. This can include

1. The exterior exit door
2. The door to an enclosed exit stair
3. The door of a horizontal exit
4. The door to an enclosed exit passageway
5. The door to the exit access corridor (for common path of travel)

Maximum travel distances can increase in length in certain occupancies when additional requirements are met. (Refer to the specific codes.) The most obvious is the addition of an automatic sprinkler system. The *UBC* and the *IBC* have a rule not currently used by the other codes. It allows an additional 100 feet to reach these exits if the last portion of the travel distance is entirely within a one-hour fire resistive corridor or exit passageway. That means the 200-foot travel distance for a sprinklered building can be increased to 300 feet. Since a number of occupancy classifications typically require this rated corridor, the 100-foot rule often applies in these jurisdictions.

Example: The floor plan in Figure 4.15 gives an example of measuring travel distances in a space that requires only one means of egress. The plan is that of an accounting firm that occupies part of one floor in a four-story sprinklered building. It is considered a

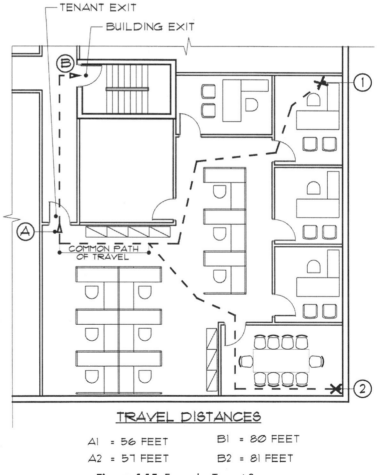

TRAVEL DISTANCES

A1 = 56 FEET   B1 = 80 FEET
A2 = 57 FEET   B2 = 81 FEET

Figure 4.15. Example: Tenant Space.

Business occupancy. Since it is a new occupancy and separate from the other tenants in the building, it must have a travel distance acceptable to code.

The dashed line on the floor plan indicates the common path of travel distance. The travel distance measurement starts at the most remote point, in other words, the farthest point from the exit. It is indicated by the "X" on the floor plan. The first calculation is to determine if this tenant space will require a second exit. (Only one is required by the occupant load.) In this case the exit is the door leading from the tenant space to the exit access corridor as indicated by "A". Therefore, the travel distance measurement ends at the center of this door. Since the tenant has two points that seem to be about the same distance from the exit, both must be measured. You start one foot from the wall at the farthest corner and move toward the exit using the most direct path and staying one foot away from any obstacles. Obstacles can include walls, corners, furniture, fixtures, equipment, and machinery.

Once the travel distance line is drawn as directly as possible, measure the line to get the travel distance measurement. In the example in Figure 4.15, the longest travel distance and the common path of travel distance is 57 feet. Since it does not exceed the 75 feet, a second exit is not required.

The next calculation is to determine the travel distance to the exit for the building floor. In this case the exit is the door leading to the exit stair as shown by "B". Therefore, the travel distance measurement begins at the same point as before, but ends at the center of this exit stair door. The distance is measured along the longest path and extends to the stairwell. In this example, the travel distance is 81 feet. You then compare this to the maximum travel distances allowed by the codes. Using Figure 4.1, the *SBC* table indicates that for Business occupancies the travel distance limit is 250 feet for sprinklered buildings. The design of the accounting firm meets the codes, since both measurements are below the maximum travel distance allowed. (Note that if this had been an unsprinklered building, the travel distance would have still met the code.)

Dead End Corridors

A dead end corridor is a corridor with only one direction of exit. In other words if a person turns down a dead end corridor, there is no way out except to retrace his or her path. It is also the distance a person must travel before a choice of two exits or two paths of travel is given. An example of a dead end corridor has been indicated on the floor plan in Figure 4.16.

Note

In the adjacent example, if the longest travel distance within the space to the tenant entry door exceeds 75 feet, the space would require two exits.

Note

If you are designing a number of different tenant spaces in the same building, the travel distance must be measured for each tenant. It does not matter if the tenants are all the same occupancy. If they are separated from each other by a demising wall, they must be treated separately.

TRAVEL DISTANCE FACTORS

Travel distance measurement is not based on a code formula. Rather it is based on the space or building as a whole. The *Life Safety Code Handbook* (1997) lists the factors on which the required code travel distances are based. They are

1. The number, age, and physical condition of building occupants and the rate at which they can be expected to move

2. The type and number of obstructions—display cases, seating, and heavy machinery—that must be negotiated

3. The number of people in any room or space and the distance from the farthest point in that room to the door

4. The amount and nature of combustibles expected in a particular occupancy

5. The rapidity with which fire might spread—a function of the type of construction, the materials used, the degree of compartmentation, and the presence or absence of automatic fire detection and *extinguishing systems*

Obviously, travel distances will vary with the type and size of occupancy and the degree of hazard present.

Note

Some of the codes allow a dead end corridor longer than 20 feet when sprinklers are present. It depends on the type of occupancy.

Note

Some occupancy classifications allow only one means of egress. When this occurs, the dead end rule typically does not apply, since there is only one way to exit.

The codes set maximum lengths for dead end corridors because they can be deadly in an emergency. When a corridor is smoke filled it is difficult to read exit signs. A person can waste valuable time going down a dead end corridor only to find out he or she has gone the wrong way and must turn back. If a dead end corridor is long, the person can easily get trapped by fire and/or smoke.

Each of the building codes and the *LSC* either describe the dead end limits within the text or list them in a table such as the *SBC* table in Figure 4.1. The most common dead end length is a maximum of 20 feet. It is measured one foot from the end of a corridor, following the natural path of travel, to the centerline of the corridor that provides the choice of two means of egress.

Although it would be best to eliminate dead corridors altogether, it is not always possible—especially in older, existing buildings. If one becomes necessary, locate the rooms or spaces that are the least used at the end of the corridor. When a dead end corridor longer than 20 feet is unavoidable, which can sometimes happen in older buildings, be sure to contact the code officials in that jurisdiction.

Example: A second travel distance example is an entire floor of a hotel in a sprinklered building. The floor plan in Figure 4.16 indicates that there are two exits. Both are enclosed stairways. (In this example it is assumed that the elevator does not constitute an exit

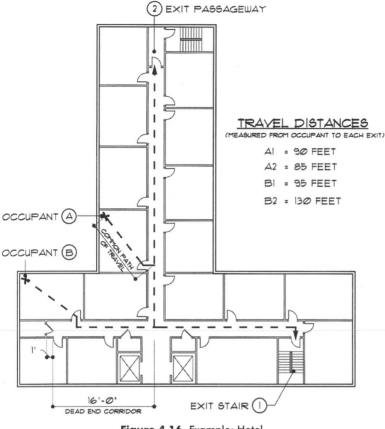

② EXIT PASSAGEWAY

TRAVEL DISTANCES
(MEASURED FROM OCCUPANT TO EACH EXIT)

A1 = 90 FEET
A2 = 85 FEET
B1 = 95 FEET
B2 = 130 FEET

OCCUPANT Ⓐ

OCCUPANT Ⓑ

COMMON PATH OF TRAVEL

1'

16'-0"
DEAD END CORRIDOR

EXIT STAIR ①

Figure 4.16. Example: Hotel.

in an emergency). Refer back to the *SBC* table in Figure 4.1. Under the Residential occupancy (Group R) for hotels, the maximum travel distance allowed is 250 feet for a sprinklered building. This means that an occupant located anywhere on the floor of this hotel cannot travel more than 250 feet to reach the closest exit.

In this example several measurements must be made. Point A as indicated on the floor plan is midway between the two exits. An occupant in this location must be able to reach at least one exit within 250 feet. In both cases (A1 and A2) the total distance is less than this.

Point B must also be within 250 feet from the enclosed exit stairs. Note, however, that the point is located in a dead end corridor. You must first check to make sure the dead end length is not longer than the 20 feet specified in the table in Figure 4.1. Since the dead end length is 16 feet you can proceed to measure the travel distance. The travel distance to both exits falls under the 250-foot maximum distance.

Note

In some jurisdictions, the placement of freestanding furniture and panel systems does not create dead end corridors. It is assumed that in an emergency this furniture can be moved or climbed over.

Common Path of Travel

Note

If a floor plan does not meet the maximum travel distance, you need to change the floor plan to meet the requirements. Often moving a wall or relocating equipment is all it takes. Adding or increasing an exit passageway is another solution. If all else fails, work closely with the local code officials.

Some of the codes set maximum lengths for common paths of travel. The specified length depends on the occupancy and can apply to either of the following types of common paths of travel. The first type occurs when a person can travel in only one direction to reach the point where there is a choice of two exits. For example, a dead end corridor can be considered a common path of travel. Any room that has only one exit door also has a common path of travel. The common path is measured similarly to travel distance, starting one foot from the wall at the most remote location. It is the distance from this point measured along the natural path of travel to the centerline of the first corridor that provides a choice of two paths of travel to remote exits, as indicated in Figure 4.16.

The second definition of a common path of travel is an exit access where two paths merge to become one. The merged path becomes the common path of travel. For example, a reception area in a tenant space typically becomes a common path of travel. Two corridors accessing the various rooms and/or offices would merge together at the reception area to arrive at the door exiting the space. This is shown in Figure 4.15. Most exit discharges can be considered a common path of travel, such as a lobby or vestibule where other means of egress must converge to leave the building.

Note

Some exterior exit doors, such as those found in main lobbies or vestibules, may not require an exit sign if they are clearly identifiable. However, this must be approved by a code official.

SIGNAGE

Note

Some code jurisdictions are beginning to require *floor-level exit signs* in addition to regular exit signs in some occupancies. These are typically placed eight inches above the floor near the exit door so that they are easy to read in emergencies with heavy smoke. Look for additional uses in the future.

Exit signs are typically required wherever two or more exits are required for a particular floor space. They must be installed at the doors of all stair enclosures, exit passageways, and horizontal exits on every floor. They must also be installed at all exterior exit doors and any door exiting a space or area when the direction of egress is unclear. (Some smaller occupancies may not require them.)

The building codes and the *LSC* specify the placement, graphics, and illumination of exit signs. The *ADAAG* also has specific regulations. As the designer, it is your responsibility to make sure the signage products you specify meet the requirements for your jurisdiction. Since the manufacturer usually supplies options with every sign, make sure you specify the correct one. For example, contrast letters are usually available in green and red; some jurisdictions, however, allow only red.

When placing exit signs the most common requirement is that no point within the exit access can be more than 100 feet (3048 mm) from the nearest visible sign. Therefore, if you have a long corridor or a large space, additional exit signs may be required. Also remember to use exits signs with arrows when it is necessary to indicate a direction. The general rule is to use a regular exit sign at exit or exit access doors and directional exit signs at all other locations (i.e., corridors, open areas.) The signs can be ceiling mounted or wall mounted. The signs must be placed a certain distance above the floor as well.

Other signs in addition to exit signs are usually required, especially when a means of egress is confusing. For example, if a regular door or stairway can be mistaken for an exit, a "NO EXIT" sign may be required. (Supplemental lettering such as "STOREROOM" or "TO BASEMENT" can be used to indicate the name of the area as well.) Still other required signage can include identification of stairways, floor numbers at each level, labeling entrance, exit doors, locked doors, and so on. When any of these signs are permanent, the *ADAAG* specifies sign proportions, lettering heights, mounting locations, lettering contrast, and, in certain cases, the use of Braille.

EXIT LIGHTING

Like exit signage, exit lighting is typically required whenever two or more exits are present. Exit lighting is also known as emergency lighting because it must be connected to a backup system in case of power failure during an emergency. This could mean connection to a backup generator or battery packs located within the light fixture. Generally, the codes require exit lighting to be provided at all exits and any aisles, corridors, passageways, ramps, and lobbies leading to an exit. Both general exit lighting and the lighting of exit signs must be lit at all times a building is in use. The codes specify minimum lighting illumination levels. Lower levels might be allowed for certain building types, such as theatres, concert halls, and auditoriums. (Chapter 8 describes emergency lighting in more detail.)

CHECKLIST

Although a means of egress is made up of number of components, the ultimate goal is to provide a direct route or exit to the exterior of a building. The checklist in Figure 4.17 has been designed to help you research and calculate the necessary means of egress for an interior project. It should be used to determine the types of means of

MEANS OF EGRESS CHECKLIST

PROJECT NAME: _____

TYPE OF SPACE: ____ BUILDING ____ FLOOR ____ TENANT ____ ROOM

OCCUPANCY TYPE(S): _____ _____ _____

OCCUPANCY LOAD(S): _____ _____ _____

TYPES OF MEANS OF EGRESS (Check and research those that apply):

EXIT ACCESS	EXIT	EXIT DISCHARGE
___ Doors	___ Exterior Doors	___ Main Lobby
___ Stairs	___ Exit Stairs	___ Foyers
___ Ramps	___ Horizontal Exits	___ Vestibules
___ Corridors	___ Exit Passageway	___ Discharge Corridors
___ Aisles		___ Exit Courts
___ Intervening Rooms		

TYPICAL CODE AND ACCESSIBILITY REQUIREMENTS (Research):

___ Doors: Type, Swing, Size, Hardware, Threshold, Clearances, Fire Rating

___ Stairs: Type, Riser Height, Tread Depth, Nosing, Width, Handrail, Guardrail, Fire Rating

___ Ramps: Slope, Rise, Landings, Width, Edge Detail, Finish, Handrail, Guardrail

___ Corridors: Length, Width, Protruding Objects, Fire Rating

___ Aisles: Fixed Seats, No Fixed Seats, Ramp(s), Steps, Handrails

___ Intervening Rooms: Type, Size, Obstructions, Fire Rating

EGRESS CAPACITIES (Calculate):

NUMBER OF EXITS:
___ MINIMUM OF TWO EXITS
___ ONE EXIT EXCEPTION
___ REQUIRED NUMBER OF EXITS
___ NUMBER OF EXITS PROVIDED

EXIT WIDTH:
OCCUPANCY LOAD X VARIABLE = TOTAL WIDTH
___ LEVEL VARIABLE
___ STAIR VARIABLE
___ OTHER VARIABLE
___ CALCULATED WIDTH @ EACH EXIT LOCATION
___ TOTAL WIDTH REQUIRED

TRAVEL DISTANCE:
___ 1/2 DIAGONAL RULE
___ DEAD END CORRIDOR
___ COMMON PATH OF TRAVEL
___ MAXIMUM TRAVEL DISTANCE FOR SPACE
___ MAXIMUM TRAVEL DISTANCE FOR BUILDING FLOOR

NOTES:

1. ATTACH ANY FLOOR PLANS AND OTHER PAPERWORK INDICATING THE REQUIRED CALCULATIONS.

2. CHECK SPECIFIC OCCUPANCY CLASSIFICATIONS FOR SPECIAL REQUIREMENTS THAT MAY APPLY.

Figure 4.17. Means of Egress Checklist.

egress, to indicate which components must be researched, and to remind you of the required calculations.

The first line of the checklist is used to distinguish the size of the project. For example, if you check "floor," that means you are designing an entire floor of a building. You must calculate the egress capacities for everything on that floor, including the exit stairs leaving the floor. If you are designing a portion of a floor, such as a "tenant" space on a multitenant floor, your main concern will be that tenant.

The next two lines of the checklist leave spaces to indicate the type(s) of occupancy you are working with and their occupancy loads. If you are working with just one occupancy classification, list it and determine its occupancy load. (See Chapter 2.) If you are working with more than one occupancy, list each one so a total occupancy load can be obtained.

Next, the main types of means of egress are listed. Checking those found in your interior project will remind you which codes must be researched. The following section of the checklist outlines the different components of a means of egress. By checking which ones apply to your project, you will know which codes and accessibility requirements you must research. You can then concentrate on only those you need. Be sure to check the building codes, and/or the *LSC*, the *ADAAG*, and the ANSI standards, and any other required local codes. In addition, pay particular attention to any exceptions or other requirements *necessary* for the occupancy classification(s) you listed at the top of the checklist.

The last part of the checklist indicates the main means of egress capacities that must be calculated. Check any that apply and use the codes and the accessibility standards as well as this book to determine everything required for your project. Many of the calculations should be "scaled off" and completed right on the project's actual floor plans. All of the required calculations and special code information should be attached to the checklist and kept with the project records.

After reading this chapter you should know that it is your responsibility to carefully plan the means of egress on interior projects. Any project can pass the basic code requirements if executed correctly. However, it takes that extra planning to reach the optimum solution. For example, any occupancy can have the correct number of exits placed to meet the half-diagonal rule, but if they are not placed as remotely as possible based on the layout of the space, you do not have adequate exits. It is also a good idea to keep the exit discharges to a minimum, allowing as many exits as possible to exit directly outside.

Note

Particular attention should be given to the type of occupancy when determining any means of egress requirement, since the codes may allow exceptions or require more severe regulations depending on the occupancy.

Note

Once a building occupant is brought into the protected portion of a means of egress, the level of protection cannot be reduced or eliminated unless an exception is allowed by your jurisdiction.

In addition, be sure to coordinate the means of egress require-ments with the fire and smoke separation requirements of the codes. Chapter 5 explains this in more detail. Chapter 9 discusses the restrictions on finishes and furnishings in a means of egress. Above all, remember that codes are minimum requirements. Add extra protection wherever it is functionally feasible and finan-cially possible. You are protecting the occupants of the building, the owner, and yourself.

CHAPTER 5

FIRE RESISTANT MATERIALS AND ASSEMBLIES

Approximately 75 percent of all codes deal with fire and life safety. Their enforcement affects virtually every part of a building, focusing first on prevention and then on early suppression and detection as the primary means of providing safe buildings. Interior fire codes focus on protecting the occupants of the building, allowing time to evacuate during a fire as well as access for fire fighters and equipment. The ultimate goal of the fire codes is to confine a fire to the room of origin, and therefore limit the spread of the fire and prevent flashover.

Fire codes include provisions for both fire protection and smoke protection. Smoke control is a relatively new field compared to fire control. Yet smoke can be just as deadly as fire, if not more so, because of how fast it can travel. The toxicity of the smoke is a large factor as well. Whether a fire is full blown or just smoldering, the smoke it produces can travel quickly and cause harm to the occupants of the building before the fire ever reaches them. The smoke causes asphyxiation and obstruction of sight, making evacuation difficult.

Because the control of fire and smoke is such a serious life safety issue, the prevention of fire and smoke spread is addressed in the codes in several ways. The codes and standards place strict requirements on the materials that are used to construct a building. The construction type of a building as discussed in Chapter 3

Note

More people die from asphyxiation due to smoke than from burns due to fire.

assigns an hourly fire rating to almost every structure element in a building, including walls and floor assemblies. Other parts of the codes place restrictions on the building materials used inside the building. These materials include everything from windows and doors to ductwork, wiring, and plumbing pipes. Interior finishes and furniture, as discussed in Chapter 9, are regulated by codes and standards as well.

In addition to regulating the materials that go into a building or space, the codes require various "systems" that are intended to aid in fire safety. Generally, fire safety systems can be divided into four main categories: prevention systems, detection systems, suppression systems, and exiting systems. The specific issues of each category are listed below.

✦ **Prevention Systems:** Focus on prohibiting and containing fires. They include fire and smoke barriers (i.e., walls, floors, ceilings), opening protectives (i.e., window, doors), and through-penetration protectives (i.e., firestops, draftstops, dampers). These are discussed in this chapter. Fire-rated finishes can also be considered a prevention system and are discussed in Chapter 9.

✦ **Detection Systems:** Consist of devices to notify occupants and fire officials; they include smoke detectors, fire alarms, and audio systems. (These are discussed in Chapter 6.)

✦ **Suppression Systems:** Consist of means to control and extinguish fires, such as fire extinguishers, fire hoses, and sprinkler systems. (These are discussed in Chapter 6.)

✦ **Exiting Systems:** Consist of means of evacuation such accessibility features, signage, and emergency lighting. Although some exiting systems are mentioned in this chapter, they are described in more detail in Chapter 4.

Before the various types of prevention systems are discussed, you must understand the concept of *compartmentation.* The main way that prevention systems control the spread of fire and smoke within a building is through compartmentation. This system creates self-contained areas within a building. Rated materials and assemblies such as walls, doors, and windows are used to separate one area from another. As a result, the fire and smoke can spread to only a limited area before meeting resistance from the rated assemblies. When one area of a building is separated from another by the use of fire rated assemblies, it is referred to as a compartment or a fire area. The codes and standards will specify interior construction and structure elements that must be used to separate these areas.

These rated assemblies can be considered a continuous rated membrane, which is created by either a single construction assembly, such as a wall, floor, or ceiling, or by a combination of carefully installed assemblies used together, such as walls, doors, and firestops. For example a rated wall is typically required to extend from the floor structure to the floor/ceiling structure above and would pierce a suspended ceiling. Although a door would be allowed in the rated wall, both the door and the door frame would be required to be rated as well. Together these elements create a compartment that helps to contain fire and smoke. Different types of compartments are required, depending on the type of occupancy and the construction type of the building.

This chapter will discuss how compartmentation works to provide protection by the use of such items as rated partitions, doors, and windows in interior projects. Collectively these are known as the prevention system. The various prevention systems discussed in this chapter have been divided into four categories: fire barriers, smoke barriers, opening protectives, and through-penetration protectives. Detection and suppression systems will be discussed in the following chapter.

DEFINITIONS

Below are some common terms used when discussing fire and smoke separation. You should be familiar with them.

ASSEMBLY, CONSTRUCTION: Refers to a number of building materials used together to create a structure element such as a wall or ceiling. One of the most common assemblies combines metal studs with gypsum board on both sides to create a wall assembly. It can also include other building parts. For example, a door assembly consists of the door, frame, and related hardware.

ASSEMBLY, FIRE-RATED: Refers to a combination of parts that make up an entire rated assembly, such as a fire door, a fire window, a firestop, or fire damper, including all required hardware, anchorage, frames, and sills. A wall or floor system can also be considered a fire-rated assembly if constructed in a certain way.

COMPARTMENTATION: The process of creating confined spaces or areas within a building for the purpose of containing fire or smoke to create safe areas of refuge. (See inset titled *High-Rise Buildings* on page 72.)

DAMPER: A device installed in ducts that closes upon detection of heat or smoke to interrupt airflow and restrict the passage of flame.

FIRE AREA: The aggregate floor area enclosed and bounded by fire walls, fire barriers, exterior walls, or fire resistant-rated horizontal assemblies of a building.

FIRE BARRIER: A continuous fire-rated vertical or horizontal assembly of materials designed to restrict the spread of fire.

FIRE BLOCKING: Building materials installed to resist the passage of fire to other areas of the building through concealed spaces.

FIRE LOAD: Amount of combustible material present that can feed a fire.

FIRE RESISTANCE: When materials or their assemblies prevent or retard the passage of excessive heat, hot gases, or flame.

FIRE RESISTANCE RATING: The time in hours, or fraction of an hour, that materials or assemblies will resist fire exposure as determined by a fire test. Also referred to as fire protection rating.

FIRESTOP: Assembly or material used to prevent the spread of fire and smoke through penetrations in fire resistive assemblies.

OPENING PROTECTIVE: A rated assembly, such as a door or window, placed in an opening located in a rated building element, such as a wall assembly, designed to maintain the fire resistance of the building element.

SELF-CLOSING: An opening protective, door or window, that will automatically close after use or in the event of activation of the fire alarm. For example, doors that are required to be rated are usually required to be self-closing.

SMOKE BARRIER: A continuous membrane, either vertical or horizontal, such as a wall, floor or ceiling assembly, that restricts the movement of smoke.

THROUGH-PENETRATION: An opening that passes through an entire assembly, such as a wall, ceiling or floor.

THROUGH-PENETRATION PROTECTIVE: A system or assembly installed in or around a through-penetration to resist the passage of flame, heat, and hot gases for a specified period of time.

COMPARING THE CODES

Each of the building codes—the *BOCA National Building Code (NBC)*, the *Standard Building Code (SBC)*, *Uniform Building Code (UBC)*, and the *International Building Code (IBC)*—has one or more chapters pertaining to fire protection. A number of requirements can also be found in the means of egress chapter within each code. The *Life Safety Code (LSC)* has two chapters on fire protection as well. When it comes to protecting a building from fire, it is typically the building codes that set the regulations, specifying the types of materials and assemblies and where they should be used. When specific testing and installation methods are required, both the building codes and the *LSC* refer you to various NFPA standards. The ones that are geared more to the interior of a building are listed in Figure 5.1.

Most code requirements for fire and smoke protection are based on occupancy classifications. The codes will determine how compartmentation and systems must work together for a particular occupancy type. For example, if a building is equipped with a fully automatic sprinkler system, some fire ratings may be reduced. (See the section on Sprinkler Systems starting on page 163.)

The *American with Disabilities Act Accessibility Guideline (ADAAG)* and other accessibility standards do not play a major role in fire prevention requirements. However, many of the fire resistant components such as fire doors and enclosed stairwell are still required to meet the accessibility requirements. Since Chapter 4

Note

A number of cities and some states have adopted their own fire codes. Some of the strictest include California, Boston, Florida, Massachusetts, New Jersey, New York City, and New York State. Be sure to check the jurisdiction of your project and use the strictest codes.

Note

The *UBC* has its own set of standards, many of which correspond to the NFPA standards.

NFPA 80:	Fire Doors and Fire Windows
NFPA 92A:	Smoke Control Systems
NFPA 92B:	Smoke-Management Systems in Malls, Atria, and Large Areas
NFPA 105:	Installation of Smoke-Contol Door Assemblies
NFPA 204:	Smoke and Heat Venting
NFPA 221:	Fire Walls and Fire Barrier Walls
NFPA 251:	Standard Methods of Tests of Fire Endurance of Building Construction and Materials
NFPA 252:	Fire Test of Door Assemblies
NPFA 255:	Method of Test of Surface Burning Characteristics of Burning Materials
NFPA 257:	Fire Test for Window and Glass Block Assemblies
NFPA 259:	Standard Test Method for Potential Heat of Building Materials
NFPA 271:	Standard Method of Test for Heat and Visible Smoke Release Rates for Materials and Products Using an Oxygen Consumption Calorimeter
NFPA 703:	Fire Retardant Impregnated Wood and Fire Retardant Coatings for Building Materials

NOTE: There are a number of NFPA standards not listed above that are specific to an occupancy, such as Health Care, or certain types of hazardous equipment. Many other standards pertain to the inspection and maintenance of a system.

Figure 5.1. Common NFPA Standards.

has already discussed the accessibility requirements related to doors, stairs, and other means of egress, this chapter will only mention the *ADAAG* a few times.

FIRE BARRIERS

Fire barriers are fire-rated building elements. (See Chapter 3.) They are walls, ceilings, or floor systems that prevent the spread of flame and heat through the use of structure materials that have fire resistance ratings. These structure materials are tested and rated as a whole construction assembly or a combination of materials used together. (See the section on Test Ratings starting on page 144.)

For fire barriers, these ratings are known as fire resistant ratings. Some of these ratings are given by the codes in their construction type tables. (See Figure 3.1, page 60.) However, each of the codes has additional requirements either in other tables or within their text. These additional requirements typically have to be compared with the construction type tables and with each other to determine the strictest requirements. For example, Figure 5.2 is a table from the *SBC* that lists some of the most common interior components and their fire ratings. Notice it lists a number of additional tables that must be referenced to determine the accurate requirements. Be sure to refer to the correct codes in your jurisdiction.

Whether a fire barrier is existing or added later, it becomes important during an interior project. The codes limit the number of penetrations in a fire-rated wall. (See the section on Through-Penetration Protectives starting on page 140.) Therefore, you must be able to determine the correct rating of the fire barrier if you are planning to add a new one or make any changes to an existing one. The actual fire rating of the wall depends on the occupancy classification, the location of the wall in the occupancy or space, and if the space or building has sprinklers.

Fire barriers can be divided into three types: fire walls, fire separation walls, and floor/ceiling assemblies. *Fire walls* have the highest fire ratings and are typically built as part of the building shell. They include party walls and occupancy separation walls. *Fire separation walls* are more likely to be added or changed during an interior project. They include tenant separation walls, corridor walls, vertical shafts, and room separation walls. Usually the fire ratings of *floor/ceiling assemblies* can be determined by the construction type and/or occupancy classification. In addition, it can also be dependent on the rating of a specific room. Each of these fire

Note

Keep in mind that fire and smoke barriers are an important component of a means of egress. A safe means of egress as required by the codes is a combination of the requirements discussed in Chapters 4, 5, and 6 of this book.

Note

Fire and smoke barriers are given fire *resistant* ratings and through-penetrations are given fire *protection* ratings.

Note

When walls are added to an existing structure it may be necessary to determine if the existing design load of the building will support these walls. See *Design Loads*, p. 47.

TABLE 705.1.2

MINIMUM FIRE RESISTANCE OF WALS, PARTITIONS, AND OPENING PROTECTIVES[1] (HRS)

COMPONENT	WALLS AND PARTITIONS[9]	OPENING PROTECTIVES
SHAFT ENCLOSURES (including stairways, exits, and elevators)		
4 or more stories	2	1½
less than 4 stories	1[2]	1[2]
all refuse chutes	2	1½
WALLS AND PARTITIONS		
fire walls[3]	4	3
within tenant space	Sec. 704.2.3	
tenant space (see also 704.3)	1	¾
horizontal exit	2	1½
exit access corridors	See Note 4, 5	20 min.[10,11]
smoke barriers	See 409.1.2	
refuse and laundry chute access rooms	1	¾
incinerator roooms	2	1½
refuse and laundry chute termination rooms	1	¾
hazardous occupancy control areas	1	¾
high rise buildings	See 412	
covered mall buildings	See 413	
assembly buildings	See Note 2	
bathrooms and restrooms	See Note 6	
OCCUPANCY SEPARATIONS[7]	Required fire resistance	
	4	3
	3	3
	2	1½
	1	¾
EXTERIOR WALLS[8]	All	¾

Notes:

1. Table 600 may require greater fire resistance of walls to insure structural stability.
2. All exits and stairways in Group A and H occupancies shall be 2 hours with 1½-hour door assemblies.
3. See also 503.1.2
4. See 704.2.3 and 704.2.4.
5. See 409 for sprinklered Group I-buildings
6. Fire rated bathroom/restroom doors are not required when opening onto fire rated halls, corridors, exit access provided:
   a. no other rooms open off the bathroom/restroom, and
   b. no gas or electric appliances are located in the bathroom/restroom, and
   c. the walls, partitions, floor and ceiling of the bathroom/restroom have a fire rating at least equal to the rating of the hall, corridor or exit access, and
   d. the bathroom/restroom is not used for any other purpose than it is designed.
7. See 704.1.
8. See Table 600, 705.1.1 and 503.4.8
9. See 704.2.2.3 for walls and partitions in Group R4 occupancies.
10. In Group R4 Large Facility occupancies, sleeping room doors shall resist the passage of smoke but closers are not required.
11. See 705.1.3.1.

Figure 5.2. *Standard Building Code (SBC) Table 705.1.2, "Minimum Fire Resistance of Walls, Partitions, and Opening Protectives (hrs)." (Reproduced from the 1999 SBC with permission of the copyright holder, Southern Building Code Congress International, Inc., all rights reserved.)*

barriers is used to create compartments that limit the spread of fire and restrict the movement of smoke in an emergency. As various fire ratings are discussed, keep in mind that the presence of an automatic sprinkler system may allow for lower ratings. The most common fire barriers are described below.

Fire Walls

Also called party walls, the main purpose of a fire wall is to provide continuous fire protection from the foundation of the building to the roof and each exterior wall. Fire walls can be used to subdivide a building into two separate types of construction or to create building divisions within the same construction type for the purpose of calculating larger allowable building areas. (See Chapter 3.) They are built so that if the construction on one side of the wall fell during an emergency, the construction on the other side would remain standing. Fire walls are typically planned and built during the actual construction of the building.

On interior projects you will usually be required to determine the rating of a fire wall only for the purpose of making penetrations. The most common required fire rating for fire walls is three to four hours. To determine the actual rating, there are several code tables that can be referenced similar to the table in Figure 3.1 of Chapter 3. However, it may be easier to refer to the original construction documents or contact the original architect to obtain the actual rating.

The rating of a fire wall can also be affected by the occupancy classification in the building. When this occurs another code table must be consulted. Figure 5.3 is Table 707.1, "Fire and Party Wall Fire Resistance Ratings," from the *NBC*. Each building code

> **Note**
>
> When an exterior wall becomes part of a required fire-rated enclosure the interior wall rating requirements do not typically apply to the exterior wall.

> **Note**
>
> Fire walls are not usually added to existing buildings. They are very costly because the wall must extend continuously from the foundation of the building up to or through the roof.

Table 707.1
FIRE AND PARTY WALL FIRERESISTANCE RATINGS

Use Group[a,b]	Minimum fireresistance rating (hours)
A-1, A-2, A-3, A-4, A-5, B, E, F-2, H-4, I-1, I-2, M, R, S-2	2
F-1, H-3, I-3, S-1, U	3
H-2	4

Note a. For requirements for Use Group H-1, see Section 707.1.1.
Note b. For requirements for aerosol warehouses, see Section 707.1.2.

Figure 5.3. *BOCA National Building Code (NBC)* Table 707.1, "Fire and Party Wall Fireresistance Ratings." (Copyright 1999, Building Officials and Code Administrators International, Inc., Country Club Hills, Illinois, *BOCA National Building Code/1999*. Reproduced with permission. All rights reserved.)

provides similar information. You may have to compare the required code table to the construction type tables to determine the strictest rating. If the wall is between two different occupancies, the stricter rating applies.

Occupancy Separation Walls

Occupancy separation walls separate areas that are classified as different occupancy types within the same building. An occupancy separation wall can be used in two distinct ways. It can separate tenants of different occupancy types, such as a restaurant located next to a retail store in a multitenant building. It might also be used to separate different uses within one type of occupancy or building, such as a retail store that has storage area similar in size to its showroom area. If one occupancy type is considered a minor occupancy to the other, separation by rated walls may not be required.

Typically, occupancy separation walls must a have a one- or two-hour fire rating. If there are two different occupancies adjacent to each other, the wall separating them must be the higher rating specified. For example, if you refer to *SBC* Table 704.1, "Occupancy Separation Requirements," as shown in Figure 5.4 to determine the fire rating of a wall between a Business occupancy and an Educational occupancy, you would find that you need to use a two-hour rated wall. The *NBC* lists similar information in its construction

TABLE 704.1
OCCUPANCY SEPARATION REQUIREMENTS

Large or Small Assembly	2 hour
Business	1 hour
Educational	2 hour
Factory-Industrial	2 hour
Hazardous	See 704.1.4
Institutional	2 hour
Mercantile	1 hour
Residential	1 hour
Storage, Moderate Hazard S1	3 hour
Storage, Low Hazard S2	2 hour
Automobile Parking Garages[1]	1 hour
Automobile Repair Garages	2 hour

Note:
  1. See 411.2.6 for exceptions.

Figure 5.4. *Standard Building Code (SBC)* Table 704.1, "Occupancy Separation Requirements." (Reproduced from the 1999 *SBC* with permission of the copyright holder, Southern Building Code Congress International, Inc., all rights reserved.)

types table with the rest of the structure elements as shown in Figure 3.1, in Chapter 3. Each code lists this information differently.

Tenant Separation Walls

Also known as demising walls, tenant separation walls are used to separate two tenants with the same occupancy or two dwelling units in the same building. Their most common fire rating is one hour. However, the exact rating required depends on the occupancy involved. Each code lists the demising wall requirements in different areas of the text. You may have to compare several tables and written requirements to determine the highest rating to use. Sprinkler systems will also affect the rating.

Corridor Walls

Corridor walls are often required to be rated because they form part of the means of egress. Their ratings range from one or two hours, depending on how the corridors are used, the occupancy of the space, and if the building is sprinklered. Typically corridors used as exits, such as *exit passageways* must have a two-hour fire rating. When required to be fire-rated, corridors used as *exit accesses* are typically rated one hour. Each code provides a table similar to *SBC* Table 704.2.4, "Fire Resistance Rating of Exit Access Corridors," as shown in Figure 5.5, to indicate the fire rating of a corridor wall. However, since some corridor walls act as the demising wall for a space, you may also have to compare these ratings to those in other tables.

Horizontal Exits

Although similar to other types of fire separation walls, a horizontal exit is a special method of providing an exit from a particular space. In this case, in the event of an emergency, occupants are not expected to leave the building but to pass to the other side of this fire-rated wall to an area of refuge. The wall usually must extend to the exterior walls. Typically, the required rating of the wall is two hours. (See Figure 4.8 and Chapter 4 for additional information.)

Vertical Shaft Enclosures

The walls that create vertical shaft enclosures for such things as stairwells, elevators, dumbwaiters, and mechanical chases provide another type of fire separation. The fire ratings for vertical

Note

A fire wall can act as a fire separation wall because of its high fire rating.

Note

Within a single tenant space, rated corridors are typically not required.

Note

When dead space below a fire-rated stairway is used for storage, it cannot block the means of egress in any way. That means the door into the storage must be outside the stair enclosure. And the storage compartment must be totally surrounded by fire-rated assemblies that have the same rating as the stair enclosure.

TABLE 704.2.4
FIRE RESISTANCE RATING OF EXIT ACCESS CORRIDORS

OCCUPANCY	OCCUPANT LOAD	FIRE RESISTANCE RATING (hours)	
		Sprinklered	Unsprinklered
A,B,F,M,S	less than 30	0	0
A	30 or more	1	1
B,F,M,S	30 or more	0	1
R1,R2,R3	less than 10, Note 1	0	0
R1,R2	10 or more, Note 1	1/2	1
R4	16 or less	0	0
R4	more than 16, Note 1	0	1
E	Note 2	1	1
I Unrestrained	All	0	N/A
I Restrained	All	0	0, Note 3
H	All	1	1

Notes:
1. Corridors within guest rooms or dwelling units need not be rated.
2. Corridors need not be rated in Group E occupancies with rooms used either for instruction with at least one exit door directly to the exterior at ground level or for assembly purposes with at least one-half of the required exits directly to the exterior at ground level.
3. Unsprinklered use condition 5 shall have exit access corridors of 1-hour fire resistance.

Figure 5.5. *Standard Building Code (SBC)* Table 704.2.4, "Fire Resistance Rating of Exit Access Corridors." (Reproduced from the 1999 *SBC* with permission of the copyright holder, Southern Building Code Congress International, Inc., all rights reserved.)

shaft enclosures are primarily determined by the number of floors that it penetrates. These walls are usually continuous from the bottom of the building to the underside of the roof deck.

Typically, the walls that enclose *exit stairs* as described in Chapter 4 must have a one-hour rating if the stairs are three stories or less and a two-hour rating if they are four or more stories. An *exit access stair* may also require a fire-rated enclosure if it connects more than two floors. These walls must be vertically continuous through each floor and fully enclose the stair. To protect the fire ratings of the walls, only limited penetrations are allowed. In addition, when a large building has more than one enclosed exit stairway one may be required to be smoke proof. (See the next section on Smoke Barriers.)

The codes limit the number of *elevators* in a single shaft or hoistway enclosure to usually no more than two to four elevators. Each shaft requires specific venting, smoke detection, and standby powers. (See inset titled *Elevators* on page 85.) In addi-

Note

Shafts used for refuse and laundry chutes have additional requirements. Refer to the building codes.

tion, most buildings require special fire separation provisions between elevator lobbies, areas of refuge, and other exit access corridors (Refer to the codes.)

Room Separation

Note

The quantity and cost of fire-rated walls are reduced by designing rooms with like fire ratings adjacent to each other, for example, an employee locker room next to the kitchen.

Not many individual rooms within a building require fire-rated walls; however, the codes consider some standard rooms to be hazardous. These rooms are sometimes called incidental rooms, usually due to the contents of the room. Some examples include boiler rooms, furnace rooms, and large storage rooms. The codes typically specify a fire separation wall with a fire rating of one hour and up to two hours to separate such rooms from the rest of the occupancy or building.

Each building code has a table similar to *NBC* Table 302.1.1, "Specific Occupancy Areas," shown in Figure 5.6. The *SBC* uses Table 409.1.5, titled "Protection from Hazardous Areas," the *UBC* uses Table 3-C, titled "Required Separation of Specific Use Areas in Group I," and the *IBC* uses Table 302.1.1, titled "Incidental Use Areas." The codes may include additional requirements for the separation of specific areas within their text as well. The *LSC* lists similar information within each occupancy chapter.

Floor and Ceiling Assemblies

Note

Some occupancies do allow vertical fire barriers (i.e., walls) to terminate at the underside of a fire-rated floor/ceiling assembly. Usually this is permitted if the fire rating of the underside of the floor/ceiling assembly is equal to that of the fire barrier. This is the exception, not the rule.

Similar to walls and partitions, fire-rated floors and ceilings are rated as an assembly. They are classified together either as a floor/ceiling or as a roof/ceiling assembly. (See Chapter 3.) It consists of everything from the bottom of the ceiling material to the top of the floor or roof above. In a commercial building, a floor/ceiling assembly often consists of a concrete slab or steel framing. A finished floor is applied to the top and a suspended ceiling, such as acoustical tile or gypsum board, may be installed below. Sometimes the concrete slab itself creates the rating required between the two floors. In other instances, a suspended ceiling may be part of the rated assembly. You should verify the required elements of the rated floor/ceiling assembly. Between the slab and the suspended ceiling are a number of additional elements such as ducts, piping, and wires that need to be considered as well. (See Through-Penetration Protectives starting on page 140.)

The fire ratings for floor/ceiling assemblies and for floor/roof assemblies are controlled by the construction type (as shown in Chapter 3) for the building and the walls that surround the assembly. Typically, the construction type tables will supply the fire rat-

Table 302.1.1
SPECIFIC OCCUPANCY AREAS

Room or area[b]	Separation[a]/protection
All use groups:	
Paint shops in occupancies other than Use Group F employing hazardous materials in quantities less than those which cause classification as Use Group H	2 hours; or 1 hour and automatic fire suppression system
Waste and soiled linen collection rooms and chute termination rooms	1 hour and automatic fire suppression system
Waste and soiled linen chute access rooms	1 hour; or automatic fire suppression system with smoke partitions
Boiler and furnace rooms	1 hour; or automatic fire suppression system with smoke partitions
Incinerator rooms	2 hours and automatic fire suppression system
Use Groups A, B, E, I-1, R-1, R-2:	
Storage rooms more than 50 square feet in area but not more than 100 square feet in area	1 hour; or automatic fire suppression system with smoke partitions
Storage rooms more than 100 square feet in area	Automatic fire suppression system with smoke partitions
Physical plant maintenance shop and workshop	2 hours; or 1 hour and automatic fire suppression system
Use Groups I-2, I-3:	
Boiler and furnace rooms	1 hour and automatic fire suppression system
Handicraft shops, kitchens, and employee locker rooms	1 hour; or automatic fire suppression system with smoke partitions
Laundries greater than 100 square feet in area	1 hour and automatic fire suppression system
Storage rooms more than 50 square feet in area but not more than 100 square feet in area	Automatic fire suppression system with smoke partitions
Storage rooms more than 100 square feet in area	1 hour and automatic fire suppression system
Physical plant maintenance shop and workshop	1 hour and automatic fire suppression system
Use Group I-2:	
Gift/retail shops and laboratories employing hazardous quantities less than those which cause classification as Use Group H	1 hour; or automatic fire suppression system with smoke partitions
Use Group I-3 padded cells	1 hour and automatic fire suppression system

Note a. For requirements for fireresistance rated separations and smoke partitions, see Section 302.1.1.1.
Note b. 1 square foot = 0.093 m².

Figure 5.6. BOCA *National Building Code (NBC)* Table 302.1.1, "Specific Occupancy Areas." (Copyright 1999, Building Officials and Code Administrators International, Inc., Country Club Hills, Illinois, BOCA *National Building Code/1999.* Reproduced with permission. All rights reserved.)

ings, but you may need to use other tables to determine the wall ratings. If you are adding a ceiling to a space, you may need to determine the ratings of the surrounding walls and use the same rating at the ceiling. For example, in a two-hour rated stairwell, the ceiling must have a two-hour rating as well.

SMOKE BARRIERS

Smoke barriers are a prevention system designed to restrict the movement of smoke and fire gases. Fire barriers, as described in the previous section, can help restrict the passage of smoke, but they do not necessarily make an effective smoke barrier. Just because a wall is fire rated does not mean it will automatically resist smoke. Additional precautions are required.

Note

When fire separation walls extend through a suspended or dropped ceiling to the underside of the floor slab above, usually the ceiling within the space can have a lower fire rating than the walls.

A smoke barrier can consist of either a *wall assembly* or a *full enclosure*. A full enclosure consists of walls, ceilings, and floor assemblies that create a continuous smokeproof compartment. To make them smoke resistant, only limited openings are allowed. In full enclosures additional mechanical functions are required for ventilation and air circulation. A smoke detector typically activates the ventilation system and automatically closes all doors with a closing device.

The most common smoke barrier uses are described below. Some of these requirements are specified in the building codes. For other, more specific codes, be sure to consult a mechanical engineer. (See Chapter 7.) Additional requirements are specified in the NFPA standards: *NFPA 92A: Smoke Control Systems* and *NFPA 92B: Smoke Management Systems in Malls, Atria, and Large Assemblies.*

Wall Assemblies

A wall used as a smoke barrier must be continuous from outside wall to outside wall and from floor slab to floor slab. It is used mostly in Institutional occupancies to subdivide floors used by patients for sleeping or treatment for greater safety. Each compartment created by a smoke barrier is considered a smoke compartment and provides an area of refuge from the adjacent compartment. Horizontal exits in Institutional occupancies also use a fire and smoke barrier, which provides another way to protect the occupants in the event of a fire. Other requirements include specific swing-type doors, automatic release door closures, and smoke dampers at mechanical ducts.

Vertical Shafts

Vertical shaft enclosure for stairs, elevators, and waste and linen chutes must be smokeproof, especially if a building is over a certain height. As mentioned earlier, the walls and openings of all vertical shafts must be fire rated. To make them smokeproof, all openings into the shaft must automatically close upon detection of smoke. A *smokestop door* may also be required. This is a door specially designed to close tightly and inhibit the passage of smoke. (See section on Fire Doors beginning on the next page.)

Vestibules

Any vestibule used adjacent to a smokeproof stairwell or elevator hoistway, between the shaft and the exterior exit door, must also be smokeproof. The codes require the vestibule to be a certain size. The doors must also be fire rated, have self-closing devices, and have a drop sill to minimize air leakage.

Note

The types of vestibules used in conjunction with the stair shaft or elevator hoistway and the presence of an automatic sprinkler system can affect the codes required for smokeproof enclosures.

SMOKE AND HOW IT TRAVELS

To gain a better understanding of smoke control systems and how they work, it is important to know how smoke moves. The Council on Tall Buildings and Urban Habitat, in the book *Fire Safety in Tall Buildings*, describes five major driving forces that cause smoke movement. They are briefly described below:

1. *Buoyancy:* As the temperature of smoke increases during a fire it becomes buoyant due to its reduced density. As the buoyancy increases a pressure builds and the smoke is forced up through any available leakage paths to the floor above and to adjacent areas.

2. *Expansion:* As a fire develops it emits gases. These gases expand and create pressure causing smoke to be forced out of an enclosed fire compartment.

3. *HVAC:* As a fire progresses, the HVAC system can transport smoke to every area it serves. The system can also supply air to a fire, increasing its intensity.

4. *Stack Effect:* Stack effect is a result of exterior air temperature. Generally, if it is cold outside there is usually an upward movement of air within the building shafts, such as stairwells, elevators, and mechanical shafts. When the outside air is warmer than the building air, the airflow moves downward. This air movement can move smoke a considerable distance from a fire.

5. *Wind:* Windows frequently break during a fire, causing outside wind to force smoke through doors into adjacent spaces and other floors.

In a fire situation smoke movement can be caused by one or more of these driving forces. That is why the correct use and placement of smoke barriers can be critical. (The three stages of a fire are explained in the inset titled *Stages of Fire Development* on page 220.)

The ceiling of the vestibule must be high enough so that it serves as a smoke and heat trap and allows an upward-moving air-flow. Ventilation is required as well. It might be as simple as an opening in an exterior wall for *natural* ventilation. The most common is *mechanical* ventilation with vents opening to the out-side air. The codes regulate a number of items such as the type of system used, the amount of supply and exhaust air, and the loca-tion of duct openings. (See Chapter 7.)

OPENING PROTECTIVES

An opening protective is a rated assembly that prevents the spread of fire or smoke through an opening in a rated wall. An opening protective is usually a door or a view window. The rating of the opening protective component is determined by the rating of the wall. Not only are the ratings important to the integrity of the entire wall during a fire to stop the spread of fire and smoke, but they are also crucial for the evacuation of the occupants during a fire. Opening protectives can also be considered a type of through-penetration system, which is discussed later in the chapter. Through-penetration components control openings required by wiring, ducts, pipes, and similar penetrations in a building. Both are components that are intended to maintain the integrity of the rated wall.

The fire protection ratings for opening protectives are deter-mined by the same codes that determine construction assemblies. Each of the building codes has a table similar to *IBC* Table 714.2, "Opening Protective Fire Protection Rating," as shown in Figure 5.7. It indicates which rated opening protective is required for each type of rated construction assembly. (Note how the rating of the opening protective is typically lower than the construction assembly.) Both the building codes and the *LSC* also direct you to a number of NFPA publications, such as *NFPA 80 Standard for Fire Doors* and *Windows*.

The intent of the codes and other standards is to regulate open-ings in rated walls so that the required rated construction does not lose its effectiveness. The most common opening protectives are described below.

Fire Doors

As mentioned in Chapter 4, the codes actually describe doors as door assemblies. A typical door consists of four main components: door, frame, hardware, and doorway (or wall opening). Other doors, such as the ones listed in Figure 5.8, will consist of even

TABLE 714.2
OPENING PROTECTIVE FIRE PROTECTION RATING

TYPE OF ASSEMBLY	REQUIRED ASSEMBLY RATING (HOUR)	MINIMUM OPENING PROTECTION ASSEMBLY (HOUR)
Fire walls and fire barriers having a required fire resistance rating greater than 1 hour	4 3 2 1 ½	3 3[b] 1 ½ 1 ½

Fire barriers of 1 hour fire resistance rated construction :
    Shaft and exit enclosure walls
    Other fire barriers
	
	1
	
	1
		
		1
		
		3/4

Fire partitions: Exit access corridor enclosure wall	 1 ½	 1/3[a] 1/3[a]
Other fire partitions	1	3/4

Note a. For testing requirements, see Section 714.2.2.
Note b. Two doors, each with a fire protection rating of 1 ½ hours, installed on opposite sides of the same opening in a building separation wall, shall be deemed equivalent in fire protection rating to one 3-hour fire door.

Figure 5.7. *International Building Code (IBC)* Table 714.2, "Opening Protective Fire Protection Rating." (Written permission to reproduce this material was granted by the copyright holder, International Code Council, Inc., 5203 Leesburg Pike, Suite 708, Falls Church, VA 22041.)

REGULATED FIRE-RATED DOORS	REGULATED FIRE-RATED WINDOWS
ACCESS DOORS	BORROWED LIGHTS
ACCORDIAN/FOLDING DOORS	CASEMENT WINDOWS
BI-PARTING DOORS	DOUBLE-HUNG WINDOWS
CONVEYING SYSTEM DOORS	GLASS BLOCK
CHUTE DOORS	HINGED WINDOWS
DUTCH DOORS	PIVOT WINDOWS
HOISTWAY DOORS	SIDE LIGHTS
HORIZONTAL DOORS	STATIONARY WINDOWS
REVOLVING DOORS	TILTING WINDOWS
ROLLING STEEL DOORS	TRANSOM LIGHTS
SERVICE COUNTER DOORS	VIEW PANELS
SWINGING DOORS	
VERTICAL SLIDING DOORS	

Figure 5.8. Types of regulated fire doors and fire windows.

more parts. All these parts make up an assembly. If the door is a fire door, the whole assembly must be tested and rated as one unit. However, each component has certain characteristics that make it fire-rated.

Door and Frame: The *door* itself is typically flush and either solid core wood or hollow metal. Very few panel doors meet the fire resistant requirements, although some are available. Depending on the hourly rating, some rated doors can be clad in plastic laminate. Fire-rated frames can be wood, steel (i.e., hollow metal), or aluminum. The most commonly specified rated frame is hollow metal. A rated door will have a label or marking on the vertical edge to confirm that it is a rated component. (See Figure 5.13.)

Hardware: The most common *hardware* includes hinges, latches and locksets, pulls, and closures. Hinges, latch sets, and closing devices are the most stringently regulated. For example, fire-rated hinges must be steel or stainless steel and a specific quantity are required for each door. Both the hinges and the latch set are important to hold a fire door securely closed during a fire. To be effective they must be able to withstand the pressure and heat that are generated during a fire.

Fire-rated exit doors also require a specific type of latch. The most common is called fire exit hardware. Fire exit hardware is tested and rated. A similar type of hardware is called panic hardware. However, panic hardware is not tested and should not be used on fire-rated doors. Both consist of a panel or bar that must be pushed to release the door latch. The most common occupancy classifications that require fire exit hardware are Assembly and Educational. Although the codes do not require it in every occupancy it is often used on exit doors. In occupanices that are not required to use fire exit hardware, lever hardware can be used.

Other issues can affect the choice of hardware on a door, including locking methods for security. The requirements of the *ADA* should also be considered in the final section of hardware. However, providing the proper means of egress and maintaining the fire rating of the doors is most important.

The codes require that fire-rated doors be self-closing. This means that the door must have a device called a closer that closes the door after each use. Closers, in general, can be surface mounted or concealed within the door, frame, or floor. You should verify that the closer application does not violate the rating of the door assembly in each case. If it is desirable that certain rated doors be open all the time, an electromagnetic or pneumatic hold-open device can be

Note

Typically no openings except for a limited number of doors are allowed in fire walls that require a three- to four-hour rating.

Note

When selecting fire-rated door hardware, be sure you are meeting the additional requirements set in the *ADAAG*, such as the shape of the item and height of installation. (See Chapter 4.)

Note

If a building is fully sprinklered, the codes may allow an exit door to have an automatic closure with a longer than standard time delay.

used. This device holds the door in an open position until an emergency occurs. Either a fusible link is triggered by heat or the activation of a smoke detector causes the door to close.

Doorway: During construction other parts are added to the door assembly, such as a lintel and a sill. These become part of the *doorway.* The rating of each of these components is based on specific requirements found in the code. For example, the construction of the sill can vary, depending on the type of construction of the floor on either side of the door. Other components depend on the rating of the wall that the doorway is penetrating. In addition, the *NFPA 80: Standard for Fire Doors and Fire Windows* places restrictions on the height that kickplates or other protection devices can be installed on fire doors. Although not directly a fire code issue, the *ADA* height restrictions on thresholds should be considered as well.

Door Ratings: Since fire protection ratings are assigned to the entire door assembly, fire doors are typically specified and sold by the manufacturer as a whole assembly. To obtain a rating, the door must undergo a fire test as specified in *NFPA 252: Standard Method of Fire Test of Door Assemblies.* The *UBC* and *IBC* currently require fire-rated doors to be tested by a positive pressure test that better resembles actual fire conditions than previous tests. When smokestop doors are used in smoke barriers, they must undergo additional testing as required in *NFPA 105: Installation of Smoke-Control Door Assemblies.* Any door that passes the required tests is assigned a fire protection rating and receives a permanent label. An example of this label is shown in Figure 5.13.

In the most recent codes, doors were classified by the fire protection rating and the typical use of the door in a building using a letter and number designation. The letter designation indicates the use of the door. The number represents the length of time the door will withstand the effects of fire according to testing. These door classes are listed in Figure 5.9. (Figure 5.9 also indicates which door class allows glass lites within the door.) A 1½ hour door could be classified as a B or D door; however, the B door is for use in the interior of the building and the D door is for use as an exterior door.

Most newer editions of the codes, including the *IBC,* are no longer using the letter designation and are simply referring to the hourly rating of the door. If you are working on a project that refers to an older edition, you may be required to refer to the classifications as well as the hourly rating. On interior projects ¾-hour (previously called Class C) and 20-minute doors are the most common.

Note

Oversize doors cannot be labeled because of their size. Instead their approval is based on a certificate of inspection furnished by an approved testing agency.

Note

Many codes are requiring positive-pressure testing of fire-rated doors. This test better represents the conditions of a fire that would cause flames to penetrate through cracks and openings in a fire door.

CLASS	FIRE RATING	LOCATION AND USE	GLASS LITE SIZE ALLOWED		
			AREA	HEIGHT	WIDTH
A	3 Hour	Fire walls separating buildings or various fire areas within a building. 3 to 4 hour walls	None Allowed	None Allowed	None Allowed
B	1½ Hours (H.M.) 1 Hour (other)	Vertical shafts and enclosures such as stairwells, elevators, and garbage chutes. 2 hour walls	100 inches	33 inches	10–12* inches
B	1 hour	Vertical shafts in low-rise buildings and discharge corridors. 1 to 1½ hour walls	100 inches	33 inches	10–12* inches
C	¾ hour	Exit access corridors and exitway enclosures. 1 hour walls	1296 inches	54 inches	54 inches
N/A	20-minute (⅓ hour)	Exit access corridors and room partitions. 1 hour walls	No Limit	No Limit	No Limit

* Final size depends on code publication used

Figure 5.9. Interior Fire-Rated Doors and Glass Lites.

The fire door rating depends on the fire rating of the wall in which it is being placed. If the wall is fire rated, the door must be rated as well. For example, all doors located in the shaft walls of an exit stair require a fire rating. If they are located in a stair enclosure that serves more than three floors, the enclosure is required to be rated 2 hours and door must be rated 1½ hours. Many exit access doors need to be rated 20 to 45 minutes. Since doors usually undergo more stringent testing and make up only a portion of an entire wall, their ratings are not as strict as those of the walls in which they are located. (Chapter 4 discusses doors in relation to size, swing, accessibility, and the means of egress concerns.)

Fire Windows

Windows can be a part of a door assembly, such as a transom, sidelight, or vision panel, or can be a completely separate entity. These and other types are listed in Figure 5.8. A fire window is considered an opening protective. It is an assembly that typically consists of a frame, approved rated glazing material, and hardware. The most common interior applications for a fire-rated window are openings in corridor walls, room partitions, and smoke barriers.

Fire windows are given a fire protection rating similar to doors and are usually classified by hourly designations. The established testing requirements are typically specified in *NFPA 80: Fire Doors and Fire Windows* or *NFPA 257: Standards on Fire Test of Window and Glass Block*. The required rating of a window depends on the location within the building. Generally, such fire resistant ratings are not greater than one hour. When the codes require a rated window assembly, the assembly must have a permanent label applied by the manufacturer guaranteeing its fire rating.

Rated Glazing

The fire codes set specific requirements for the size, thickness, location, and types of glazing materials that can be used in a rated fire window. For example, Figure 5.9 shows you the typical area and dimension restrictions for glass lites used in fire-rated doors. Glazing products for use in a fire-rated assembly are assessed by their ability to stay in place in the event of a fire, resistance to thermal shock in a hose stream test, strength against human contact, and resistance to heat transfer to the unexposed side. There are a wide variety of different types of glass. When glass products are used in a rated wall, they must meet the requirements of *NFPA 257*. Three types of glazing are considered fire rated—wire glass, glass block, and fire-rated glazing.

Wire Glass: Wire glass consists of wire mesh sandwiched between two layers of glass. The steel wire helps to distribute heat and increase the strength of the glass. Wired glass is rated for up to 45 minutes. Each of the codes sets requirements on the sizes allowed in rated assemblies specific to the use of wired glass. Until recently, wire glass was the only acceptable glazing for a rated opening protective. It still is an affordable and dependable material for a rated window.

Glass Block: Glass block is typically given a rating of 45 minutes, although, it may be allowed in a wall with more than a one-hour rating. There are new types of glass block that have 60- to 90-minute ratings, but glass block with this type of fire resistance rating may not be addressed in the codes. The use of performance codes will provide more opportunities to use these new products as long as the code official agrees that an adequate level of protection is provided. Where glass block is allowed, there are often restrictions on the area of glass block used as an interior wall. The codes also set limits when glass block is used as a view panel in a rated wall and may require the block to be installed in steel channels.

Note

If a window is large enough that it can be mistaken for a door, the codes require a rail to be installed across the window at a specific height.

Note

Standard fire-rated glass, such as wire glass and glass block, are given fire *protection* ratings, while other types of glass block and fire-rated glass are typically given fire *resistance* ratings. (Refer to the section on Test Ratings in this chapter.)

Note

In addition to fire resistance, heat transfer must be considered when using large amounts of glass.

Note

Be sure to check with the NFPA and the local code officials for the specifics on this new type of glass—fire-rated glazing. It may not be allowed in every situation.

Fire-Rated Glazing: Fire-rated glazing includes newer products, such as tempered glass, clear ceramics, insulated glass, and multilayer laminated glass, which have been developed as alternatives to wire glass. Each has unique attributes as an opening protective, as a design element and as a cost-effective material. These products are available in 60- and 90-minute ratings instead of the typical 45 minutes for wire glass and glass block. Some manufacturers have developed a glazing assembly that meets the requirements of a 2-hour rated wall assembly. Other products can provide only a 20-minute rating but allow greater resistance to impact. They all provide fire-rated glazing options that are wireless and transparent, but these products are typically more expensive than wire glass.

The new glazing materials provide the designer with a number of new interior window applications. Because of their high ratings, larger sheets of glass can be used. However, some of these sizes may exceed the current maximum listings of fire-rated glazing found in the building codes. Similar to the use of glass block, as performance-based requirements develop there will be more opportunity to use these materials in ways that vary from the set limitations. (See inset titled *Using Performance Codes* on page 12.) The *IBC*, for example, requires glazing other than wired glass to comply with the size limitations in *NFPA 80* and the requirements of *NFPA 257*. You should work closely with the code official and manufacturers to determine which glazing product is best for your project and to assure that the glazing material you choose will provide the protection required. All fire-rated glazing must pass the appropriate tests and standards and have a permanent label etched into the glass.

THROUGH-PENETRATION PROTECTIVES

A though-penetration is defined as an opening that pierces the entire thickness of a construction assembly, such as a wall or ceiling. When these construction assemblies are fire-rated, the codes require the penetrations to be protected with fire assemblies such as firestops, draftstops, and fire dampers. (The codes may also include shutters as a common opening protective.) These fire assemblies act as prevention systems and are referred to as through-penetration protection systems. Through-penetration protection systems are required to have a fire protection rating. Not only are the ratings important to the integrity of the entire wall during a fire to stop the spread of fire and smoke, they are also crucial for the evacuation of the occupants during a fire. The most common through-penetration protectives are described below.

Firestops

Firestops are a type of through-penetration protection system that is required in fire and smoke barriers. They are used as a means of restricting the passage of smoke, heat, and flames in concealed spaces. They seal and protect any opening created by penetrations, such as plumbing pipes, electrical conduit and wire, HVAC ducts, cables, and similar building service equipment that pass through walls, floors, and ceilings. They may also be required in concealed spaces between walls and at connections between horizontal and vertical planes.

The *NEC* and the *LSC* require the use of listed and approved firestops in fire and smoke barriers. They are rated under *ASTM E814: Standard Test Method for Fire Tests of Through-Penetration Fire Stops.* (Prior to this standard being issued, they were tested under *ASTM E119.*) This test established two ratings. An *F-rating* is based on the number of hours the firestop resists flame and hot gases, a hose stream performance, and whether it remains in the opening. The *T-rating* is stricter and includes the F-rating criteria plus a maximum temperature riser. When specifying a firestop you need to either list one of these ratings or list the specific devices or system. Each code has slightly different criteria.

A number of noncombustible materials can be used to create firestops. These include silicone foam, mortar, mineral wool, fire resistive board, wire mesh, collars, and clamp bands. They can be divided into two groups: systems and devices. A *firestop system* is typically constructed in the field and added after the through-penetration has been installed. The most common way to create a firestop is to fill the open space between the penetrating item and the fire barrier with fire-rated material and finish it with a sealant. The amount of damming materials and noncombustible sealant are specific to the location of the penetration, the dimension of the opening, the type of smoke or fire barrier, and the type and size of the penetrating item.

A *firestop device* is factory built and is typically installed as part of the through-penetration. There are two types that prevent the spread of flame and smoke while retarding the rise in temperature as required by a T-rating. Endothermic fire-stops release water when exposed to heat. This causes a cooling effect that enables the installation to meet the fire rating required by the code. An intumescent fire-stop expands in volume under fire conditions, forming a strong char. This expansive caulk seals the gaps created as the penetrating items melt away.

Draftstops

Note

Firestops and draftstops are similar but not the same. Firestops are used in all types of buildings to close off small spaces. Draftstops are required in combustible construction to close off large concealed spaces.

Draftstops are similar to firestops in that they prevent the passage of fire, heat, and smoke; however, draftstops are not required to be noncombustible; in fact, they are typically required in buildings with construction types that include combustible materials. Draftstops are placed between the ceiling and the floor above, attic spaces, and other concealed spaces. They are used to create separate spaces or areas to prevent the movement of air. The codes specify when draftstops are required and the size of the spaces they divide.

Damper Systems

A damper is another type of opening protective and can also be considered a type of smoke barrier. (See inset titled *Smoke and How It Travels* on page 133.) It is used specifically in HVAC ductwork and is typically specified by the mechanical engineer. It is a device arranged to automatically interrupt the flow of air through a duct system during an emergency so that it restricts the passage of smoke, fire, and heat.

There are two kinds of fire or smoke damper systems: static and dynamic. A static damper automatically shuts down during a fire, whereas a dynamic damper system remains in operation even during a fire. Dynamic dampers can be used in either static or dynamic HVAC systems; but static dampers can be used only in static systems. Depending on their installation, fire and smoke dampers may also be used to control the volume of air for the heating and cooling system during normal use. When a fire occurs, the dampers then stop or regulate the potential flow of heated air, smoke or flame through the duct system. There are three main types of dampers used in HVAC systems: fire dampers, smoke dampers, and ceiling dampers. (There is a fourth new type of damper called a corridor damper, but since it is used primarily in California, it is not discussed in this book.)

Fire Dampers: Fire dampers are required by the codes in several locations. They are typically required in ducts that penetrate rated partitions or extend through rated floor assemblies and at air transfer openings in partitions. In other words, a damper must be installed whenever a duct passes through a wall, ceiling, or floor that is part of a fire-rated assembly. It can be installed within the duct or on the outside as a collar fastened to the wall or ceiling. The most common fire damper includes a fusible link on either side of the assembly the duct is penetrating. This fusible link melts during a fire when an area reaches a certain temperature, causing the fire damper to close and seal the duct.

The rating of a damper can range from 1½ hours to 3 hours. The length of the rating is determined by the codes and depends on the rating of the fire-rated construction assembly the duct is passing through. Figure 5.10 is a table from *NBC* titled Table 718.1, "Fire Damper Rating," that indicates required fire damper ratings. Fire tests for fire dampers include *UL 555* and *UBC 43-7*. These standards are typically used to determine the hourly fire rating of the fire damper. Installation of fire dampers in HVAC systems is regulated by *NFPA 90A: Standard for Installation of Air Conditioning and Ventilating Systems* and *NFPA 90B: Standard for Installation of Warm Air Heating and Air Conditioning Systems.*

Smoke Dampers: Smoke dampers are similar to fire dampers, but they are activated specifically by smoke rather than heat. They are typically required when ducts penetrate a smoke barrier. Since smoke barriers are not required by the codes as often as fire-rated partitions and assemblies, smoke dampers are not used as often as fire dampers. When the smoke damper is required, it is installed with a smoke detector. The smoke detector is typically located inside the duct so that when it detects smoke it causes the smoke damper to close off the duct. *NFPA 90A, NFPA 90B,* and *UL 555S* regulate smoke dampers. They are specified by four classes (Class I,

**Table 718.1
FIRE DAMPER RATING**

Type of penetration	Minimum damper rating (hour)
Fire partitions less than 1 hour	
Unprotected floor assemblies (see Section 714.3.1.1)	½
Single membrane of a 1-hour fireresistance rated assembly	
1-hour fireresistance rated assemblies	1
2-hour fireresistance rated assemblies	1½
3-hour or greater fireresistance rated assemblies	3

Figure 5.10. *BOCA National Building Code (NBC)* Table 718.1, "Fire Damper Rating." (Copyright 1999, Building Officials and Code Administrators International, Inc., Country Club Hills, Illinois, *BOCA National Building Code/1999.* Reproduced with permission. All rights reserved.)

Class II, Class III, and Class IV), with Class I being the most effective. If required, combination fire and smoke dampers are available.

Ceiling Dampers: Ceiling dampers, sometimes referred to as ceiling radiation dampers, are used in suspended ceilings that are part of the rated floor/roof and ceiling assembly. They prevent heat from entering into the space between the ceiling and the floor or roof above. They also prevent the heat from traveling through the duct system. The ceiling damper closes when the heated air tries to move up through the damper. Ceiling dampers are regulated by *UL 555C*.

TEST RATINGS

Chapter 3 discussed the use of construction types and how each type specifies fire ratings for the structure elements within a building. These structure elements are made up of various construction assemblies. The assemblies are assigned ratings that are determined by fire tests. The purpose of the test is to determine the rating of an assembly by registering its performance during the test and examining its fire resistive properties. The fire resistance rating is assigned according to the time lapsed when the test is terminated. For wall, partition, and floor/ceiling assemblies the ratings used are known as fire *resistant* ratings (FRR). For window and door assemblies and other opening protectives and through-penetration protectives, the ratings are called fire *protective* ratings (FPR). The ratings for both are based on hourly increments.

The American Society for Testing and Materials (ASTM), the National Fire Protection Association (NFPA), and Underwriters Laboratories (UL), in conjunction with the American National Standards Institute (ANSI), have established a wide variety of standard fire endurance tests. These tests are performed by fire testing agencies. (Some of the more common testing agencies are listed in Figure 5.11.) Manufacturers use these agencies to confirm that their products meet specific requirements. For example, walls, floors, roofs, columns, and beams that are constructed of masonry, metal, or composite structural materials are tested in a furnace under controlled laboratory conditions. The most standard test is *ASTM E119: Test Methods for Fire Tests of Building Construction and Materials*. Similar tests being used today are *ANSI/UL 263*, *NFPA 251*, and *UBC Standard 43-1*.

ASTM E119 generally evaluates how long an assembly will contain a fire, retain its own structural integrity, or both. The test measures the performance of construction assemblies in three

Note

The International Conference of Building Officials (ICBO) has developed a number of its own standards for use in jurisdictions using the *UBC*.

Commercial Testing Company
Factory Mutual Research Corporation
National Institute of Standards and Technology
The Ohio State University
Portland Cement Association
Radco, Inc.
Standard Fire Test, Fire Prevention Research Institute
University of California
Underwriters Laboratories, Inc.
Underwriters Laboratories of Canada
Warnock Hersey International, Inc.

Figure 5.11. Fire Testing Agencies.

areas: (1) the temperature rise on the protected side of the assembly, (2) the smoke, gas, or flames that pass through the assembly, and (3) the structural performance during exposure to the fire. If the assembly being tested is a load-bearing assembly, the test measures the load-carrying ability during exposure to fire. In addition, if a wall or partition obtains a rating of one hour or more, it is subject to a hose stream test to see if it will resist disintegration. Other components, such as certain doors, may have to pass a pressure test.

Opening protectives and through-penetration protective systems must also pass specific tests. For example, fire doors must conform to the test requirements of *ASTM E152* and fire windows and shutters must meet the requirements of *ASTM 257*. Other common fire tests are listed in Figure 5.12.

The most important distinction between the tests in Figure 5.12 is the different types of glazing. In the past, tests for glass set fire exposure limits to 45 minutes and did not test the radiant heat created by the glass during the fire. With the recent development of fire-rated glazing and newer types of glass block with higher fire ratings, stricter tests are required, especially when large amounts of the glass are being used. You typically should request the stricter tests as indicated in the chart when using these types of glazing.

Any assembly that passes the required tests shown in Figure 5.12 must have a permanent label attached to it to prove it is fire rated. Figure 5.13 is an example of one of these labels used for a fire-rated door. Any such label must indicate the manufacturer, the test rating, and in some cases the maximum transmitted temperature. The label often indicates the seal of the testing agency as well. When a required assembly such as a fire door is not sold as an assembly or is only partially complete, it is up to you to make sure that each of the additional required components has the proper rating and that each is appropriately labeled.

Note

In the past fire door tests were conducted in furnaces under a neutral pressure. Now, most tests require a positive pressure test.

Note

Fire-rated labels are either permanently affixed to the product or directly etched into the fire assembly.

FIRE-RATED ASSEMBLIES AND OTHER MATERIALS	REQUIRED FIRE TESTS[a]
Wall assemblies Ceiling assemblies Floor assemblies	ASTM E119 UL 263 NFPA 251 UBC 43-1
Fire doors[b]	ASTM E152 UL 10B NFPA 252 UBC 43-2
Fire windows and shutters Wire glass Glass block[c]	ASTM E163 UL 9 NFPA 257 OR 80 UBC 43-6
Firestops	ASTM E814 UBC 43-4
Fire-rated glazing[c]	ASTM E152 OR E119 NFPA 257

Note a: UBC tests may be required only in jurisdictions using the UBC.
Note b: 20-minute doors do not require a hose-stream test.
Note c: If large amounts of glass are used, radiant heat should be tested

Figure 5.12. Summary of Fire Tests.

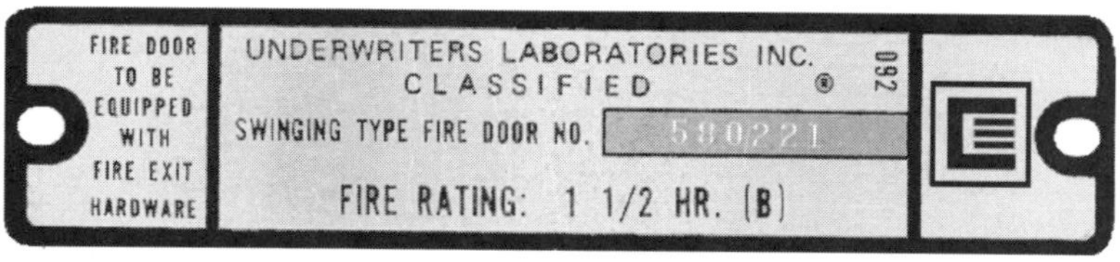

Figure 5.13. Typical Label for a Fire-Rated Assembly. (Reproduced with permission from Ceco Door Products.)

USING RATED MATERIALS

Several organizations in the United States publish lists of tested assemblies. These organizations have a wide variety of assemblies that have been tested and assigned the appropriate hourly fire rating. Included assemblies are walls and partitions, floor/ceiling systems, roof/ceiling systems, beams, girders, and truss protection systems, column protection systems, and door and window assemblies. Three of the most widely used publications are indicated below.

✦ Underwriters Laboratories: *Fire Resistance Directory, Vol. I* for beams, columns, floors, roofs, and partitions and *Fire Resistance Directory, Vol. II* for through-penetration firestop systems
✦ Gypsum Association: *Fire Resistance Design Manual*
✦ Factory Mutual: *Specification Tested Products Guide*

These publications use line drawing and detailed descriptions for the rated assemblies. They indicate specific materials, workmanship, and detailed sizes and dimensions. An example of a common one-hour wall assembly is shown in Figure 5.14. Each rated assembly is assigned a file or design number specific to that assembly and organization and an hourly rating. It is your responsibility to refer to the correct file number when a fire rated assembly is required by the code.

For example, if you were asked to replace some existing steps in an exit access corridor with a ramp, the codes would require you to rate the new ramp. It would become part of the existing floor/ceiling assembly. Depending on the occupancy classification and the type of construction of the building, the assembly could require from a one-hour to a four-hour rating. Once you determined the fire rating required by the building code, you would use one of the publications listed above to find the detail of the rated assembly most similar to the existing construction conditions. Use the file number of this assembly in your specifications of the new ramp.

It is important to note, however, that the test results and ratings of materials and assemblies can become invalid if the materials and assemblies are not used and maintained properly. Below are several factors to keep in mind when specifying rated assemblies.

1. If you do not use a product the way a manufacturer specifies, its rating becomes void. You must either have it retested the way it is built or add fire protection to create the rating.
2. If the construction of the joints between each assembly, such as wall-to-wall, wall-to-ceiling, or wall-to-floor, are substandard, fire and smoke can penetrate no matter how good each assembly is.
3. Conventional openings, such as electrical switches and outlets in wall assemblies and electrical raceways and pull boxes in floor/ceiling assemblies, can affect the fire endurance of an assembly. Some assemblies are tested with these penetrations; others are not.

Design No. U495
Nonbearing Wall Rating — 1 or 2 HR.
(See Items 5 and 7)

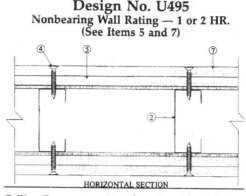

HORIZONTAL SECTION

1. **Floor and Ceiling Runners** — (Not Shown) — Channel-shaped runners, 3-5/8 in. wide (min), 1-1/4 in. legs, formed from No. 25 MSG (min) galv steel, attached to floor and ceiling with fasteners spaced 24 in. OC, max.
2. **Steel Studs** — Channel-shaped 3-5/8 in. wide (min), 1-1/4 in. legs, 3/8 in. folded back returns, formed from No. 25 MSG (min) galv steel, spaced 24 in. OC max.
3. **Batts and Blankets*** — (Optional, not shown) — Mineral wool or glass fiber batts partially or completely filling stud cavity.
   See Batts and Blankets (BZJZ) category for names of Classified companies.
4. **Screws** — Type S self-tapping screws, 1-1/4 or 2 in. long, (1 Hr) and 2-1/2 in. long (2 Hr).
5. **Building Units*** — For 1 Hr Rating — Nom 5/8 or 3/4 in. thick, 4 ft wide, faced gypsum wallboard panels with the faced side on the interior wall cavity. Panels attached to studs and floor and ceiling runners with screws spaced 8 in. OC along the edges of the panel and 12 in. OC in the field of the panel. Joints oriented vertically and staggered on opposite sides of the assembly.
   GENERAL ELECTRIC CO
   SILICONE PRODUCTS DIV —Type CoreGuard.
   NATIONAL GYPSUM CO —Type Gold Bond Fire-Shield Type X Hi-Impact Wallboard or Gold Bond Fire-Shield Type X Kal-Kore Hi-Impact Plaster Base.
6. **Joint Tape and Compound** — (not shown) — Vinyl, dry or premixed joint compound, applied in two coats to joints and screw heads; paper tape, 2 in. wide, embedded in first layer of compound over all joints.
7. **Wallboard, Gypsum*** — For 2 Hr Rating — any Classified 5/8 in. thick (minimum), 4 ft wide, wallboard applied over exterior face of Building Unit (Item 5). Wallboard to be applied vertically with joints staggered 24 in. from Building Unit (Item 5) and attached to studs and floor and ceiling runners with screws spaced 8 in. OC.
   See Wallboard, Gypsum (CKNX) Category for names of manufacturers.
*Bearing the UL Classification Marking

Figure 5.14. UL Fire Resistant Assembly. (Reprinted from the 2000 *Fire Resistance Directory, Volume 2* with permission from Underwriters Laboratories Inc. Copyright 2000 Underwriters Laboratories.)

4. A fire can impair the stability of a structure assembly. If a fire occurs and the assembly is exposed to flame and heat, this exposure can affect the strength and structural integrity of the building materials. After a fire the original fire rating may no longer be valid.

When a rated assembly is required, the building codes will often refer you to one or more of the earlier mentioned standards within their test. Some jurisdictions may prefer you to use one publication over another. However, the codes may also allow other ways to determine the appropriate construction assembly. Some codes may specify construction assemblies and their ratings in their test. For example, Table 719.1b in the *IBC* and Table 7-B in the *UBC* lists and describes walls and partitions assemblies and their ratings. And Table 719.1c in the *IBC* and Table 7-C in the *UBC* lists and describes floor/ceiling assemblies and their ratings. Some jurisdictions will allow calculations or an engineering analysis of a proposed or existing construction assembly to determine the rating of the assembly. Others may allow for the rated assembly to be approved by the local building official. This last option will become more prevalent as more and more performance codes are introduced and used. For most projects, referring to the tested assemblies represented by the publications listed above will be appropriate. For existing construction or for innovative design elements that are required to be rated, the other methods may be required.

CHECKLIST

Figure 5.15 is a fire resistance checklist that can be used on your interior projects or as a guideline to make your own checklist. It indicates each type of fire barrier, smoke barrier, opening protective, and through-penetration protective typically regulated by the codes. The checklist can be used to remind you of what to look for and research on a project, as well as give you a place to record the necessary code information for future reference. Remember, however, that it must be used in conjunction with the codes and standards classification of the project and the construction type of the building.

The checklist begins with the standard blanks for project name, occupancy classification of the project, and the construction type of the building. (If necessary, refer to Chapters 2 and 3 to determine these.) The remainder of the checklist lists the various types of interior assemblies and protectives. To the left of each component is a blank space so you can check off each of the components being used in your project.

Then for each system that is "required," fill in the necessary information. If the assembly or component already exists in the building make a note in the "existing" column. This will be helpful

FIRE RESISTANCE CHECKLIST

PROJECT NAME:_____

OCCUPANCY (new or existing):_____

TYPE OF CONSTRUCTION:_____

REQUIRED FIRE PROTECTION (check those that apply)	EXISTING (yes or no)	LOCATION IN BUILDING	TYPE OF MATERIAL OR ASSEMBLY REQUIRED (list information)	HOURLY RATING OR FIRE TEST REQUIRED (list type)
FIRE BARRIERS: __ Fire Wall(s) __ Occupancy Separation Wall(s) __ Tenant Separation Wall(s) __ Corridor Walls __ Horizontal Exit(s) __ Vertical Shaft Enclosure(s) __ Room Separation(s) __ Floor/Ceiling Assembly(ies) __ Other:_____				
SMOKE BARRIERS: __ Wall Assembly(ies) __ Vertical Shaft(s) __ Vestibule(s) __ Other:_____				
OPENING PROTECTIVES: __ Fire Door(s) __ Fire Window(s) __ Rated Glazing __ Other:_____				
THROUGH-PENETRATION PROTECTIVES: Engineer Required? ___YES ___ NO __ Firestop(s) __ Draftstop(s) __ Damper System(s) __ Other:_____				

NOTE: Refer to codes and standards for specific information. Also check the *ADAAG* for mounting locations.

Figure 5.15. Fire Resistance Checklist.

when you need to match existing conditions. Use the next column to indicate the location of the system. For example, indicate which vertical shafts require a smoke barrier.

The next two columns indicate the specific types of systems or material used and the types of tests and/or ratings required by the codes and standards. This information will help you to select the correct products as you are specifying for the project. For example, you can indicate the type of firestop to be used and the rating it must provide, or indicate the size and type of rated glazing that will be used and the specific tests it must pass.

As you are filling out the checklist, you may have to consult engineers or other professionals to determine exact requirements. Use this form throughout the project as a guideline and a reminder of items to be researched and completed. When complete, be sure to file the checklist and any other pertinent testing and code information required with the project paperwork for future reference. (See Chapter 10.)

Your design may not require every means of fire resistance listed in this chapter to be used. Each project will be different. In addition, there are other variables not discussed in this chapter such as detection systems, suppression systems, interior finishes and exiting systems. Although each of these topics is discussed in other chapters, they are important as they relate to the fire resistance of an assembly. Remember that every component used in the design and construction of a building or space will affect the overall fire resistance of the building or space.

CHAPTER 6

FIRE PROTECTION SYSTEMS

As mentioned in the previous chapter, fire and smoke are the primary threats to the safety of the occupants in a building. Fire and smoke can travel quickly both horizontally and vertically unless special efforts are made to prevent this from happening. The codes direct most of their regulations to safety issues that may occur in the event of a fire. The previous chapter described the four main types of prevention systems that are used in the control of fire and smoke within a building. This chapter will discuss two other types of systems: detection systems and suppression systems.

All of the systems discussed in this chapter are directly tied to the plumbing, mechanical, or electrical system of a building. For this reason, an engineer is typically involved in this portion of a project. (This was also the case with dampers, as discussed in Chapter 5.) However, as the designer you will often need to designate preferred locations of devices, coordinate location of various design elements, and be involved in other decisions that may affect your project. Some examples may include locating fire extinguishers, selecting the type of sprinkler heads, and coordinating the location of sprinkler heads with the location of the light fixtures.

DEFINITIONS

Below are some common terms used when discussing detection and suppression systems. You should be familiar with them.

AUTOMATIC FIRE SUPPRESSION SYSTEM: A system using carbon dioxide, foam, wet or dry chemical, a halogenated extinguishing agent, or an automatic sprinkler system to suppress a fire when activated by a smoke or fire detector system.

AUTOMATIC SPRINKLER SYSTEM: A system using water to suppress a fire when activated by a smoke or fire detector system.

DELUGE SYSTEM: An automatic sprinkler system that delivers a large amount of water to an area upon detection of fire by a separate automatic detection system.

FIRE DETECTOR: A device that detects one of the signatures of fire. This could include smoke, heat, or toxic gases.

FLASHOVER: Simultaneous ignition or explosion that occurs during a fire when all the combustible materials become heated to their ignition temperature. Also called back draft. (See inset titled *Stages of Fire Development* on page 220.)

FUSIBLE LINK: A connecting link of a low-melting alloy that melts at a predetermined temperature. For example, it holds sprinkler heads closed and fire doors and dampers open until a fire occurs.

RADIANT HEAT: The heat that is transferred through an object to the other side. For example, if a fire occurs in a room, radiant heat may be transmitted through the wall or door to the adjacent corridor.

SMOKE DETECTOR: A device that detects the presence of smoke as an indicator of fire. It may work as a single unit or as part of a system of devices.

COMPARING THE CODES

With the use of fire protection systems such as an automatic sprinkler system within a building, the building codes and the *LSC* allow for greater flexibility in construction types, rating of interior walls, and overall area and building heights as discussed in previous chapters. The building codes also specifically address requirements for the use of fire dampers, fire alarm systems, and automatic sprinkler systems within a building as part of the total fire protection system of a building. There are additional codes and standards that specify the use and installation of these systems. Some of these codes are most often used by a mechanical or electrical engineer, but understanding the scope of these codes is important in the development of the design.

When specific testing and installation methods are required, both the building codes and the *LSC* refer to a number of the standards published by the National Fire Protection Association (NFPA). The NFPA standards specify locations, design details, and installation requirements, as well as testing standards that must be followed. Some of the standards deal with fire prevention. Others refer to detection and suppression systems. The ones most used for interior projects have been listed in Figure 6.1 for your reference. These will be included in the discussion of each type of system.

The *American with Disabilities Act Accessibility Guidelines (ADAAG)* and other accessibility standards do not play heavily in the development of fire protection systems. The main accessibility requirement for fire prevention has to do with fire alarms and accessible warning systems. Also keep in mind that any suppression system device installed for occupant use must be placed at accessible reaching heights and locations and cannot project more that four inches in certain locations. Signage and operational mechanisms are also important.

DETECTION SYSTEMS

Fire detection systems include smoke detectors, fire alarms, audio systems, and accessible warning systems. They are systems that detect fires and warn the building occupants. They signal a warning allowing time for evacuation and possibly time to extinguish

NFPA 10:	Portable Fire Extinguishers
NPFA 12:	Carbon Dioxide Extinguishing Systems
NFPA 13:	Installation of Sprinkler Systems
NPFA 13R:	Installation of Sprinkler Systems in Residential Occupancies up to and Including Four Stories in Height
NFPA 14:	Installation of Standpipe, Private Hydrants, and Hose Systems
NFPA 20:	Installation of Stationary Pumps for Fire Protection
NFPA 70	National Electric Code
NFPA 72:	National Fire Alarm Code
NFPA 110:	Emergency and Standby Power Systems
NFPA 111:	Stored Electrical Energy Emergency and Standby Power Systems
NFPA 170:	Fire Safety Symbols

NOTE: There are a number of NFPA standards not listed above that are specific to an occupancy, such as Health Care, or certain types of hazardous equipment. Many other standards pertain to the inspection and maintenance of a system.

Figure 6.1. Common NFPA Standards.

Note

Never paint over smoke detectors or other fire safety equipment. It can hamper their effectiveness. Many operate by fusible links. Paint may keep the fusible links from melting.

the fire manually. Many detection systems also notify the local fire department and are connected to the building sprinkler system for automatic fire extinguishing.

Fire detection and alarm systems have changed dramatically over the last several decades due to technological advances. Today, they can employ everything from programmable computers to remote controls so fire, smoke, heat, and gases can be detected. These modern detection systems have resulted in better protected buildings. They have also resulted in a multitude of new codes, regulations, and standards.

The building codes generally specify where manual or automatic fire signaling systems or fire alarm systems are required. Fire codes specify the required systems as well as provide testing data. The two most used detection systems are fire alarms and smoke detectors. As you read the following types of detection systems, note that they are usually tied into the electrical system of a building. Also note that today's advanced technology can allow integration of fire and smoke detection systems with other building controls, such as the mechanical system or the security system. Computers are used to tie the systems together to monitor and control the various activities in a building in a comprehensive way. The development of software and products to work within an integrated system is ongoing. However, this type of system is

CARBON MONOXIDE DETECTION

Carbon monoxide is produced by incomplete combustion of organic materials. Prolonged exposure to carbon monoxide can be fatal. The first sign of a problem is often occupants experiencing flu-like symptoms. Continued and prolonged exposure will cause drowsiness to the point of unconsciousness and ultimately death.

Exposure to this gas occurs most frequently from appliances or engines powered by gas, such as automobiles, lawnmowers, stoves, and hot water heaters. These types of systems are used most often in Residential occupancies. Detection is not yet required by any of the building codes. Even if detection systems were required, the standards for the manufacture and installation of CO_2 detectors are still emerging, such as *UL 2034 Standard for Safety, Single and Multiple Station Carbon Monoxide Detectors*. It is unclear what level of exposure to the gas should be considered dangerous. Carbon monoxide detectors are available to the public for use in residential settings. They rely on the occupants to report to authorities, usually the fire department, when alarms indicate a high level of carbon monoxide. As detection systems develop and additional standards are set, carbon monoxide detection will be required in Residential occupancies and others. You should continue to be aware of current requirements that may affect your project.

complex and most suitable for complex projects. If you are design-ing an extensive project you will typically involve an electrical engineer. (See Chapter 8 for more information.)

Smoke Detectors

The best way to protect the occupants in a building from the dan-gers of a fire is to know that there is a fire as early as possible. This of course allows more time to contain the fire and remove the occupants, if necessary, before the danger escalates. Since smoke and toxic gases are the main killers in a building fire, fire and smoke detectors are important in every design. (See inset titled *Carbon Monoxide Detection.*) Smoke detectors are especially effec-tive in detecting smoldering fires that do not produce enough heat for sprinkler activation.

There are two methods of using smoke detectors. A *single-station* smoke detector will sound alone when it senses smoke without ringing the general alarm. Individual units are mostly used in Residential occupancies such as hotels and dormitories. This way minor alarms due to cooking or shower vapors do not alarm the whole building. A *multiple-station* system interconnects all the detectors so that when one goes off a general alarm will sound.

Most of the codes require smoke detectors to be tied into the fire alarm system. (See the following section.) Other smoke detec-tors may be required to activate automatic doors. They act as releasing devices during the presence of smoke so that the door will self-close. Both multiple- and single-station detectors must be tied into the building's power source.

Although the codes specify which occupancies require smoke detectors, they do not always specifically state where to locate them within a space or building. You need to determine the best placement. For example, in a cooking area you do not want to place the smoke detector where standard cooking procedures may activate the alarm. In addition, do not place detectors too close to the intersection of a wall and ceiling or too close to a doorway because air currents may cause smoke and heat to bypass the unit. When mounted on a wall, smoke detectors should typically be between 6 and 12 inches from the ceiling. When unusual design situations occur, work with the manufacturer as well as the code officials in your jurisdiction to locate the detectors.

Fire and smoke detection systems, whether simple or com-plex, are essential elements of providing safety for the occupants of any building in the event of a fire. Depending on the level of com-

Note

Smoke detectors will increase in importance as more finishes and furnishings become flame resistant. (See Chapter 9.) Such materials will be more likely to smolder for long periods of time without a flame at temperatures too low for sprinklers to respond.

Note

Battery-operated smoke detectors are typically not allowed by the codes unless they are an added precaution not required by the codes or they are added to an existing one- or two-family house.

FIRE TECHNOLOGY

For more complex or larger projects, expanding technology is allowing for more ways to recognize the presence of fire because fire creates more than just smoke and heat. Fire actually produces various types of symptoms. These include molecular gases (smoke that includes carbon dioxide), aerosols, heat conduction, thermal radiation (heat), and acoustic waves. New technology allows for the detection of multiple symptoms of fire to determine if a fire really exists. This allows for better detection of a fire and also reduces the number of false alarms.

For example, just because there is smoke does not necessarily mean that there is a fire. Someone with a cigarette standing directly below a smoke detector could cause it to alarm. More sophisticated detection systems will then compare that input with the presence of other symptoms of fire or whether another smoke detector nearby indicates that there is smoke. If no other symptoms of fire exists, the detection system may delay setting off the fire alarm until another symptom is present or the smoke continues.

Technology, especially the use of microprocessing, has allowed not only advancements in the individual detectors but the detection systems as well. Now, systems can check each detector individually to see if it is working properly and in the event of a fire determine the exact location of the fire, not just the floor on which the fire originated. The sensitivity of particular zones of detectors can be modified to allow for different levels of heat or smoke that might be present in normal conditions.

Note

Some jurisdictions may require the older NFPA standard *NFPA 74: Installation, Maintenance, and Use of Household Fire Warning Equipment* for use with smoke detectors.

Note

The traditional manual fire alarm box is a pull device. New accessible types of boxes are available. Instead of pulling a handle to activate the alarm, the devices require pushing with minimal effort. Both types must be red.

plexity that your project requires, you may need to review your design with engineers, manufacturers and the local code official.

Fire Alarms

A fire alarm system can be activated either *manually* by the use of a "pull" device or *automatically* upon the operation of an automatic sprinkler system, fire detection system, or smoke detection system. The codes will specify which type of system is required for a particular occupancy classification. Some occupancies may require both types of activation. Many will require a strobe light that is a part of the alarm. These strobes are typically required to be mounted at specific heights on a wall. The codes also specify the type of alarm, its location, and the wiring required. For installation of the fire alarm the codes refer to the standard *NFPA 72: National Fire Alarm Code.*

Although they must be audible in all parts of a building, the alarms must be placed in a natural path of escape in a position for maximum visibility. Each required exit from a building must have a fire alarm, usually not more than five feet from the entrance to an exit, because the noise from the alarm helps the occupants during a fire to locate the exits. The *ADAAG* sets some additional require-ments as well, such as the mounting height of the pull device so that it is accessible. (See the section on Accessible Warning Sys-tems below.)

Audio Systems

Some occupancies and building types require an audio system to be tied into the fire alarm system. These include factories, large storage facilities, occupancies in high rise buildings and other Hazardous occupancies. An audio system is basically an intercom system that directs the occupants out of the building during an emergency. Some systems may also indicate the location of the emergency. If you are working in this type of occupancy, be sure to check for specific code requirements.

Accessible Warning Systems

Whenever an emergency warning system such as a smoke detec-tor or a fire alarm is required by the codes in public or commercial buildings, the *ADAAG* requires that the system be both audible and visible. The *audible* alarm must be set within a certain decibel range so that it exceeds the prevailing sound level in the room or space it is used. The distance all occupied spaces are from the origin of the alarm and any doors that would reduce the level of sound should be considered in the placement of the accessible warning systems.

Visual alarms are basically white or clear flashing lights used as an alarm signal and are sometimes referred to as strobes. The *ADAAG* sets a number of requirements for visual alarms. First of all, they need to be of a certain type. This includes the color, inten-sity, flash rate, and pulse duration. They also must be placed in specific locations—certain heights above the floor and certain dis-tances apart. When required they must be provided in at least each restroom, hallway, and lobby of a building in addition to other common use areas such as meeting rooms, break rooms, examination rooms, and classrooms. In occupancies with multiple sleeping units a certain percentage of the units must be equipped with a visual alarm as well.

SUPPRESSION SYSTEMS

Suppression systems provide for the control and extinguishment of fires once they occur. Like detection systems, their installation often needs to be coordinated with other trades and professionals.

Note

Visual alarms can be referred to in a number of different ways. Depending on the publication and the manufacturer, they can be called visual alarm signals, visible signal devices, visual signaling appliances, or visual notification appliances.

Note

Visual alarms must typically be installed in more locations than audible alarms, since a visual alarm can be observed only in the space in which it is installed.

Since most of them use water, a mechanical engineer usually needs to be involved. Typically, the engineer will design the system and reference the appropriate codes. (See Chapter 7.)

It is your responsibility to be familiar with these codes. In addition, be aware that the *ADAAG* sets certain requirements as well. When a suppression system is meant to be used by an occupant, it must be mounted at accessible heights and be located within accessible reaches from a front or side approach. Also, it cannot protrude more than four inches into a path of travel. This may eliminate bracket-mounted fire extinguishers and surface-mounted fire protection cabinets in certain areas.

The most common suppression systems include fire extinguishers, stand pipes, fire hoses, amd sprinkler systems. These are explained below.

Fire Extinguishers

Portable fire extinguishers are one means of fire suppression. Since they are movable and do not require access to plumbing lines, they are usually specified by the designer on interior projects. They can be surface mounted where space allows or recessed within a wall using a special cabinet. The cabinet must either have a vision panel or be clearly marked with a sign, because the fire extinguisher must be visible at all times. Since it is meant to be used by the building occupant, it must be mounted so that all operating parts are accessible. The fire extinguisher must also be tested and have an approved label.

> **Note**
>
> When surface mounting a fire extinguisher be sure you note *ADAAG* height and projection requirements.

The building codes specify which occupancies and types of building uses require fire extinguishers. Most occupancies do require an extinguisher, but specific types of areas require them as well. For example, most commercial kitchens as well as smaller kitchens and break rooms require fire extinguishers.

For additional requirements the codes refer to *NFPA 10: Standard for Portable Fire Extinguishers.* This standard indicates more detailed information including specific numbers, sizes, and extinguisher types. The most common requirement specifies that no occupant can be more than 75 feet from a fire extinguisher when fire extinguishers are required. Other NFPA publications provide fire extinguishers requirements for special occupancies.

Standpipes and Fire Hoses

Standpipes and fire hoses are typically installed during the construction of a building. They are a manual, fixed fire suppression system. Some are easily recognized by the glass-enclosed cabinet and the folded fire hose. Others are simply a large diameter pipe that extends vertically through a building with connections for fire hose hookup. The system supplies water for extinguishing fires and can be used by the fire fighters or the building occupants, depending on the class and type of system.

Class of Standpipes: Three classes of standpipes are classified by the codes. The classes are based on the purpose and intended use of the system.

+ **Class I:** Designed for fire department use or limited building personnel trained in its operation, Class I standpipes consist of pipes with high pressure 2½-inch (63-mm) outlets for hookup to fire department hoses.
+ **Class II:** Primarily designed for building occupants, Class II standpipes have hoses attached that are usually limited to 1½ inches (38 mm) in diameter or smaller. They are designed for small scale fire protection and are mostly used in buildings that do not have a sprinkler system.
+ **Class III:** Class III is a combination of Class I and Class II standpipes. It is designed for use by the building occupants or the fire department. Both a 2½-inch (63-mm) outlet for fire department hookup and a 1½-inch (38-mm) outlet with 1½-inch (38-mm) hose and nozzle are included.

Types of Standpipes: There are also five different types of standpipe systems.

1. **Automatic wet system**: An automatic wet system has a water supply within the piping system that is ready upon demand.
2. **Automatic dry system**: An automatic dry system is normally filled with pressured air. The use of a hose valve is required to admit water into the system.
3. **Manual wet system**: A manual wet system does not have water in the pipes themselves, but rather is connected to a water supply that must be pumped into the pipes by the fire department.
4. **Manual dry system**: A manual dry system does not have water within the pipes or in an attached supply. The water must be pumped in from the fire department.
5. **Semiautomatic dry system**: A semiautomatic dry system is similar to an automatic dry system, but a remote control located at the hose connection is required to activate the valve to admit water into the system.

Note

A standpipe riser (i.e., pipe) may also serve as a sprinkler system riser if specific codes requirements are met.

The type and class of a required standpipe depends on the code, the type of occupancy, the height of the building, and the presence of a sprinkler system. Some types of buildings that may require standpipes include multistory buildings with or without sprinklers, high-rises (see inset titled *High-Rise Buildings* on page 72), storage buildings, and certain other spaces. Each code sets slightly different requirements for standpipes.

The *UBC* Table 9-A, "Standpipe Requirements," is shown in Figure 6.2. It specifies which types of buildings and occupancies will require a standpipe and which class to use. The *NBC*, the *SBC* and the *IBC* list their requirements within their texts. The codes also refer to the standard *NFPA 14: Installation of Standpipes Private Hydrants and Hose Systems.* This standard specifies the number, type, and locations for standpipes. Most standpipes are located on each

TABLE 9-A
STANDPIPE REQUIREMENTS

Occupancy	Nonsprinklered Building[1]		Sprinklered Building[2,3]	
×304.8 for mm ×0.0929 for m²	Standpipe Class	Hose Requirement	Standpipe Class	Hose Requirement
1. Occupancies exceeding 150 feet in height and more than one story	III	Yes	I	No
2. Occupancies four stories or more but less than 150 feet in height, except Group R, Division 3[6]	[I and II[4]] (or III)	[5] Yes	I	No
3. Group A Occupancies with occupant load exceeding 1,000[7]	II	Yes	No requirement	No
4. Group A, Division 2.1 Occupancies over 5,000 square feet in area used for exhibition	II	Yes	II	Yes
5. Groups I; H; B; S; M; F, Division 1 Occupancies less than four stories in height but greater than 20,000 square feet per floor[6]	II[4]	Yes	No requirement	No
6. Stages more than 1,000 square feet in area	II	No	III	No

1. Except as otherwise specified in Item 4 of this table, Class II standpipes need not be provided in basements having an automatic fire-extinguishing system throughout.
2. The standpipe system may be combined with the automatic sprinkler system.
3. Portions of otherwise sprinklered buildings that are not protected by automatic sprinklers shall have Class II standpipes installed as required for the unsprinklered portions.
4. In open structures where Class II standpipes may be damaged by freezing, the building official may authorize the use of Class I standpipes that are located as required for Class II standpipes.
5. Hose is required for Class II standpipes only.
6. For the purposes of this table, occupied roofs of parking structures shall be considered an additional story. In parking structures, a tier is a story.
7. Class II standpipes need not be provided in assembly areas used solely for worship.

Figure 6.2. *Uniform Building Code (UBC)* Table 9-A, "Standpipe Requirements." (Reproduced from the 1997 edition of the *Uniform Building Code*, copyright 1997, with permission of the publisher, the International Conference of Building Officials.)

landing in the building's exit stair enclosure or smokeproof vestibule. Not only does this provide easy access, it also provides fire protection for one to two hours. Class II standpipes may require additional locations for accurate coverage with the fire hose. Since Class II standpipes are meant for use by a building occupant, placing the fire hose cabinet so that it is accessible also becomes important.

Sprinkler Systems

Automatic sprinkler systems are invaluable in the containment of a fire. Research shows that the number of lives lost during a fire when automatic sprinklers are present is greatly reduced. As a result, more occupancies and use groups are increasingly required to install automatic sprinkler systems where previously these systems were optional. In addition, most are required to be tied into an alarm system so that the occupants, the appropriate building personnel, and the fire department are notified in an emergency. Although water damage may occur from the release of water by the sprinkler system (5–25 gallons/minute depending on the type of sprinkler), it will be considerably less than the damage that would occur if it is necessary for the fire department to assist to extinguish the fire by a fire hose (200–250 gallons/minute).

The NFPA is the main source for sprinkler requirements. *NFPA 13: Standard for Installation of Sprinkler Systems* is the standard most referenced by the codes and is used throughout the country. It lists detailed design and installation requirements and references a number of other NFPA standards. One of the newest requirements is that an identification number be located on each sprinkler head. This number identifies the specific type and function capabilities of that sprinkler head, which allows the designer and the code official to verify that the correct sprinkler head has been installed. On the other hand, it is the building codes and *LSC* that specify when an automatic sprinkler system is required. Each code specifies the number of occupancies, types of buildings, and special rooms that generally require sprinklers. The type of construction may also make a difference.

Uses and Occupancies Requiring Sprinkler Systems: The most common occupancies that require sprinklers are Factory, Hazardous, and Storage occupancies. Other occupancies require sprinklers if large groups of people will be present. These include Assembly and Institutional occupancies as well as large Mercantile and Residential occupancies. The requirements are typically based on the number of occupants, the mobility of the occupants, and the types of hazards present. Other common uses are listed below.

Note

Since automatic sprinklers have been in use since the beginning of the century, some older buildings may have systems that are considered antiquated. Ultimately, a code official must decide whether an old system needs to be replaced to meet the codes.

Note

Depending on the occupancy, the amount of hazards and the type of system, most sprinkler systems require each sprinkler head to cover and protect 90 to 200 square feet. The typical distance between the sprinkler heads ranges from 12 to 15 feet. It is usually up to the plumbing engineer to determine the exact requirements.

Buildings

- ✦ Aircraft hangers
- ✦ Amusement buildings
- ✦ Basements
- ✦ Covered malls
- ✦ High-rise buildings
- ✦ Underground structures
- ✦ Unlimited-area buildings
- ✦ Windowless buildings

Special Rooms and Areas

- ✦ Atriums
- ✦ Drying rooms
- ✦ Duct systems exhausting hazardous materials
- ✦ Furnace and boiler rooms
- ✦ Hazardous materials
- ✦ Incinerator, trash, and laundry collection areas
- ✦ Kitchen exhaust systems
- ✦ Spray painting shops or booths
- ✦ Stages
- ✦ Tops of chutes
- ✦ Unenclosed vertical openings

Note

Sprinkler requirements for some occupancies may result in a partial system or a "limited area" sprinkler system, where only a part of a building is covered by sprinklers to meet minimum code requirements. However, this is usually not recommended and must be approved by the code officials.

Types of Sprinkler Systems: An engineer typically determines which type of sprinkler system to use. Using the codes and the NFPA standards the engineer also determines the size and number of pipes and the spacing of the sprinkler heads. Most systems are one of the four types described below.

1. **Wet pipe system:** A wet pipe system is the most common system. It uses water to extinguish a fire and consists of pipes that are water filled at all times. When a fire occurs the heat from the fire activates the sprinkler. The heat melts the fuse link, causing water to discharge immediately.

2. **Dry pipe system:** A dry pipe system is used in unheated occupancies to prevent freezing. Instead of water, the pipes are filled with pressurized air or nitrogen. When activated by the heat of a fire, the air is released and water floods the pipes to extinguish the fire.

3. **Deluge system:** A deluge system is a closed-head foam/water system. The deluge system discharges foam to control severe fires. It is usually activated by a detection system and used in hazardous situations where water is dangerous (i.e., electrical situations).

Note

The typical wet pipe sprinkler system is usually equipped with a fire department connection as a secondary source of water supply when 20 or more sprinklers are present.

4. **Preaction system:** A preaction system is a combination of wet and dry systems to allow delayed reaction and warning signals. Like the deluge system, it is activated by a detection system. The delayed reaction allows the system to be intercepted and turned off if the sprinklers are not necessary. It is used primarily in areas where property is susceptible to water damage or where sprinkler pipes are likely to get damaged.

Both wet and dry systems require the same piping. The risers supply the water from the building's incoming water supply to the cross mains at each floor. The cross mains supply the branch lines. Sprinkler heads are at the end of each branch line.

Sprinkler Design Issues: Although adding a sprinkler system is expensive, it usually saves money in other areas of construction. The codes allow automatic sprinkler systems as a trade-off for other code requirements. It may be a major trade-off, such as constructing a larger building, or a smaller trade-off, such as not having to rate a wall. For example, in some jurisdictions a nonrated door in a rated

---

CONSTRUCTION TYPES
May allow lower fire resistance requirements of some structure elements resulting in less strict construction types and lower construction costs.

BUILDING AREA
May allow one story and some two story buildings to increase in size horizontally resulting in more square feet per building.

BUILDING HEIGHT
May allow one story to be added to the height of a building.

MEANS OF EGRESS
May allow an increase in the distance of travel from the most remote point to the exit, certain escalators are permitted without enclosure, accessible elevators may not need an area of refuge, possibly longer dead end corridors.

FIRE AND SMOKE SEPARATION
May allow up to three floor levels of stairways and other openings between floors not to be fully enclosed, may eliminate separate means of venting smoke in elevators, omit fire dampers, larger areas of glazing, lower fire ratings of assemblies, lower rating of opening protectives, less comparmentation in high-rise buildings, reduce number of fire alarms, reduce number of draftstops, eliminate or reduce number of standpipes.

INTERIOR FINISHES AND FURNITURE
May allow a lower flame spread resulting in a lower finish classes, eliminate firestops behind raised finishes, additional foam plastic insulation, lower furniture ratings.

Figure 6.3. Common Sprinkler Trade-Offs.

corridor may be used when additional sprinklers are used on both sides of the door. Other common sprinkler trade-offs have been listed for you in Figure 6.3. Be sure to refer to the specific codes if any of them pertain to an interior project and make sure it is allowed by your jurisdiction.

Sprinklers may not be appropriate in every situation. Fires can begin in enclosed spaces or in locations where they are shielded from the sprinkler head. Other fires ignite and travel too quickly. Some types of fires should not be extinguished with water. For example, sprinklers should not be used in rooms or areas that contain electrical equipment such as computer and telephone equipment rooms. Restaurant kitchens and other rooms with the potential for a grease fire should also limit the use of wet pipe sprinklers that use water. One of the other systems that discharge foam or dry chemicals may be more appropriate.. Other buildings that contain extremely valuable items, such as libraries and museums, may eliminate sprinklers, limit their use, or use delayed reaction sprinklers.

When a sprinkler system does not use water, the system is often referred to in the codes as non-water-based fire extinguishing. In the past, systems that discharged halon were widely used in situations where a water-based system was not desirable. But since halon has been determined to contribute to the erosion of the ozone layer, the production of halon ended. However, systems that use halon may still be in place in existing buildings. Recycled halon is still available for use in these systems, since replacing existing systems with alternatives can require redesign of the entire system. The current alternative systems include chemical agents, inert gases, powder, or water mist systems. Each differs from halon in various ways and has different characteristics that affect its suitability for use in each situation.

Sprinkler Heads: There are several different styles of sprinkler heads or escutcheons. They can either improve the function of the sprinkler system or simply change the aesthetics of the head. The different types of heads include pendant, fast response, large drop, upright, side wall, extended coverage, residential, and early-suppression–fast-response (ESFR). Even tamper resistant sprinkler heads are available for Institutional occupancies. There are also different types of cover plates that can be used to conceal the sprinkler head. Although it is not within the scope of this book to present a complete outline of the differences between various sprinkler types, a few characteristic are important to note.

Note

In a multistory building it is possible to have a sprinkler system installed in one story and not another.

Note

If you are working on a project in which a sprinkler system may be inappropriate, be sure to research other fire suppression systems as well as automatic fire detection systems.

Selecting the correct sprinkler head and the correct type of sprinkler system depends on the situation and the code requirements. These decisions are typically made by a sprinkler contractor or an engineer. As the designer you should work closely with the mechanical or fire suppression engineer. It is especially important to verify sprinkler head locations, since you must provide adequate clearance at each head. Typically the codes require 18 inches of clearance below the sprinkler deflector. This becomes significant in areas where wall cabinetry or shelving is used, such as storage rooms, kitchens, or libraries, and any other special design elements.

For interior projects, minor or large scale changes to an existing space can affect the proper layout of the sprinklers. If the occupancy type in a space has changed, the existing layout of sprinklers may not be adequate. Or, if you are making changes to an existing space, the existing sprinkler system or layout may not be compliant with the most current codes for that occupancy type or space. For example, the addition or removal of walls may affect the required sprinkler locations and spacing for proper areas of coverage, or the addition of suspended ceiling may require a change in the type of sprinkler head. The affect of modifications to a sprinklered space should always be considered in the design.

Note

A project may have more than one type of sprinkler head. For example, you may want to use a concealed head in a decorative ceiling and an exposed pendant in less public areas.

CHECKLIST

Figure 6.4 is a fire protection checklist that can be used on your interior projects or as guideline to make your own checklist. It indicates each main type of detection and suppression system required by the codes. The checklist can be used to remind you of what to look for and research on a project, as well as give you a place to record the necessary code information for future reference. Remember, however, that it must be used in conjunction with the codes and standards required in your jurisdiction as well as the *ADAAG*.

The checklist begins with the standard blanks for project name, occupancy classification of the project, and the construction type of the building. (If necessary, refer to Chapters 2 and 3 to determine these.) The remainder of the checklist lists the types of detection and suppression systems and each major component of the system. To the left of each component is a blank space so you can check off the systems required in your project.

Then for each system that is "required" fill in the necessary information. If the system or component already exists in the

FIRE PROTECTION CHECKLIST

PROJECT NAME:_____

OCCUPANCY (new or existing):_____

TYPE OF CONSTRUCTION:_____

REQUIRED FIRE PROTECTION (check those that apply)	EXISTING (yes or no)	LOCATION IN BUILDING	TYPE OF SYSTEM REQUIRED (list information)	QUANTITIES REQUIRED (new or additional)
DETECTION SYSTEMS: Engineer Required? ___YES ___ NO __ Smoke Detector/Alarm(s) __ Fire Alarm(s) __ Audio System(s) __ Accessible Warning System(s) __ Other:_____				
SUPRESSION SYSTEMS: Engineer Required? ___YES ___ NO __ Fire Extinguisher(s) __ Standpipe(s) __ Fire Hose(s) __ Sprinkler System(s) __ Types of Sprinkler Head(s) __ Other:_____				

NOTES:

1. Refer to codes and standards for specific information. Also check the *ADAAG* for mounting locations and alarm details.

2. If automatic sprinkler systems are used, check for possible code trade-offs.

3. Consult and coordinate detection systems with electrical engineers and supression systems with mechanical engineers.

Figure 6.4. Fire Protection Checklist.

building make a note in the "existing" column. This will be helpful when you need to match existing conditions. Use the next column to indicate the location of the system. For example, indicate which areas of the building or space require a sprinkler system.

The next two columns indicate the specific types of systems or components that may be required. As you are filling out the checklist, be sure to consult with the appropriate engineer or other experts to determine the exact requirements necessary for your project.

There has been much debate over the years as to how many fire protection systems must be present in one building. For example, some jurisdictions are requiring sprinklers in almost every new structure. Of course the codes set minimum standards, yet some argue that there is too much overlap between prevention, detection, and suppression systems. Others believe that sufficient trade-offs, such as the sprinkler trade-offs shown in Figure 6.4, help to eliminate overprotection. As new products come on the market other redundancies may occur as well.

However, more advanced testing methods are also being developed. These tests along with computer simulations (see Chapter 10) will be more accurate and will better represent what would happen in a real fire. Combined, they will help to streamline the type of fire prevention system used in a building. This will also allow for better protection of the occupants. When necessary rely on experts as well as your common sense to use the best combination of these systems to enhance the safety of a building and protect its occupants.

Other variables not discussed in this chapter are interior finishes and exiting systems. Interior finishes are an important part of the prevention system, since they are applied to the surface of the building materials and construction assemblies. Finishes and furniture are often the first to make contact with a fire. Both have strict regulations and testing requirements. Chapter 9 discusses interior finishes as they relate to fire codes. Exiting systems are discussed in Chapter 4. Some of the most important elements during an emergency include exit signage and emergency lighting.

CHAPTER 7

PLUMBING AND MECHANICAL REQUIREMENTS

This chapter covers two separate code items—plumbing codes and mechanical codes. Unlike most of the codes already discussed in the previous chapters, the mechanical and plumbing codes address issues that concentrate on health and welfare concerns instead of life safety. In the past each of the major code organizations published a separate plumbing code and mechanical code. This changed when the International Code Council (ICC) published the first *International Plumbing Code (IPC)* in 1997 and the *International Mechanical Code (IMC)* in 1998. Depending on the jurisdiction of your project, you could be using one of the older model codes or the newest version of the international code books. In addition, each of the building codes sets a few general requirements for plumbing and mechanical systems.

Typically, you will not be required to know or research most of the plumbing and mechanical codes. On interior projects that include major plumbing or mechanical work, you will usually require the services of a registered engineer. Even on smaller projects that do not require the services of an engineer, a licensed plumbing or mechanical contractor will know the plumbing codes. Yet, as the designer, you should be aware of a number of plumbing and mechanical requirements. One of the most important is how to determine the required number of plumbing fixtures.

The first part of this chapter is dedicated to the plumbing codes required for interior projects. It covers the quantities and

Note
Some code jurisdictions may still be using older versions of the codes that were published by the model code organizations. The most current codes are the *IPC* and the *IMC*.

Note

Whether an engineer is required depends on the jurisdiction of the project. Each jurisdiction has specific requirements for professional services and stamped drawings. (See Chapter 10.)

types of plumbing fixtures required by the plumbing codes and discusses the accessibility standards for each. The second part of the chapter discusses the main types of mechanical systems and how the codes are used. The last part of the chapter introduces a checklist that incorporates both.

PLUMBING REQUIREMENTS

There are only a few references to plumbing requirements in the building codes (mostly referring to sprinkler systems and accessibility requirements). Most of the actual requirements needed to design a plumbing system are found in the plumbing codes. Until recently, most of the code organizations published a plumbing code. They included the *BOCA National Plumbing Code (NPC)*, the *Standard Plumbing Code (SPC)*, and the *Uniform Plumbing Code (UPC)*. With the introduction of the *International Plumbing Code (IPC)*, these other codes are no longer being updated and will eventually by phased out. In addition, some local jurisdictions have developed additional regulations that modify the requirements of the plumbing code. (This will be discussed later in the chapter.) You should verify which plumbing code and regulations your jurisdiction enforces.

As the designer you will use typically refer to certain sections of the plumbing code. When an interior project requires a substantial amount of plumbing work, you will generally use the services of a licensed engineer. You will design the space and place the fixtures, and the engineer will design the corresponding plumbing system. (See inset titled *The Basic Plumbing System* on page

B	BIDET		H.W.	HOT WATER
B.S.	BAR SINK		H.W.T.	HOT WATER TANK
B.T.	BATH TUB		L. or LAV.	LAVATORY
C.W.	COLD WATER		K.S.	KITCHEN SINK
C.W.M.	CLOTHES WASHING MACHINE		SH.	SHOWER
D.F.	DRINKING FOUNTAIN		S.P.	SWIMMING POOL
D.W.	DISH WASHER		S.S.	SERVICE SINK
E.W.C.	ELECTRIC WATER COOLER		U. or URN.	URINAL
F.E.C.	FIRE EXTINGUISHER CABINET		W.C.	WATER CLOSET
F.H.C.	FIRE HOSE CABINET		W.H.	WATER HEATER
F.S.P.	FIRE STANDPIPE			

Figure 7.1. Plumbing Abbreviations.

178.) Smaller design projects, like adding a breakroom, a small toilet facility, or relocating a few sprinkler heads, may not require the services of an engineer. Instead a licensed plumbing contractor will do the work directly from your drawings or, if required, supply plumbing shop drawings. To assist you, Figure 7.1 indicates the most common plumbing fixture abbreviations.

The part of the plumbing code that you need to know as the designer can basically be narrowed down to one similar chapter in each of the plumbing codes. It is the chapter on plumbing fixtures. Each code describes the types of fixtures and supplies a table that indicates the number and type of plumbing fixtures required for each occupancy classification. This table is discussed later in this chapter.

However, the plumbing codes are not the only resource for plumbing requirements. The building codes discuss sprinkler systems, standpipes, fire hoses, and fire extinguishers and often refer you to various standards. (These are explained in Chapter 6.) In addition, specific accessibility standards must be followed when selecting and locating plumbing fixtures. Both the *Americans with Disabilities Act Accessibility Guidelines (ADAAG)* and the American National Standards Institute (ANSI) accessibility standards list similar requirements. They include such things as minimum clearances, location requirements, ease of control use, and other accessibility standards. Both the plumbing codes and the corresponding accessibility regulations are explained as plumbing fixtures and toilet facilities are discussed below.

Note

Engineers and contractors must follow a number of other plumbing standards in addition to the codes. One of the more comprehensive standards is *ANSI-A40,* also known as the *A40 Plumbing Code.* Other standards are listed and referenced within each plumbing code.

Note

When determining clearances and specific dimension requirements for accessible toilet facilities, pay particular attention to whether they are minimum, maximum, or absolute dimensions. Many of these dimensions are critical.

Definitions

When working with plumbing codes and plumbing fixtures you should be familiar with the following terms.

BRANCH: Any part of a piping system other than a main, riser, or stack pipe. It is typically a small pipe that leads to or from these larger pipes.

CLEANOUT: An access opening in the drainage system to remove obstructions.

DRAIN PIPE: Any pipe that carries waste water in a building.

MAIN: The principal artery of any continuous piping system to which branches may be connected.

RISER: A water pipe that extends vertically one full story or more to supply water to branches or fixtures.

SOIL PIPE: A pipe that carries sewage containing solids.

STACK PIPE: A vertical main that can be used as a soil, waste, or venting pipe.

TRAP: A device that creates a liquid seal at a plumbing fixture to prevent the emission of sewer gases. Water and sewage can still flow through the trap.

VALVE: A device used to start, stop, or regulate the flow of liquid or gas into piping, through piping, or from piping.

VENT PIPE: A pipe or system of pipes installed to provide a flow of air to or from a drainage system or circulation of air within the system to protect trap seals from siphonage or backpressure.

WASTE: The discharge from any plumbing fixture that does not contain solids.

Quantity of Plumbing Fixtures

Determining the quantity of plumbing fixtures is the first step when designing an interior project that requires plumbing fixtures. Not only will the quantity of fixtures required by the code determine the types of plumbing fixtures, but it will also affect the number of accessible fixtures. All these factors will affect your design. For example, the number of standard and accessible water closets will affect the size of a restroom, and the type of drinking fountain may affect the width or shape of a corridor. The plumbing code table is explained first, followed by a discussion of the *ADAAG* requirements.

The Table: The number of plumbing fixtures required by the codes must be calculated when there is new construction, when a building addition is made, and when an occupancy classification changes. The number and type of fixtures are determined by a table in the plumbing code. As previously mentioned, the plumbing code will often correspond with the required building code. However, since the *International Plumbing Code (IPC)* was one of the first international family of codes to be published, some jurisdictions may enforce the *IPC* in conjunction with a different building code. You should verify which code and edition is being enforced in the jurisdiction of your project.

Each of the plumbing codes has a table similar to *IPC* Table 403.1, "Minimum Number of Plumbing Facilities," as shown in Figure 7.2. For each occupancy classification, the table lists the number of water closets for males and females, the number of lavatories, drinking fountains, bathtubs, showers, washing machines, and other miscellaneous fixtures. The number of required fixtures is based on the occupant load within the building or space. (See

TABLE 403.1
MINIMUM NUMBER OF PLUMBING FACILITIES[a]
(see Sections 403.2 and 403.3)

	OCCUPANCY	WATER CLOSETS (Urinals, see Section 419.2) Male	Female	LAVATORIES	BATHTUBS/ SHOWERS	DRINKING FOUNTAINS (see Section 410.1)	OTHERS
A S S E M B L Y	Nightclubs	1 per 40	1 per 40	1 per 75	—	1 per 500	1 service sink
	Restaurants	1 per 75	1 per 75	1 per 200	—	1 per 500	1 service sink
	Theaters, halls, museums, etc.	1 per 125	1 per 65	1 per 200	—	1 per 500	1 service sink
	Coliseums, arenas (less than 3,000 seats)	1 per 75	1 per 40	1 per 150	—	1 per 1,000	1 service sink
	Coliseums, arenas (3,000 seats or greater)	1 per 120	1 per 60	Male 1 per 200 Female 1 per 150	—	1 per 1,000	1 service sink
	Churches[b]	1 per 150	1 per 75	1 per 200	—	1 per 1,000	1 service sink
	Stadiums (less than 3,000 seats), pools, etc.	1 per 100	1 per 50	1 per 150	—	1 per 1,000	1 service sink
	Stadiums (3,000 seats or greater)	1 per 150	1 per 75	Male 1 per 200 Female 1 per 150	—	1 per 1,000	1 service sink
	Business (see Sections 403.2, 403.4 and 403.5)	1 per 50		1 per 80	—	1 per 100	1 service sink
	Educational	1 per 50		1 per 50	—	1 per 100	1 service sink
	Factory and industrial	1 per 100		1 per 100	(see Section 411)	1 per 400	1 service sink
	Passenger terminals and transportation facilities	1 per 500		1 per 750	—	1 per 1,000	1 service sink
I N S T I T U T I O N A L	Residential care	1 per 10		1 per 10	1 per 8	1 per 100	1 service sink
	Hospitals, ambulatory nursing home patients[c]	1 per room[d]		1 per room[d]	1 per 15	1 per 100	1 service sink per floor
	Day nurseries, sanitariums, nonambulatory nursing home patients, etc.[c]	1 per 15		1 per 15	1 per 15[e]	1 per 100	1 service sink
	Employees, other than residential care[c]	1 per 25		1 per 35	—	1 per 100	—
	Visitors, other than residential care	1 per 75		1 per 100	—	1 per 500	—
	Prisons[c]	1 per cell		1 per cell	1 per 15	1 per 100	1 service sink
	Asylums, reformatories, etc.[c]	1 per 15		1 per 15	1 per 15	1 per 100	1 service sink
	Mercantile (see Sections 403.2, 403.4 and 403.5)	1 per 500		1 per 750	—	1 per 1,000	1 service sink
R E S I D E N T I A L	Hotels, motels	1 per guestroom		1 per guestroom	1 per guestroom	—	1 service sink
	Lodges	1 per 10		1 per 10	1 per 8	1 per 100	1 service sink
	Multiple family	1 per dwelling unit		1 per dwelling unit	1 per dwelling unit	—	1 kitchen sink per dwelling unit; 1 automatic clothes washer connection per 20 dwelling units
	Dormitories	1 per 10		1 per 10	1 per 8	1 per 100	1 service sink
	One- and two-family dwellings	1 per dwelling unit		1 per dwelling unit	1 per dwelling unit	—	1 kitchen sink per dwelling unit; 1 automatic clothes washer connection per dwelling unit[f]
	Storage (see Sections 403.2 and 403.4)	1 per 100		1 per 100	(see Section 411)	1 per 1,000	1 service sink

a. The fixtures shown are based on one fixture being the minimum required for the number of persons indicated or any fraction of the number of persons indicated. The number of occupants shall be determined by the *International Building Code*.

b. Fixtures located in adjacent buildings under the ownership or control of the church shall be made available during periods the church is occupied.

c. Toilet facilities for employees shall be separate from facilities for inmates or patients.

d. A single-occupant toilet room with one water closet and one lavatory serving not more than two adjacent patient rooms shall be permitted where such room is provided with direct access from each patient room and with provisions for privacy.

e. For day nurseries, a maximum of one bathtub shall be required.

f. For attached one- and two-family dwellings, one automatic clothes washer connection shall be required per 20 dwelling units.

Figure 7.2. *International Plumbing Code (IBC)* Table 403.1, "Minimum Number of Plumbing Facilities." (Written permission to reproduce this material was granted by the copyright holder, International Code Council, Inc., 5203 Leesburg Pike, Suite 708, Falls Church, VA 22041.)

Chapter 4 for more information on occupant load.) Typically, every floor in a building will require at least one toilet or restroom, but the actual number of facilities depends on the type of occupancy and the number of occupants. In addition, some tenant spaces may require their own toilet facilities. It depends on the occupancy of the tenant and if the tenant has access to the common building facilities.

The *NPC, UPC,* and the *IPC* base the number of occupants on the occupant load found by the occupant load calculation determined in the building code. (See Chapter 2.) The *SPC* requires a separate calculation of "occupancy content" as specified in the plumbing code instead of the building code. The *SPC* provides an occupant content factor, which is divided into the occupiable area of the building or space. The occupiable area does not include areas used for building utilities, toilet rooms, corridors, stairways, vertical shafts, public kitchens, or equipment rooms. In many cases, this would differ from the occupant load determined by the building codes.

Once you know the occupancy classification or use group of a project and have estimated the total number of occupants as required by the code in your jurisdiction, use the plumbing fixture table to determine the quantity and type of plumbing fixtures required. If any fixture total results in a fraction, *round up* to the nearest whole number. For example, if you are working on a school that will have 620 occupants, you would refer to the Educational occupancy section of the table in Figure 7.2. It requires one water closet for every 50 people. By dividing 620 by 50 and rounding up, you know that you will require a minimum of 13 water closets.

When determining plumbing fixtures, you should also be aware of the following:

1. Urinals are required in some male restrooms, depending on the occupancy of the building or space. Common examples include schools, restaurants, lounges, transportation terminals, auditoriums, theaters, and churches. Each plumbing code gives specific requirements.
2. Certain occupancies with limited square footage and minimal occupants will allow a single facility with one lavatory and one water closet. Common examples include offices, retail stores, restaurants, laundries, and beauty shops. This facility must be unisex and fully accessible.
3. A separate toilet facility provided for a tenant cannot be deducted from the total common facilities required on the floor or in the building.

4. Separate plumbing fixtures for toilet facilities can be combined into one common restroom (separate for males and females) if all applicable building occupants have access to them. For example, if five female water closets are required on a floor, they can be combined into one women's restroom. However, in a large building, maximum travel distances might limit the number of fixtures that can be grouped together.

5. When a building requires toilet facilities for its customers, patrons, or visitors, employee facilities can either be separate or included in the public customer facilities. The most common occupancies that require customer facilities include restaurants, night clubs, places of public assembly, and mercantile buildings.

6. If a particular occupancy or use group is not covered by the plumbing fixture table, you must consult a local code official for the specific requirements. (If you want to get an estimate, use the type of occupancy most similar to your project; however, remember that the code official makes the final decision.)

7. An adjustment may be made to the total number of fixtures or to the ratio of male to female facilities in certain cases. Some jurisdictions have "potty parity" regulations that allow modification to the values provided within the code tables. These regulations often apply to Assembly occupancies. Modifications take into account factors like the probable division of the male and female population using the facilities, the frequency of use by each gender, and the difference in time it takes each gender to utilize the facilities. An example would be a sports stadium. With approval from the building official, you may also be able to modify the allocation of fixtures in facilities that are used predominately by one gender, such as an all female health club or an all male dorm. In each case, you must provide satisfactory data to the code officials.

8. The code publications require separate unisex toilet and bathing facilities for certain occupancies, such as Assemblies and Mercantile. They are intended to allow someone who is elderly or disabled, or even a child, to be assisted by someone of the opposite sex. Depending on the publication you are using, this requirement is located either within the accessibility chapter of the building code or in the plumbing code. For example, unisex toilet facilities are usually required when more than six water closets are provided.

Note

Remember that the plumbing fixture tables specify *minimum* requirements. You may want to include more fixtures, especially in Assembly occupancies where it is normal for large groups of people to use the restrooms all at the same time, such as during intermissions.

These facilities are counted in the total number of plumbing fixtures required, not in addition to the required amount, and are usually noted by a sign such as "Family" or "Unisex."

Note

If an elevator does not service the floors above the ground floor of a building, the toilet facilities on these floors may not have to be accessible.

ADAAG **Percentages:** Which fixtures are required to be accessible depends on the number of fixtures, the distribution of fixtures within a facility, and the type of occupancy classification. When there are multiple fixtures, the *ADAAG* requires a percentage of them to be accessible. This typically results in a certain number of accessible fixtures in a multifacility restroom. When an occupancy has a number of individual units, such as hotels and apartment buildings in Residential occupancies and hospitals in Institutional occupancies, the percentage of units that are required to be fully accessible are also given in the *ADAAG*. (See Chapter 2 for more information on occupancy classifications.)

In some existing buildings it may be necessary to add a single toilet facility that is accessible when it is not possible to adapt existing facilities. For example, more than one existing water closet may need to be removed to make room for an accessible one;

THE BASIC PLUMBING SYSTEM

All plumbing systems can be broken down into three main components.

DRAINAGE SYSTEM: This part of the plumbing system is usually referred to as the DWV or "drain–waste–vent" system. It consists of wide pipes, since it operates on gravity, starting at the plumbing fixture and ending at the public sewage system. It consists of three parts: *Traps* are used at the discharge of each fixture to prevent odors, gases, and insects from entering the building. *Branch* and *stack pipes* are required to transport the used water from the trap to the sewer. (It is a soil stack if it carries solid human waste. Waste stacks carry other wastes.) And vertical stack *vents* penetrate the roof of a building and allow harmful gasses to escape as water is discharged.

WATER SUPPLY SYSTEM: This system consists of small diameter pipes that use pressure to convey hot and cold water. First is the *main water line,* which brings water into the building from the public water system. Once in the building, it splits into two *distribution lines.* One leads cold water directly to the plumbing fixtures, and the other leads to the hot water heater for the water to be heated before it is distributed to a fixture. This system is controlled by *valves* both at the entry into the building and at each fixture.

PLUMBING FIXTURES: The fixtures are the beginning of the drainage system and the end source for the water supply system. They consist of water closets, lavatories, urinals, sinks, drinking fountains, bathtubs, showers, dishwashers, clothes washers, and other miscellaneous fixtures.

this in turn may reduce the total number of fixtures to below what is required by the plumbing code. In such a case you might need to add a new single accessible toilet facility. It is typically allowed to be unisex so that it covers male and female requirements. Also note, as mentioned earlier, that the building or plumbing codes may require a separate single accessible unisex toilet facility in addition to and separate from the other required accessible facilities. This facility should follow the *ADAAG* guidelines, since its primary intention is for elderly or disabled individuals.

Types of Plumbing Fixtures

Once you know the quantity and the type of fixtures required by the plumbing code table and the number of fixtures that have to be accessible, you must research the specific requirements for each fixture. The codes set certain requirements. If a fixture is to be accessible, you must follow the accessibility regulations as well. Both the *ADAAG* and the ANSI accessibility standards give specific dimension and location requirements.

The most common plumbing fixtures are water closets, urinals, lavatories, sinks, drinking fountains, bathtubs, and showers. The one code requirement that they all have in common is that each fixture must be finished with a smooth, nonabsorbent material. Other code and accessibility requirements for each of these fixtures are described below and in the next section. (Be sure to refer to the plumbing codes, the *ADAAG*, and the ANSI standards for the specific requirements.)

Water Closets: The codes typically require every floor in a building to have at least one water closet (i.e., toilet). The plumbing code requirements for water closets include the types allowed and the clearances for installation. The most common requirement is that all water closets specified for public use must have an elongated bowl and a seat with an open front. Clearances include specific dimensions at each side and in front of the bowl.

For accessible water closets, specific floor clearances around the water closet are required. The amount required depends on whether the fixture is positioned for a front approach, a side approach, or both. It also depends on whether the water closet is by itself or in a toilet stall and whether it is wall hung or floor mounted. (Refer to section on Toilet Facilities and Restrooms later in this chapter.) Typically, 18 inches is required between the centerline of the bowl and the side wall to allow access to the grab bars. (See Figure 7.3.) Extra clearance is required to the front

Note

The local Health Department may also place requirements on certain fixtures in some occupancies, especially in restaurants.

Note

Additional plumbing fixtures that are not as common include spas, hot tubs, whirlpools, baptisteries, ornamental and lily pools, aquaria, and fountains. They have specific code requirements as well. Consult an engineer or plumbing contractor when required.

and/or other side of the bowl for maneuverability. If a manual flush valve is used, it must be located on the "open side" of the toilet. The *ADAAG* also specifies the height to the top of the toilet seat and sets additional requirements for grab bars, flush controls, and toilet paper dispensers.

Urinals: Urinals are not required by the plumbing codes in every occupancy. They are typically found in the male restrooms of schools, restaurants, clubs, lounges, transportation terminals, auditoriums, theaters, and churches. If they are required, they are usually substituted for one or more of the required water closets.

When urinals are provided, the *ADAAG* requires at least one to comply to accessibility requirements. It must either be a stall type or a wall hung fixture with an elongated rim at a maximum height above the floor. In addition, clear floor space allowing front approach must be provided. The flush control requirements are similar to those on water closets.

Lavatories: Anywhere a water closet is used, a lavatory must also be installed, but the same ratio is not always used by the codes. Therefore, in larger restrooms you usually end up with more water closets and/or urinals than there are lavatories.

The *ADAAG* requires at least one lavatory on each floor to be accessible. In many of the newer restrooms where a continuous counter or vanity is provided, the entire run of lavatories is made accessible. Specific clearances and heights are required. Most important is the clear floor space leading up to the lavatory and the kneespace and toespace underneath. Because kneespace is required, all hot water and drain pipes must be covered to prevent contact. Faucets controls must also be of a certain type (i.e., lever) for ease of use.

Sinks: Sinks required by the codes are usually considered miscellaneous fixtures. They can include service sinks, utility sinks, kitchen sinks, and laundry basins. Some are required by the code, depending on the occupancy. For example, in a Business occupancy a utility sink (i.e., janitor sink) is typically required. Others are installed even when they are not required by the plumbing code. For example, kitchen or bar sinks in breakrooms are fairly common additions to an interior project.

Most of the *ADAAG* requirements are for kitchen-type sinks. These requirements are similar to lavatories except that the height and clearance dimensions are slightly different. This is especially important when designing pantry areas in a break room or lunch-

Note

Although not required by the *ADAAG*, the use of automatic water and flushing controls that activate upon movement are also considered accessible and are becoming more popular, especially in Assembly occupancies.

Note

There are at least three different ways to prevent contact with hot water and drain pipes under a lavatory: (1) wrap them with insulated material, (2) create an enclosure around the pipes, or (3) reconfigure the location of the pipes.

Note

Additional sink requirements for some occupancies are set by the local health department within a jurisdiction.

room where the counter height is typically 36 inches above the floor. The accessible requirement is a maximum of 34 inches at the sink, which means you either need to use a bilevel counter or lower the whole counter to 34 inches above the floor. Another requirement sets the maximum depth of an accessible sink to 6 inches.

Drinking Fountains: One drinking fountain is typically required for every 75 occupants. If there is more than one floor, each floor must have its own. The main plumbing code requirement for drinking fountains is that they cannot be installed in toilet rooms or the vestibules leading to the toilet room. One of the most common locations for a drinking fountain is the corridor outside the restroom area. This typically provides a central location for the user and easy access to the plumbing pipes.

The *ADAAG* requires at least one drinking fountain on every floor of a building to be accessible. If there is only one it must be either a "hi–low" fountain with water spouts at wheelchair and standard heights, or an accessible drinking fountain with an adjacent water cooler. If there is more than one drinking fountain on the same floor, usually 50 percent of them must be accessible.

An accessible drinking fountain also requires a spout at a particular height and location and has front or side controls that are easy to operate. In addition, specific amounts of clear floor space must be provided. Cantilever drinking fountains must allow a front approach and minimum kneespace, and free-standing units must allow specific floor space for parallel approach.

Bathtubs: Bathtubs are rarely required by the plumbing codes. When bathing facilities are required, often a shower can be used in its place. Bathtubs are most commonly found in Residential occupancies such as hotels, dormitories, and apartment buildings. If a bathtub is required in an accessible toilet room the *ADAAG* sets certain standards. They include a certain amount of clear floor space in front of the tub, a secure seat within the tub, specific location of controls and grab bars, a shower spray unit that can convert from a fixed to a hand-held unit, and specific types of bathtub enclosures.

Showers: Like bathtubs, showers are typically required by the plumbing code in Residential occupancies. (In some cases they may be allowed to replace the bathtub.) Some Assembly occupancies, such as gymnasiums and health clubs, require showers as well. In addition, manufacturing plants, warehouses, foundaries,

Note

Some jurisdictions allow an alternate source of water in lieu of a drinking fountain (e.g., water cooler, accessible sink).

Note

One of the best types of accessible bathtub seats is one that extends from outside the tub into the head of the tub. It allows a person to do the maneuvering outside the tub before sliding in.

Note

When safety showers are required, you must also refer to *ANSI Z58.1: Emergency Eyewash and Shower Equipment.*

and other similar establishments may require showers if employees are apt to be exposed to excessive heat or skin contamination. The plumbing code specifies the type of shower pan and drain that must be used.

When there is more than one shower, at least one must be accessible. The *ADAAG* allows two types of showers: transfer showers and roll-in showers. Each must be a certain size. Depending on the type of shower, specific seats, grab bars, and controls must be used. In addition, the *ADAAG* specifies the type of shower spray unit, curb height, and shower enclosure.

Dishwashers and Clothes Washers: There are very few requirements for dishwashers and clothes washers. Clothes washers are typically required in certain Residential occupancies. Dishwashers are rarely required but, when specified, must meet certain installation requirements. Although there are no accessibility requirements for these appliances, it may be helpful to specify front load washers for ease of loading.

Toilet Facilities and Restrooms

In addition to the requirements for each plumbing fixture, specific plumbing code and accessibility standards must be met in the construction and layout of a toilet facility or restroom. The plumbing codes give specific privacy and finish requirements as well as minimum clearance dimensions. When an accessible fixture or facility is required, you must refer to the *ADAAG* and the ANSI standards. They typically set stricter fixture clearances (as described above) as well as specific requirements for toilet stalls, grab bars, and accessories.

Note

When a 60-inch diameter turning space is not possible, a T-shaped space is usually allowed. See the *ADAAG* and ANSI standards for specific requirements.

The codes require privacy both at the entrance to the restroom and within the restroom when there are multiple fixtures. When a restroom is connected to a public area or passageway, it must be screened so that no one can look directly into the toilet facility. This is usually accomplished with either a vestibule leading into the restroom or a deliberate arrangement of walls. In addition, the *ADAAG* requires all restrooms, whether they are fully accessible or only partially accessible, to be directly accessible to the public. This includes minimum door clearance into the space and an unobstructed turning space within the space.

Single-Toilet Facilities: Most *single-toilet* facilities must be accessible or at least be adaptable. (For example, the lavatory, counter, and mirror may be adjustable for later conversion when required.) In fully accessible single-toilet facilities, all fixtures, accessories, and grab bars must be mounted at accessible heights and specific floor clearances must be provided. Figure 7.3 indicates the requirements of a typical accessible single-toilet facility. Both ANSI and the *ADAAG* give specific dimensions for floor clearances depending on the layout of the room and the swing of the door. In addition, an unobstructed turning space within a 60-inch diameter circle is required. This circle can overlap at fixtures where toespace is provided and should be drawn directly on the floor plan to indicate compliance.

Multiple-Toilet Facilities: If a *multiple-toilet* facility is required, the water closets must be separated from each other and from the rest of the room by *toilet stalls.* There are many ways to design the layout of a multi-toilet facility. Figure 7.4 shows one type of layout. The codes require the stall partitions to be made of impervious materials. (The most common options are laminate or painted metal partitions.) Certain minimum clearance dimensions and doors with privacy locks are required as well. Urinals must also be separated by a partial screen, but no doors are required.

> **Note**
>
> Toilet facilities with only one water closet and one lavatory do not normally require additional partitions inside the space.

> **Note**
>
> Doors swinging into accessible restrooms or toilet stalls cannot reduce the clear floor space required for each fixture. However, depending on which standard you are using, the door is sometimes permitted to swing into the 60-inch diameter turning space. (See Figure 7.3.)

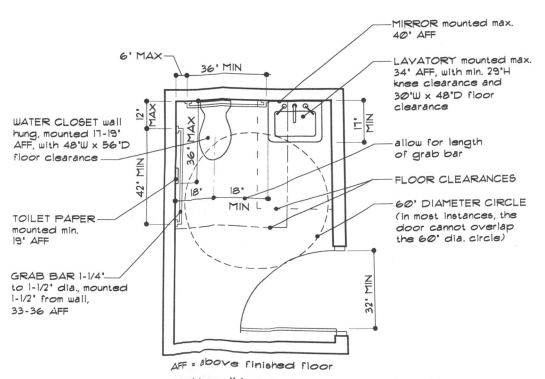

Figure 7.3. Typical Accessible Toilet (using ADAAG requirements).

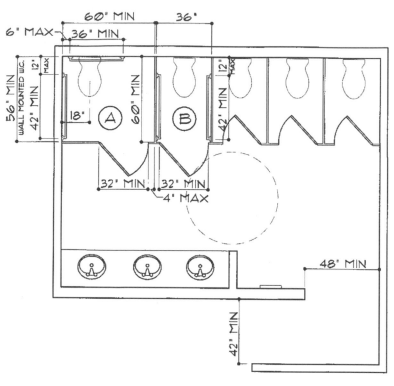

A = WHEELCHAIR ACCESSIBLE STALL

B = AMBULATORY ACCESSIBLE STALL
(also referred to as an "alternate" stall)

Figure 7.4. Example of Multi-toilet Facility (using ADAAG requirements).

Note

A standard accessible stall and the "alternate" stall are shown in Figure 7.4. However, the use of the "alternate" stall is not required by *ADAAG* unless six or more stalls are provided.

If the stalls are required to be accessible, additional regulations must be met. When one accessible stall is required, it must allow for the use by a person in a wheelchair. The typical size of this stall is 5' × 5' or 5' × 8', depending on the swing of the doors. Toe clearances and specific grab bar locations are important as well. If a second accessible stall is required the "alternate stall" as described in the *ADAAG* can be provided. This stall is not as wide and the arrangement of grab bars is different. The alternate stall configuration provides for a person with a mobility disability but who does not necessarily use a wheelchair. The *ADAAG* includes additional requirements for urinals, such as mounting heights and clearances. Privacy screens used at urinals must also provide enough clearance.

Accessories and Grab Bars: Restroom accessories are also regulated by the *ADAAG* and the ANSI standards. These include mirrors and medicine cabinets, controls, dispensers, receptacles, disposal units, air hand dryers, and vending machines. Of course, in single accessible toilet facilities all accessories must be accessible. This includes specific heights, clear floor space, and operation requirements of each accessory. In multifixture facilities only a percentage of the accessories must be accessible; however, many new facilities provide all accessories at accessible heights for consistency of design.

Grab bars are also regulated by the *ADAAG* and the ANSI standards. Grab bars are required at water closets, showers, and tubs that are required to be accessible. They must be located beside and/or behind the water closet and within reach ranges for bathing facilities. Grab bars must also be mounted at specific heights. Depending on the location of the grab bar, the specific length, spacing, and orientation (horizontally or vertically) are specified. The size and strength requirements of the grab bar are also regulated. In addition, some jurisdictions or licensing requirements may require grab bars in locations other than those specified by the *ADAAG*. For example, a diagonal bar may be required over a tub to assist in getting in and out of the tub.

Signage: Signage varies with the type of facility. When all facilities are not accessible, accessible toilets and restrooms must be identified by a sign showing the International Symbol of Accessibility as shown in Figure 7.5. The entrance to the room must have a sign, and if it is a multi-toilet facility, the accessible stalls within the room must have a sign as well. In addition, any nonaccessible restroom must indicate the location of the nearest accessible facility. All signs must also meet the typical accessible requirements for signage, such as sign proportions, lettering size and contrast, mounting locations, and use of Braille. (See the *ADAAG* for specifics.)

> **Note**
>
> Additional grab bars may be required by certain code jurisdictions over and above what is required by the *ADAAG*.

> **Note**
>
> Although the diameter of a grab bar can vary slightly, the 1½-inch distance from the wall cannot. This distance is a safety clearance that prevents arms from slipping through when a person braces for support.

Figure 7.5. International symbol of accessibility.

MECHANICAL REQUIREMENTS

Although there are some references to mechanical systems in the building codes, most of the actual requirements are found in the mechanical codes. Until recently, each of the code organizations published a new edition of the mechanical code every three years. They included the *BOCA National Mechanical Code (NMC)*, the *Standard Mechanical Code (SMC)*, and the *Uniform Mechanical Code (UMC)*. With the introduction of the *International Mechanical Code (IMC)* these other codes are no longer being updated and will eventually be phased out. In addition, some states have developed their own mechanical codes. Be sure to check with the jurisdiction to see which code is enforced.

The mechanical codes contain the requirements for the installation and maintenance of heating, ventilation, cooling, and refrigeration systems. As the designer you will very rarely, if ever, refer to the actual mechanical code publications. Instead, the mechanical codes are typically used by mechanical engineers and licensed mechanical contractors, as are a number of standards and other resources. These include those from the American National Standards Institute (ANSI) and the American Society of Heating Refrigeration, and Air Conditioning Engineers (ASHRAE). These and other standards are referenced in the back of each code publication.

When collaborating with an engineer, you will design the interior space, which typically includes locating the supply diffusers and return grilles, and the engineer will design the corresponding mechanical system. On projects that require minimal mechanical work, such as adding or relocating supply diffusers and return grilles to an existing system, the mechanical contractor may be able to work directly from your drawings or supply the required "shop" drawings. It may be necessary to coordinate your preliminary design with the engineer to make sure you allow enough clearance for equipment, especially as it affects ceiling heights.

Note

Although the *ADAAG* does not specify requirements for mechanical systems, the *ADA* in general may require parts of the mechanical system, such as the controls or registers, to be adjusted to accommodate an individual person.

Definitions

Before continuing with this section, be sure you are familiar with the following mechanical terminology.

DAMPER: A valve installed inside an air duct to regulate the flow of air.

DUCT: An enclosed rectangular or circular tube used to transfer hot and cold air to different parts of a building.

EXHAUST AIR: Air *removed* from a conditioned space through openings, ducts, plenums, or concealed spaces to the exterior of the building.

PLENUM: Any enclosed portion of a building that forms part of an air distribution system, including areas above ceiling, below floors, and in vertical shaftways.

RETURN AIR: Air *removed* from a conditioned space through openings, ducts, plenums, or concealed spaces to the heat exchanger of a heating, cooling, or ventilation system.

SUPPLY AIR: Air *delivered* to a conditioned space through openings, ducts, plenums, or concealed spaces from the heat exchanger of a heating, cooling, or ventilation system.

VENTILATION: The process of supplying or removing air by natural or mechanical means to or from any space.

VENTILATION AIR: The portion of supply air that comes from the outside plus any recirculated air that has been treated to maintain the desired quality of air within a space.

ZONE: A space or group of spaces within a building with heating and/or cooling requirements that are similar and are regulated by one heating or cooling device/system.

Code Considerations

All types of mechanical systems will need to meet certain code requirements. Some of these are a part of the building codes. For example, Chapter 5 and Chapter 6 discussed ventilation of vertical shafts, firestopping, and fire dampers. Other provisions are found in the mechanical codes. The main mechanical requirements you should be aware of as a designer are discussed below.

Mechanical Rooms: Mechanical rooms can include furnace or boiler rooms, fan rooms, and refrigeration rooms. Depending on the size of the building and the type of mechanical system used, these rooms can be separate or combined into one. It is the size and location of mechanical room(s) that are important. The codes specify that each room must have minimum door widths so equipment can be easily replaced. In addition, minimum working space along the control side of the equipment is required. If you need to locate a mechanical room on an interior project, be sure to work closely with the mechanical engineer to size the room correctly. Mechanical rooms are not typically required to be handicap accessible. (See Chapter 5 for fire rating requirements.)

Note

Not all buildings require a mechanical room. Many smaller buildings have their HVAC units either on the roof or on the ground adjacent to the building. Consult an engineer for the options.

TYPES OF MECHANICAL SYSTEMS

Mechanical systems are often referred to as HVAC systems. (This acronym stands for heating, ventilation, and air conditioning.) They can be separate or combined into one system. A wide variety of HVAC systems are available. The system that is selected and used in a particular building depends on a number of factors, including the size and use of the building, the number of occupants, the cost, and the maintenance. Below is a description of the three main types of mechanical systems.

✦ **ALL-AIR SYSTEMS:** This system uses *centrally* located fans to circulate hot and cold air to and from a space through long runs of ductwork. All-air systems are the most widely used mechanical system in large buildings. They include the variable air volume system (VAV), which is the most popular, and the constant air volume system (CAV).

✦ **ALL-WATER SYSTEMS:** This system uses pipes to transport hot and cold water to and from each space where the air is *locally* circulated by a convector or fan to create the hot and cold air. The most common all-water system is the electric baseboard convector system found in private residences. Other systems include fan-coil terminals, closed loop heat pumps, and hydronic convectors.

✦ **AIR AND WATER SYSTEMS:** A combination system that uses a central fan to circulate fresh air to a space where it is heated or cooled by water before entering the space. The most common combination system is the air–water induction system.

Most mechanical systems will require some type of ductwork to supply the air, registers to distribute the air, and grilles to retrieve the return air. Some buildings use ductwork to return air as well. This is called a *duct* system. Other buildings use a *plenum* system, whereby the open space above the suspended ceiling and/or the enclosed vertical shafts are used to collect the return air. In a plenum system ducts are still required to supply the air.

Note

Existing ductwork can hinder the placement of fire separation walls. You may have to work with a mechanical engineer or contractor to reroute the ducts.

Cooling Loads: The cooling load refers to how much energy is required to cool a space. It is one of the main factors in determining the size and type of a mechanical system. As you are designing a space be aware that there are a number of items that can affect the cooling loads of a space or building. They include the number and size of exterior windows, the type of glazing, the quantity and type of lighting fixtures, the amount of equipment, the number of people, and the size of the space. These and other factors are used by the mechanical engineer in conjunction with the codes to determine the size of the ducts and the number of supply diffusers and return grilles required. It is important to work closely with the mechanical engineer, since the results will affect ceiling heights and the location of other ceiling fixtures.

Zoning and Thermostat Locations: Different areas of a building may be zoned separately to provide different levels of comfort. Typically, parts of a floor or building with similar temperature requirements are grouped into the same zone. For example, perimeter rooms that have exterior windows are typically zoned separately from interior spaces. Other rooms may have particular requirements and need to have a separate zone. Some may even have a separate supplemental system because of their special needs. Some examples include a kitchen in a restaurant, a locker room in a sports complex, a computer room in a school, and a conference room in an office space.

Each mechanical zone has a separate thermostat. The codes do not specify the location of a thermostat. Instead, it is typically determined by the engineer and depends on the surrounding heat sources. Some thermostat sensors can even be located above the ceiling. The *ADAAG* does not specifically regulate the location of a thermostat either. However, when it is placed in general areas where changing the temperature is common, the thermostat should be located within accessible reaching heights.

Note

It is often required that spaces adjacent to exterior walls and windows be zoned separately from interior spaces. Solar heat and outside temperatures typically cause different temperatures in perimeter rooms.

Exhaust Requirements: Whenever air is removed from a building or space the process is considered exhaust. An exhaust system is usually required by the code in specific types of rooms and in certain occupancies. An exhaust system can remove air that contains smoke, germs, chemical, odors, or other unhealthy or contaminated components. This is especially important in more hazardous types of occupancies. Exhaust systems are also typically required in all restrooms and in designated smoking areas. The rate at which air must be removed from an area is generally based on the activity or type of air that is being exhausted.

Ventilation Requirements: Whenever air from the outside is added to a building or space that process is considered ventilation. It can be brought in by natural air flow through operable windows, vents, or louvers or by the mechanical system. The mechanical codes regulate both. The code regulates the size of the window, vent, or louver and the amount of required outside air according to the floor area of the space that is being ventilated. If natural ventilation is not possible, then the space is typically required to be ventilated mechanically.

The requirements are generally based on the use or occupancy of the space. A common example is a computer room or a telephone room. These rooms typically require ventilation. When someone occupies one of these rooms on a regular basis, outside air is usually required. However, if no one occupies the room, the code may allow mechanical ventilation. Other examples include atriums and vestibules.

Plenum Requirements: Most air type HVAC systems use either a duct or a plenum for return air. (See *Types of Mechanical Systems* on page 188.) When there are no ducts attached to the return grilles, the open space between the ceiling and the floor above creates a ceiling plenum that acts as the duct and collects the return air. When this plenum system is used, it must be limited to specific fire areas within the building. For example, a plenum cannot pass through a stairwell. The important thing to remember is that if an opening is cut in a rated wall to allow the return air to continue across the ceiling cavity, a fire damper must be added to that opening. (See Chapter 5.) The building codes prohibit the use of combustible materials in the plenum space. In addition, only certain types of cabling are allowed. These include any electrical, telephone, and communication wires. (See Chapter 8.)

Duct Requirements: If the mechanical system uses ducts to retrieve the air as well as to supply conditioned air to a space, the codes place fewer restrictions on the types of materials allowed in the ceiling space. However, the codes place restrictions on the ducts themselves. The building codes set some requirements, such as the use of firestops and fire dampers when ducts pass through fire-rated walls. (See Chapter 5.) The mechanical codes specify such things as the size of the ducts, types of rated materials allowed, and mounting and clearance requirements. They also prohibit the use of mechanical ducts in certain locations.

Access Requirements: Certain components of a mechanical system, including ductwork and specific duct connections, must allow adequate access for maintenance. Replacement of major components must be permitted without substantial damage to existing building materials. Suspended ceiling grids, for example, allow easy access to ductwork. When solid ceilings such as gypsum board are used, an access door may be required at specific locations. For example, access must usually be provided at all fire dampers located in the ductwork, at air volume boxes located in the ceiling, and at any shut off valves used on water type systems.

CHECKLIST

The checklist in Figure 7.6 combines a number of plumbing and mechanical code requirements. For each project the checklist asks you if an engineer is required. This will depend on the size of the project, the amount of plumbing or mechanical work, and the jurisdiction of the project. (See Chapter 10.) The checklist begins by asking you the project name, the occupancy classification, building type, and occupant load of the space or building you are designing. (These are all explained in Chapter 2.)

The first section of the checklist concentrates on plumbing fixtures. The main types of plumbing fixtures are listed. Use the plumbing code and the *ADAAG* to determine how many of each plumbing fixture are required. List these required quantities in the standard and accessible fixtures columns on the checklist. When necessary, use the adjacent column to note how many are already existing in the building. Refer to these quantities as you are locating the fixtures in your design.

The next section of the checklist indicates some of the other plumbing requirements that may need to be examined in a project. These include the type of sprinkler system, the type(s) of sprinkler heads, the number and type of standpipes and fire hoses, and the number and type of fire extinguishers. (These requirements are discussed in Chapter 6.) If these systems are existing, record the appropriate types and quantities as required. You may need to work with an engineer to see if additional systems are required. If it is a new building, record the systems to be installed.

The last section of the checklist concentrates on the mechanical system of a project. It lists the main mechanical items you should look for in an existing building. Fill in the necessary information and refer to it as you plan your design. If it is a design project in a new building, work with the engineer to determine these items.

The purpose of the plumbing and mechanical codes is to establish standards that protect the health and welfare of the occupants of a building. Although you will typically only refer to these codes when you are placing plumbing fixtures, it is important for you, as the designer, to understand the general codes. You must often coordinate the location of plumbing fixtures, sprinklers, fire extinguishers, air diffusers and returns, and other plumbing and mechanical elements within a building. This will require working closely with an engineer or a licensed mechanical contractor.

PLUMBING AND MECHANICAL CHECKLIST

PROJECT NAME:_____

OCCUPANCY (new or existing):_____

BUILDING TYPE:_____

OCCUPANCY LOAD:_____

PLUMBING REQUIREMENTS:*   Engineer Required? ___ yes ___ no

TYPE AND QUANTITY OF PLUMBING FIXTURES (Check those that apply and insert quantities):

FIXTURE	Standard Fixtures		Accessible Fixtures	
	REQUIRED	EXISTING	REQUIRED	EXISTING
___ Water Closet	_____	_____	_____	_____
___ Urinal	_____	_____	_____	_____
___ Lavatory	_____	_____	_____	_____
___ Sink	_____	_____	_____	_____
___ Drinking Fountain	_____	_____	_____	_____
___ Bathtub	_____	_____	_____	_____
___ Shower	_____	_____	_____	_____
___ Other _____	_____	_____	_____	_____
___ Other _____	_____	_____	_____	_____

TYPE OF SPRINKLER SYSTEM: _____

___ Existing   ___ New   ___ Not Required

TYPE OF SPRINKLER HEADS: _____

___ Existing   ___ New   ___ Not Required

TYPE OF STANDPIPE/FIRE HOSE (Class I, Class II, Class III): _____

___ Existing   ___ New   ___ Not Required

NUMBER OF FIRE EXTINGUISHERS: _____

___ Existing   ___ New   ___ Not Required

MECHANICAL REQUIREMENTS:*   Engineer Required? ___ yes ___ no

TYPE OF MECHANICAL SYSTEM: _____

LOCATION OF MECHANICAL ROOM: _____

TYPE OF AIR CIRCULATION (Duct or Plemun): _____

SPECIAL VENTILATION REQUIRED: _____

SPECIAL EXHAUST SYSTEM REQUIRED: _____

CEILING HEIGHT(S) REQUIRED: _____

LOCATION OF SUPPLY DIFFUSERS (Ceiling, Wall, Floor): _____

LOCATION OF RETURN GRILLS (Ceiling, Wall, FLoor): _____

NUMBER AND LOCATION OF THERMOSTATS/ZONES: _____

---

* Refer to Chapter 6 Checklist for additional requirements.

NOTES:

1. Refer to codes and standards for specific information. Also check the *ADAAG* for mounting locations.

2. If automatic sprinkler systems are used, check for possible code trade-offs.

3. Be sure to note on floor plans the location of fire rated walls for placement of required fire dampers and fire stops.

Figure 7.6. Plumbing and Mechanical Checklist.

As you proceed to Chapter 8 remember that plumbing, mechanical, and electrical systems are often planned simultaneously, especially in large buildings. A number of building elements must often be arranged to house these systems so they can move vertically and horizontally through the building. For example, building cores and stairwells create vertical shafts for the distribution of the systems. Suspended ceilings and flooring systems allow horizontal movement of these systems. Planning for these systems in the early stages of a project is important. They also affect the selection and placement of finished ceilings, walls, and floor systems.

Note

It is often necessary to meet with an engineer in the preliminary stage of a design project so that your design can be coordinated with new and existing plumbing, mechanical, and electrical systems.

CHAPTER 8

ELECTRICAL AND COMMUNICATION REQUIREMENTS

This chapter covers electrical and communication code requirements. Although some of these requirements are found in the building codes, most of the codes are found in the *National Electric Code (NEC)*. The *NEC* is also referred to as *NPFA 70* and is published by the National Fire Protection Association (NFPA). The code is unique in that it is the main electrical code referred to in the United States. It also references other NFPA standards within its text. Most jurisdictions have either adopted the *NEC* or are enforcing a part of the *NEC* in addition to local code requirements. The *ICC Electrical Code—Administrative Provisions (IEC)*, developed by the ICC, may be used in conjunction with the *NEC*. The *IEC* is not a separate code; rather it acts as an administrative supplement that can be used with the *NEC*.

A number of other standards organizations have additional electrical standards as well. The most common are the American National Standards Institute (ANSI), the National Electrical Manufacturers Association (NEMA), and Underwriters Laboratories (UL). In addition to providing supplemental design and installation procedures, these standards organizations develop standards for the fixtures themselves, as well as provide specific testing and labeling procedures for electrical and communication equipment.

As the designer you will rarely refer to the *NEC* or the electrical standards. On interior projects you will generally be responsible for determining the location and types of outlets, fixtures, equipment, and appliances used in a project. In some cases, you will also need to coordinate the location of equipment rooms. However, when a project requires substantial electrical work, an electrical engineer is required to design the electrical system. On smaller electrical projects, such as some residential homes or minimal changes to a tenant space, that do not require the services of an engineer, a licensed electrical contractor will know the codes.

This chapter covers the codes and standards requirements with which you should be familiar. The first part of the chapter concentrates on electrical requirements. The second half of the chapter briefly discusses different communication systems and how they are affected by the codes. These systems include voice, data, and security systems. Any necessary *Americans with Disabilities Act Accessibility Guidelines (ADAAG)* regulations are mentioned as well. (The *ADAAG* mostly controls the mounting height of the outlets and fixtures.)

DEFINITIONS

Before continuing with this chapter, be sure you are familiar with the following electrical terms.

BOX: A wiring device that is used to contain wire terminations where they connect to other wires, switches, or outlets. A *junction box* is where several wires are joined together.

CABLE: A conductor, consisting of two or more wires combined in the same protective sheathing and insulated to keep the wires from touching.

CIRCUIT: The path of electrical current that circles from the electrical source to the component (i.e., outlet, fixture) and back to the source. A number of circuits are used within a building to evenly distribute the electrical load. A *branch circuit* supplies electricity to a number of components or outlets.

CIRCUIT BREAKER: A safety device that opens and breaks a circuit to stop the flow of electricity when an overload or fault occurs.

CONDUCTOR: A cable or insulated wire that carries and distributes electricity.

CONDUIT: A raceway or pipe that houses and protects electrical wire and cables, typically made of metal or plastic.

FEEDER: A conductor that supplies electricity between the service equipment and the branch panel boards.

FUSE: A safety device that contains metal that will melt or break when the current exceeds a specific value for a specific time period, causing the flow of electricity to stop.

OUTLET: A box in which electrical wiring is connected to an electrical component. A *fixture outlet* is used to connect electricity to a hard-wired light fixture or receptacle outlet. A light switch is also sometimes referred to as a fixture outlet. A *receptacle outlet* allows the connection of a plug-in appliance or equipment.

RACEWAY: An enclosed channel designed to hold wires and cables.

TELEPHONE BANK: Two or more adjacent public telephones, often installed as one unit.

ELECTRICAL SYSTEMS

An electrical system consists of a distribution system (also known as a transmission system) and a premises wiring system. The *distribution system* is controlled by the electrical utility company and originates in huge generators. From these generators, high voltage wires transport the electricity to transformers. The utility transformers convert the electricity to lower voltages before it enters a building. The utility distribution system ends at the service entrance connection point to the building and usually includes the utility meter.

The *premises wiring system* is the electrical system within the building. Premise wiring begins where the utility service connection is made and extends to the building's main electrical panel and to the outlets used throughout the building for fixtures, appliances, and equipment. In larger buildings, where higher voltages are provided by the utility company, additional interior transformers may be used before or after the electricity reaches the panel board. This panel board is typically contained in an electrical room and may consist of a main disconnect switch, secondary switches, fuses, and circuit breakers.

Cables and wires run from this electrical panel to various locations throughout a building. In smaller buildings, these cables or branch circuits are directly connected to the electrical outlets. In large buildings, feeder conductors are used to distribute the electricity horizontally and vertically to a number of smaller panel boards. These panel boards supply electricity to separate areas within the building. Branch circuits are used to connect the panel boards to the various electrical outlets.

The *NEC* regulates only the portion of the electrical system that is controlled by the building. It does not include any part controlled by the electrical utility company.

ELECTRICAL REQUIREMENTS

Electrical Panels/Rooms

Three types of electrical panels can be used in a building. The first and largest is the service entrance *switchboard*. It is the main electrical panel that distributes the electricity from the utility service connection to the rest of the building. The *NEC* regulates the size of the room that contains this panel. For example, one of the most typical requirements is that there must be at least 3'-0" clearance in front of the panel. When the switching panel is two-sided, the code requires enough working room on both sides of the panel. Additional space is required if any transformers are used. (See inset titled Electrical Systems on the preceding page.) The switchboard room must also be ventilated to control heat building up from the equipment. If it is located on an outside wall, ventilation can be done directly to the outside. If not, ducts and fans must be used to provide outside air ventilation. (Refer to *NEC* for duct location restrictions.)

Power panel boards are used throughout a building to distribute electricity to each floor and/or tenant space. They are one-sided electrical panels that are typically housed in electrical closets or in cabinets that are placed in or against a wall. In multistory buildings the electrical closets should be stacked directly above each other on each floor so that the electrical systems can be vertically distributed.

Each floor may also have one or more smaller *branch panel boards* that supply electricity to a particular area or tenant. Typically, closets that contain only panel boards do not have to be rated. Closets that contain large transformers and panel boards are required to be rated.

All these requirements are important to know, especially if you are creating a layout for a new space or building and one or more electrical closets must be located. You would work closely with an engineer to make sure the closets are located as required for distribution. You will also need to confirm that the sizes of the rooms allow for the electrical panels and other equipment to have the correct clearances.

> **Note**
>
> An electrical panel is a common place for a fire to start. When designing interiors be careful not to locate electrical panels next to stairwells or other main means of egress.

Electrical Wiring and Conduit

To distribute electricity to all areas that it is needed, electrical wiring must pass through many construction elements. When electrical wiring is installed, the diameter of any hole created for the passage of wire cannot be more than $\frac{1}{8}$ inch larger than the

TYPE AC:	Armored Cable (BX)
TYPE ALS:	Aluminum Sheath Metal-Clad Cable
TYPE CS:	Copper Sheath Metal-Clad Cable
TYPE FC:	Flat Cable Assemblies
TYPE FCC:	Flat Conductor Cable (FLAT WIRE)
TYPE IGS:	Integrated Gas Spacer Cable
TYPE MC:	Metal-Clad Cable
TYPE MI:	Mineral-Insulated, Metal-Sheathed Cable
TYPE MV:	Medium-Voltage Cable
TYPE NM or NMC:	Nonmetallic-Sheathed Cable (ROMEX)
TYPE PLTC:	Power-Limited Tray Cable
TYPE SE or USE:	Service-Entrance Cable
TYPE SNM:	Shielded Nonmetallic-Sheathed Cable
TYPE TC:	Power and Control Tray Cable
TYPE UF:	Underground Feeder and Branch-Circuit Cable

Figure 8.1. Types of Electrical Cables.

diameter of the wire, cable, or conduit passing through the hole. When these wires pass through a rated floor, ceiling, or wall assembly, the building codes require the use of a rated firestop. (See Chapter 5 for more information on firestops.)

The *NEC* specifies the types of electrical wiring or cables that can be used, depending on where they are located inside the building. Figure 8.1 gives you an idea of how many different types of cables there are. (Many of these cable types also have subcategories.) Which electrical cable to use is typically determined by the electrical engineer or contractor. Noncombustible cable is required in most conditions. In addition, certain areas within a building may require special cables. For example, special rules apply for wiring in ducts, plenums, and other air handling spaces. (See Chapter 6.) You should be familiar with the most common cables as described below. They are listed by their more common trade names.

1. **Romex:** Romex is a trade name for nonmetallic-sheathed cable (Type NM or NMC). It consists of two or more insulated conductors and should include a ground wire surrounded by a moisture-resistant plastic material. The *NEC* limits this cable mostly to Residential one- and two-family dwellings and multiunit dwellings not exceeding three floors. Typically these are wood frame buildings.

2. **BX or Flex:** BX is a type of armor cable. It is a flexible cable (Type AC) that consists of two or more conductors wrapped in heavy paper or plastic and encased in a continuous spiral-wound metal jacket. It is commonly used in commercial applications. In new installations, the *NEC* requires BX to be secured in intervals, but in existing installations you may find that the cable was just fished through walls, floors, and ceilings. In addition, BX is often used to connect 2 × 4 light fixtures in suspended ceiling grids to allow relocation flexibility. In most instances, the *NEC* will limit the length of flex wiring to 6 feet in length; however, other jurisdictions may be stricter.

3. **Metal-Clad Cable:** Metal-clad cable (Type MC) is often used when BX cable is restricted. It looks similar to BX cable, but MC cable has an additional green ground wire that provides extra grounding. As a result, it can be used in more applications than BX cable.

4. **Flat Wire:** Flat wire is the common name for flat conductor cable (Type FCC). It is a small cable in a flat housing that allows it to be used under carpet tiles without protruding. Flat wire can be used in many applications. It is often used to rework obsolete wiring systems in existing buildings. The *NEC* prohibits the use of flat wire in wet and hazardous areas and in residential, hospital, and school buildings.

Another option often used when wiring large residential and commercial buildings is *conduit*. Conduit is a fire-rated metal piping used to house and protect plastic conductors or cables. It is available in plastic, too, but plastic is typically allowed only in nonrated applications. More than one wire or cable can be fished through the conduit. The conduit may also act as a system ground (see the section on Grounding on page 204) and may protect surrounding building materials should a wire overheat. There are a number of different types of conduits, including rigid metal conduit, flexible metal conduit, rigid plastic conduit, and even preassembled cables in nonmetallic conduit.

The type of conduit required depends on where it will be used and the types of hazards present. The rigid and flexible metal conduits are the most common. Although the length of flexible conduit may be limited by the code, the code may set other limitations as well. For example, some jurisdictions require all low voltage wiring to be run through conduit. (See the section on Low Voltage Wiring starting on page 209.)

Circuitry

The distribution of electricity is managed and organized by creating different circuits. Separate circuits are created by wiring (or cable) that branches from the main electrical source to different areas of the building or space. Each circuit feeds electricity to a series of light fixtures, outlets, equipment, and/or appliances before it returns to the branch panel or power panelboard. Each circuit may be carrying a different voltage and amperage of power. For example, a washing machine will require a 220-voltage circuit, which must be separate from the 120-voltage circuit required for the lights in the room.

The codes limit the number of volts or amperage that is allowed on a single circuit. Therefore, it is important to supply an engineer with the correct quantity and types of equipment in a space or building so that the circuitry can be designed correctly. This can affect the number of light fixtures that can be switched together and how many fixtures can be controlled by dimmers. Certain equipment may require circuits that serve only a single outlet. This is called a *dedicated circuit*, sometimes referred to as a dedicated outlet. It is also known as "clean power."

Electrical Boxes

Electrical boxes include outlet boxes and switch (or device) boxes. *Outlet boxes* can be wall- and/or floor-mounted for electrical receptacles or wall- and/or ceiling-mounted for light fixtures. *Switch boxes* are typically wall-mounted and control the lighting outlet box. The control can be in the form of a toggle, dimmer, or remote. The surface area of these boxes cannot exceed 16 square inches. Most are either 2 × 4 inches or 4 × 4 inches. Both the *NEC* and the building codes typically specify that no more than 100 square inches of electrical boxes can be installed for every 100 square feet of wall surface. In fire-rated walls, when boxes are used on opposite sides of the same wall, the boxes must be separated horizontally by 24 inches.

The boxes are usually mounted within a wall by fastening the box to a stud. For example, in a metal stud and gypsum board wall, the outlet box and the switch box are mounted to the metal stud and a hole is cut around the gypsum board to allow access to the box. The code specifies that the opening in the wall cannot exceed ⅛ inch clearance between the box and the gypsum board. In a rated wall, this gap must be fire caulked.

Because the needs of residences are somewhat consistent, the codes provide more specific requirements. For example, the *NEC*

Note

Another common type of electrical box is a junction box. It houses the connection of wires and allows access to these connections.

specifies the minimum number of electrical boxes to be provided. The code specifies that all occupiable rooms must have a switch outlet that controls the lighting. Receptacle outlet boxes must be installed so that no point along the horizontal floor line in any space is more than six feet from an outlet. In most dwelling spaces the rooms are small enough so that placing receptacle outlets as shown in Figure 8.2 will comply with the code. Hallways, on the other hand, require at least one receptacle outlet. In addition, the *NEC* and the *IRC* require specific location of outlets in bathrooms, kitchens, and laundry areas. (Also see the section on Grounding and GFIs.)

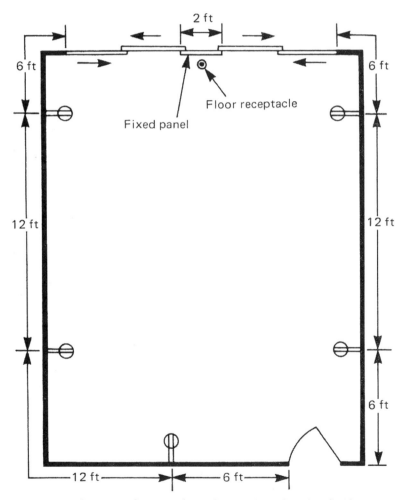

Figure 8.2. Plan View of Receptacle Outlet Locations. (Reprinted with permission from *National Electrical Code Handbook*, Copyright 1993, National Fire Protection Association, Quincy, MA 02269. This reprinted material is not the complete and official position of the National Fire Protection Association on the referenced subject, which is represented only by the book in its entirety.)

Since the needs and requirements in commercial facilities vary with the activities and equipment needs of a particular tenant or user, the codes do not provide as many specific requirements as for Residential occupancies. For example, the *NEC* does not specify the frequency of electrical boxes or switch outlets. Their placement is determined by specific equipment requirements and convenience considerations. For example, the typical length of a cord on a vacuum cleaner may be a good guideline for placement of receptacle outlets within a long corridor.

The mounting height of the electrical boxes is regulated by the *ADAAG*. When mounted on a wall, the *ADAAG* requires that the outlet box be located at the least 15 inches above the floor. Switch boxes must be located within the accessible reaching height above the floor. When designing accessible work areas, such as study carrels in public libraries and office workstations, careful placement of the outlets is important. They must be located within the appropriate reach ranges. Whenever possible, locate the outlets above the worksurface or counter. You may also be able to mount a special outlet toward the front edge under the worksurface.

According to the *ADAAG*, not all electrical devices may be required to be accessible. It will depend on the location and use of the device, the type of equipment connected to it, and if it is meant for use by employees. An example of a nonaccessible outlet may be an outlet or switch in a janitor's closet or an outlet behind a permanent copier. You need to consider if there is a possibility that the employee who would use the device could be disabled and need the device within the reach ranges. On the other hand, if the outlets or devices are to be used by clients or the general public, they should be accessible. You may need to discuss this issue with the owner to decide.

Junction Boxes

As the designer, another type of electrical box you need to be aware of is a *junction box*. A junction box is used by an electrician to tie several wires together. For example, a main cable run that leaves the electrical panel will at some point need to branch off to electrify several light fixtures. At the point where these wires come together, a junction box is used to protect the various cable connections and to allow for future access. The standard 4 × 4 metal box is typically used.

Although junction boxes are usually specified by an electrical engineer, some codes that pertain to the junction box can affect your design. Depending on your design, you want to review and

Note

In residential occupancies when a wall is broken by a doorway, fireplace, or similar opening, each continuous wall space of two or more feet must be considered separately for the placement of a receptacle outlet.

Note

All junction boxes must be easily accessible, whether they are located in the floor, wall, or ceiling. You must plan your design accordingly.

Note

If an outlet has special power requirements, you may want to specify a dedicated circuit so that it will be wired separately. This will prevent electrical disturbances from other nearby electrical equipment.

coordinate the location of junction boxes either with the engineer or in the field with the electrical contractor.

The most important requirement to know is that a junction box must be accessible at all times. Junction boxes are most often located on or near the ceiling slab. If you are using a suspended ceiling grid with removable tiles, access becomes very easy. However, if a junction box is located in an area where you are planning to use a drywall ceiling, an access panel must be added to allow access to the junction box. The size of the panel depends on how easily the box can be reached from the underside of the ceiling.

Grounding and GFIs

The electrical code requires that all electrical systems be *grounded*. This is accomplished by a third wire that always accompanies a cable. In general, this ground wire redirects live currents into the ground to prevent a person from getting shocked when there is a short circuit. However, the presence of water makes it easier for an electrical current to flow. If the circuit or outlet is wet or if the person touching the outlet or adjacent appliance is wet or standing in water, there is a much higher chance of getting shocked. As a result, the *NEC* requires special grounded circuits in rooms where water will be present.

Note

A third type of GFI is one that plugs into an existing outlet. It should be used only on a temporary basis and is often used on a construction site before the permanent wiring has been installed.

These circuits are called *ground fault circuit interrupters*, also commonly known as GFI or GFCI. The GFI is a device that is able to detect small current leaks. If a current leak occurs, the GFI disconnects the power to the circuit or appliance and thus prevents an electrical shock from occurring. The GFI can be installed in the electrical panel as part of a circuit breaker, or it can be installed as a special type of receptacle at the electrical outlet.

The *NEC* requires that exterior receptacle outlets be GFIs. On interior projects, typically all standard 120-volt duplex receptacle outlets located in areas where there is water should be specified as GFIs. These areas could include bathrooms, kitchens, break rooms, bar areas, laundry rooms, and even pools or spas. Every outlet within the room, unless not readily accessible, must be specified as a GFI on your electrical floor plans.

Light Fixtures

Light fixtures have a number of additional code and standard requirements. Only fire tested and labeled light fixtures should be used on interior projects. The most widely accepted standards are created by Underwriters Laboratories (UL). Each light fixture manufactured in the United States is tested to be used in specific environments or locations and is then assigned a UL rating or seal of approval. (See inset titled UL Labels on page 23.) For example, a fixture installed in a damp location must be marked "Suitable for Wet Locations." Other light fixtures are specifically marked for wall mounting, undercabinet mounting, ceiling mounting, and covered ceiling mounting.

As the designer, it is important to specify UL-approved light fixtures. UL tested and labeled fixtures have undergone rigorous testing. Some jurisdictions allow only UL-approved fixtures on a project. However, even if they are not required, you should be specifying them. You cannot assume every light fixture is UL approved. You need to look carefully when specifying fixtures supplied by countries outside the United States and fixtures made by custom fabricators. In addition, you must choose the fixture appropriate to the location in which it will be used.

The attachment of a light fixture to an outlet box is related to its weight and the type of fixture. Light fixtures that weigh less than 50 pounds are usually supported by the outlet box that serves the fixture. Additional support of the outlet box is required for heavier fixtures. The *NEC* also places strict requirements on the access of electrical components. All electrical boxes must allow access so that repairs and wiring changes can be made at any time. All light fixtures must be placed so that both the lamp (i.e., light bulb) and the fixture can be replaced when needed. This becomes especially important when light fixtures are used within an architectural element such as ceiling coves.

In fire-rated ceiling and wall assemblies, only certain types of light fixtures are allowed. For example, when light fixtures are recessed into a ceiling that has a one-hour rating, the mechanical part of the fixture must be rated or a fully enclosed rated box must be built around the housing to maintain the one-hour rating of the ceiling. In other instances, noncombustible material must also be sandwiched between the fixture and the finished surface. In addition, when using 2 × 4 fluorescent light fixtures and they are placed end to end, there cannot be a gap between the fixtures. (Note that side-by-side installation of 2 × 4 light fixtures is not always considered safe.)

Emergency Electrical Systems

Emergency electrical systems are required in most buildings. They are used to back up the normal electrical system in case of an emergency. The emergency electrical system must have the capac-

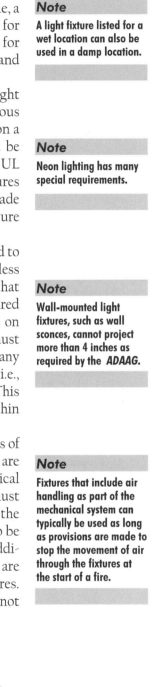

Note

A light fixture listed for a wet location can also be used in a damp location.

Note

Neon lighting has many special requirements.

Note

Wall-mounted light fixtures, such as wall sconces, cannot project more than 4 inches as required by the *ADAAG*.

Note

Fixtures that include air handling as part of the mechanical system can typically be used as long as provisions are made to stop the movement of air through the fixtures at the start of a fire.

ity to operate such equipment as means of egress lighting, exit signs, automatic door locks, and other emergency equipment.

Each of the building codes and the *Life Safety Code (LSC)* specify emergency lighting requirements. The requirements are found in the means of egress chapters of the codes. (See the section on Exit Lighting on page 115.) Each code specifically states the following basic requirements:

1. Artificial lighting must be present in the path of exit discharges when a building is in use. (There are exceptions for Residential occupancies.) The intensity of the emergency lighting cannot be less than 1 footcandle (11 lux) at the floor level on the path of egress. (This can be reduced at times of performance in some Assembly occupancies.)

2. Exit signs must be located and illuminated in a way that they can direct occupants safely out of the building. Exit signs can be externally illuminated, internally lit, or self-luminous. Exit signs must be illuminated by not less than 5 footcandles (54 lux) or the equivalent light level. Typically, a contrast level of 0.5 must be provided as well.

3. Provisions must be made so that in case of power loss, emergency or exit lighting will be available for a certain time. Most codes require that exit lighting be connected to an emergency power source that will assure illumination usually for 1 to 1½ hours in case of power failure, depending on the jurisdiction. For example, in Business occupancies, a battery pack can usually be used as the emergency source of power. In some occupancies, such as in Assembly, Institutional, or Hazardous occupancies, a separate source of emergency power, such as an emergency generator, must be provided for the exit signs.

Note

It may be necessary for the code official in the jurisdiction of your project to designate which exit accessway must be illuminated with emergency lighting.

The easiest method of creating emergency lighting in a design project is to include some of the existing light fixtures on a separate circuit designated for emergency lighting. That means that the separate circuit is connected to a backup power source. You must also make sure that if one light fixture burns out it will not leave an area in darkness. Some ways to ensure this are to use dual lamp light fixtures, to use fixtures with battery packs, or to design an overlapping light pattern.

The *NEC* provides additional requirements for emergency electrical systems. The main requirement specifies that when the power changes from the main power source to the emergency system, the delay cannot be longer than 10 seconds. It also specifies the types of backup systems that can be used. Which system to use is typically determined by the electrical engineer.

Standby Power Systems

Standby power systems are similar to emergency electrical systems. They are used to supply power when the normal power source fails in an emergency. However, instead of operating the emergency systems, standby power is used for other building systems, such as the mechanical system, fire pumps, general lighting, communication systems, elevators, and other standby equipment.

Typically the standby power system must operate 60 seconds after the failure of the normal power supply. The building codes specify when a standby power system is required and the *NEC* specifies the type of system and how it is installed. Typically, an electrical engineer would design this type of system.

COMMUNICATION REQUIREMENTS

A building's communication system can consist of a number of different systems. These include intercoms, telephones, computers, security, background music, and television systems, such as surveillance equipment, cable services, and satellite hookups. In some cases, fire alarms are integrated into the building's communication system as well. A communication system also includes assistive listening systems required by the *ADAAG* in Assembly occupancies. The *NEC* and the standards organizations set some requirements for these communication systems. However, these systems are not as heavily regulated as electrical systems, because

Note

In some occupancies, such as hospitals and businesses with critical computer systems, the 10-second power delay may not be acceptable. It may be necessary to add an uninterrupted power supply (UPS) that keeps the electricity flowing during the 10-second transition time.

Note

An important source for standby power systems is *NFPA 110: Emergency and Standby Power Systems.*

LOW VOLTAGE CABLING SYSTEMS

The type of cabling system used within a building to support voice, data, video and security systems is called structured cabling. It is also known as integrated cabling or universal cabling. The system is made up of backbone cabling and horizontal cabling. Backbone cabling carries the signals to the main distribution areas of the building or space. It begins where the public utility enters the building, goes to the main equipment room and then to the local communication closet. In large commercial projects, fiber cabling is typically used for backbone cabling.

The cables that are pulled to each workstation or outlet are known as horizontal cabling. Connections to the individual desktops or outlet can be made through the horizontal cabling system using fiber optic or copper cabling. However, because copper is less expensive for individual connections, it is more widely used in horizontal cabling. In cases that support complex systems, fiber optics should be considered for horizontal cabling. (See the section titled Low Voltage Wiring on page 209.)

the wiring for communication systems is so low in voltage that it poses very few safety problems. The primary concern is the fire hazard caused by the spread of fire along the cables or circuits.

Similar to the electrical system, the *NEC* does not regulate the transmission of signals or the connection of communication services to the building. It regulates only the parts of these systems that are inside the building. Many of the rules for these systems include the type of cable or wiring used, the clearance for power conductors, and the proper grounding procedures. Other requirements may be regulated by industry standards or on a local level.

Computers and advanced electronics are becoming an essential part of a project both in residential and commercial spaces. Some projects may require a communication consultant to adequately plan the system. Depending on your role in the design of the communication system, it is important to understand the current and future needs of the client and to coordinate your design with the company doing the installation of the system. The electrical implications as well as the local regulations need to be considered. Some projects may require an electrical engineer.

The remainder of this section concentrates on voice and data systems, including telephones and computer systems, and concludes with a section on security systems. Keep in mind, however, that since the technology is constantly changing, you must closely coordinate communication systems with local vendors and/or consultants.

Note

In the future, as computers continue to change and grow more powerful, additional code provisions will probably be added for the use and the wiring of computers.

Communication Rooms

Note

Many of the newer telephone systems operate by computer. Additional space may be required to house a computer inside or directly outside the switching room. Other systems may allow you to network to the main computer system.

Every building requires a central area where the incoming communication services are connected to the building's communication system. In the past, this was primarily the telephone service and the space was referred to as the telephone switching room. Because advances in technology and communication have expanded the area of communication, the incoming communication service may include telephone, computer data, and similar electronic information relay. This room or area is typically located in the basement or on the ground floor as close as possible to the communication service entrance. In small buildings, only a small panel located in the mechanical room or a closet may be required. In larger buildings, a central switching room is required. The size of the room depends on the number of telephones and other connections that must be serviced and the size of the switching panel. When determining the size of the room, you should consult the various companies installing the communication systems (i.e., telephone, computer, security).

In buildings with multiple floors, each floor has its own *communications closet* that feeds off the main switching room. There may be separate closets for telephone and computer equipment or one room that combines both. Like electrical rooms, these communication closets are usually stacked on top of each other to allow for continuous vertical wiring. The closet provides a central location to distribute cabling throughout the floor, either directly to each telephone and computer or to one or more satellite closets. A *satellite closet* is often used within separate tenant spaces to allow the separation of utilities. It also allows easier distribution of cables in large buildings.

Low Voltage Wiring

Cables used for communication systems are different than electrical cables, because of the lower voltages required for communication systems. Some of the common types are listed in Figure 8.3. As the designer, you will rarely specify a type of cable, but rather will work closely with the client and their communication consultants or vendors. You should know, however, that there are a number of standards that apply to the use and installation of cabling systems. Typically, the type of cable needed depends on where it is used. For example, if a cable is used in a mechanical plenum space (see Chapter 7), it must be marked as a plenum cable. Each of these communication cables must meet certain fire ratings and be appropriately labeled. Listed below are the three main types of cables and/or connections used today. Each type has a different characteristic that will affect the design of the system.

1. **Fiber optic cable:** A fiber optic cable transmits light along ultrathin glass or plastic strands. Each strand is composed

TYPE MPP:	Multipurpose Plenum Cable
TYPE CMP:	Communications Plenum Cable
TYPE MPR:	Multipurpose Riser Cable
TYPE CMR:	Communications Riser Cable
TYPE MP or MPG:	Multipurpose General Purpose Cable
TYPE CM or CMG:	Communication General Purpose Cable
TYPE MP:	Multipurpose General Purpose Cable
TYPE CMX:	Communications Cable, Limited Use
TYPE CMUC:	Undercarpet Communications Wire and Cable

Figure 8.3. Types of Communication Cables.

of layers of fibers protected by a cabling jacket and a plastic coating. Fiber optic cables provide higher bandwidth than other types of cable, which yields higher speed and capacity. And, because they are smaller and lighter and can withstand greater pulling tension, they are easier to use than copper. In addition, fiber optics are not affected by electromagnetic and radio frequency interference. For future expansion of the data or communication system, additional fibers can easily be included in the initial installation.

2. **Copper Cabling:** Copper cabling provides less capacity and speed than fiber optics, but it is still the most common type of low voltage cabling used today. Copper wire is twisted into pairs and encased in a protective sheathing. It is rated by "category," which indicates its bandwidth performance. Manufacturers are continually developing copper cabling with more capacity. In the past, Category 3 (CAT 3) was commonly used for data cabling. Now, it is used more for voice systems, while Category 5 (CAT5), Category 5E (CAT5E), and Category 6 (CAT6) are currently used more for data installations.

3. **Wireless:** Wireless systems connect to the individual outlets by transmitters and receivers instead of actual cabling. They use infrared or radio transmission. Sometimes microwave and laser signals are used between facilities. Wireless systems work well in situations where reorganization occurs frequently. However, wireless systems can be much slower and are more expensive. In addition, in areas where buildings are close together, interference from other wireless systems can cause problems.

When communication cables are installed throughout a building, they must be kept separate from electrical cabling. In most cases communication cables cannot be placed in any raceway, compartment, conduit, outlet box, or junction box used for electric light or power. When cables are run through walls, many jurisdictions require the low voltage cables to be run in a separate metal conduit. For example, in a typical room the area for the communication cables is often located next to an electrical outlet. Two conduits would be installed in the wall: one for the electrical wiring and one for the low voltage. When running communication cables horizontally across a ceiling, cable trays or J-hooks are typically used. Often these cables can remain exposed. The various communication vendors will share this common path until they reach their respective outlet locations.

PUBLIC TELEPHONES

Public telephones are not regulated by the *NEC*. Instead, the *Americans with Disabilities Act (ADA)* sets a number of regulations. Title IV of the ADA deals specifically with telecommunication services and sets regulations for accessible public telephones. (Refer to Chapter 1.) In addition, the *ADAAG* sets specific clearance and reach requirements.

Public telephones can include public pay telephones, public closed circuit telephones, or other telephones for public use. Although the installation of public phones is usually the responsibility of the telephone company, there are a variety of public phones and not all are accessible. As the designer, you must be aware of the *ADAAG* and *ADA* requirements and be able to specify the correct type of public phone. Whenever one or more public telephones are provided, at least one telephone must be accessible. When one or more banks of telephones are provided, additional phones may need to be accessible.

Accessible public telephones must provide either front or side access. The ADAAG indicates that in both cases a clear floor space of at least 30 × 48 inches must be provided. Bases, side enclosures, fixed seats, and other protruding objects cannot reduce this floor space. The actual height of the telephone depends on the type of access and the depth of any obstruction (i.e., shelf). Other accessible requirements include volume controls, text telephones, push-button controls, position of telephone books, length of cord, and signage displays.

Voice/Data Outlets

The termination of the low voltage cable is the telephone outlet and computer outlet, often called voice and data outlets, respectively. Usually the cables are all run through the same conduit to one box. Depending on the type of cover plate, a typical 2 × 4 or 4 × 4 electrical box is used. In either instance, it is not unusual to have an outlet with four jacks—two for voice and two for data.

The main requirement for mounting voice and data outlets is found in the *ADAAG*. In accessible areas, the outlet must be mounted at least 15 inches above the floor to allow for easy reach. (See section on Electrical Boxes earlier in this chapter for more accessibility requirements.)

Security Systems

Although security systems are not required by the code, some aspects of their use and installation are controlled by the codes. Because it is an issue of life safety, the *Life Safety Code (LSC)* and the building codes regulate security systems when they affect exiting. A number of standards must be followed as well. One of the big-

Note

In addition to providing a clear floor space at the accessible public telephone, you need to make sure the telephone is located on an accessible route within the building.

Note

Required text telephones are based on the number of interior and exterior telephones. See the *ADAAG* for additional information.

gest concerns is that the locking of doors for security reasons cannot interfere with the required means of egress. However, whether part of a standard security system or special security system (i.e., psychiatric hospitals or prisons), the doors within the means of egress may require locks. In these cases, there are various locking systems that will serve the security issues while not endangering the occupants.

You first need to determine if the lock is fail safe or fail secure. The lock is considered to be fail safe if the door automatically unlocks when power goes out, such as in the event of a fire. If the lock is fail secure, the door will remain locked even in the event of the loss of power. This type of lock may interfere with exiting if additional precautions are not provided, such as constant monitoring by personnel.

Three types of locks are typically used for security: mechanical, electrical, and pneumatic locks.

1. **Mechanical Locks:** Mechanical locks are opened either with a key or by a code entered into a push-button mechanism. These types of locks are not usually allowed on an exit door unless there is constant supervision of the door.

2. **Electrical locks:** Electrical locks can be electromechanical or electromagnetic. Two of the more common types of *electromechanical locks* include delayed egress or alarmed doors. Since they can be fail safe or fail secure, you must specify the proper action if the door is required for exiting. Standards that apply to electromechanical locks include *ANSI/UL 1034 and ANSI/BHMA 156.5. Electromagnetic locks*, often referred to as "maglocks," use a magnetic field to hold the metal plate on the door or jamb in place. (These locks are similar to electromagnetic door holders, which are used to hold open fire-rated doors and release them to close when the fire alarm is activated.) Since they have no mechanical parts and depend on electricity, they are considered fail safe and can be safely connected to the fire alarm system and the security system. Standards that apply to electromagnetic locks include *ANSI/BHMI A156.23* and *ANSI/BHMA A156.24.* Remember, since these doors do not rely on a mechanical latch for closure, additional hardware may be needed on a rated door to properly latch the door as required by the code.

3. **Pneumatic Locks:** Pneumatic locks use electromechanical devices and pneumatic air pressure. They are used largely in Institutional occupancies such as hospital and prison facilities. These locks can be locked and released electronically and manually.

Note

The NFPA is in the process of creating a standard to regulate premises security.

Security systems continue to become more complex as entry and control systems are more data based. Electronic codes and card readers are already common. In situations that require higher level of security and control, biometric readers that read voice, fingerprint, or other physical characteristics are in use. These products are most often used for entry control and may not be required to monitor exiting. These products will become more cost effective as technology and demand continue, yet the concern about proper exiting must always be addressed.

When security systems are installed as part of an automated building, they cannot disrupt other systems that affect life safety. Automated building systems combine the control of the automatic systems within a building, such as fire alarm, sprinkler system and HVAC systems. These are then controlled by a single source of data. Establishing the proper relationship and prioritizing the systems can be complex. In most cases, the fire alarm must take precedent over the security issues. For instance, if a fire activated the fire alarm, certain doors that are locked must be allowed to open for proper egress. And because the codes affect all the systems of a building in different ways, each system must continue to meet the code requirements.

The *ADA* requires that most spaces, including high security spaces, be accessible. This requirement will affect the location, size, shape, and texture of handles, levers, locks, keypads, card readers, and other equipment. This equipment must be within the

NEWEST COMMUNICATION TECHNOLOGY

The growth in communication technology may be the fastest changing element in the design industry and in our daily lives. Developments in computers and the Internet are ongoing and will continue to affect the design of buildings in the way of communication. Codes and standards will continue to change to address these new uses, particularly as they affect safety in use and installation.

Innovations such as broadband communications systems, which allow voice, audio, video, data, and Internet connections to travel along a single cable at a faster rate, will bring new requirements. Because fiber optic cables are an efficient transmitter of data, their use will expand. Zoned cabling will continued to be developed to coordinate the efficiency of open office design and the technological requirements of individual workstations.

As more systems within a building are controlled by computer programs and data input, more interrelated systems will be developed. The management of multiple systems such as mechanical, fire protection, communication, and security systems together in a "total building system" is already causing consideration of new regulation.

reach ranges. (Refer to the *ADAAG* for specifics.) In addition, the required area for clearances can affect the location of doors and the use of turnstiles. Visual and audible accessibility must be considered as well.

CHECKLIST

The checklist in Figure 8.4 combines a number of electrical and communication code requirements. For each project the checklist asks you if an engineer is required. This will depend on the size of the project, the amount of electrical or communication work, and the jurisdiction of the project. (See Chapter 10.) The checklist begins by asking you the project name and its occupancy classification.

The first part of the checklist concentrates on the electrical requirements. It notes the main electrical items you should determine in your project. The checklist does not get into specific code requirements since most of them are determined by the engineer or contractor. However, you should know where the electrical panels are and their sizes. In addition, determine and note any building conditions, such as a plenum mechanical system, that will affect the type of wiring used. Other checklist items are to remind you of the types of outlets and equipment that should be labeled or noted on your drawings.

The second half of the checklist pertains to communication systems. Since most of the details are determined by the engineer or the company installing the system, this part of the checklist is to help you keep these systems organized. Spaces are provided for you to fill in the names of the companies installing the system as well as where the main part of the system will be located. This can include the location of the communication room or the location of the surveillance monitors for the security system. Any other systems considerations should also be noted, such as the type of wiring used.

As the designer it will be your responsibility to locate in your drawings all electrical outlets, switches, light fixtures, and large equipment or appliances. You must also indicate the placement of any communication systems, such as public phones, voice outlets, data outlets, and security card readers. In addition, indicate any special type of outlets, such as dedicated or GFI, and the type of light fixtures. On projects in new buildings, you may be responsible for locating and sizing equipment rooms, such as switching rooms and electrical closets, in conjunction with an engineer.

ELECTRICAL AND COMMUNICATION CHECKLIST

PROJECT NAME:_____

OCCUPANCY (new or existing):_____

ELECTRICAL REQUIREMENTS: Engineer Required? ___ yes ___ no

TYPES OF ELECTRICAL PANELS (Check those that apply and note locations, sizes):

    ___ SWITCHBOARD: _____

    ___ PANEL BOARD(S): _____

    ___ BRANCH PANEL BOARD(S): _____

SPECIAL WIRING CONDITIONS: _____

LOCATION OF RECEPTICAL OUTLETS: _____

    ___ Existing   ___ New   ___ Not Required

LOCATION OF SWITCHES: _____

    ___ Existing   ___ New   ___ Not Required

SPECIAL TYPES OF OUTLETS/CIRCUITS (Check those that apply and note locations):

    ___ DEDICATED OUTLETS: _____

    ___ GROUND FAULT CIRCUIT INTERRUPTERS: _____

    ___ OTHER: _____

TYPES OF REQUIRED EQUIPMENT (Check those that apply, list new and existing, specify if over 120V):

    ___ LIGHT FIXTURES: _____

    ___ APPLIANCES: _____

    ___ EQUIPMENT: _____

    ___ OTHER: _____

TYPE OF EMERGENCY ELECTRICAL SYSTEM: _____

    ___ Existing   ___ New   ___ Not Required

TYPE OF UNINTERRUPTED POWER SUPPLY SYSTEM: _____

    ___ Existing   ___ New   ___ Not Required

TYPE OF STANDBY POWER SYSTEM: _____

    ___ Existing   ___ New   ___ Not Required

COMMUNICATION REQUIREMENTS: Engineer Required? ___ yes ___ no

TYPE OF COMMUNICATION SYSTEMS (Check those that apply and insert information):

SYSTEM	MANUFACTURER OR INSTALLATION COMPANY	CENTRAL LOCATION OF SYSTEM	SPECIAL CONSIDERATIONS
___ Intercom System	_____	_____	_____
___ Computer System	_____	_____	_____
___ Surveillance System	_____	_____	_____
___ Cable TV Services	_____	_____	_____
___ Satellite System	_____	_____	_____
___ Building Telephone System	_____	_____	_____
___ Public Telephone System	_____	_____	_____
___ Assistive Listening System	_____	_____	_____
___ Other _____	_____	_____	_____

NOTES:

1. Refer to codes and standards for specific information. Also check the *ADAAG* for mounting locations.

2. Be sure to note on floor plans the location of fire rated walls for placement of required firestops.

Figure 8.4. Electrical and Communication Checklist.

The electrical engineer will design the electrical system based on your drawings. You should supply the engineer with as much information as possible. The engineer will determine such things as the number of circuits required to carry the electrical load, the types and sizes of electrical cables and materials, the size and location of conduit, and the placement of the cables and equipment throughout the building. The communication vendors will also use your drawings to locate the appropriate communication systems.

CHAPTER 9

FINISH AND FURNITURE SELECTION

Over the years there have been many fatal fires in the United States due to flammable finishes and upholstery. One of the most noted incidents is the 1942 fire in Boston's Coconut Grove Nightclub, which claimed the lives of 492 people. In response to that deadly fire, Boston established regulations dealing with interior finishes, known today as the Boston Fire Code. A number of other cities and states have their own finish and furnishings regulations. In addition, each of the building codes and the *Life Safety Code (LSC)* has a section or chapter dedicated to interior finishes. These chapters also refer to a variety of standards.

Building codes and standards give strict instructions on the selection of finishes, since finishes often ignite and rapidly spread a fire. A wallcovering, for example, that is *not* flame resistant can spread a fire down the length of an entire corridor in a matter of seconds, setting other flammable items, such as draperies and upholstery, on fire and creating deadly smoke, heat, and toxic fumes.

Chapter 5 discussed fire prevention through the use of rated interior building materials and assemblies. This chapter concentrates on the products that are either placed on top of the building materials or set within the compartments created by the building materials and structure elements.

Finishes and furniture are given fire ratings similar to building materials. However, these ratings are usually obtained by smaller scale flame tests rather than full scale fire tests. This chapter discusses the various finish and furniture tests and how to select products based on the ratings. Other code restrictions and accessibility requirements are also discussed.

It is important to understand the codes that affect interior finishes and furniture. Interpreting charts, understanding test requirements, and selecting materials that meet the codes are critical. Furniture, which was not as heavily regulated in the past, is becoming just as important. Remember, your client's safety is in your hands.

DEFINITIONS

Below are some definitions you should be familiar with before continuing this chapter.

BACK COATING: The process of coating the underside of a fabric or finish to improve its durability, enable it to serve as a heat barrier, or both.

FIRE BLOCK: A separate material used behind or underneath the primary finish or other building material for the purpose of creating a fire barrier.

FLAME RESISTANCE: When a finish or piece of furniture restricts the spread of a flame when exposed to a flame or nonflaming source. It includes resisting the flame or terminating the flame following ignition.

FLAME SPREAD: The propagation of flame over a surface.

FLAMMABILITY: The amount of flame spread during test conditions.

HEAT BARRIER: A liner used between upholstery and the filling below to prevent the spread of flame or smoldering heat. It may be applied as a backcoating.

INTERIOR FINISH: Includes interior wall and ceiling finish and interior floor finish, but does not include trim.

MOCK-UP, FURNITURE: A representation of a finished piece of furniture that utilizes the same frame, filling, and upholstery as the finished piece. It can be a full or partial mock-up.

SMOLDERING: Combustion that occurs without a flame that generates smoke, toxic gases, and heat. It usually results in a charred area.

TRIM: Picture molds, chair rails, baseboards, handrails, door and window frames, and similar decorative or protective materials used in fixed applications.

> **Note**
>
> The terminology used to describe products that are more resistant to fire has changed over the years. *Flameproof* is a common term that is usually incorrect, since very few products are totally unaffected by fire. The correct terms are *flame retardant* and *flame resistant*.

TYPES OF FINISHES AND FURNISHINGS

Interior finishes and furnishings covered by the codes and standards include a variety of materials and products and can be divided into six categories: interior ceiling finishes, interior wall finishes, interior floor finishes, window treatments, furnishing finishes, and furniture. They are listed and defined below and are discussed throughout this chapter.

1. **Interior Ceiling Finishes:** Exposed interior surfaces of a building, including suspended ceiling grids and coverings that can be applied to fixed and movable ceilings, soffits, beams, space frames, and other similar elements.
2. **Interior Wall Finishes:** Exposed interior surfaces of a building, including coverings that may be applied over fixed or movable walls and partitions, columns, and other similar elements.
3. **Interior Floor Finishes:** Exposed interior surfaces of a building, including coverings that may be applied over a finished or unfinished floor, stair (including risers), ramp, and other similar elements.
4. **Window Treatments:** Decorative elements that control the amount of light from a window area. These can include draperies, liners, blinds, or shutters. These elements can be made of textiles, wood, vinyl, and other similar materials.
5. **Furnishing Finishes:** Exposed finishes found in case goods furniture, systems furniture, and soft seating, such as fabrics, wood veneers, and laminates. This category also includes nonexposed finishes, such as the foam in seating, liners in drapery, and other similar elements.
6. **Furniture:** Whole pieces of furniture rather than separate parts and finishes. This category usually includes upholstered products, such as seating and panel systems. Also included are mattresses, which consist of the whole mattress composition, including fabric, padding, and coils, and similar bedding assemblies.

Until recently codes often regulated only the first four categories. However, this is changing. As requirements are getting stricter, more standards are being developed. Some jurisdictions (discussed later in this chapter) are already regulating furnishings and finishes. The building codes are also beginning to reference more of these standards. It is your responsibility to check the requirements and select furnishings and their finishes wisely using your knowledge of codes and standards.

COMPARING THE CODES

The two main sources for interior finish regulations are the building codes and the *Life Safety Code (LSC)*. Each of the building codes and the *LSC* have a chapter or section dedicated to interior finishes. Similar to codes for construction materials as discussed in Chapter 5, the regulations often refer you to various standards. Note, however, that the codes concentrate more on finishes than furniture. As you will see later in this chapter, in addition to the standards referred to in the codes, there are a number of other industry standards that you must follow as well. Figure 9.1 indicates the number of NFPA standards alone. In addition, many individual cities and states also have their own regulations. Some of the most stringent ones include California, Boston, Florida, Massachusetts, New Jersey, New York City, and New York State. Be sure to check the jurisdiction of your project to see if there are more stringent requirements.

The next section of this chapter will describe the various finish and furniture standards. How to use this information is described in more detail later in the chapter. (See section on Using the Codes, page 230.)

STAGES OF FIRE DEVELOPMENT

To gain a better understanding of how a fire can harm a human being and why fire codes are necessary, it is important to review the different stages in the development of a fire. They can be divided into three stages:

STAGE 1: Known as the time of ignition, this first stage is the *initial growth* of a fire. Smoke produced during this stage can travel many feet from the room of origin and pose a threat to humans.

STAGE 2: This is the *growth stage* when the fire begins to ignite material in the immediate area, including finishes and furniture. As a fire starts to consume a large part of a room, the heat generated may *flashover,* or simultaneously ignite surrounding rooms and corridors. This explosion usually occurs when a fire reaches the 1200-degree range.

STAGE 3: In this stage the fire is *fully developed,* causing the entire building to quickly become dangerous. Smoke, heat, toxic gases, and possible structural collapse can harm those who remain within range.

The rate at which these stages of fire development can progress varies tremendously with the construction of a building and the finishes and furniture used within. However, the first 5 to 10 minutes of a fire are the most critical. The materials and finishes you select can either contribute to the growth or prevent the spread of a fire. The goal is to lengthen the amount of time during which the occupants can safely evacuate a building.

NFPA 253:	Test for Critical Radiant Flux of Floor Covering Systems Using Radiant Heat Energy Source
NFPA 255:	Method of Test of Surface Burning Characteristics of Burning Materials
NFPA 258:	Research Test Method for Determining Smoke Generation of Solid Materials
NFPA 260:	Method of Tests and Classification System for Cigarette Ignition Resistance of Components of Upholstered Furniture
NFPA 261:	Method of Test for Determining Resistance of Mock-Up Upholstered Furniture Material Assemblies to Ignition by Smoldering Cigarettes
NFPA 265:	Fire Tests for Evaluating Room Fire Growth Contribution of Textile Wall Coverings
NFPA 266:	Method of Test for Fire Characteristics of Upholstered Furniture Exposed to Flaming Ignition Source
NFPA 267:	Method of Test for Fire Characteristics of Mattresses and Bedding Assemblies Exposed to Flaming Ignition Source
NFPA 272:	Standard Method of Test for Heat and Visible Smoke Release Rates for Upholstered Furniture Components or Composites and Mattresses Using an Oxygen Consumption Calorimeter
NFPA 286:	Methods of Fire Tests for Evaluating Room Fire Growth Contribution of Wall and Ceiling Interior Finish
NFPA 701:	Methods of Fire Test for Flame Propogation of Textiles and Films

Figure 9.1. Common NFPA Standards.

STANDARDS AND TESTING

The codes do not go into a lot of specifics about finishes and furniture. Instead they refer you to a number of standards that you must follow. Remember that the codes set *minimum* requirements, and sometimes there will be a stricter standard available. In some cases as the designer, it will be up to you to follow the strictest standards within the industry. (See section on Documentation and Liability in Chapter 10, page 262.) This section describes the various standards and related tests referred to by the codes and/or required by certain jurisdictions.

Each test has a particular purpose. That may mean that the results of the test may not be consistent with the use of the material in your design. For example, one of the more common standards, *Steiner Tunnel Test,* is considered a small-scale test and is not appropriate for all finish applications. The *Radiant Panel Test,* on the other hand, is for finishes applied to floors and does not take into account flooring finishes used in other applications, such as on walls. It is important to know the intent of the test and recognize the limitations of the test results.

The standard tests that are described below have been grouped by the common test name. Within each category specific test names will be mentioned, depending on the standards organization that provides the test. For example, the American Society for Testing and Materials (ASTM), the National Fire Protection Association (NFPA), and the Underwriters Laboratories (UL) each have their own written standard for many of the same tests. These test names are each labeled with the organization's initials and test number.

As you read through this section, refer to Figure 9.2. It summarizes the various finish and furniture tests discussed. Along the left hand side of the chart are the common test names for the various tests that apply to finishes and furniture. The specific standard names as published by the various standard organizations are listed in the next column according to the type of test. The right hand side of the chart lists whether the tests result in a pass/fail rating, a class rating, or a ranked rating. (See section on Obtaining Test Results, page 235.)

Steiner Tunnel Test

The *Steiner Tunnel Test* is the principal test used to determine both the flame spread and smoke developed ratings in the classification of interior wall and ceiling finishes. (It is also the oldest interior finish test.) As one of the first interior finish tests, its name comes from the fact that finishes are tested in a tunnel-like apparatus. The finish is tested in a horizontal or in a 45-degree position.

Flame spread ratings indicate the speed at which a fire may spread across the surface of a material. *Smoke developed* ratings determine how much visibility there is in a given access route when a material is on fire and creating smoke. The ASTM, NFPA, and UL standards organizations all use the same ratings in their tests. These tests are *ASTM E-84*, *NFPA 255*, and *UL 723*.

The test defines the flame spread and smoke development ratings of finishes by comparing the burning characteristics of two known materials, glass-reinforced cement board and red oak flooring. Arbitrarily, the cement board is given a flame spread of 0 and red oak flooring is assigned a flame spread of 100. All other materials are assigned values based on those ratings. Using these ratings, interior wall and ceiling finishes are grouped into the following classes, Class A being the most strict and Class C being the least:

✦ **Class** A: Flame spread 0–25, smoke developed 0–450. Includes any material classified at 25 or less on the flame spread test scale and 450 or less on the smoke test scale.

Note

Finish and furniture testing is constantly changing. Older tests are being improved and new tests are being developed. It is critical to keep abreast of the changes to make sure you continue to specify finishes and furniture that pass the appropriate tests.

Note

Labeled wood that has been treated with a fire retardant typically qualifies as a Class A interior finish. Most untreated wood has a Class C flame spread rating.

COMMON TEST NAMES	STANDARD NAME/NUMBER	TYPE OF RATING
CORNER TEST (applied finish)	NFPA 265 UBC 42-2 NBC "Room/Corner Fire Test" SBC "Standard Test Method for Evaluating Room Fire Growth Contribution of Textile Wallcoverings"	Pass or Fail
(upholstered materials)	NFPA 286	Ranked
MATTRESSES	NFPA 267 ASTM E1590 CAL 129	Ranked
	FF 4-72	Pass or Fail
PILL TEST	DOC FF1-70 DOC FF2-70	Pass or Fail
RADIANT PANEL TEST	ASTM E648 NFPA 253 NBS IR75-950	Class Rating
SMOLDER RESISTANCE TEST (applied finish)	NFPA 260 (was 260A) CAL 116 ASTM 1353	Pass or Fail
(mock-up)	NFPA 261 (was 260B) CAL 117 ASTM 1352	Class Rating
SMOKE DENSITY TEST	ASTM E662 NFPA 258	Class Rating
STEINER TUNNEL TEST	ASTM E-84 NFPA 255 UL 723 Chamber Test or UL 992	Class Rating
TOXICITY TEST	LC 50 PITTS TEST	Ranked
UPHOLSTERED SEATING TESTS (full scale)	NFPA 266 CAL 133 ASTM E1537 UL 1056	Pass or Fail
(small scale)	NFPA 272 (was 264A) ASTM 1474	Ranked
VERTICAL FLAME TEST	NFPA 701 ASTM D6413	Pass or Fail

NOTES:

1. Any number of the above tests may be required by a jurisdiction depending on the occupancy and its location within a building.
2. There may be other tests and/or test names not listed above that are more specific to a jurisdiction.

Figure 9.2. Summary of Tests.

Note

Class A, B, and C designations for wall and ceiling finishes used by the *LSC* and the *Standard Building Code (SBC)* correlate directly with the Class I, II, and III designations used by the *National Building Code (NBC)* and the *Uniform Building Code (UBC)*.

✦ **Class B:** Flame spread 26–75, smoke developed 0–450. Includes any material classified at more than 25 but not more than 75 on the flame spread test scale and 450 or less on the smoke test scale.

✦ **Class C:** Flame spread 76–200, smoke developed 0–450. Includes any material classified at more than 75 but not more than 200 on the flame spread test scale and 450 or less on the smoke test scale.

Note that the smoke rating remains the same for each. It is the flame spread scale that distinguishes the difference in each class.

An alternative test sometimes used instead of the tunnel test is the *Chamber Test.* It uses a different index rating and rates only Class B (0–4) and Class C (5–8). This test is also known as UL 992.

Radiant Panel Test

The *Radiant Panel Test* is used to rate interior floor finishes. Standards have been created by three different standards organizations. The tests are *NFPA 253, ASTM E648,* and *NBS IR75-950.* They determine the critical radiant flux by measuring the minimum energy required to sustain flame on a floor covering in watts per square centimeter. Although flooring is not considered a major cause of fire spread, the flooring material in exit access corridors can be of concern because it has been determined to add to fire growth. Therefore, the test provides a measure of a floor covering's tendency to spread flames if located in a corridor and exposed to the flame and hot gas (also considered radiant heat) from fire in an adjacent room. Test results determine two class ratings, with Class I being the stricter of the two.

✦ **Class I:** Critical radiant flux, minimum of 0.45 watts per square centimeter.

✦ **Class II:** Critical radiant flux, minimum of 0.22 watts per square centimeter.

Not all occupancies require a floor finish that has been tested. If it is required, only exits and access to exits are typically regulated. (See section titled Using the Codes and Figure 9.3 later in this chapter.) This is due to the fact that traditionally finished floors and floor coverings, such as wood floors and resilient floor covering (i.e., VCT), are unlikely to become involved in the early growth of a fire. And so, they do not prove to present an unusual hazard.

Pill Test

In addition to the Radiant Panel Test, all carpets manufactured for sale in the United States have been required, since 1971, to meet the *Federal Flammability Standard*. Also known as the *Pill Test*, it uses a methenamine pill to ignite the carpet during the test. This pass/fail test regulates the ease of surface ignition and surface flammability. There are two separate tests. *DOC FF1-70* regulates wall to wall carpeting and *DOC FF2-70* is for area rugs. Both of these tests are required by the federal government and therefore are some of the few tests that apply to both commercial and residential projects. Other flooring finish regulations are required for occupancies that warrant more careful restrictions or where a codes official deems it necessary for a particular situation. (See previous section.)

Note

When carpet is used as a finish other than on a floor more tests will be required.

Vertical Flame Test

Vertical flame tests are generally required for *vertical treatments*, such as curtains, draperies, window shades, large wall hangings or tapestries, and plastic films used for decorative purposes. Any vertical finish that is exposed to air on both sides is considered a vertical treatment. The vertical flame tests include *NFPA 701* and *ASTM D6413*, which are more realistic than the tunnel test because the flame source is used to create a vertical burning of the finish rather than the horizontal or 45-degree burning used in the *Steiner Tunnel Test*.

Note

NFPA 260A/B is now two separate standards: *NFPA 260* and *NFPA 261*.

NFPA 701 is divided into two separate pass/fail tests. The small scale test is required for straight hanging pieces. The large scale test is for fabrics that are used in folds, such as gathered drapery, fabric blackout linings, and large scale fabric such as banners. It also includes table linens, display booth separators, plastic films, and textile wall hangings. The large scale test takes into account the effect of air trapped between fabric layers. Note, however, that when the vertical treatments cover a large area they may also be required to pass the *Steiner Tunnel Test*.

Corner Test

Another test must be used when napped, tufted, or looped textiles or carpets are used on walls and ceilings. Although each building code and the *LSC* have adopted a different name for the same basic test, it is generally referred to as the *Corner Test*. These tests determine how an interior finish material will add to fire growth (including heat and smoke), create combustion products such as gases, and may cause flashover or fire spread beyond the initial fire location.

The test uses a simulated corner of a room for more accurate representation of an actual finish installation. It is a pass/fail test.

One of the tests considered a type of corner test is *NFPA 265*, which tests when textile wall coverings are used on an interior surface. In the year 2000, NFPA introduced a new test titled *NFPA 286*. Although it is similar to *NFPA 265* and is still considered a corner test, it was developed to test finishes that are used in a slightly different way. *NFPA 286* tests wall and ceiling interior finishes other than textiles, such as expanded vinyl wallcovering. *NFPA 286* also uses a stronger flame source that better tests the finish in a ceiling application. The results of the test provide a ranking of the finish materials based on their performance. (Combining these two tests into one is being considered by NFPA.)

Note

If you add a backing during installation to an approved textile you must have it retested. The backing makes the original test invalid.

Smolder Resistance Test

Smolder resistance tests are also known as *Cigarette Ignition Tests.* A cigarette ignition test analyzes the smoldering resistance of a finish. It is a nonflame test that uses an actual lit cigarette as the ignition source to see how a product will smolder before either flaming or extinguishing. This test determines the flammability of upholstered furniture by testing individual textiles or finishes as well as furniture mock-ups. Each type is explained below.

Finishes: When a smolder resistance test is used on individual finishes or textiles, it is a pass/fail test. These tests include *NFPA 260, CAL 116,* and *ASTM 1353.* (Note that *NFPA 260* was first developed as *NFPA 260A.*) It measures the char size left on the fabric or material. For example, if the ignited cigarette creates a char mark on the product that is larger than the specified standard, the product would fail the smolder resistance test.

This test applies to cover fabrics, interior fabrics, welt cords, decking materials as well as filling/padding materials. These materials can be natural or man-made fibers, foamed or cellular materials, or loose particulate filling materials such as shredded polyurethane or feathers and down. Although the test provides a cigarette resistance classification, Class I or Class II, it is essentially a pass/fail test. If the material passes the test, it is classified as Class I. Any material that does not pass the test is classified as Class II.

Mock-ups: Other smolder resistance tests were developed specifically for furniture mock-ups. The most common names for these tests include *NFPA 261, CAL 117,* and *ASTM 1352.* (Note that *NFPA 261* was originally developed as *NFPA 260B* but was renumbered as

NFPA 261 in 1989.) These are rated tests that test the individual mock-ups of seat cushion crevices, armrests, backs and other similar furniture configurations. They give a better indication of how a whole piece of furniture will react rather than just the top finish layer.

Smoke Density Test

Smoke density tests determine whether a solid material will hold a flame or smolder and how much smoke it will emit. The test measures the actual optical density of the smoke, how thick and how dark, to determine the amount of visibility during a fire. It is a rated test. The best known versions of the test are *NFPA 258* and *ASTM E662.*

Toxicity Test

Toxicity testing is currently required only in a few states. The *Pitts Test* or *LC-50* is the most commonly used test and was developed by the University of Pittsburgh. It measures the amount of toxicity a material omits when it is burned. The testing covers a wide range of materials in addition to finishes and furniture. Included are wall, ceiling, and floor finishes, furniture upholstery, mattresses, and bed pads as well as electrical wire and conduit, mechanical ductwork, thermal insulation, and plumbing pipes.

The test determines an *LC-50* rating in addition to other variables. Although it is a rated test, at this time there are no set standard ratings. Therefore, when selecting a finish or furnishing you should compare two or more products with *LC-50* ratings. The higher the test score the better, since higher ratings are less toxic. Some jurisdictions try to stay within or above the natural wood ratings of *LC16* through *LC25.*

Toxicity testing is a relatively new. Some manufacturers are starting to list *LC-50* ratings on their products, however, in many cases the results may not be readily available. New York State was the first to enforce the test and keeps a database of all the finishes and products that have been tested. To sell in New York State, manufacturers are required to register the test results with New York's Department of State, Office of Fire Prevention and Control in Albany, New York. To obtain the *LC-50* rating for a product, you must first get the Department of State (DOS) or Listed Pending Review (LPR) number from the manufacturer and then contact New York State to receive a report containing the testing information for that product.

> **Note**
>
> The *LSC* and the building codes do not necessarily mention or require every finish and furniture test mentioned here, yet many are required locally.

Upholstered Seating Test

Upholstered seating (and mattresses) are tested in full scale tests or small scale tests. A full scale test can use a mock-up of the piece of furniture or an actual piece of furniture, whereas a small scale test uses smaller mock-ups of parts of a piece of furniture.

Full Scale Tests: Tests that are considered full scale tests include *Cal 133, NFPA 266, ASTM E1537,* and *UL 1056.* The *California Technical Bulletin 133,* also referred to as either *CAL 133* or *TB 133,* was the first test of its kind. The test is a pass/fail test of a *whole* piece of furniture rather than of an individual finish or material. It was originally developed for furniture used in public spaces in the state of California, but it has become a more common requirement throughout the country and in a number of different occupancies. It is intended for furniture in public buildings in any area or room that contains 10 or more pieces of seating furniture. This applies to prisons, health care facilities, nursing homes, day care facilities, stadiums, and auditoriums, public assembly areas in hotels and motels.

The aim of the test is to eliminate the flashover that occurs in the second phase of a fire. It is a flame resistance test that measures the carbon monoxide, heat generation, smoke, temperature, and weight loss of an entire piece of furniture. It is up to manufacturers to have their furniture tested and appropriately labeled. Note that the individual materials that make up the furniture cannot be approved for individual use. The entire piece of furniture must be tested and approved. (See inset titled Using CAL 133 on the facing page.) Since this is a requirement not typically found in the building codes, it is up to you to select furniture that passes this test when it is required.

Since its conception a number of cities and other states have followed California's lead and are also enforcing *CAL 133* or one of the other similar standards. More are planning to follow suit. Those that already have or are soon planning to pass the legislation for *CAL 133* include California, Illinois, Massachusetts, Minnesota, New Jersey, Ohio, the Port Authority of New York and New Jersey, and the city of Boston. Be sure to check with the jurisdiction of your project.

Small Scale Tests: *NFPA 272* is a small scale test that applies to both upholstered furniture and to mattresses. *NFPA 272* was formerly issued as *NFPA 264A.* ASTM's version of the test is known as *ASTM 1474.* This test measures how quickly upholstered furniture and mattresses will ignite. It also measures the rate of heat release.

> **Note**
>
> Not all upholstered furniture will require *CAL 133* testing. Some may just require a smolder resistance test. The results of both tests can be improved with the use of certain fabric backcoatings, interliners, fire blockers, and special rated foams.

> **Note**
>
> Many furniture manufacturers currently offer *CAL 133*-compliant products. It is required of all members of both the Business and Institutional Furniture Manufacturers Association (BIFMA) and the American Furniture Manufacturers Association (AFMA).

USING CAL 133

Whether or not CAL 133 is required in your jurisdiction, you may want to specify CAL 133-tested products whenever possible. Furniture testing is becoming more accepted and enforced throughout the country. As laws and standards are getting stricter, there are more areas of liability for the designer. (Refer to the section on Documentation and Liability on page 262.) Here are some issues to consider:

1. Selecting a special fabric or "C.O.M." (customer's own material) will change the CAL 133 test results of a piece of furniture. The cost of retesting by the manufacturer may be passed on to you. The lead time or length of production may also be extended.

2. You may have the option of specifying a fire block liner to make a piece of furniture CAL 133 compliant. Fire block liners are often used between the foam and upholstery instead of using a flame retardant foam. You must work with the manufacturer.

3. Buildings with sprinklers are not always required to have CAL 133 tested furniture. However, if a fire occurs, the lack of tested furniture can become an issue.

4. Be aware that specifying custom furniture, as well as having furniture reupholstered, can be a problem. Unless you build a mock-up and have it tested there is no way a one-of-a-kind piece of furniture can be tested under CAL 133. It ruins the piece being tested.

The test applies to upholstered furniture and mattresses in commercial, institutional, and high risk occupancies.

Mattresses

Although mattresses can be tested using the small-scale tests mentioned in the previous section, there are other tests that apply only to mattresses. These include *NFPA 267, ASTM E1590, California Technical Bulletin 129* (or *CAL 129*), and *FF4-72*. The first three tests are used to determine the heat release, smoke density, generation of toxic gases (carbon monoxide) and weight loss that occur when an individual mattress or mattress with its foundation is exposed to a flame. This test method uses a full scale mattress in an open calorimeter environment and applies to bedding used in public occupancies, such as hotels and dormitories.

The *FF4-72* test, also called the *Standard for Flammability of Mattresses*, is required by the government and is applicable to mattresses used in single-family dwellings as well as commercial projects. It is a pass/fail test that measures the char size created when exposed to a lit cigarette. It is required for most types of mattresses as well as mattress pads.

Note

For more technical information on testing procedures and performance criteria you may wish to consult S.C. Reznicoff's *Specifications for Commercial Interiors.*

Other tests may be required for both finishes and furniture. The required test for a finish depends on the application of the finish. For example, the same fabric will need a different test or more than one test, depending on whether it is used as a drapery, an upholstery, or a wall covering. (See Figure 9.9.) Furnishings have their own tests, depending on where they are used. Certain jurisdictions may also require other tests not listed here. Be sure to check with the local code official.

Additional tests continue to be developed as concerns for other safety issues are identified. The government, standard organizations, and industry representatives must consider if new regulations are warranted. Often their decisions are based on actual occurrences that cause unreasonable risk of death, injury, or significant property loss.

USING THE CODES

As mentioned earlier, each of the building codes and the LSC have a chapter on interior finishes. Each chapter is organized to include wall and ceiling finishes, floor finishes, and decorations and trim. Some of the standards and tests described earlier in this chapter are required by the codes. These will be listed within the text of each code. Which one you need to use will depend on what type of finish you are using and where it is being applied. (Also note that interior finishes may be referred to in other chapters of the building code, such as the chapter on Plastics, and in the plumbing code.)

Each building code chapter also includes a table that specifies required finishes for certain means of egress and types of buildings. For example, the table in Figure 9.3 is Table A.10.2.2, "Interior Finish Classification," from the appendix of the LSC. Each of the building codes contains similar information. The NBC uses Table 803.4, "Interior Finish Requirements," the SBC uses Table 803.3, "Minimum Interior Finish Classification," the UBC uses a similar Table 8-B, "Maximum Flame-Spread Class," and the IBC uses Table 803.4, "Interior Wall and Ceiling Finish Requirements by Occupancy."

The Table

Depending on the jurisdiction of your project, you may need to compare the requirements of the building code and the LSC. The LSC table is more comprehensive than the building codes in that (1) it specifies finish classes for interior floor coverings, using

Classes I and II, in addition to Classes A, B, and C for interior wall and ceiling finishes, and (2) it has divided the occupancy classifications into new and existing buildings. To use the table in Figure 9.3 correctly you need to be familiar with the five different finish classes. There are three classes for wall and ceiling finishes (Classes A, B, and C), which are obtained using the *Steiner Tunnel Tests*, and two separate classes for interior floor finishes (Classes I and II), which are obtained using the *Radiant Panel Tests*. (Refer to sections earlier in this chapter.) These different classes recognize that when escaping a fire within a building, people must move away from the flames while traveling through the means of egress toward an exit. It is important for the exits to be free of fire and smoke for safety and visibility. Therefore, the assigned classes become stricter as you move toward an exit and are the strictest at the exit.

Before using the *LSC* table you need to determine both the occupancy classification of your building and whether it is considered "new" or "existing." (This is described in Chapter 2.) Once you know the occupancy, the table lists the finish classes allowed in each area of the building. Each of the codes divides these areas the same way. They consist of exits, accesses to exits, and other rooms or spaces. (Refer to the section on Types of Means of Egress on page 78 for a description of each.) As you read across the table in Figure 9.3 for a particular occupancy it will tell you which class of finishes is allowed in each of these areas. Generally, the closer you get to the exterior of a building or exit discharge, the stricter class rating and fire resistance the finish must have.

Notice in the table that some occupancies have a symbol or footnote following the recorded class. This indicates that the occupancy has further finish restrictions or requirements. Further research will be required in the *LSC* or the building codes under the specified occupancy. These occupancies typically include

Health Care
Detentional/Correctional
Residential—Hotels and dormitories
Residential—Apartment buildings
Unusual Structures

The general rule of thumb is that stricter finishes are required in occupancies where the occupants are immobile or have security measures imposed on them that restrict freedom of movement, such as Health Care facilities and Detentional/Correctional facili-

Note

If you are working on a building in one of the cities or states having its own code, you must check that jurisdiction for further requirements. (More states are beginning to increase their standards as well.)

Note

The *LSC* and the building codes have different rules on sprinklers. See Chapter 6 and the codes for more information.

ties, or where occupants are provided with overnight accommodations, such as hotels and dormitories. In contrast, more relaxed requirements are found in Industrial and Storage occupancies where occupants are assumed to be alert, mobile, and fewer in number.

Note also at the bottom of the table how automatic sprinklers used throughout a building can change the required finish class ratings. Some of the tables used by the building codes specify this information more clearly within the table. Therefore, it is important to know if the building you are working on is sprinklered and where the sprinklers are located.

Example

Figure 9.4 is a floor plan of a grade school without a sprinkler system. If you were designing the interiors of this existing school, you would refer to a code table such as the table in Figure 9.3. Under "Educational—Existing" in the occupancy column of this table it tells you the following:

Table A.10.2.2 **Interior Finish Classification Limitations**

Occupancy	Exits	Access to Exits	Other Spaces
Assembly — New			
>300 occupant load	A	A or B	A or B
≤300 occupant load	A	A or B	A, B, or C
Assembly — Existing			
>300 occupant load	A	A or B	A or B
≤300 occupant load	A	A or B	A, B, or C
Educational — New	A	A or B	A or B, C on low partitions†
Educational — Existing	A	A or B	A, B, or C
Day-Care Centers — New	A I or II	A I or II	A or B NR
Day-Care Centers — Existing	A or B	A or B	A or B
Group Day-Care Homes — New	A or B	A or B	A, B, or C
Group Day-Care Homes — Existing	A or B	A, B, or C	A, B, or C
Family Day-Care Homes	A or B	A, B, or C	A, B, or C

Figure 9.3. *Life Safety Code (LSC)* Table A.10.2.2, "Interior Finish Classification Limitations." (Reprinted with permission from 2000 *Life Safety Code*, Copyright 2000 National Fire Protection Association, Quincy, MA 02269. This reprinted material is not the complete and official position of the National Fire Protection Association on the referenced subject, which is represented only by the standard in its entirety.)

Table A.10.2.2 Interior Finish Classification Limitations *(Continued)*

Occupancy	Exits	Access to Exits	Other Spaces
Health Care — New (sprinklers mandatory)	A or B	A or B C on lower potion of corridor wall[†]	A or B C in small individual rooms[†]
Health Care — Existing	A or B	A or B	A or B
Detention and Correctional — New	A[†] I	A[†] I	A, B, or C
Detention and Correctional — Existing	A or B[†] I or II	A or B[†] I or II	A, B, or C
1- and 2-Family Dwellings, Lodging or Rooming Houses	A, B, or C	A, B, or C	A, B, or C
Hotels and Dormitories — New	A I or II	A or B I or II	A, B, or C
Hotels and Dormitories — Existing	A or B I or II[†]	A or B I or II[†]	A, B, or C
Apartment Buildings — New	A I or II[†]	A or B I or II[†]	A, B, or C
Apartment Buildings — Existing	A or B I or II[†]	A or B I or II[†]	A, B, or C
Residential, Board and Care — *(See Chapters 32 and 33.)*			
Mercantile — New	A or B	A or B	A or B
Mercantile — Existing Class A or Class B	A or B	A or B	Ceilings — A or B, walls — A, B, or C
Mercantile — Existing Class C	A, B, or C	A, B, or C	A, B, or C
Business and Ambulatory Health Care — New	A or B I or II	A or B I or II	A, B, or C
Business and Ambulatory Health Care — Existing	A or B	A or B	A, B, or C
Industrial	A or B	A, B, or C	A, B, or C
Storage	A or B	A, B, or C	A, B, or C

NR: No requirement.
Notes:
1. Class A interior wall and ceiling finish — flame spread 0–25, (new) smoke developed 0–450.
2. Class B interior wall and ceiling finish — flame spread 26–75, (new) smoke developed 0–450.
3. Class C interior wall and ceiling finish — flame spread 76–200, (new) smoke developed 0–450.
4. Class I interior floor finish — critical radiant flux, not less than 0.45 W/cm².
5. Class II interior floor finish — critical radiant flux, not less than 0.22 W/cm² but less than 0.45 W/cm².
6. Automatic sprinklers — where a complete standard system of automatic sprinklers is installed, interior wall and ceiling finish with flame spread rating not exceeding Class C is permitted to be used in any location where Class B is required and with rating of Class B in any location where Class A is required; similarly, Class II interior floor finish is permitted to be used in any location where Class I is required, and no critical radiant flux rating is required where Class II is required. These provisions do not apply to new health care facilities.
7. Exposed portions of structural members complying with the requirements for heavy timber construction are permitted.
[†]See corresponding chapters for details.

Figure 9.3. Continued.

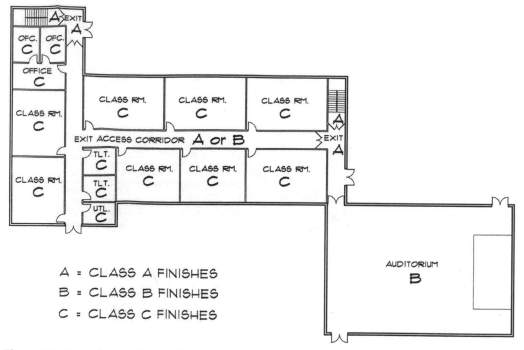

A = CLASS A FINISHES

B = CLASS B FINISHES

C = CLASS C FINISHES

Figure 9.4. Example: Grade School.

◆ Class A wall and ceiling finishes must be used in all exit areas of the school.

◆ Class A or B finishes are both allowed in access areas such as corridors and stairs.

◆ Any of the three classes (A, B, or C) is allowed in all the remaining spaces, such as classrooms, offices, and so on.

However, many grade schools are a mixed occupancy because of the gymnasiums, auditoriums, and/or cafeterias typically built with them. If this grade school has an auditorium, for example, that holds between 150 and 300 people, the finish requirements for this area must be found in the table under "Assembly—Existing" in the occupancy column. In this case, Class C finishes will not be allowed in the general areas of this assembly space.

If you were selecting wallcoverings, for example, for the grade school, you would have to decide whether to (1) use a different type of wallcovering in the auditorium assembly and access areas so you could possibly use less expensive Class C wallcovering in the remainder of the school or (2) upgrade all general area wallcovering in the educational part of the school to a Class B so the wallcoverings in the school would match those of the auditorium. (Class A wall and ceiling finishes will still be required in the exit areas.)

Notice that the table does not specify a particular class of interior floor finish for either of the occupancies mentioned above. On the other hand, you could be designing the interior of a new day care center. Although this is still an Educational occupancy, the table indicates that you must use floor coverings that have been tested using one of the standard *Flooring Radiant Panel Tests*. (See Figure 9.2.)

OBTAINING TEST RESULTS

Some of the standards and tests mentioned earlier in this chapter are specifically referenced and, therefore, required by the code. Others are industry standards that you must be familiar with so that you know when to reference and use them. Regardless, the results of all the tests described in this chapter can be listed in several ways: some of the tests are pass/fail, while others determine and assign a specific class or ranked rating. For example, the *CAL 133* and the *NFPA 701* tests are strictly pass/fail tests. If a finish passes, you are allowed to use it; if it fails, you cannot use it.

Other tests, such as the *Steiner Tunnel Test* and the *Radiant Panel Test*, assign class ratings to the tested finishes. Still others, such as *LC-50*, provide you with a ranked number rating. In both these cases, the manufacturer must supply you with the letter or number rating for these tests. For example, a tunnel test will result in an A, B, or C rating. You then compare these ratings to what is required by the codes. (When selecting finishes you need to make sure you are given the correct information by the manufacturer.)

Figure 9.2 indicates which tests are pass/fail and which provide class or ranked ratings. The important thing to remember is that most manufacturers typically test their products before putting them on the market. Manufacturers realize that their finishes and furnishings must meet code requirements if you are going to specify them. To use these products it is crucial for you to know how to find and obtain the required test results.

Pretested Finishes

Many manufacturers either list the test results on their samples and products or are able to provide the information to you upon request. Some examples include the written information on the back of carpet books and on cards attached to fabric samples. You

> **Note**
>
> As the designer, it is important that you keep abreast of the most current testing and code requirements. Even if your jurisdiction does not require it, you should specify the most advanced tests and materials. If you are ever held liable you must prove you used the most advanced requirements at the time you designed the project. (See Chapter 10.)

Note

Manufacturer representatives can be very helpful in determining technical and code information on their products. Remember, manufacturers need to comply with the industry standards to remain competitive.

can find similar labels and information on most wall coverings, floor coverings, ceiling coverings, and other finishes. Even certain furniture must be labeled with the required tests.

Figure 9.5 is a copy from the back of two different fabric samples made by KnollTextiles. Along with other necessary information, each KnollTextiles label indicates the standard tests the fabric has passed.

If you refer to the sample A in Figure 9.5, you are able to determine immediately which tests the fabric passes. Each test standard that this fabric meets is listed under "Flame Retardant Ratings." To determine the type of tests the fabric in sample B has passed, you need some additional information. Note the five symbols near the bottom of the label. Each of the symbols indicates that the fabric has passed certain industry standards.

These symbols were created by the Association for Contract Textiles (ACT). ACT was founded in 1985 to provide the design industry with information to help designers choose the right products for their projects. Concentrating on the contract interiors market, ACT sets standards for upholstery, wallcoverings, panels and upholstered walls, and drapery. The five symbols shown in Figure 9.6 are voluntarily used by a large number of textile manufacturers on their products. The symbols indicate a material's characteristics in flame resistance, colorfastness, physical properties (such as pilling, breaking, and seam slippage), and

Name	Quadrate
	Hazel Siegel Design ©1990
Style Number	K643/3
Color	Navy
Content	Cotton 52%, Rayon 48%
Width	52 inches
Repeat	3¼ inches horizontal, 3¼ inches vertical

Flame Retardant Rating: ASTM E-84. Class "A" flamespread rating. Passes. UL #723, NFPA #255, ANSI #2.5, California Bulletin #117.

Light Fastness: Meets 40 hour NAFM requirement. AATCC-16A test method.

Durability: Exceeds 70,000 double rubs. NAFM requirement 15,000 double rubs. Wyzenbeek Test Method.

KnollTextiles. A Division of Knoll International. P.O. Box 157 East Greenville, PA 18041   800 523.0346 / 800 343.KNOLL

A

Name	Calligraphy
Style Number	K369/9
Color	Iris
Content	Rayon 51%, Polyester 49%
Width	54 inches
Repeat	5 inches vertical, 6¾ inches horizontal
Primary Use	Upholstery

Flame Retardant Rating: California Technical Bulletin #117 - Section E.

Colorfastness: AATCC-8, Wet Crocking, Class 4.5. Dry Crocking, Class 5.

Lightfastness: AATCC-16E, Class 5 at 40 hours.

Physical Properties: Brush pill ASTM D3511. Breaking strength ASTM D3597-D1682-6. Seam slippage ASTM D3597-D434-75.

Durability: Exceeds 70,000 double rubs Wyzenbeek Method.

Cleaning Code: S

†Copyright: This style is a copyrighted textile design. ©Knoll 1998. All rights reserved.

KnollTextiles.   P.O. Box 157 East Greenville, PA 18041
Knoll   1 800 343-5665

B

Figure 9.5. Sample Finish Labels. (Reprinted with permission from KnollTextiles.)

Flame Resistance

Flammability testing determines a fabric's resistance to burning.

APPLICATION	PASSES
Upholstery	California 117 Section E
Direct Glue Wallcoverings	ASTM E 84 (adhered method)
Panels and Upholstered Walls	ASTM E 84 (unadhered method)
Drapery	N.F.P.A. 701 Small Scale

Colorfastness to Wet & Dry Crocking

Colorfastness to wet & dry crocking refers to the rubbing off of color from the fabric onto clothing, hands or other materials and can occur under wet or dry conditions.

APPLICATION	PASSES
Upholstery	AATCC 8 Dry Crocking, Class 4 minimum Wet Crocking, Class 3 minimum
Direct Glue Wallcoverings	AATCC 8, Class 3 minimum
Panels and Upholstered Walls	AATCC 8, Class 3 minimum
Drapery	AATCC 8 (solids) AATCC 116 (prints) Class 3 minimum

Colorfastness to Light

Colorfastness to light is the degree to which fabric will retain its color when exposed to light.

APPLICATION	PASSES
Upholstery	AATCC 16A or AATCC 16E Class 4 minimum at 40 hours
Direct Glue Wallcoverings	AATCC 16A or AATCC 16E Class 4 minimum at 40 hours
Panels and Upholstered Walls	AATCC 16A or AATCC 16E Class 4 minimum at 40 hours
Drapery	AATCC 16A or AATCC 16E Class 4 minimum at 60 hours

Physical Properties

3 physical property tests include: brush pill test to determine a fabric's pilling. Breaking/tensile strength is the ability of a fabric to withstand tension without breaking or tearing. Seam slippage is the pulling apart of fabrics at the seams.

APPLICATION	PASSES
Upholstery	Brush pill ASTM D3511, 3 minimum Breaking strength ASTM D3597-D1682-64 50 lbs. minimum in warp & weft Seam slippage ASTM D3597-D434 25 lbs. minimum in warp & weft
Panels and Upholstered Walls	Breaking strength D5034 Grab Method 35 lbs. minimum in warp & weft Seam slippage ASTM D3597-434 25 lbs. minimum in warp & weft
Drapery	Seam slippage ASTM D3597-434 for fabrics over 6 oz./sq. yard 25 lbs. minimum in warp & weft Seam slippage ASTM D3597-434 for fabrics under 6 oz./sq. yard 15 lbs. minimum in warp & weft

Abrasion

Abrasion is the ability of a fabric to withstand damage from wear and rubbing. There is a general contract specification as well as a heavy duty specification.

APPLICATION	PASSES
General Contract Upholstery	ASTM 3597 modified (#10 cotton duck) 15,000 double rubs Wyzenbeek Method
Heavy Duty Upholstery	ASTM 3597 modified (#10 cotton duck) 30,000 double rubs Wyzenbeek method ASTM D4966 (21 oz. weight) 40,000 rubs Martindale method

heavy duty   general contract

Figure 9.6. ACT Textile Performance Guidelines. (Reprinted with permission from Association for Contract Textiles.)

abrasion. For each symbol, ACT indicates the test(s) or standard(s) that the material must meet in order to bear the symbol.

Although all this information is important to you as the designer, the main symbol that relates directly to the codes is the flame resistance symbol. In Figure 9.6, beside the symbol for the flame resistance, the type of application for the interior finish and the standards that it meets are listed. The flame symbol indicates that a fabric has passed the *Steiner Tunnel Test* (*ASTM E 84*), the vertical flame test (*NFPA 701*), and the smolder resistance test (*California Bulletin 117*). So, if a material's specifications or tag indicate the flame symbol, then you automatically know that the material passes those tests.

Referring back to sample B in Figure 9.5, since the label has a flame symbol, you are now able to tell which tests that fabric has passed. (Under the category "Flame Retardant Ratings," *CAL 117* is listed as well. This is redundant, since the flame symbol already indicates the same requirements.) Once you are familiar with the symbols, it will make selection of flame resistant materials easier.

Nontested Finishes

Note

Certain finishes may also be required in toilets and restrooms, but these are usually specified in the plumbing codes.

There will be situations when testing information is not available. For example, you may select a finish that is geared toward residential use where codes are not as strict, or a finish from a smaller manufacturer that makes specialty items and cannot afford to test all of its finishes. In these cases it is up to you to have the finish tested or make sure it is properly treated.

The standards organizations can help you determine where to get your finishes tested. There are a number of *testing companies* throughout the country that will perform the tests necessary to classify a material. Figure 9.7 provides a list of some of these flame testing agencies. (Note that some are treatment companies as well.)

Applied Textiles Lab Services
Better Fabrics Testing Bureau
Building Technologies (Finland)
CSTB (France)
Inchape Testing Services
Kiesling-Hess Fabric Service Company, Inc.
Southwest Research Institute
United States Testing Company
Warnock Hersey International, Inc.

Figure 9.7. Flame Testing Agencies.

However, these tests can be very costly since they need to be performed under conditions simulating actual installations. For example, a wallcovering should be tested with the adhesive that will be used to secure it to the wall, or a carpet with the padding that will be used underneath it. The alternative is to have the finish treated instead. This is often much more cost effective.

There are several *treatment companies* that will add fire retardant coatings, also known as flame resistant finishes, to materials that have not initially passed the required tests. (Ask your local manufacturer's representative for locations.) These retardants can be either a surface treatment or a fire resistant coating applied as a backing. They will delay ignition of a material and slow flame spread without changing the basic nature of the material. They can also lower the smoke development value. You send the treatment company your fabric or any other finish and tell them which tests your finish must comply with. The treatment company will add the appropriate fire retardant coating. (See inset titled Fire Retardant Treatments on page 242.)

For example, if you know a fabric wallcovering needs to have a Class B rating, tell the company it must meet the *Steiner Tunnel Test*'s B rating. If you are working in one of the stricter jurisdictions, such as New York City you can tell the testing company that your fabric needs to pass Port Authority regulations or any of the other required codes.

The fire retardant treatments can usually upgrade nonclassed finishes and can even improve the performance of some rated materials to a higher class. Upon completion of the work, the treatment company will send you a Certificate of Flame Resistance, similar to the one shown in Figure 9.8, indicating which tests the fabric will pass.

Similar steps must be taken for any finish or furnishing when the necessary test results are not given by the manufacturer. This can include, but is not limited to, any of the finishes listed in Figure 9.9.

FINISHES VERSUS FURNITURE

As mentioned earlier, some cities and states issue their own regulatory standards on upholstered furniture. For example, New York state has created strict codes relating to toxicity. In addition, more cities and states are also beginning to adopt the *California Technical Bulletin 133*, as discussed earlier.

Whether or not you are working in one of the more stringent fire code jurisdictions, it is important to determine if you are

Note

Whenever concentrated amounts of furniture are used in a project, be sure to check the design load of the building or space. (See Design Loads, p. 47.) Some examples include library areas, file rooms, and assembly seating.

Resistflame Finishing Company
7115 Miami Ave
Cincinnati, OH 45243

Certificate of Flame Resistance

We certify the following material was treated for:

Bill To:

Ship To:

HOLY FAMILY CHURCH FLAMEPROOFING

Invoice Number	Ship Date	Order Number	Customer PO

Description of Treated Material:

					Qty	Pieces
1	Yards	MULTI	21 ASSORTED DRAPERY PANELS	MULTI		
	RESISTFLAME	Minimum Charge			1	1

TEST RESULTS OF THIS MATERIAL MEETS NFPA REQUIREMENTS FOR FLAME RETARDANT, CODE 701 (SMALL SCALE). TESTS MADE OF FABRICS WHICH HAVE BEEN TREATED DEMONSTRATE THAT FLAME RESISTANCE WILL WITHSTAND UP TO TWENTY (20) SOLVENT DRYCLEANINGS.

Resistflame Finishing Company
7115 Miami Ave
Cincinnati, OH 45243

THOMAS L. APPLEGATE II
PRESIDENT

Figure 9.8. Sample Certificate of Flame Resistance. (Reprinted with permission from Keisling-Hess.)

FINISH CATEGORY	FINISH EXAMPLES	TYPICAL TEST REQUIRED
CEILING TREATMENTS	Ceiling Tiles Special Finishes	Steiner Tunnel Test Corner Test
WALL COVERINGS	Vinyl Wallcoverings Fabric Wallcoverings Wood Paneling Wood Veneers	Steiner Tunnel Test Corner Test
FLOOR COVERINGS	Carpets Rugs Carpet Padding Hard Surface Flooring Resilient Flooring	Pill Test Radiant Panel Test Steiner Tunnel Test
WINDOW TREATMENTS	Draperies Liners Blinds Wood Shutters	Vertical Flame Test Steiner Tunnel Test
UPHOLSTERIES	Fabrics Vinyls Battings Welt Cords Foams Interliners Fillings	Steiner Tunnel Test Smolder Resistance Test Smoke Density Test
FURNITURE	Seating Panel Systems Mattresses	Smolder Resistance Test Upholstered Seating Test Mattress Test

NOTE: Any of the finish or furniture applications listed above may also require a toxicity test.

Figure 9.9. Typical Regulated Finishes.

selecting a finish or a furnishing. This is not always a simple task. There are certain items that may take on different meanings, depending on your jurisdiction and your project. When necessary, be sure to get clarification from the code officials in the jurisdiction where your project is located.

Below are some of the most common discrepancies:

1. **Carpet:** In some jurisdictions a carpet is considered a furnishing if it is installed over a finished floor. Yet in other instances it is considered an interior finish, such as when it is installed directly over concrete.

2. **Movable Partitions:** Movable walls or panel partitions come in a variety of styles and sizes. In some jurisdictions these may be classified as furnishings; in others they may

be classified as temporary walls. (When classified as walls you must refer to the fire separation sections of the codes.)

3. **Draperies/Wall Hangings:** Most window treatments are not regulated by codes unless they cover large portions of a wall. Many codes consider draperies a finish only if they cover more than 5 to 10 percent of wall area. Tapestry and any other textile hangings are considered the same. (See the discussion of *NFPA 701* in the earlier section on Standards and Testing.)

4. **Built-In Cabinetry and Seating:** When there is a continuous expanse of plastic laminates and wood veneers due to custom millwork, many jurisdictions will regard these surfaces as interior finishes. In addition, high back upholstered restaurant booths can also be restricted in certain jurisdictions.

Note

If a regulation defines a carpet as a floor covering only, do not specify it as a wallcovering without further clarification or testing. (See the discussion of the Corner Test earlier in this chapter.)

ACCESSIBILITY REGULATIONS

The *ADAAG* and the accessibility standards from the American National Standards Institute (ANSI) put very few accessibility restrictions on finishes and furniture. The pertaining regulations can be broken down into three categories: floor finishes, seating, and work surfaces. These are described below. Be sure to check

FIRE RETARDANT TREATMENTS

Fire retardant treatments can alter finishes and furniture in various ways. Below are a number of problems that can occur when a fire retardant is added to a fabric:

1. The fabric may shrink.
2. The hand or feel of the fabric may change, perhaps resulting in stiffening of the fabric.
3. The strength of the fabric may decrease, causing it to tear easier.
4. If a fabric has a texture, the texture may flatten or become distorted.
5. The fabric may give off toxic fumes, especially in the presence of fire.
6. A wet treatment may cause the dye in the fabric to bleed or possibly change or fade in the future.

If you are concerned about any of these issues, consult the company treating the fabric and, when necessary, submit a sample for testing prior to purchasing or treating the entire amount. The results are often based on the content of the fabric and the type of treatment used. (It is also better to have a fabric treated prior to applying it to a surface or furniture in case there are any problems.)

the *ADAAG* regulations and the ANSI standards for the specifics and the strictest requirements.

Currently, floor coverings are the main type of finish regulated by the *ADAAG*. The *ADAAG* requires that the floor surface along accessible routes and in accessible rooms be slip-resistant. Other floor finishes, such as carpet and padding, cannot be too thick or too loose and must be securely fastened at the edges. This is often accomplished in commercial projects by using carpet that directly glues to the floor (without padding). The *ADAAG* requires beveled transitions or ramps for even slight changes in elevation that can occur between different floor surfaces. (The *ADAAG* and ANSI standards give specific dimensions.) The goal is to make sure wheelchairs have easy access.

Flooring surfaces that create detectable warnings may also be required in certain occupancies. A detectable warning consists of a change in floor finish to alert someone with poor vision of an approaching obstacle or change in level. The warnings typically consist of strips of contrasting textures, such as alternative smooth and rough stone or grooved concrete. Although they are mostly required on the exterior of a building, they can apply to the interior as well, for example, at an entrance to a hazardous area or at the top of an escalator or exposed stairway.

Accessibility regulations for furniture can be divided into seating and work surfaces. It is not the type of seat that is regulated, but rather the number and location that are provided for wheelchairs. Currently, in all accessible public and common use areas a certain amount of the seating spaces must be provided for wheelchairs. For example, restaurants must provide wheelchair access to the tables. The placement of the surrounding furniture must also allow the required maneuvering areas, even though the furniture may seem movable, and all fixed-seating areas must allow for wheelchair placement at various seating locations. This is especially important in Assembly occupancies. (Refer to the *ADAAG* for more specific requirements.)

Worksurface regulations refer to tables and desks as well as counter tops. To be accessible their heights must range between 28 and 34 inches above the floor, with at least 27 inches to be clear for kneespace. There are also depth and width restrictions.

Note

Directly gluing a carpet to the floor instead of using a pad will help to eliminate thickness problems as well as future warping or binding of the carpet during wheelchair use.

Note

Although other finishes are not currently regulated by the *ADAAG*, you may want to do additional research on finishes that can be helpful, especially in public spaces. For example, darker baseboards may be helpful in corridors for those who are visually impaired.

OTHER RESTRICTIONS

Below are some universal code restrictions used by most of the building codes. However, you will always run into exceptions and

Note

When considering more specific code requirements remember that some jurisdictions are still using older editions of the code publications. These editions are not always as strict as the newer ones.

Note

Vinyl wallcovering is regulated in all thicknesses because of its burning characteristics. It has a high smoke density.

Note

Often, the Sprinkler Rule is not accepted by the building codes, even though the *LSC* allows it. Check with your jurisdiction.

Note

When renovating an existing space you should always remove existing finishes before installing new.

unusual circumstances. For these you should consult your local code official. The importance of knowing what is expected and enforced by the officials in the jurisdiction of your project cannot be stressed enough.

1. **10 Percent Rule**: When trims and decorative finishes are kept to a minimum of 10 percent of the wall and ceiling areas of a space, they can usually have a lower rating than what is typically required. The finishes must be evenly distributed, such as crown molding or wainscoting. If they are concentrated in a specific area, such as a paneled law office, this rule does not apply.

2. **$\frac{1}{28}$ Inch Rule**: Any wall or ceiling covering that is more than $\frac{1}{28}$ inch thick is to be treated as an interior finish. Therefore, thermally thin finishes such as paint and most wallpapers (not vinyl wallcoverings) when applied to noncombustible building material do not have to be rated. Noncombustible building materials include gypsum board, brick, and concrete. (This rule does not apply when finishes are continually applied on top of each other.)

3. **Furring Strips**: When interior finishes are applied to furring strips instead of directly to noncombustible building material, the furring strips cannot exceed a thickness of 1¾ inches. In addition, the intervening spaces between the strips must be filled with a fire-rated material or fire blocked at intervals not more than 8 feet.

4. **Sprinkler Rule**: When a building has an automatic sprinkler system, finish class ratings may be lowered, and finishes without ratings may sometimes replace rated finishes. (Be sure to check with the jurisdiction of your project.)

5. **Means of Egress**: All exits and paths of travel to and from the exits must be clear of furnishings, decorations, or other objects. This includes no draperies on or obscuring exits doors and no mirrors on or adjacent to exit doors. In addition, attention must not be drawn away from the exit sign.

6. **Structural Building Elements**: Exposed building structural members, such as wood columns, heavy timber beams, and girders, are typically allowed, since they occur on specific spacings and do not constitute a continuous surface to allow flame spread. (These architectural regulations are specified by the structural sections of the codes.)

7. **Foam Plastics**: Cellular or foamed plastic materials cannot be used as wall or ceiling finishes unless positively tested

or unless they comply with the 10-percent rule. (Some minimal exceptions do apply in the building codes.)

Interior finishes may be further restricted by the occupancy classification of a building. Certain building occupancies require stricter codes and more specific requirements. These additional requirements are addressed by the building codes, the *LSC*, the *ADAAG*, and the ANSI standards in specific occupancy sections.

Generally, occupancies where the occupants have evacuation difficulties have stricter requirements than occupancies with fully mobile occupants. The occupancies that allow overnight provision for multiple occupants are usually the strictest. These include Health Care facilities, Detentional/Correctional facilities, and most Residential occupancies (except single-family homes). For example, hotels must use additionally rated finishes and furnishings such as bedding and draperies.

CHECKLIST

The checklist in Figure 9.10 has been designed to help you with any project that requires finish and/or furniture selection. It can be used for one particular project, or a separate checklist can be used for each space or room within the project. This is helpful if you have a variety of rooms or spaces, each with its own finishes and furnishings. It is also helpful when some rooms or areas have stricter requirements than others. For example, a project may include exits and exit accesses. Not only are the requirements for these more public areas stricter, but you will typically select finishes and furniture for these areas that are different from those of the other areas within the project.

The first part of the checklist asks you for the project name, the space name or number (when required), the occupancy classification of the project (and whether it is new or existing), and the building type. It is important to determine the occupancy and the building type in the beginning, since both are needed to determine which tests are required by the codes.

The rest of the checklist assists you with finish selection and testing research. The first column lists the most common wall finishes, ceiling finishes, floor coverings, draperies, and furnishings. Check the ones that will be used in your room or project so you can narrow down the amount of finishes and furnishings that must be researched, tested, or treated. Blank spaces have been left to fill in items not listed on the checklist.

FINISHES AND FURNITURE CHECKLIST

PROJECT NAME:_____ SPACE: _____

OCCUPANCY (new or existing):_____

TYPE OF SPACE (check one): _____ EXIT _____ EXIT ACCESS _____ OTHER SPACE

REGULATED FINISHES AND FURNISHINGS (check those that apply)	TEST METHOD REQUIRED (fill in test name)	MANUFACTURER AND CATALOG #	MANUFACTURER TESTED (yes or no)	FINISH TREATMENT (yes or no)	DATE COMPLETED
WALL COVERING __ Vinyl Wallcovering __ Fabric Wallcovering __ Wood Paneling __ Wood Veneers __ Carpet __ Decorative Molding __ Other:_____					
FLOOR COVERING __ Carpet __ Rugs __ Carpet Padding __ Vinyl Tile __ Hardwood __ Other:_____					
CEILING FINISH __ Ceiling Tile __ Linear Ceiling __ Decorative Molding __ Other:_____					
WINDOW TREATMENT __ Draperies __ Liners __ Blinds __ Wood Shutters __ Other:_____					
FURNISHINGS __ Fabric __ Vinyl __ Batting __ Welt Cord __ Interliners __ Filling __ Seating __ Mattresses __ Other:_____					

NOTES:

1. Refer to codes and standards for specific information. Also check the *ADAAG* for finish and furniture requirements.

2 . Attach all testing verification including copies of manufacturer labels and treatment certificates.

Figure 9.10. Finishes and Furniture Checklist

Once you know the types of finishes and furnishings you will be selecting, use the charts in Figure 9.2 and 9.9 and refer to the codes to determine which tests are required. For example, if you are using direct glue carpet on the floor you may need only to verify that it passes the *Pill Test*. In other types of spaces it may require a Class I or Class II rating; or if it is being used as a wall finish, the *Corner Test* must be verified as well. Write down the name of the test required for each finish and furnishing you checked off in the first column, and if it is a rated test include the rating required by the code. (See Figure 9.2 for specific test names.)

You should not start selecting finishes or furniture until you have determined the tests required for each area. Then as you select them refer to the checklist to see if the specific finishes and furniture meet the testing requirements. Indicate the manufacturer and the catalog number of the finish or piece of furniture you select in the space provided on the checklist. Use the remaining part of the checklist to indicate either the test results verified by the manufacturer or the name of the treatment company that will treat the finish.

For each finish or furnishing listed, be sure any necessary tests are completed. If required tests are listed on the manufacturer's label make a copy of the label. If the manufacturer cannot verify that a finish has passed a required test, you will need to have the finish treated and make sure the treatment company sends you a certificate verifying its compliance with the test.

After you have gathered all the testing information and have the required documentation, you should attach it to the checklist and file it with your project files in case this information is required in the future. In addition, check the *ADAAG* to determine if any special regulations must be met and document these as well.

According to Jackman and Dixon's *The Guide to Textiles for Interior Designers*, other situations that may require additional consideration when selecting finishes include (1) areas where smoking is permitted, (2) areas that accommodate seating for extended periods of time, such as planes, buses, rapid transit systems, transportation terminals, cocktail lounges, restaurants, and lounge areas in public buildings, and (3) areas where the level of light is low.

Remember that codes are *minimum* standards. Even though the enforcement of codes is different for every jurisdiction, you should always take into consideration the welfare of your clients when selecting interior finishes and furnishings. Whenever possible, even if not required, you should select those that have been fire tested and rated with the strictest test requirements. Much of the testing is fairly recent and more tests are constantly being devel-

Note

Remember that if a manufacturer cannot verify that a furnishing passes the *CAL 133*, there is no way to have it treated. (Refer to Using CAL 133, p. 229, and the discussion preceding it.) You must find furniture that is built according to the *CAL 133* requirements.

Note

Although codes for interior finishes are much stricter on commercial projects, they should be considered *equally as critical* in residential projects. Deaths occur more often in residential fires.

oped. You may need to prove in the future that you used the most advanced test available at the time of finish and furniture selection. (Refer to the section on Documentation and Liability in Chapter 10.)

CODE OFFICIALS AND THE CODE PROCESS

Each chapter in this book deals with a specific step in the code process, beginning in Chapter 1 with determining the publications required by a code jurisdiction and ending in Chapter 9 with finish and furniture requirements. Throughout each chapter references are made to code officials and the code approval process. This chapter concentrates on the code process as a whole. It introduces you to the different types of code officials and various steps that should be undertaken for a smooth approval of your design. (Also see inset titled The Administrative Chapter on page 251.)

As you read this chapter, the important thing to remember is that as the designer it is your responsibility to design the interior of a building in conjunction with the codes, standards, and federal regulations required in that jurisdiction. You must make sure your research of these regulations is thorough and properly recorded in your project drawings and specifications. It is your responsibility to make sure your design meets the intent of the codes. It is the codes official's job to review your drawings and verify their code compliance. Although the code official is there to guide you and answer your questions, it is not the official's responsibility to design the space or to do the research for you. You must learn to apply the various code requirements properly and work in conjunction with the code officials.

Note

There are various types of code consultants who can be used to provide added expertise during code research, especially on large projects.

THE CODE OFFICIALS

A code official, also known as a building official, is someone who has the authority to administer, interpret, and enforce the provisions of the adopted and/or amended code within a particular jurisdiction. This jurisdiction could be a state, county, city, or other political subdivision created by law. The term "code official" has been used throughout this book as a general term to describe a broad number of different people and functions.

In reality, the role of code official can consist of a variety of people, each with a different job title. The number of code officials will vary by jurisdiction. In smaller jurisdictions one person may have several responsibilities. In larger jurisdictions there may be several people with the same title grouped into a department, each with his or her area of expertise. The most common types of code officials are described below.

PLANS EXAMINER: A code official who checks your floor plans and construction drawings both in the preliminary stages and the final permit review stage of a project. The plans examiner checks for code and standards compliance. As the designer, you will be working most closely with the plans examiner.

FIRE MARSHAL: A code official who typically represents the local fire department. A fire marshal checks your drawings in conjunction with the plans examiner during both the preliminary stages and the final permit plan review. The fire marshal reviews the drawings for fire code compliance.

BUILDING INSPECTOR: A code official who visits the project job site after a permit is issued to make sure all construction complies with the codes as specified in the construction drawings and in the code publications.

With the growing complexity of the building industry, the role of the code official has increased in scope. Most jurisdictions require code officials to have specific levels of experience in the design or construction industry. Code officials must understand how the building's structural system, means of egress, fire alarm and detection systems, and similar aspects work together to conform to the code requirements to protect the occupants of the space or building. They must also understand the actual building process.

In the past, three of the major code organizations, Building Officials Code Administrators International (BOCA), Southern Building Code Congress International (SBCCI), and the International Conference of Building Officials (ICBO), have had individual processes for code officials to be certified for different roles. The positions include plans, building, electrical, and mechanical inspectors for their specific code publication. In some jurisdictions, this type of certification has become mandatory to be employed as a code official. The Council of American Building Officials (CABO) also developed the Certified Building Official program to establish professional qualifications for a building official working under their separate publications. Likewise, the International Code Council (ICC) formed the Board for International Professional Standards to provide similar testing and certification for code officials enforcing the international family of codes. As the various international codes are adopted and enforced by jurisdictions throughout the United States and the existing model codes are phased out; the model code organizations will revise their independent certifications.

With the introduction of new materials and new types of integrated systems, the job of the building official is requiring a new level of design knowledge. Like other professionals involved with the construction industry, building officials attend continuing education seminars to keep up with changes in the codes and technology. It is becoming more and more important for the code official to be involved early in the design process in order to

THE ADMINISTRATION CHAPTER

The first chapter in each of the building codes—SBC, NBC, UBC, and IBC—is the Administration chapter. This chapter discusses the qualifications and responsibilities of the code official and the code process. There are subtle differences in the requirements between the publications, but for the most part are very similar. Below is a list of typical requirements included in each of the administrative chapters.

- ✦ Scope of Work Requiring Code Compliance
- ✦ Duties and Powers of the Code Official and the Code Department
- ✦ Fees and Permits
- ✦ Construction Documents Requirements
- ✦ Demolition of Structures
- ✦ Inspections
- ✦ Certificate of Occupancy
- ✦ Means of Appeals
- ✦ Violations
- ✦ Stop Work Order

The administrative chapter of the building codes is the one that is most often modified by local jurisdictions.

develop the best design. This will become increasingly true with the use of performance codes. There will be situations in which neither the designer nor the code official will be able to rely on the straight-forward approach of the prescriptive code for a particular design solution. (See inset titled Using Performance Codes on page 12.)

CODE ENFORCEMENT

Each code jurisdiction adopts its own set of codes. Once adopted, these codes and the standards they reference become law and are enforceable by that jurisdiction. For example, many *state* jurisdictions either adopt one of the main family of codes or develop their own codes and standards. Typically, the state will enforce these regulations on state-owned buildings. The *county, city,* or *municipal* jurisdictions within these states either usually adopt the state requirements as they are or add their own amendments. The code becomes a local law and is enforced by the local code department within the jurisdiction.

A single project can be under the jurisdiction of several agencies. For example, in addition to the code departments there may be other *local agencies* that enforce their own regulations and establish separate jurisdictional boundaries. On interior projects the most common is the local health department. It may enforce its regulations on a state, county, or city level. Some zoning and historical ordinances can also affect an interior project. These are typically enforced by different groups on a municipal level.

The enforcement of federal laws and regulations is a little more complicated. Each federal agency enforces its regulations in federal buildings; beyond that there is no specific enforcement procedure. Each federal agency does not have the manpower to enforce its laws in every local jurisdiction. Therefore, many state and local jurisdictions formally adopt the federal regulations or create laws that are stricter than the federal requirements so that they can legally enforce them.

The *Americans with Disabilities Act (ADA)* is especially important since it affects most design projects. Jurisdictions that modify their laws to incorporate the accessibility standards may try to get them certified by the Department of Justice (DOJ) to determine if they are equivalent to the *ADA,* but this is a long process. Even when a local jurisdiction does not enforce the *ADA* or other federal laws, it is still your responsibility as the designer to know what the laws are and to incorporate them into your projects. (See Appendix E for more information on *ADA.*)

QUALITY CODE DEPARTMENTS

In 1995 a new system to assess code departments was introduced by the nation's insurance agencies in conjunction with the Federal Emergency Management Agency (FEMA). Known as the Building Code Effectiveness Grading System (BCEGS), it is a rating system that reviews how a code jurisdiction handles code administration, plan review, and field inspections. Detailed questionnaires are sent to each jurisdiction. The administration section concentrates on the building codes adopted, modifications through local ordinances, personnel qualifications, experience, education, contractor licensing requirements, public awareness programs, participation in code development activities, and administrative policies and procedures.

The plan review and field inspection sections of the questionnaire focus more on staffing issues and details of the code review process. Each jurisdiction is responsible for filling out the questionnaire, which is then reviewed and rated on a point system, giving an overall rating to the code jurisdiction. (The ratings range from 1 to 10 with 1 being the best.) Ultimately, the code jurisdiction can use the results to determine which areas need improvement. A jurisdiction can also ask to be reevaluated as it makes improvements to try to increase its overall rating—making for a better code department.

THE CODE PROCESS

Although the process for code approval may change slightly, depending on the type of project and the jurisdiction in which you are working, the ultimate goal is to meet all the code requirements so that a building permit can be obtained. Most interior projects, unless they consist strictly of finish and furniture selection, cannot be constructed without a permit.

To obtain a permit with minimum delay or difficulty you should use the process encouraged by the code officials in the jurisdiction of your project. Learn to work with the code officials as you move through the code process explained below. Several steps are done directly by the designer, which include the initial project research, preliminary review, and any appeals that may be necessary. The other steps in the process directly affect the construction contractor and include the permit approval, the inspection process, and the final approval, which allows the space to be occupied. Each step is explained below.

> **Note**
>
> A jurisdiction may allow some interior projects to be built without stamped and sealed drawings. The decision is usually based on a maximum square foot and building height requirement.

Initial Project Research

Since codes, standards, and federal regulations affect most interior projects, you need to do code research before you start design-

Note

Some projects may require the code official(s) to walk through the existing building at the beginning of a project to determine code compliance. This is especially important in older buildings that require updating. (See Appendix B.)

Note

Many code departments sell copies of the code publications they have adopted. These copies should indicate all required amendments. (See Appendix D for additional sources.)

ing your project. The research should be done in the programming stage of the design process at the same time you are collecting client and building information. You should write down or copy the main sections of the codes that apply to your project and keep them with your project files. (Refer to the section on Documentation and Liability later in this chapter.) This documentation, along with the use of the checklists provided in this book, will help you remember code issues that affected the design of the project. This can be especially useful if questions arise later in the process.

The first thing you must determine is the jurisdiction of the project. (See section on Code Enforcement on page 252.) You will need to call or visit the local codes department and ask them which codes, standards, and federal regulations are enforced. Each jurisdiction can make amendments, deletions, and additions that alter the original code publication. You need to know what these changes are. For example, a jurisdiction that adopts the *BOCA National Building Code (NBC)* may have some local ordinances that override specific *NBC* requirements. You should also ask if any local codes or ordinances will affect your project. For example, local health codes usually apply to projects that include food preparation.

In addition, you will need to know which edition of the codes are being used and how often new editions are adopted. As described in Chapter 1, most codes and standards have major updates every two or three years and minor changes on a yearly basis. Since each jurisdiction will adopt these changes on a different schedule, it is important to know when any changes occur. Some jurisdictions have mailing lists and provide notices when updates occur.

As you are determining the code publications and the editions required, you should also determine what is required by the jurisdiction to obtain a final project approval. For example, depending on the size and the scope of a project, specific floor plans and specifications may be required. They typically include stamped construction drawings indicating demolition plans, partition plans, reflected ceiling plans, and power and communication plans. The specifications can be part of the drawings or included as a separate document. On certain interior projects, specific details, stamped engineering drawings, and engineering calculations may be required as well. (See section on Construction Documents later in this chapter.)

Most jurisdictions have strict requirements as to who can design a project and what types of drawings are required for an interior project. For example, many drawings must be stamped by a licensed architect and/or licensed engineer registered within the state of the project. In some jurisdictions registered interior designers are allowed to stamp drawings as well. Other projects may not require a professional stamp. These are typically projects in buildings that have three stories or less and have a minimum number of square feet such as small commercial buildings and residential single-family homes. To meet these various requirements many firms employ a variety of designers and other professionals. As an individual you may have to collaborate with other designers and professionals to complete a project.

Preliminary Review

Most code jurisdictions have some form of preliminary plan review procedure that occurs in the early stages of a project. Although you may not require a preliminary review on all projects, for some projects this might be crucial. It may be as informal as faxing a floor plan indicating the pertinent code issues or as formal as a meeting with a number of code officials. When arranging a preliminary review meeting you should request the plans examiner, the fire marshal, and any other necessary official to be present so all code concerns can be addressed at once.

The plan review should occur in the preliminary stages of the design process, typically during the schematic design phase. You should have completed a majority of your code research and be prepared to discuss and clarify specific code issues. The preliminary floor plans should be to scale and have enough detail to discuss the major code topics. (See Figure 10.3.) For example, the overall size of the building or space should be provided and the division of occupancies and the arrangement of exits should be indicated. If you are designing only a portion of a building, be sure to have a location plan that indicates the layout of the remaining portions of the floor or building.

The purpose of the preliminary review meeting is to review the major code issues and to determine if the conclusions drawn from your research are valid. For example, discuss any code discrepancies you may have found in your research. Also ask the code officials if they have any concerns with your design and if they foresee any potential problems. Likewise, if you know there is a situation that cannot easily meet the code requirements, be prepared with your own alternative solutions. It is not wise to rely on code officials to solve the problem, because they may come up with a solution that meets the intention of the code but that does not fit with your design intentions.

Note

The National Conference of States on Building Codes and Standards (NCSBCS) publishes a directory of state building codes and regulations. (See Appendix D.)

Note

If two required codes have conflicting requirements, usually the most restrictive requirement applies. However, the code official has the authority to make the final decision.

Note

Most code officials are more than happy to meet with you, but not every jurisdiction endorses the preapproval process described in this section. You should request a meeting whenever you find it necessary to clarify code issues after doing your own code research.

During the meeting take notes so you can make the necessary changes to your design. It is also important to prepare a summary of the meeting for your records. After the meeting you should send a copy of the summary to each attending code official and ask him or her either to sign off on the summary, indicating acceptance, or to send you a written confirmation of the summary. On smaller projects you may be able to make the necessary corrections and notations directly on the preliminary floor plan and ask the code officials to sign their approval on it. In either case, it is important to get all approvals and permissions in writing, since each code official can have a different interpretation of the same code, as discussed in the following section on the appeals process.

In some cases, you have to obtain a review by sending a project to the actual code organization that publishes the code being enforced in that jurisdiction. The SBCCI, for example, will review specific issues of a project, such as fire protection, sprinklers and standpipes, means of egress, light and ventilation, and other similar issues. The project would be reviewed to see if it is in compliance with each of the codes published by that code organization, including building, mechanical, electrical, and plumbing. This type of service is offered to design professionals and the state and local jurisdictions enforcing the codes. However, there is a fee for this type of review.

Most of the time a review is best handled through the local code officials. On the other hand, a more formal review service may help identify particular design problem areas. (Jurisdictions may also use these services when work loads may cause a delay in the permitting process.)

As the designer it is your responsibility to know the codes and to plan your design in accordance with the codes. However, it is important to clarify all code issues at the beginning of a project. The preliminary code review helps you to do this. In addition, it typically results in a smoother permit approval. (See the section on the Permit Process later in this chapter.) Not only will you have incorporated the necessary codes, standards, and regulations in your drawings, but the code officials will be familiar with the project before the plans are brought in for a permit plans check.

Appeals Process

All codes, standards, and regulations are written for the safety and protection of the occupant. However, they are not always as specific as you would like them to be. Often a code provision can have more than one interpretation. Usually these discrepancies can be settled with the help of a code official. Code officials undergo training and attend code review classes and, therefore, can usually provide additional insight to a specific code provision. They also have access to the expertise of other officials.

However, you may not always agree with the code official's interpretation. For example, there may be an alternative method of achieving the same code compliance. This will be even truer as more performance codes are adopted. (See inset titled Using Performance Codes on page 12.) In addition, no code will be able to address every design situation. You may be working in an older building where making changes can be cost prohibitive, or you may want to use a new building material or finish material that is not covered by the code. In most cases it is to your benefit to try to work out a solution with the code official. But if a mutual solution cannot be reached, you may decide to use the appeals process.

The appeals process is a formal request made in writing either through a code official or directly to a Board of Appeals. Each of the codes have specific reasons why an appeal can be made. They also regulate who can make the appeal, usually the owner or representative of the owner. As the designer, you can represent the owner and make the appeal to the board. The Board of Appeals consists of a variety of professionals that meet to review code discrepancies. The board does not have the authority to waive a code requirement. Rather it is the board's responsibility to review the appeal, listen to both sides, and decide whether or not the appeal follows the interpretation of the code.

Figure 10.1 is a building code appeals form indicating the typical information required. (Usually separate appeal requests must be made for building, plumbing, mechanical, and electrical codes.) Once the Board of Appeals receives your appeal, both the designer and the code official are scheduled to present their side of the issue. As the designer, you must be prepared to explain the current code interpretation and how you specifically plan to comply with the code within your design project. If your appeal is accepted, the board grants a variance for your particular project. This variance applies only to the situation at hand; for other projects you must go through a similar process.

Permit Process

A permit is typically required for any interior project that requires construction. This includes but is not limited to

1. Construction or alterations made to a building
2. Change in occupancy
3. Installation of regulated equipment

Note

Interpretations of the codes, standards, or federal regulations can usually be obtained from the organizations that publish them. However, this can be time-consuming and there is no guarantee that the local code official will agree with the interpretation.

Note

Often a good source for justifying an appeal is a code publication used by another jurisdiction. For example, you may be able to find an alternative code or method in the *Life Safety Code (LSC)*.

Note

The words "variance" and "appeal" are sometimes used interchangeably. However, variances usually apply to local zoning laws and appeals apply to the codes.

METROPOLITAN GOVERNMENT OF NASHVILLE AND DAVIDSON COUNTY, TENNESSEE
DEPARTMENT OF CODES ADMINISTRATION

APPEAL UNDER THE FIRE AND BUILDING CODES

CASE NO.: _____

MAP: _____

PARCEL: _____

COUNCIL DIST _____

TO THE METROPOLITAN BOARD OF FIRE AND BUILDING CODE APPEALS:

 The undersigned hereby appeals the decision of the Director of the Department of Codes Administration, Metropolitan Government of Nashville and Davidson County, Tennessee, wherein a BUILDING PERMIT and/or CERTIFICATE OF OCCUPANCY are refused for _____

_____

_____

located at _____

_____

_____

in accordance with plans, application, and all data heretofore filed with the Director of the Department of Codes Administration, all of which are hereto attached and made a part of this appeal.

 Said BUILDING PERMIT and/or CERTIFICATE OF OCCUPANCY was denied for the reason

_____

_____

_____

_____

_____

_____

_____

_____

_____

_____

 Based on the powers and duties generally of the Metropolitan Board of Fire and Building Code Appeals, as set out in the Code of the Metropolitan Government of Nashville and Davidson County, Tennessee, Section 2.80.080, a variance, interpretation or exception is hereby requested in the above requirement as applied to this property.

Date _____   Please Sign Below

Appeal Taken By _____   _____

Please Print Name   Address and Zip   Phone

Appellant _____   _____   _____

Represented By_____   _____   _____

Owner _____   _____   _____

Lessee _____   _____   _____

Indicate who should receive certified notice: _____

BOARD OF FIRE AND BUILDING CODE APPEALS MEETS ON THE 2ND TUESDAY OF EVERY MONTH AT 9:00 A.M. ON THE 1ST FLOOR (AUDITORIUM) OF THE METRO HOWARD OFFICE BUILDING; 700 2ND AVENUE, SOUTH; NASHVILLE, TENNESSEE. APPEAL FORM MUST BE FILLED OUT AND FEE OF $50.00 RECEIVED BY THE LAST DAY OF THE MONTH TO BE PLACED ON THE NEXT MONTH'S AGENDA. A REPRESENTATIVE MUST BE PRESENT AT THE MEETING TO GIVE REASONS WHY THE BOARD SHOULD GRANT THE REQUEST AND TO ANSWER ANY QUESTIONS.

Figure 10.1. Sample Code Appeal Form.

The permit is issued based on your construction documents that consist of drawings, specifications, and any other documentation that may be required. In most cases the permit is obtained by a licensed contractor, but it can also be obtained by the building owner or a registered design professional. Figure 10.2 is an example of a building permit. Each jurisdiction requires slightly different information. Most jurisdictions also require separate permits for plumbing, electrical, and mechanical work. These are usually obtained by the appropriate subcontractors, since these permits make each subcontractor legally responsible for the specified work.

To obtain the permit the contractor must submit a permit application, a permit fee, and a specific number of construction documents. It is at this stage that the code officials fully review the drawings and specifications. Therefore, it is important that all relevant code correspondence made during the preliminary review and any granted appeals be attached to the application or noted directly on the construction drawings. This is especially helpful if the same code officials are not checking the plans in both the preliminary check and the permit plan check.

The whole process can take one day or several weeks, depending on the size of the project, the number of code officials that must check the project, and the work load of the code department. The set of drawings is typically checked by both a plans examiner and the fire marshal. Some jurisdictions will have more than one examiner check the drawings. For example, there may be separate building, mechanical, plumbing, and electrical code examiners as well as other local and/or state code examiners.

If there are any code discrepancies on the drawings, the building official will require corrections to be made before the permit is issued. This will necessitate making the appropriate changes and submitting the updated documentation. Upon approval, the code official(s) will stamp or write "approved" on the drawings. One set of drawings is kept by the code department and at least one set must be kept on the job site at all times. In addition, the permit itself must clearly be posted at the job site during construction.

Note

In some jurisdictions it is almost imperative that an expeditor is used as a go-between between the contractor and the codes department in order to obtain a permit.

Note

Many jurisdictions have computerized the permit process. Instead of filling out a form, the code department enters your project information directly into a computer.

Note

To accommodate tight construction schedules, some jurisdictions allow building permits to be issued in phases. This becomes especially important in new buildings where construction can begin while designers complete the interior details.

Inspection Process

The code process does not stop with the issue of a permit. During the construction of a project several inspections of the job site must be made by a building official. This is done to guarantee that the work matches what is required by the construction documents and that the work continues to comply with the codes.

FOR DEPARTMENTAL USE ONLY

CITY AND COUNTY OF SAN FRANCISCO
DEPARTMENT OF BUILDING INSPECTION

APPLICATION FOR BUILDING PERMIT

BLDG. FORM 1/2

APPLICATION NUMBER

FORM 1 ☐ TYPE I - II - III - IV Building

FORM 2 ☐ _____ Story TYPE V Building

APPLICATION IS HEREBY MADE FOR PERMISSION TO BUILD IN ACCORDANCE WITH THE PLANS AND SPECIFICATIONS SUBMITTED HEREWITH AND FOR THE PURPOSE SET FORTH HEREIN:

ADDRESS

SIDE _____ ST. AVE.

FT. _____ FROM _____ ST. AVE.

NEAREST CROSS STREET

OSHA APPROVAL REQ'D
APPROVAL NUMBER: ☐

DATE FILED	FILING FEE RECEIPT NO.	TYPE OF CONSTRUCTION	ASSESSOR'S BLOCK & LOT NO.
PERMIT NO.	ISSUED	ESTIMATED COST	REVISED COST
			BY: DATE:

BUILDING DESCRIPTION

SIZE OF LOT: FRONT _____ FT. REAR _____ FT. AVE. DEPTH _____ FT.

IS ANY OTHER BUILDING ON LOT? YES ☐ NO ☐ (IF YES, SHOW ON PLOT PLAN)

IS AUTO RUN-WAY TO BE CONSTRUCTED? YES ☐ NO ☐

USE OF BUILDING

BLDG. CODE OCCUP. CLASS.

DOES BUILDING EXTEND BEYOND PROPERTY LINE? YES ☐ NO ☐

GROUND FLOOR AREA _____ SQ. FT.

HEIGHT AT CENTER LINE OF FRONT OF BUILDING

WILL STREET SPACE BE USED DURING CONST'N? YES ☐ NO ☐

IS BUILDING DESIGNED FOR ADDITIONAL STORIES? YES ☐ NO ☐ HOW MANY?

NUMBER OF DWELLING UNITS

NUMBER OF STORIES OF OCCUPANCY

NUMBER OF BASEMENTS

WILL SUB-SIDEWALK SPACE BE USED? YES ☐ NO ☐

GENERAL CONTRACTOR _____ ADDRESS

CALIFORNIA LICENSE NUMBER _____ EXPIRATION DATE _____ TELEPHONE

ARCHITECT OR ENGINEER (DESIGN) _____ ADDRESS

CALIFORNIA CERTIFICATE NUMBER _____ TELEPHONE

ARCHITECT OR ENGINEER (FOR CONSTRUCTION) _____ ADDRESS

CALIFORNIA CERTIFICATE NUMBER _____ TELEPHONE

OWNER'S NAME _____ ADDRESS

TELEPHONE

CONSTRUCTION LENDER (ENTER NAME AND BRANCH DESIGNATION IF ANY, IF THERE IS NO KNOWN CONSTRUCTION LENDER, ENTER "UNKNOWN".) _____ ADDRESS

NORTH STREET

WEST STREET

EAST STREET

SOUTH STREET

DESIGN LIVE LOAD FOR FLOORS:
(TO BE POSTED IN COMMERCIAL AND INDUSTRIAL BLDGS.)

IMPORTANT NOTICES

No change shall be made in the character of the occupancy or use without first obtaining a Building Permit authorizing such change. See San Francisco Building Code and San Francisco Housing Code.

No portion of building or structure or scaffolding used during construction, to be closer than 6'0" to any wire containing more than 750 volts. See Sec. 385, California Penal Code.

Pursuant to the San Francisco Building Code, the building permit shall be posted on the job. The owner is responsible for approved plans and application being kept at building site.

Grade lines as shown on drawings accompanying this application are assumed to be correct. If actual grade lines are not the same as shown revised drawings showing correct grade lines, cuts and fills together with complete details of retaining walls and wall footings required must be submitted to this department for approval.

ANY STIPULATION REQUIRED HEREIN OR BY CODE MAY BE APPEALED.

BUILDING NOT TO BE OCCUPIED UNTIL CERTIFICATE OF FINAL COMPLETION IS POSTED ON THE BUILDING OR PERMIT OF OCCUPANCY GRANTED, WHEN REQUIRED.

APPROVAL OF THIS APPLICATION DOES NOT CONSTITUTE AN APPROVAL FOR THE ELECTRICAL WIRING OR PLUMBING INSTALLATIONS. A SEPARATE PERMIT FOR THE WIRING AND PLUMBING MUST BE OBTAINED.

THIS IS NOT A BUILDING PERMIT. NO WORK SHALL BE STARTED UNTIL A BUILDING PERMIT IS ISSUED.

In dwellings all insulating materials must have a clearance of not less than two inches from all electrical wires or equipment.

CHECK APPROPRIATE BOX
☐ OWNER ☐ ARCHITECT ☐ ENGINEER
☐ LESSEE ☐ AGENT WITH POWER OF ATTORNEY
☐ CONTRACTOR ☐ ATTORNEY IN FACT

APPLICANT'S CERTIFICATION

I CERTIFY THAT I HAVE READ THIS APPLICATION AND STATE THAT THE ABOVE INFORMATION IS CORRECT. I AGREE THAT IF A PERMIT IS ISSUED FOR THE CONSTRUCTION DESCRIBED IN THIS APPLICATION, ALL THE PROVISIONS OF THE PERMIT AND ALL LAWS AND ORDINANCES THERETO WILL BE COMPLIED WITH.

NOTICE TO APPLICANT

HOLD HARMLESS CLAUSE: The permittee(s) by acceptance of the permit, agree(s) to indemnify and hold harmless the City and County of San Francisco from and against any and all claims, demands and actions for damages resulting from operations under this permit, regardless of negligence of the City and County of San Francisco, and to assume the defense of the City and County of San Francisco against all such claims, demands or actions.

In conformity with the provisions of Section 3800 of the Labor Code of the State of California, the applicant shall have coverage under (I), or (II) designated below or shall indicate item (III), or (IV), or (V), whichever is applicable. If however item (V) is checked item (IV) must be checked as well. Mark the appropriate method of compliance below:

I hereby affirm under penalty of perjury one of the following declarations:

( ) I. I have and will maintain a certificate of consent to self-insure for workers' compensation, as provided by Section 3700 of the Labor Code, for the performance of the work for which this permit is issued.

( ) II. I have and will maintain workers' compensation insurance, as required by Section 3700 of the Labor Code, for the performance of the work for which this permit is issued. My workers' compensation insurance carrier and policy number are:

Carrier _____

Policy Number _____

( ) III. The cost of the work to be done is $100 or less.

( ) IV. I certify that in the performance of the work for which this permit is issued, I shall not employ any person in any manner so as to become subject to the workers' compensation laws of California. I further acknowledge that in the event that I should become subject to the workers' compensation provisions of the Labor Code of California and fail to comply forthwith with the provisions of Section 3800 of the Labor Code, that the permit herein applied for shall be deemed revoked.

( ) V. I certify as the owner (or the agent for the owner) that in the performance of the work for which this permit is issued, I will employ a contractor who complies with the workers' compensation laws of California and who, prior to the commencement of any work, will file a completed copy of this form with the Central Permit Bureau.

Signature of Applicant or Agent _____ Date _____

Figure 10.2. Sample Application for Building Permit Form.

Inspections must be made at certain intervals during the construction, before the work is concealed or covered up by the next phase of construction.

It is typically the responsibility of the contractor to notify the codes department when it is time to make an inspection. On interior projects, these intervals usually include

1. **Framing Inspection**: The walls are usually framed and completed on one side. The side that is open allows the inspector to check the construction materials, firestops, and other opening protectives.
2. **Systems Inspection**: Separate inspections are made for the plumbing, mechanical, and electrical installations. This inspection can be made at the same time as the framing inspection if these systems are complete. There is usually a preliminary inspection before the walls are closed and then a final inspection at the end of construction as part of the final inspection.
3. **Gypsum Board/Lath Inspection**: When all the gypsum board or lathing is in place but before any taping or plaster is done, the inspector will check to make sure all walls, especially fire-rated walls, are built to code.
4. **Final Inspection:** Once the project is complete the inspector will do one final walk-through to confirm compliance of all remaining codes and to make sure the space is ready to be occupied.

At each inspection check, the construction can continue only if the inspector grants an approval. If the inspector finds the project is not acceptable, a correction notice is issued and another inspection is scheduled. If the inspector feels that a condition is unsafe or that the construction is not being carried out in an acceptable manner, a stop work order will be issued. This means that no other work on the site can occur until the specific problem is addressed.

Certificate of Occupancy

A Certificate of Occupancy (C of O) is issued after the final inspection has been completed. It is typically requested from the code official by the person who requested the building permit, usually the contractor. If during the final inspection the code inspector is satisfied that the building or space complies with the code and the construction is complete, a certificate is issued. In some jurisdictions, the Certificate of Occupancy is also referred to

Note

As the designer, you should also be periodically checking the construction of your project to ensure that it is following your design and code instructions. This should be part of every construction administration.

Note

Unfortunately, there is no guarantee that preapproved plans or even plans that receive a permit will be approved in the field. An inspector may see a code noncompliance in the field that was missed on the construction drawings. If this occurs, either the designer must work out the discrepancy with the appropriate code official or the contractor is required to make the changes necessary to comply to the code.

as a Use and Occupancy (U and O) letter. Although some occupancies are exempt, the certificate is typically required before the tenant can occupy the building or space, and it must be posted in a conspicuous location in the building. Once the Certificate of Occupancy is issued the code process is complete.

Temporary Certificate of Occupancy

Note

A temporary certificate of occupancy may be issued on projects when part of a building can be safely occupied before the completion of the remainder of the project.

For a larger project, construction may be done in phases. The client may not want to wait until all portions of the overall project are completed to occupy the facility. Or, a certain aspect of the project cannot be completed because of delay in the arrival of material or equipment, for example, custom granite countertops or water fountains. In those cases, some jurisdictions will issue a Temporary Certificate of Occupancy. This will allow portions of the project to be occupied as long as the code official feels that the occupants will not be in any danger because the entire project is not complete. The Temporary Certificate of Occupancy is also known as a Partial Certificate of Occupancy or Partial Use and Occupancy Permit.

Certificate of Completion

This certificate is issued when the structure or systems are complete within a space or building. This type of certificate is usually necessary to connect to local utilities. It does not give the right to occupy the space or building. A Certificate of Occupancy must still be issued to occupy the space or building.

DOCUMENTATION AND LIABILITY

Note

Some code departments will not issue a permit if you incorporate more stringent codes not currently enforced by that jurisdiction. If that is the case, be sure to document all correspondence.

Building codes and the standards they reference are continually being updated, especially those that pertain to interiors. For example, many of the testing requirements for interior finishes and furniture are fairly recent and more tests are constantly being developed. It is crucial when designing interior projects to keep current with the regulations. Even if the jurisdiction of your project does not yet require some of the stricter codes or standards, you should know what they are and use them. Not only are people's lives at stake, but you will be held liable should an incident occur. You need to prove that you used the most advanced test or strictest requirement available at the time you designed the project.

ECONOMIC OPTIONS IN CODES

Thorough code research is imperative for the safety of building occupants, but a number of options are allowed by the code that can affect the cost of the project. These options are frequently overlooked, resulting in needless construction costs. In his book *Building and Safety Codes for Industrial Facilities,* Joseph N. Sabatini lists a number of reasons for overlooked cost savings in industrial buildings. They can be generalized to include all design projects:

1. **Options Not Clear in the Codes:** Sometimes options, alternatives, or exceptions are scattered throughout the chapters, and finding them requires familiarity and expertise.

2. **Nonfamiliarity and Infrequent Use of Codes:** Many designers merely spot-check the codes on an intermittent basis because they do not have the time to review them thoroughly.

3. **Some Trade-offs Are Interdisciplinary:** Since some designers are scheduled to participate in planning on a staggered basis, poor communication and coordination result.

4. **Lack of Preliminary Meetings Involving All Disciplines:** Sound economic decisions can be made only if all disciplines are involved in the early planning stages.

5. **Design Time Is Too Short:** Because of committed investments, interest payments, and the income that the facility will bring as soon as it is in operation, design time is often abbreviated, and therefore comprehensive code reviews are often not done.

6. **Overkill:** Because of item 5, conscientious professionals use overkill and include items in the design that are not always mandated by the building codes, regulations, and enforced standards.

It is important to reference specific code sections and standard numbers. When conducting a code review, it is a good idea to make copies of all chapters and/or paragraphs that apply to the project. On larger projects you may want to summarize these sections on cover sheets. In addition, collect written evidence of any materials that must meet certain regulation. For example, when you are requesting the results of a performance test from a manufacturer or an outside source, it is your responsibility to obtain the results in writing. Equally important is to have your documentation organized to show the research you have done for each code compliance.

The development of a performance checklist or a standard evaluation form is very useful, since the ease of establishing compliance with standards is in direct proportion to the quantity and quality of your documentation. You should have a general check-

Note

Properly and consistently prepared code documentation is imperative should any liability issues occur after a project is completed.

Note

The length of time to keep project records and code documentation is highly debatable. However, according to *Guidelines* published by Victor O. Schinnerer & Co., Inc., many states have a *statute of repose*, which sets a time limitation on how long after a project is completed a suit can be brought against a designer or design company.

list, such as the one in Figure 10.3, to make sure each code topic has been covered in every project.

Use this checklist in conjunction with the more specific checklists introduced in each chapter of this book. You may want to add to these checklists or develop your own. It is impossible to put every code requirement on a checklist, since the requirements will be different on every project. Instead, the purpose of the checklist is to remind you of the code and standard requirements that must be researched and documented on your drawings and in your specifications. When necessary, you should always attach the appropriate backup. The backup could consist of a copy of the manufacturer's warranty or specifications, a product label listing the codes with which the product complies, or a copy of a certificate from a testing agency similar to the one in Figure 9.6.

The importance of documenting every project in construction drawings, specification books, and project files cannot be stressed enough. Even if you follow all the codes thoughout an entire project, if you cannot prove it when asked, the research was useless. Be sure to keep all your research, correspondence with the code officials, and other documentation on file with the project records.

INTERIOR PROJECT CHECKLIST

1 DETERMINE WHICH CODES ARE REQUIRED (Chapter 1)
___ Building Code and Other Code Publications
___ Standards and Tests
___ Government Regulations
___ Local Codes and Ordinances

2 OCCUPANCY REQUIREMENTS (Chapter 2)
___ Determine Type of Occupancy Classification(s)
___ Calculate Occupancy Load(s)
___ Review Specific Occupancy Requirements
___ Compare Code and Accessibility Requirements

3 MINIMUM TYPE OF CONSTRUCTION (Chapter 3)
___ Determine Construction Type
___ Determine Ratings of Structural Elements
___ Calculate Maximum Floor Area (as required)
___ Calculate Building Height (as required)
___ Check All Enforced Standards

4 MEANS OF EGRESS REQUIREMENTS (Chapter 4)
___ Determine Quantity and Type of Each Means of Egress
___ Calculate Travel Distance
___ Calculate Minimum Widths
___ Determine Required Signage
___ Compare Code and Accessibility Requirements
___ Check All Enforced Standards

5 FIRE RESISTANT REQUIREMENTS (Chapter 5)
___ Determine Fire and Smoke Barriers
___ Determine Through Penetration Opening Protectives
___ Review Types of Fire Tests and Ratings Required
___ Compare Code and Accessibility Requirements
___ Check All Enforced Standards

6 FIRE PROTECTON REQUIREMENTS (Chapter 6)
___ Determine Fire and Smoke Detection Systems
___ Determine Fire Supression Systems
___ Review Possible Sprinkler Tradeoffs (as required)

7 REVIEW PLUMBING REQUIREMENTS (Chapter 7)
___ Determine Types of Fixtures Required
___ Calculate Number of Each Fixture Required
___ Compare Code and Accessibility Requirements
___ Coordinate with Engineer (as required)

8 REVIEW MECHANICAL REQUIREMENTS (Chapter 7)
___ Determine Access and Clearance Requirements
___ Figure Zoning and Thermostate Locations
___ Determine Type of Air Distribution System
___ Check for Accessibility Compliance
___ Coordinate with Engineer (as required)

9 REVIEW ELECTRICAL REQUIREMENTS (Chapter 8)
___ Determine Location of Outlets, Switches, and Fixtures
___ Determine Emergency Power and Lighting Requirements
___ Determine Types of Communication Requirments
___ Check for Accessibility Compliance
___ Coordinate with Engineer (as required)

10 FINISH AND FURNITURE REQUIREMENTS (Chapter 9)
___ Review Tests and Types of Ratings Required
___ Determine Special Finish Requirements
___ Determine Special Funiture Requirements
___ Compare Code and Accessibility Requirements
___ Check All Enforced Standards

NOTE: Consult the jurisdiction having authority at any step in question.

Figure 10.3. Interior Project Checklist.

CONSTRUCTION DOCUMENTS

Throughout this book, it has been noted when code issues should be documented both in your records and in the construction documents. These documents include drawings, specifications, and any additional documentation required by a code jurisdiction. The checklists at the end of each chapter are specifically meant to help you with your code research and documentation. Having certain information documented on the drawings makes the review by code officials easier. They automatically know which code issues were considered in the development of the design.

Some codes actually require certain information to be included in the construction documents. Other information is required by the jurisdiction. Below is a list of the most typical code information that should be included in your construction documents either on the drawings or in the written specifications. Note, however, that this list is not all inclusive.

Cover Sheet
- ✦ Applicable code publication(s) and edition(s) (recognize local or state amendments)
- ✦ Construction type(s)
- ✦ Area of space designed
- ✦ Area limitations
- ✦ Occupancy classification(s)
- ✦ Sprinkler status of building or space (i.e., sprinklered or unsprinklered)
- ✦ Occupancy load per floor (or area if necessary)

Drawings
- ✦ Location plan (when designing a portion of a floor or building)
- ✦ Compartmentation of the fire areas
- ✦ Location of rated walls and type of rating
- ✦ Location of rated doors, windows, and other through-penetrations
- ✦ Exit sign locations
- ✦ Emergency lighting and/or systems
- ✦ Accessibility clearances and critical dimensions
- ✦ Sections of rated assemblies (walls, ceilings, etc.)
- ✦ Details for penetrations (electrical, plumbing, environmental and communication conduits, pipes, and systems)

Specifications and Schedules
- ✦ Types of rated doors, frames, and hardware
- ✦ Types of rated windows and through-penetrations
- ✦ Types of light fixtures, such as emergency lights and exit signs

Note

Although rarely done, a permit can be revoked after construction begins if it is discovered that information used to grant the permit was in error, even if the error was made by a code official.

Note

Certain sections of the *IBC* indicate specific information that must be included in the construction document prior to code review.

✦ List of required standards and tests

Additional information may be required for review by the code official for approval of the design. Because this documentation is usually developed by an engineer or consulting professional, the information may not be located in your drawings or specifications. This may include

✦ Sprinkler riser diagram
✦ Sprinkler coverage calculations
✦ Mechanical load calculations
✦ Plumbing fixture calculations

FUTURE TECHNOLOGY

Note

As performance codes gain more acceptance, computer models will become even more important as a tool.

Computers are quickly becoming a powerful force in code enforcement. A number of software packages are currently available. Each of the code organizations sells computerized versions of its code publications. These software packages assist you in your code research by providing you with search capabilities. For example, you can do a word search for a particular code topic, or have the computer bring up specific code reference numbers or tables.

Currently, computers are also being used in fire research and testing. Many of today's fire and flame tests do not mimic true emergency situations. Building fires incorporate a number of additional variables that are not present in the testing labs. These variables include a number of combustible materials, furniture, and finishes that add to the fuel of a fire. Computer models can be used to create possible fire scenarios. The user is able to control and change a number of variables, such as types of building materials, wall locations, and use of smoke barriers, and watch the screen to see how a fire will react. A number of items can be determined from these computer simulations, including the relationship between the time required to escape and the time available to escape during a fire.

Computer models can also reconstruct real fires to analyze what happened and develop ways to prevent future fires. In the future as software and hardware prices decrease, computer models will be more readily accessible to designers. Computer models can be used as a tool for designers to convince code officials of acceptable alternatives to existing codes. In addition, as the enforcement of performance codes becomes more common, computer analysis, calculations, and modeling will help to provide support for design solutions.

Codes, standards, and federal regulations will remain an important part of the design process as we move into the future. An early and comprehensive code research at the beginning of each interior project is crucial to the smooth development of a project, not to mention the safety of the building occupants. In addition, a thorough documentation of your research is a must.

Remember, code officials have the same goal—the safety of the building occupants. It is important to build a good relationship with the code officials. Since not every jurisdiction is the same, you need to learn the local system. Learn how to work within the system and with the various personalities. Code officials are a valuable resource. Working together you can usually determine design solutions that comply with the required codes, standards, and federal regulations.

APPENDIX **A**

FAMILY
RESIDENCES

Single- and double-family residences are considered Residential occupancies by the building codes. However, they are covered by a totally separate code publication. Prior to the development of the international codes, the residential code was called the *One and Two Family Dwelling Code (OTFDC)*. It was published by the Council of American Building Officials (CABO). However, it is now part of the international code family as published by the International Code Council (ICC). (See Chapter 1.) Starting in the year 2000, the newest edition of the code is titled the *International Residential Code (IRC)*. The *IRC* is the main code used for single-family homes, two-family homes, duplexes, and townhouses that have their own means of egress.

The *IRC* covers a wide variety of codes, including building, plumbing, mechanical, and electrical codes. It also refers to a variety of standards and other publications. Although family residences do not have as many regulations as other buildings, a number of interior codes and standards are still required. A brief description of the most common interior codes is discussed below. (They are listed in the same order as the rest of the book.)

CONSTRUCTION TYPES

Family residences are typically wood structures. In some areas metal framing is starting to gain popularity as well, especially where seismic codes are enforced. However, most houses today still consist of wood framing. Concrete and concrete block are typically used to create the foundation of the structure. Other materials, such as brick, stucco, and wood siding, may be used for aesthetic reasons. The *IRC* specifies the types of material that can be used. A code official must approve any alternative materials. Most interior structure elements consist of wood studs with gypsum board, or lathe and plaster in older homes. (See Chapter 2 for additional information.)

BUILDING HEIGHT AND AREA

To be considered a family residence covered by the *IRC*, the structure typically cannot be more than three stories high. (If more than three stories, the building codes will apply.) To find the actual height and area requirements, you must refer to the building codes. (See Chapter 3.) In addition, the *IRC* places minimum square footage requirements and minimum ceiling heights in each habitable room within the residence. For example, the ceiling height in a habitable room must typically be a minimum of 7'-0" above the finished floor.

MEANS OF EGRESS

Note

Most homes rely on exterior windows as a means of egress during an emergency. The codes set minimum requirements for the sizes, height, and operation of these windows.

The *IRC* requires a minimum of one regulated exterior exit door in each residence. It must be at least 3'-0" wide by 6'-8" high and have a specific type of landing on each side. Other doors to the exterior are allowed to have smaller widths. The width of interior doors is not regulated, but the code does set a minimum width for all hallways and exit accesses. The minimum corridor width, for example, is typically 3'-0" wide. (A larger width may be required by the accessibility standards for accessible houses.)

When sleeping areas (i.e., bedrooms) are located on an upper floor, the *IRC* requires an emergency means of egress from these areas. The code typically allows this exit to be an operable window. The bottom of the window cannot be more that 44 inches above the floor, and the window when open must have a clear opening of a certain dimension that allows a person to exit through the window in case of a fire.

Stairs and ramps within a residence are regulated as well. However, the dimensions are not as strict as the building codes. For example, tread sizes are allowed to be smaller and riser sizes are allowed to be higher than stairs in nonresidential spaces and only one handrail is usually required. In addition, the *IRC* specifies other handrail requirements, such as the height and size when they are required (i.e., when platforms are raised above a certain height).

FIRE RESISTANCE

Fire and smoke separation is required between two or more family dwellings, such as a duplex or a townhouse. Depending on whether they are side by side or above each other, they must be separated by either a fire-rated wall or a fire-rated floor assembly. Wall assemblies must extend to the underside of the roof and floor assemblies must be continuous to each exterior wall. Any required through-penetrations must be firestopped. (See Chapter 5.)

In single-family residences the main separation requirement pertains to attached garages. A one-hour assembly must separate any part of the garage that connects to the house. Other fire code requirements are specified for fireplaces, wood-burning stoves, etc.

Note

As more people turn toward home health care, additional fire hazards are being created that may not be covered by the codes. Added precautions must be taken.

FIRE PROTECTION

Fire and smoke detection in family residences typically consists of smoke detectors. All new homes require smoke detectors that are interconnected and tied into the electrical system with battery backup. If a significant renovation or addition is being made to an existing residence, the code official may require that an interconnected smoke-detecting system be added. Older homes require at least battery-operated detectors. Typically, they must be installed outside each sleeping area and on all inhabitable floors. Some stricter jurisdictions require one smoke detector in each bedroom. Others may require carbon monoxide detectors as well. (See inset titled Carbon Monoxide Detection on page 156.)

Manual fire extinguishers are the main means of fire suppression; however, some jurisdictions are beginning to require sprinkler systems in multi-tenant units. The *IRC* refers you to the National Fire Protection Association (NFPA) standard *NFPA 13D: Installation of Sprinkler Systems in One and Two Family Dwellings and Manufactured Homes* for installation standards. (In the future, more homes may require sprinkler systems.)

Note

Townhouses require stricter separation requirements than two-family dwellings.

PLUMBING

The minimum requirements for plumbing fixtures in family residences typically include one kitchen sink, one water closet, one

Note

Plastic pipes are not allowed in many jurisdictions.

lavatory, one bathtub or shower unit, and one washing machine hookup. (In a duplex one washing machine hookup may be adequate if it is available to both units.) In addition, each water closet and bathtub or shower must also be installed in a room with privacy.

Some jurisdictions may require additional plumbing fixtures, based on the number of bedrooms. The *IRC* requires minimum clearances for most of the fixtures. Usually these dimensions are less that those required by the plumbing codes in other buildings. If accessibility standards are required, there may be additional requirements.

MECHANICAL

Ventilation in a family residence is directly tied into the quantity of exterior windows and how much natural ventilation they supply. For example, when a bathroom does not have a window, a fan with a duct leading directly to the exterior of the building is required. When windows are present a certain percentage of them must be operable for both ventilation and emergency reasons. (See earlier section on Means of Egress.) Another important ventilation code has to do with dryers. A dryer exhaust must be ducted to the outside, yet the code sets very specific length requirements that may limit the location of a laundry room within the house.

The heating system of a house must be able to maintain a specific room temperature in all habitable rooms. Because of the size of a house can vary greatly, a wide variety of systems can be used. Some examples include air units, heat pumps, and baseboard heating. In addition, all heating, ventilating, and air conditioning (HVAC) equipment and appliances must meet certain standards and have a factory-applied label. They must also be located where they are easy to access and maintain.

ELECTRICAL

Note

Although often seen in older homes, exposed lamps such as pull chain and keyless fixtures are typically not required in new residential construction.

For electrical requirements the *IRC* refers to the NFPA standard *NFPA 70: National Electric Code (NEC)*. Some of these requirements were discussed in Chapter 8, such as that all electrical outlets must be certain distances apart and that GFI outlets must be used in wet areas. Other requirements are more specific to residential homes. For example, all inhabitable rooms require a wall switch to control lighting. Certain light fixtures are limited by the code as well.

One of the newest electrical requirements for residences is called the arc-fault circuit interrupter (AFCI). It is a device that protects a circuit and/or outlet from an electrical arc (or bright flash of electrical discharge), which is a cause of many electrical fires. Although relatively new, future editions of the *NEC* will start requiring AFCIs to protect at least bedroom receptacles.

A number of interior appliances also have specific electrical code and/or standards requirements. These include ranges and ovens, open-top gas broiler units, clothes dryers, and water heaters.

Note

Newer installations do not allow electrical outlets directly above baseboard heating units.

FINISHES

Requirements for finishes in residences are not nearly as strict as those required in other occupancies. The *IRC* requires that all wall and ceiling finishes, except for trims (i.e., baseboards and chair rails) and materials that are less than $\frac{1}{28}$ inch thick, are required to meet specific *ASTM F84* testing requirements as issued by the American Society for Testing and Materials (ASTM). The most popular residential finishes, wallpaper and paint, are both exempt from this requirement. Some finishes, such as wood veneer and hardboard paneling, must conform to other standards as well. Finishes in shower and bath areas are also regulated. These areas must be finished with a smooth, hard, and nonabsorbent surface (i.e., ceramic tile, marble, or vinyl tile).

ACCESSIBILITY

The *Americans with Disabilities Act (ADA)* does not apply to private residences. Instead, the *Fair Housing Act (FHA)* sets most of the accessibility standards for residences, yet it pertains mostly to multiunit housing. (See Chapter 1.) The American National Standards Institute (ANSI) also has a standards section dedicated to dwelling units.

Most private residences are not required to be accessible. However, housing built with government funds may require partial or full accessibility. Other interior projects may require a house to be "adaptable." This means that the house could easily be converted to be accessible. An adaptable house may include such things as adjustable counters, movable cabinetry, structurally reinforced areas for future grab bars, and specific fixtures and equipment, such as wall-mounted water closets and a stove with front controls. The additional maneuvering space would also have been designed into the layout of the dwelling. When a house is required to be accessible, you can refer to the *FHA* or the ANSI standards for guidance.

This appendix covers the general residential codes and accessibility regulations. Depending on the jurisdiction, you must refer to either the *IRC* or the *OTFDC* for any specific information. Since the *IRC* and the *OTFDC* cover many topics in one publication, it may not give enough information for every type of project. In some cases, the code official may refer you to other codes or standards, especially for plumbing, mechanical, and electrical requirements. At the very least, residential codes set the minimum requirements to assure that the occupants' health, safety, and welfare are addressed.

EXISTING AND HISTORIC BUILDINGS

The way codes apply to interior projects in existing buildings and historical buildings varies from the way they apply to projects in recently constructed buildings. An *existing* building is any structure that was erected and occupied prior to the adoption of the most current building code. Therefore, every building is eventually considered an existing building. Whether an existing building is *historical* depends on two things. It must either be listed in the *National Register of Historical Places* or designated as historical under a specific state or local law. Both types of buildings are briefly described below.

When working on projects in existing and historical buildings, many of the codes, standards, and federal regulations described throughout this book must still be referenced. However, some additional publications apply as well. There are two relevant code publications: the Southern Building Code Congress International (SBCCI) has the *Standard Existing Building Code*, and the International Conference of Building Officials (ICBO) provides the *Uniform Code for Building Conservation*. In addition, each of the building codes has a short chapter geared toward existing buildings. Some federal guidelines include the Department of Housing and Urban Development's (HUD) *Rehabilitation Guidelines* and the U.S. Department of Interior's (DOI) *Secretary of the Interior's Standards for Rehabilitation* written specifically for historic buildings on the *National Register*. (See Appendix D.) Also refer to the Bibliography in this book for additional sources.

EXISTING BUILDINGS

When an alteration or addition is made to a portion of an existing building, the codes do not normally require the whole building to comply with the most current building codes. New *additions* to a building must comply with the current codes. For *alterations* or repairs made to the existing building, the codes typically require only the new work to comply as long as it does not cause other portions of the building to be in violation of the code. For example, the new work cannot demolish an existing fire wall or block an existing exit. A change in *occupancy* classification can also affect a portion of an existing building. This can occur if a new tenant moves into the building or an existing tenant changes its use or classification. The space must typically meet the most current code requirements for that occupancy.

However, sometimes if the design calls for significant change, the code official can require that more of the building be brought up to code. For example, in the renovation of an older residence where a large amount of electrical work is being done, the code official can require that you update the entire electrical service and wiring. Sometimes a "50-percent" rule of thumb is used. If you are doing an extensive renovation, you may want to determine if there is a more definitive limit.

In some jurisdictions, when working on an interior project in an existing building, you may be required to have the building evaluated by a code official to determine if any changes are required. In other jurisdictions there may be a standard level of compliance required for any work performed in an existing building. What is required generally depends on the size of the alteration, the type of occupancy, and the condition of the existing building. On the other hand, if you are working on a project in an older building, you may want to have a code official walk the building with you even if it is not required. This is especially helpful when you are changing the occupancy of the entire building. An initial walk-through can give both of you a better understanding of your options as you proceed.

You must also refer to *Americans with Disabilities Act (ADA)*. The *ADA* specifically states that existing buildings must fully comply with the accessibility requirements as stated in the *ADA Accessibility Guidelines (ADAAG)*. This is especially true when additions and alterations are made. However, the *ADA* does allow exceptions where compliance with the *ADA* is either structurally infeasible, too costly, or would cause an unsafe situation. These exceptions must be fully analyzed. Refer to the *ADA* and other experts when necessary. (See Appendix E for more information.)

HISTORICAL BUILDINGS

When working on a project in a historical building additional code requirements and additional plan review procedures are required. Many jurisdictions have state or local regulations for historical buildings. It is important to check for the correct local procedures before starting a project. For example, some historical regulations control only the preservation of the exterior of a building, however, this may include any interior work that is visible from the exterior of the building.

The key to historical projects is to determine which codes must be met and what approval procedures must be followed. Communication with your code department and historic preservation organizations is imperative. Some historical organizations have the power to grant alternatives or waivers to code provisions. For example, some jurisdictions may allow safety equivalencies. In other jurisdictions, you must work closely with the code official to determine what options you have. It may be necessary to apply to the appeals or variance boards for special circumstances.

The *ADA* allows exceptions or alternative solutions for historical buildings when a requirement threatens or destroys a building's historical significance, for example, where the required change or addition would destroy a historical detail of the building or space. Some of these alternative solutions are stated in the *ADAAG*. Others may need to be discussed with your state or local historical preservation official or directly with the *ADA* Access Board (also known as the Architectural and Transportation Barriers Compliance Board or ATBCB.) Remember though, that approval of an alternative solution for one area does not exempt the whole building from meeting other requirements.

The *ADAAG* does specifically state minimum requirements that all historical buildings must meet. These include (1) at least one accessible route into the building, (2) at least one accessible toilet when toilet facilities are provided, (3) access to all public areas on the main floor, and (4) accessible displays and written information. However, all *ADA* regulations must be followed whenever possible.

There are a number of *ADAAG* requirements that can typically be met without major disruption. For example, installing compatible offset hinges to widen doorways, adding full-length mirrors and raised toilet seats in restrooms, and replacing door and faucet handles with lever controls.

When existing conditions seem to make meeting the codes and accessibility requirements difficult, the exemptions allowed for existing and/or historic buildings should be considered. It may

> **Note**
>
> A valuable resource for historic buildings is the *Catalog of Historic Preservation Publications* developed by the U.S. Department of Interior's National Park Service. (Refer to Appendix D.)

be necessary to discuss alternatives with the local officials and the ATBCB. However, whether the building is existing or historical, the overall goal when making interior changes is to make the building as safe as possible and in the process as accessible as possible.

ABBREVIATIONS

Below is a comprehensive list of abbreviations for organizations, associations, agencies, and institutions that are often used when reading code publications or talking to code officials and other professionals. Included are standards organizations, code organizations, professional associations, and government agencies. When available, web sites have been included in parentheses. The most common code, standards, and federal regulation acronyms have also been included and are highlighted with italics. The list is in alphabetical order by abbreviation.

AA   Aluminum Association (www.aluminum.org)
AAMA   American Architectural Manufacturers Association
          (www.aamanet.org)
AATCC   American Association of Textile Chemists and
          Colorists (www.aatcc.org)
ABA   *Architectural Barriers Act*
ABC   American Building Contractors
AC   Asbestos Cement Pipe Producers Association
ACI   American Concrete Institute (www.aci-int.org)
ADA   *Americans with Disabilities Act*
ADAAG   *Americans with Disabilities Act Accessibility Guidelines*
          (www.adaag.com)
AES   Audio Engineering Society (www.aes.org)
AFMA   American Furniture Manufacturers Association
          (www.afmahp.org)
AFPA   American Forest and Paper Association (formerly
          NFoPA) (www.afandpa.org)

AGA	American Gas Association (www.aga.org)
AGC	American General Contractors
AHA	American Hardboard Association (www.hardboard.org)
AHLI	American Home Lighting Institute
AHMA	American Hotel and Motel Association (www.ahma.com)
AIA	The American Institute of Architects (www.aiaonline.com)
AIBD	The American Institute of Building Design (www.aibd.org)
AISC	American Institute of Steel Construction, Inc. (www.aisc.org)
AISI	American Iron and Steel institute (www.steel.org)
AITC	American Institute of Timber Construction
ALSC	American Lumber Standards Committee
ANSI	American National Standards Institute (www.ansi.org)
APA	American Plywood Association (now Engineered Wood Association) (www.apawood.org)
ARIDO	Association of Registered Interior Designers of Ontario (www.arido.on.ca)
ASA	Acoustical Society of America (www.acoustics.org)
ASAHC	American Society of Architectural Hardware Consultants
ASCE	American Society of Civil Engineers (www.asce.org)
ASHRAE	American Society of Heating, Refrigerating, and Air Conditioning Engineers, Inc. (www.ashrae.org)
ASI	American Specification Institute
ASID	American Society of Interior Designers (www.asid.org)
ASME	American Society of Mechanical Engineers (www.asme.org)
ASSE	American Society for Safety Engineering (www.asse.org)
ASSE	American Society of Sanitary Engineers (www.asse-plumbing.org)
ASTM	American Society for Testing and Materials (www.astm.org)
ATBCB	Architectural and Transportation Barriers Compliance Board (www.access-board.gov)
AWI	American Woodwork Institute

AWPA	American Wood Preservers Association (www.awpa.com)
AWPB	American Wood Preservers Bureau
AWPI	American Wood Preservers Institute (www.awpi.org)
AWS	American Welding Society, Inc. (www.amweld.org)
AWWA	American Water Works Association (www.awwa.org)
BCMC	Board for the Coordination of Model Codes (CABO)
BFRL	Building Fire & Research Laboratory (NIST) (www.bfrl.nist.gov)
BHMA	Building Hardware Manufacturers Association
BIA	Brick Institute of America
BIFMA	Business and Institutional Furniture Manufacturers Association (www.bifma.com)
BOCA	Building Officials and Code Administrators International (www.bocai.org)
BOMA	Building Owners and Managers Association International (www.boma.org)
BP&R	Building Performance and Regulations Committee
BRAB	Building Research Advisory Board
BRI	Building Research Institute
BSI	Building Stone Institute
BSSI	Building Seismic Safety Council (www.bssconline.org)
BTECC	Building Thermal Envelope Coordinating Council
CABO	Council of American Building Officials (now ICC) (www.cabo.org)
CAH	The Center for Accessible Housing
CBD	*Canadian Building Digest* (www.nrc.ca/irc/cbd)
CCC	Carpet Cushion Council (www.carpetcushion.org)
CDA	Copper Development Association, Inc. (www.copper.org)
CFID	Council of Federal Interior Designers (now IIDA)
CFR	Code of Federal Regulations (www.access.gpo.gov/nara/cfr)
CIA	Cork Institute of America
CISC	Ceilings and Interior Systems Contractors Association (www.cisca.org)
CISPI	Cast Iron Soil Pipe Institute (www.cispi.org)
COTCO	Committee on Technical Committee Operations
CPSC	United States Consumer Product Safety Commission (www.cpsc.gov)

CRI	Carpet and Rug Institute (www.carpet-rug.com)
CS	Commercial Standards
CSI	Construction Specifications Institute (www.csinet.org)
CSPP	Committee of Steel Pipe Producers
CSRF	Construction Sciences Research Foundation (www.scrf.org)
CSSB	Cedar Shake and Shingle Bureau (www.cedarbureau.com)
CTI	Ceramic Tile Institute of America (www.ctioa.org)
DHHS	Department of Health and Human Services (www.hhs.gov)
DHI	Door and Hardware Institute (www.dhi.org)
DOC	United States Department of Commerce (www.doc.gov)
DOD	United States Department of Defense (www.defenselink.mil)
DOE	United States Department of Energy (www.doe.gov)
DOI	United States Department of Interior (www.doi.gov)
DOJ	United States Department of Justice (www.usdoj.gov)
DOL	United States Department of Labor (www.dol.gov)
DOT	United States Department of Transportation (www.dot.gov)
DWI	Durable Woods Institute
EPA	Environmental Protection Agency (www.epa.gov)
ETL	ETL Intertek Testing Services (www.etl.com)
FAA	Federal Aviation Administration (www.faa.gov)
FCC	Federal Construction Council
FCGS	Federal Construction Guide Specification
FEMA	Federal Emergency Management Agency (www.fema.gov)
FGMA	Flat Glass Marketing Association
FHA	*Federal Housing Act*
FIDER	Foundation for Interior Design Education Research (www.fider.org)
FMED	Factory Mutual Research Corporation
FM	Factory Mutual Engineering Division
FMERC	Factory Mutual Engineering and Research Corporation
FFRS	Forest Products Research Society

FR	*Federal Register*
FPL	Forest Products Laboratory (www.fpl.fs.fed.us)
FRA	Federal Railroad Administration (www.fra.dot.gov)
FS	Federal Specifications
FSPT	Federation of Societies for Paint Technology (www.coatingstech.org)
FSS	Federal Supply Service (www.fss.gsa.gov)
FTC	Federal Trade Commission (www.ftc.gov)
FTI	Facing Tile Institute
FTMS	Federal Test Method Standard
GA	Gypsum Association (www.gypsum.org)
GSA	General Services Administration
HHS	Department of Health and Human Services (also DHHS) (www.os.dhhs.gov)
HMMA	Hardware Merchants and Manufacturers Association
HPMA	Hardwood Plywood Manufacturers Association
HPSC	Home Products Safety Council
HUD	Department of Housing and Urban Development (www.hud.gov)
IAEI	International Association of Electrical Inspectors (www.iaei.com)
IBC	*International Building Code*
IBD	Institute of Business Designers (now IIDA)
ICBO	International Conference of Building Officials (www.intlcode.org)
ICC	International Code Council (www.intlcode.org)
IDC	Interior Designers of Canada (www.interiordesigncanada.org)
IDEC	Interior Designers Educators Council (www.idec.org)
IEC	*International Electrical Code*
IESNA	Illuminating Engineering Society (www.iesna.org)
IFDA	International Furnishings and Design Association (www.ifda.com)
IFMA	International Facility Management Association (www.ifma.org)
IIDA	International Interior Design Association (formerly IBD, ISID, & CFID) (www.iida.org)
IMC	*International Mechanical Code*
IPC	*International Plumbing Code*
IOTFDC	*International One and Two Family Dwelling Code*

IRC	*International Residential Code*
ISDI	Insulated Steel Door Institute
ISID	International Society of Interior Designers (now IIDA)
ISO	International Organization for Standardization (www.iso.ch)
ISP	Institute of Store Planners (www.ispo.org)
ITD	Institute of Technology Development
LIA	Lead Industries Association, Inc. (www.leadinfo.com)
LSC	*Life Safety Code*
MA	Mahogany Association, Inc.
MBNA	Metal Building Manufacturers Association
MCSC	Model Codes Standardization Council
MEC	Model Energy Code (www.energycodes.org)
MFMA	Maple Flooring Manufacturers Association (www.maplefloor.org)
MGRAD	Minimum Guideline Requirements for Accessible Design
MHI	Mobile Home Institute
MIA	Marble Institute of America (www.marble-institute.com)
MIL/MS	Military Specifications (www.dodssp.daps.mil)
MILSTD	Military Standards (www.dodssp.daps.mil)
MPS	Minimum Property Standards
MSS	Manufacturers Standardization Society of the Valve and Fittings Industry (www.techstandards.co.uk)
NAAMM	National Association of Architectural Metal Manufacturers (www.naamm.org)
NADAF	National Association of Decorative Architectural Finishes
NAIMA	North American Insulation Manufacturers Association (www.naima.org)
NAHB	National Association of Home Builders (www.nahb.com)
NAMD	National Association of Marble Dealers
NAMM	National Association of Mirror Manufacturers
NAMP	National Association of Marble Producers
NASA	National Aeronautics and Space Administration (www.nasa.gov)
NBC	*BOCA National Building Code*
NBHA	National Builders Hardware Association
NBS	National Bureau of Standards

NCD	National Council on Disability (www.ncd.gov)
NCIDQ	National Council for Interior Design Qualification (www.ncidq.org)
NCMA	National Concrete Masonry Association (www.ncma.org)
NCPI	National Clay Pipe Institute (www.ncpi.org)
NCSBCS	National Conference of States on Building Codes and Standards (www.ncsbcs.org)
NEC	*National Electric Code*
NEHRP	National Earthquake Hazards Reduction Program (www.quake.wr.usgs.gov)
NEMA	National Electrical Manufacturers Association (www.nema.org)
NES	National Evaluation Service (www.nateval.org)
NFiPA	National Fire Protection Association (also NFPA) (www.nfpa.org)
NFL	National Fire Lab
NFOR	National Forest Products Association
NFSA	National Fire Sprinkler Association (www.nfsa.org)
NG	National Gypsum Company (www.nationalgypsum.com)
NHLA	National Hardwood Lumber Association (www.natlhardwood.org)
NIAE	National Institute for Architectural Education
NIBS	National Institute of Building Sciences (www.occnibs.org)
NIH	National Institutes of Health (www.nih.gov)
NIOSH	National Institute for Occupational Safety and Health (www.niosh.gov.eg)
NIMA	National Insulation Manufacturers Association
NIST	National Institute of Standards and Technology (www.nist.gov)
NKCA	National Kitchen Cabinet Association
NLPGA	National L-P Gas Association
NMC	*BOCA National Mechanical Code*
NOFI	National Oil Fuel Institute, Inc.
NOFMA	National Oak Flooring Manufacturers Association (www.nofma.org)
NPA	National Particleboard Association
NPC	*BOCA National Plumbing Code*
NPCA	National Pest Control Association (www.pestworld.org)
NPDA	National Plywood Distributors Association

NPVLA	National Paint, Varnish, and Lacquer Association
NSC	National Safety Council (www.nsc.org)
NSF	National Sanitation Foundation Testing (www.nsf.org)
NTMA	National Terazzo and Mosaic Association (www.ntma.com)
NWMA	National Woodworking Manufacturers Association
OSHA	Occupational Safety and Health Administration (www.osha.gov)
OTFDC	*One and Two Family Dwelling Code*
PBS	Public Building Services
PCA	Portland Cement Association (www.portcement.org)
PCI	Prestressed Concrete Institute (www.pci.org)
PDI	Plumbing and Drainage Institute (www.pdionline.org)
PHS	Public Health Services (www.hhs.gov/phs)
PLIB	Pacific Lumber Inspection Bureau (www.softwood.org/PLIB)
PMA	Philippine Mahogany Association
PPI	Plastic Pipe Institute (www.plasticpipe.org)
PPFA	Plastic Pipe & Fitting Association
PPW	Ponderosa Pine Woodwork
PRF	Plywood Research Foundation
PS	*Product Standards*
PTI	Post-Tensioning Institute (www.post-tensioning.org)
PVA/BFDP	Paralyzed Veterans of America, Barrier-Free Design Program
RCSC	Research Council on Structural Connections (www.boltcouncil.org)
RFCI	Resilient Floor Covering Institute (www.rfci.com)
SBC	*Standard Building Code*
SBCCI	Southern Building Code Congress International (www.sbcci.org)
SDI	Steel Door Institute (www.wherryassoc.com/steeldoor.org)
SFPA	Society of Fire Protection Engineers (www.sfpe.org)
SGA	Southern Gas Association (www.sga-aso.com)
SGA	Stained Glass Association of America
SJI	Steel Joist Institute (www.steeljoist.org)

SMACNA	Sheet Metal & Air Conditioning Contractors National Association, Inc. (www.smacna.org)
SMC	*Standard Mechanical Code*
SPA	Southern Pine Association
SPC	*Standard Plumbing Code*
SPI	Society of the Plastics Industry, Inc. (www.socplas.org)
SSA	Social Security Administration (www.ssa.gov)
STI	Steel Tank Institute (www.steeltank.com)
TC	Tile Council of America (www.tileusa.com)
TPI	Truss Plate Institute
UBC	*Uniform Building Code*
UBPVLS	Uniform Boiler and Pressure Vessel Laws Society, Inc.
UCBC	*Uniform Code for Building Conservation*
UFAC	Upholstered Furniture Action Council (www.ufac.org)
UFAS	*Uniform Federal Accessibility Standards*
UL	Underwriters Laboratories, Inc. (www.ul.com)
ULC	Underwriters Laboratories of Canada (www.ulc.ca)
UMC	*Uniform Mechanical Code*
UPC	*Uniform Plumbing Code*
USCS	United States Department of Commerce, Commercial Standards (www.ia-usa.org/natcomm.htm)
USDA	United States Department of Agriculture (www.usda.gov)
USFA	United States Fire Administration (www.usfa.fema.gov)
VA	Veterans Administration
WA	Waferboard Association
WCLIB	West Coast Lumber Inspection Bureau (www.wclib.org)
WFIA	Wood Flooring Institute of America
WH	Warnock Hersey (www.warnockhersey.com)
WPC	Wood Protection Council
WRI	Wire Reinforcement Institute, Inc. (www.bright.net/~wwri)
WSFI	Wood and Synthetic Flooring Institute

CODE RESOURCES

Eventually you will want to start your own codes library, or you may need to find a specific book for a project you are working on. Below are the names, addresses, and phone numbers of the many codes, standards, and national organizations, government regulatory agencies, and some of the most popular professional bookstores in the United States. Many now have web sites as well.

All of the codes and standards organizations carry their own publications. Some of these sources are listed in the Bibliography of this book. Many of these organizations also sell literature and forms to complement these publications. The national organizations can provide supportive data on the codes and standards. Each of the federal regulatory agencies supplies a copy of its own regulations and provides other literature upon request. The professional bookstores carry a variety of the code publications and many other useful reference books. Most of them will mail you a free book listing or catalog upon request and will take on-line or phone orders with a credit card.

Codes Organizations

Building Officials and Code Administrators International (BOCA)
4051 West Flossmoor Road
Country Club Hills, IL 60478
(708) 799-2300
(800) 323-1103
www.bocai.org

International Code Council (ICC)
5203 Leesburg Pike
Falls Church, VA 22041
(703) 931-4533
www.intlcode.org

International Conference of Building Officials (ICBO)
5360 South Workman Mill Road
Whittier, CA 90611
(562) 699-0541
www.icbo.org

Southern Building Code Congress International (SBCCI)
900 Montclair Road
Birmingham, AL 35213-1206
(205) 591-1853
(800) 877-2224
www.sbcci.org

Federal Regulatory Agencies

Architectural and Transportation Barriers Compliance Board
(ATBCB, also known as the ADA Access Board)
1111 18th Street NW
Suite 501
Washington, DC 20036
(202) 653-7848 (Voice/TDD)
(800) 872-2253 (Voice/TDD)
www.access-board.gov

Department of Energy (DOE)
Forrestal Building
1000 Independence Avenue SW
Washington, DC 20505
(202) 586-6827
www.doe.gov

Department of Housing and Urban Development (HUD)
4M Seventh Street SW
Washington, DC 20410
(202) 619-8045
www.hud.gov

Department of Interior (DOI)
Preservation Assistance Division
National Park Service
P.O. Box 37127
Suite 200
Washington, DC 20013
(202) 343-9573
www.doi.gov

Department of Justice (DOJ)
Office of Americans with Disabilities Act
Civil Rights Division
P.O. Box 66118
Washington, DC 20530
(202) 524-0301 (Voice)
(202) 514-0381 (TDD)
www.usdoj.gov

Environmental Protection Agency (EPA)
401 M Street SW
Washington, DC 20460
(202) 382-2080
www.epa.gov

Federal Communications Commission (FCC)
1919 M Street NW
Washington, DC 20554
(202) 632-7260 (Voice)
(202) 632-6999 (TDD)
www.fcc.gov

Federal Emergency Management Agency (FEMA)
401 M Street SW
Washington, DC 20472
(202) 646-2500
www.fema.gov

National Institute of Standards and Technology (NIST)
Quince Orchard and Clopper Roads
Gaithersburg, MD 20899
(301) 975-3058
www.nist.gov

Occupational Safety and Health Administration (OSHA)
Office of Informational Safety and Consumer Affairs
200 Constitution Avenue
Room N3647
Washington, DC 20210
(202) 523-8148
www.osha.gov/index.html

Standards Organizations

American National Standards Institute (ANSI)
1130 Broadway
New York, NY 10018
(212) 642-4900
(800) 242-4140
www.ansi.org/home.html

American Society of Heating, Refrigeration, and Air Conditioning
　　Engineers (ASHRAE)
1791 Tullie Circle NE
Atlanta, GA 30329
(404) 636-8400
www.ashrae.org

American Society for Testing and Materials (ASTM)
100 Barr Harbor Drive
West Conshoshocken, PA 19428
(610) 832-9500
www.astm.org

National Fire Protection Association (NFPA)
P.O. Box 9101
Batterymarch Park
Quincy, MA 02269
(617) 770-3000
www.nfpa.org

Underwriters Laboratories (UL)
333 Pfingsten Road
Northbrook, IL 60062
(708) 272-8800
www.ul.com

National Organizations

National Conference of States on Building Codes and Standards
(NCSBCS)
505 Huntmar Park Drive
Suite 210
Herndon, VA 22070
(703) 437-0100
www.ncsbcs.org

National Institute of Building Sciences (NIBS)
1201 L Street NW
Suite 400
Washington. DC 20005
(202) 289-7800
www.occnibs.org

Professional Bookstores

CALIFORNIA

Builders Booksource
1817 Fourth Street
Berkeley, CA 94710
(510) 845-6874
(800) 843-2028
www.buildersbooksite.com

Hennessey + Ingalls
Art & Architecture Books
1254 Third Street Promenade
Santa Monica, CA 90401
(310) 458-9074

Richard Hilkert, Bookseller, Ltd.
333 Hayes Street
San Francisco, CA 94102
(415) 863-3339

Rizzoli Bookstore
951 Wilshire Boulevard
Beverly Hills, CA 90212
(310) 278-2247

Rizzoli Bookstore
3328 Santa Monica Boulevard
Santa Monica, CA 90401
(310) 393-0101

Rizzoli Bookstore
South Coast Plaza
3333 Bristol
Costa Mesa, CA 92626
(714) 957-3331

William Stout Architectural Books
804 Montgomery Street
San Francisco, CA 94133
(415) 391-6757

DISTRICT OF COLUMBIA

AIA Bookstore
1735 New York Avenue NW
Washington DC 20006
(202) 626-7475

BOMA Publications
1201 New York Avenue NW
Suite 300
Washington, DC 20005
(800) 426-6292

Home Builders Bookstore
1201 Fifteenth Street NW
Washington, DC 20005
(800) 223-2665

FLORIDA

Books & Books, Inc.
296 Aragon Avenue
Coral Gables, FL 33134
(305) 442-4408

ILLINOIS

Prairie Avenue Bookshop
418 South Wabash
Chicago, IL 60605
(800) 474-2724

Rizzoli Bookstore/Chicago
Water Tower Place
835 North Michigan Avenue
Chicago, IL 60611
(312) 642-3500

INDIANA

Architectural Center Bookstore
47 South Pennsylvania
Indianapolis, IN 46204
(317) 634-3871

MASSACHUSETTS

Rizzoli Bookstore
Copley Place
100 Huntington Avenue
Boston, MA 02116
(617) 437-0700

NEW YORK

Rizzoli Bookstore/Midtown
31 West 57th Street
New York, NY 10019
(212) 759-2424
(800) 522-6657

Rizzoli Bookstore/Winter Garden
3 World Financial Center
New York, NY 10281
(212) 385-1400

Rizzoli Bookstore/SoHo
454 West Broadway
New York, NY 10012
(212) 674-1616

Urban Center Books
457 Madison Avenue
New York, NY 10022
(212) 935-3592

OREGON

Building Tech Bookstore
8020 SW Cirrus Drive
Beaverton, OR 97008
(800) 275-2665

TENNESSEE

Davis-Kidd Booksellers
4007 Hillsboro Pike
Nashville, TN 37215
(615) 292-8251
(615) 385-2645

Professional Booksellers
2200 21st Street
Nashville, TN 37212
(615) 383-0044

TEXAS

IFMA Bookstore
One East Greenway Plaza
Suite 1100
Houston, TX 77016-0191
(713) 623-4362

WASHINGTON

Peter Miller Books
1930 First Avenue
Seattle, WA 98101
(206) 441-4114

ON-LINE BOOKSTORES

www.amazon.com
www.barnes&noble.com
www.borders.com
www.wordsworth.com

ABOUT THE ADA

As mentioned in Chapter 1, the *Americans with Disability Act (ADA)* is a federal civil law that prohibits discrimination against people with disabilities. Since it is a federal law, the code officials in a jurisdiction cannot decide whether or not it applies in their area; *ADA* is enforceable in the entire United States. The better question may be: Does the project have to conform to the *ADA* guidelines? And, to what extent must the project meet the *Americans with Disabilities Accessibility Guidelines (ADAAG)* requirements?

PLACE OF PUBLIC ACCOMMODATION

Title III is the segment of the law that requires compliance in places of public accommodation. A place of public accommodation is defined by *ADA* as any facility that is owned and operated by a private entity whose operation affects commerce and falls within one of these 12 categories:

Place of lodging
Establishment serving food
Place of exhibition or entertainment
Place of public gathering
Sale or rental establishment
Service establishment
Station for public transportation
Place of public display
Educational facility
Recreation areas
Place of exercise
Social service center

Although almost all places of public activity are included in the definition of a place of public accommodation, facilities that are owned and operated by religious entities, one- and two-family dwellings, private clubs, and certain government facilities are not required to conform to the requirements. Those entities may not be completely exempt from compliance, however, if part of their facilities is utilized as a place of public accommodation. For example, if a church rents part of its facility to a day care during the week and the day care is not operated by the church, the area that the day care leases would be required to meet *ADA* requirements. Similarly, if a part of a private residence is used as a business that is open to the public, that part of the residence that is used as the business would be required to meet the requirements even though private residences are exempt from *ADA*.

Conversely, an educational facility that is operated by a synagogue, for example, may not be required to conform with *ADA* because of the exemption for religious entities. In some cases, it may be clear whether your project needs to comply with *ADA*, whereas in other cases, you may need to discuss this further with your client to determine if the space would be considered a public accommodation. It may be wise to seek an opinion from the Access Board for projects that are not clear. (See Resources in Appendix D)

Note

The *ADA* covers other aspects of accessibility that can affect your project, including employment, communication, and equipment.

ADA ACCESSIBILITY GUIDELINES

The part of the *ADA* that gives designers specific design criteria for accessibility in all aspects of interior and architectural design is called the *ADA Accessibility Guidelines (ADAAG)*. It is not within the scope of this book to include all the requirements of the *ADAAG*. However, it is important to understand that the requirements found in the *ADAAG* are presented as either scoping requirements or technical requirements. Scoping requirements tell you how many accessible toilets, water fountains, doors, and so on you must provide. Technical requirements give you specific requirements or dimensions which have to be met for the door, sink, millwork, and so on to be accessible. The *ADAAG* also covers special occupancy sections. These include both scoping and technical provisions that are specific to the building use. (See Chapter 2 for more information.) The Access Board is responsible for making revisions to the *ADAAG* as discussed in Chapter 1.

Some aspects of a space within a public accommodation may not need to meet the *ADAAG* requirements if not used by the

Note

Revisions to the *ADAAG* made by the Access Board are enforceable only when voted into law by the Department of Justice (DOJ).

public. The level of accessibility that your project must meet should be established early in the design process. As a designer, it is your responsibility to understand and keep abreast of the most current *ADAAG* requirements.

LEVEL OF COMPLIANCE

Depending on whether your project involves new construction, an alteration of an existing space, or minor cosmetic changes to an existing facility, the *ADA* laws provide for different levels of required compliance with the *ADAAG*. Generally, the requirements for new construction are most stringent, whereas there are allowances for projects that are alterations to an existing building or space and for existing facilities not currently being modified. Below is a general overview of the varying levels of compliance for each type of construction project.

New Construction

For new construction, the design must meet all the requirements as prescribed by the *ADAAG*. A project that is from the ground up or a completely new tenant space within an existing building, for example, would both be considered new construction according to the *ADA*. In the case of new construction, there are essentially no exceptions for meeting the requirements.

Alterations

In the case of an alteration or renovation to an existing building, rules for compliance are more complex. If a project involves alterations or renovations to an existing building, changes made to the area must conform to *ADAAG* unless existing conditions make compliance impossible. Alterations to one area may require additional changes in adjacent areas. For example, if a "primary function space," such as a small auditorium in a high school, is altered and made to be more accessible, *ADA* may require that the path to the primary function area and certain support areas, such as the corridors to the auditorium and to the bathrooms, drinking fountains, and telephones, be altered to provide a similar level of accessibility.

However, if the cost of alterations to ancillary facilities and the path of travel to them exceeds 20 percent of the cost of the alteration of the primary function area, those changes would not

Note

In some cases, an alteration to an existing building would not have to meet the *ADAAG* requirements, such as, if the change is structurally infeasible or would cause an unsafe condition.

be required. The 20-percent rule may allow alterations for accessibility to be done in increments, but it is not intended to allow building owners to make a series of small alterations to an existing building in order to avoid a more costly accessibility update. To prevent this, the law specifies that the total cost of alterations in a three-year period may be accessed to determine if an appropriate allotment of cost has been spent on accessibility updates.

Existing Facilities

ADA also applies to existing buildings even if no alterations or renovations are planned. Owners may seek the advice of a design professional concerning how *ADA* applies to them. When the *ADA* law was passed, it allowed for a two-year period for the removal of "architectural barriers" from existing buildings. The intent was to allow building owners to begin to make changes to their existing buildings, such as adding ramps, widening doors, adding power-assisted doors, and fixing other existing barriers, to bring their buildings into compliance with the law and make them accessible.

Since the initial two-year period has ended, owners are now expected to evaluate their facilities and to develop a strategy to make their facility accessible to persons with disabilities in the near future. This should be documented by a written report and drawings. There are some options for accommodating the needs of persons with disabilities instead of making physical changes. However, conforming to *ADA* regulations should be pursued to the extent of "readily achievable." An accessible path to the building from the exterior, an accessible entrance into the building, an accessible path to the goods or services, accessible toilet facilities, and then direct access to the actual goods and services is the order of priority that *ADA* sets for making changes to an existing building. (Additional exceptions are allowed for existing buildings that are deemed historic. See Existing and Historic Buildings in Appendix B for more information.)

To the Maximum Extent Feasible

For all project types the law requires that an attempt to meet the *ADAAG* requirements be "to the maximum extent feasible." If the alterations needed to meet the requirements are not "readily achievable," both structurally and financially, the law allows for exceptions when the alteration could be considered an "undue burden." One example might be that during the renovation of an auditorium, it is determined that although required by *ADAAG*, an assisted listening system exceeds the budget for this phase of the project and is disproportionate to the profit that the owner receives from the auditorium.

Many times these burdens are hard to determine. They are usually decided on a case-by-case basis by the regulating authority or the courts. (Review some of the resources in the Bibliography for additional information.) When determining whether the cost of the accommodation is an undue burden, the financial resources of the facility, the number of employees, and the type of facility are taken in to account. The decision to limit the scope of accessibility should be determined by the owner as "undue burden," and should be primarily a financial decision, not a design decision. It is typically the owner's responsibility to provide the legal documentation to support this decision.

Another way that the government encourages building owners to make their existing facilities accessible is through tax incentives. Small businesses, in particular, may be able to receive tax credits for architectural and system modifications for accessibility purposes. Other provisions allow expenditures to be treated as a tax deduction instead of as a capital expenditure. Although not within the scope of this book or within the scope of typical design services, designers should be aware that these incentives are available.

REGULATION AND ENFORCEMENT

Because the *ADA* is a civil rights law, the *ADA* is enforced through the judicial system. It could occur through a private suit by an individual or by legal action taken by a federal agency in support of a discrimination claim. Because most projects must meet additional local or state accessibility requirements, many issues can be clarified as part of the code review process, but the *ADAAG* requirements are different. In most cases, there is not a local agency that will review a project for compliance with *ADAAG*. Several states have developed individual accessibility standards and submitted them for review by the Department of Justice (DOJ) for certification. Currently, Texas, Washington, Maine, and Florida have accessibility standards certified by the DOJ. If the standard is certified to sufficiently address accessibility issues consistent with the *ADAAG*, the new standard is considered "certified." Then the projects can be reviewed by local building officials for accessibility compliance. This process, however, still does not guarantee that the project is in complete compliance with *ADAAG*.

In many cases, compliance with *ADAAG* will be clearly defined. If not, you can request clarification of specific issues of concern from the Access Board. In addition, each state now has a central contact to assist with technical questions. A list of these state code contacts can be found on the Access Board's web site. (See Appendix D.) Projects can also be sent to the Department of Justice or the Access Board for review; but this process may not be practical except for significantly large projects.

RESPONSIBILITY FOR COMPLIANCE

Initially, the owner was recognized as the sole entity responsible for establishing compliance in the facility because of the language of the regulations. The language of the law represents that the owner is the one who "owns" and "operates" the facility and who is involved in the "design and construction" of the facility. The owner makes decisions about many issues that can affect the accessibility of a space or building. The owner sometimes limits the scope of work because of budget. The owner also maintains the facility after construction.

However, recent legal disputes between the DOJ and design firms suggest that the design professional and potentially others in the construction process may hold some legal responsibility for compliance with *ADA* in the future. It may be reasonable to assume that the designer is familiar with the *ADAAG* requirements in order to apply them to the design. However, the issue of responsibility under the law is still unclear. What is clear is that you should seek a complete understanding of the need for compliance as a joint effort between the client and your design efforts in the development of the project. Documenting your decisions in drawings and other written documents is important. The clarity of *ADA* is still being discovered through the judicial system and the subsequent modifications to the *ADA*, including the *ADAAG*.

In conclusion, if your project falls within the definition of public accommodation as described in the *ADA*, then the *ADAAG* requirements will apply to your project. (See the exceptions mentioned earlier.) In addition, state and local jurisdictions may have other accessibility codes or requirements that need to be considered. (See Chapter 1.) In cases where the requirements seem to conflict, the requirement that provides for the greater degree of accessibility should be used.

Note

Sometimes, additional accessibility standards, such as *ANSI*, will apply to your project. It depends on the code jurisdiction.

BIBLIOGRAPHY BY TOPIC

ACCESSIBILITY

Belbusti, John M., "The Complexity of Compliance with the ADA," *The Metropolitan Corporate Counsel*, March 2000, p. 6.

Building Owners and Managers Association International, *ADA Compliance Guidebook: A Checklist for Your Building*, New York, NY, 1991.

Carson, Wayne G., P.E., Code Comparison Charts/Accessibility Requirements for Person with Disabilities, Code Connection, Inc., Warrenton, VA, 1992.

Evan Terry Associates, P.C., *Americans with Disabilities Act Facilities Compliance Workbook*, John Wiley & Sons, Inc., New York, NY, 1994.

Kridler, Charles and R. K. Stewart, "Technics Topics Access for the Disabled: Part II," *Progressive Architecture*, August 1992, pp. 35–36.

Kridler, Charles and R. K. Stewart, "Technics Topics Access for the Disabled: Part III," *Progressive Architecture*, September 1992, pp. 45–46.

Perritt, Henry H., Jr., *Americans with Disabilities Act Handbook*, 2nd ed., John Wiley & Sons, Inc., New York, NY, 1991.

BUILDING HEIGHT AND AREA

Allen, Edward and Joseph Iano, *The Architect's Studio Companion*, John Wiley & Sons, Inc., New York, NY, 1995.

International Conference of Building Officials, *Handbook to the Uniform Building Code*, ICBO, Whittier, CA, 1998.

CODE INFORMATION AND CODE OFFICIALS

The American Institute of Architects, *An Architect's Guide to Building Codes & Standards*, 3rd ed., Washington, DC, 1991.

The American Institute of Architects, *Introduction to Building Codes and Standards*, State Government Affairs, Washington, DC, April 1987.

Building Officials and Code Administrators International, *BOCA National Building Code*, BOCA, Country Club Hills, IL, 1999.

Building Officials and Code Administrators International, Inc., International Conference of Building Officials, Southern Building Code Congress International, *Legal Aspects of Code Administration*, August 1998.

Council of American Building Officials, "National Review Process Streamlines Product Evaluation," *CABO Newsletter*, April 1996, pp. 2–3.

Dorris, Virginia Kent, "Living and Working within the Code," *Southern Building*, March/April 1999, pp. 15–17.

International Code Council, *International Building Code*, ICC, Country Club Hills, IL, 2000.

International Conference of Building Officials, *The Uniform Building Code*, ICBO, Whittier, CA, 1997.

National Fire Protection Association, *NFPA 101: Life Safety Code*, Quincy, MA, 2000.

Nelson, David S., Bruce J. Burdette, and Kathleen I. Mihelich, "Nationally Recognized Inspector Certification through ICC," *Codes Forum*, January–February 1997, pp. 48–49.

National Fire Protection Association, "Questions and Answers about NFPA codes and How They Fit into Existing Regulatory Systems," *NFPA Journal*, May/June 1996, p. 97.

Patterson, Maureen, "Know the Codes," *Building Interiors*, 1997, pp. 6–7.

Scott, David, "The New Inspector; Everywhere at Once," *NFPA Journal*, January/February 1997, pp. 84–87.

Smeallie, Peter H., "Federal Buildings Local Codes," *The Construction Specifier*, April 1990, pp. 106–110.

Southern Building Code Congress International, *Standard Building Code*, SBCCI, Birmingham, AL, 1999.

Underwriters Laboratories, Inc., *An Overview of Underwriters Laboratories*, Northbrook, IL, 1993.

Underwriters Laboratories, Inc., *Testing for Public Safety*, Northbrook, IL, 1992.

Zekowski, Gerry, "Understanding UL," *Architectural Lighting*, January 1992, pp. 35–37.

CONSTRUCTION TYPES

Allen, Edward and Joseph Iano, *The Architect's Studio Companion*, John Wiley & Sons, New York, NY, 1995.

Holland, Joseph T., III, "Fire Retardant Treated Wood," *Southern Building*, September/October, 1993, pp. 19–21.

Cote, Ron, P.E., *Life Safety Code Handbook*, 7th ed., National Fire Protection Association, Inc., Quincy, MA, 1997.

National Fire Protection Association, *NFPA 220: Types of Building Construction*, NFPA, Quincy, MA, 1999.

ELECTRICAL CODES

Cauldwell, Rex, "Electrical Handbook for Remodelers," *JLC*, January 1992, pp. 20–23.

Coxe, Sally Jewell, "Making Connections," *NFPA Journal*, September/October 1998, pp. 64–65, 68–71.

Early, Mark W., P.E. et al., *National Electric Code Handbook 1999*, National Fire Protection Association, Quincy MA, 1999.

Germershausen, Mary M., "Structured Cabling: Building Block of the New Millennium," *The Construction Specifier*, November 1999.

Holt, Michael, *Understanding the National Electrical Code*, Albany, NY, 1996.

Intertec Electrical Group, *Understanding NE Code Rules on Lighting*, Intertec Publishing Corporation, New York, NY, 1991.

Moore, Wayne D. P.C., "Systems Integration—It's Here," *NFPA Journal*, January/February 2000, p. 30.

Myers, Donald L., "Security Locking Systems," *The Construction Specifier*, CSI Net, April 1996, http://www.csinet.org.

National Fire Protection Association, *National Electric Code*, NFPA, Quincy, MA, 2000.

Ratto, F James, "Emergency Lighting—A Critical Element in Building Safety," *Architectural Lighting*, October/November 1992, pp. 39–40.

Seaton, Michelle, "Communication Is Key," *NFPA Journal*, September/October, 1998, pp. 58, 60–61.

FINISHES AND FURNISHINGS

Cote, Ron, P.E., *Life Safety Code Handbook*, 7th ed., National Fire Protection Association, Inc., Quincy, MA, 1997.

Jackman, Dianne R. and Mary K. Dixon, *The Guide to Textiles for Interior Designers*, 2nd ed., Peguis Publishers Limited, Winnipeg, Canada, 1990.

McGowan, Maryrose, AIA, IIDA, *Specifying Interiors*, John Wiley & Sons, Inc. New York, NY.

National Council of Architectural Registration Boards, *Fire Safety in Buildings*, NCARB, 1996.

National Fire Protection Association, *NFPA 260: Standard Methods of Tests and Classification System for Cigarette Ignition Resistance of Components of Upholstered Furniture*, NFPA, Quincy, MA, 1998.

National Fire Protection Association, *NFPA 261: Standard Method of Test forDetermining Resistance of Mock-up Upholstered Furniture Material Assemblies to Ignition by Smoldering Cigarettes*, NFPA, Quincy, MA, 1998.

National Fire Protection Association, *NFPA 266: Standard Method of Test for Fire Characteristics of Upholstered Furniture Exposed to Flaming Ignition Source*, NFPA, Quincy, MA, 1998.

National Fire Protection Association, *NFPA 26: Standard Method of Test for Fire Characteristics of Mattresses and Bedding Assemblies Exposed to Flaming Ignition Source*, NFPA, Quincy, MA, 1998.

National Fire Protection Association, *NFPA 701: Methods of Fire Tests for Flame-Resistant Textiles and Films*, NFPA, Quincy, MA, 1999.

National Fire Protection Association, *NFPA 272: Standard Method of Test Heat and Visible Smoke Release Rates for Upholstered Furniture Components or Composites and Mattresses Using an Oxygen Consumption Calorimeter*, NFPA, Quincy, MA, 1999.

National Fire Protection Association, *NFPA 286: Standard Methods of Fire Tests for Evaluating Contribution of Wall and Ceiling Interior Finish to Room Fire Growth*, NFPA, Quincy, MA, 2000.

New York State Department of State Office of Fire Prevention and Control, *Fire Gas Toxicity*, Albany, NY, May 1984.

New York State Department of State Office of Fire Prevention and Control, *New York State Building Materials and Finishes Fire Gas Toxicity Data File*, Albany, NY, September 1992.

Reznikoff, S. C., *Specifications for Commercial Interiors*, Billboard Publications, Inc., New York, NY, 1989.

"The Facts on TB 133," *UDM Uphoistry Design & Manufacturtng*, July 1992, pp. 28–30.

Zelinsky, Marilyn, "Update: California Technical Bulletin 133," *Interiors*, September 1992, pp. 33–34, 118.

FIRE AND SMOKE PREVENTION

Braun, Vince C., "Steel, Hollow Metal, and Composit Fire Doors and Frames," *The Construction Specifier*, April 1994, pp. 98–111.

Cooper, Martin J., II, "Firestopping," *The Construction Specifier*, May 1992, pp. 171–184.

Council on Tall Buildings and Urban Habitat, *Fire Safety in Tall Buildings*, McGraw Hill, Inc., New York, NY, 1992, pp. 17–24.

Fleming, Russell P., "Myths and Misconceptions," *NFPA Journal*, January/February 1999, pp. 20, 79.

Flaming, Russell P., "Fast Responses," *NFPA Journal*, September/October 1999, p. 28.

Gentile, Kenneth, P.E., "How to Talk Alarms," *NFPA Journal* September/October, 1998, pp. 63–65.

Gypsum Association, *Fire Resistance Design Manual*, Washington, DC, April 2000.

Hicks, Harold D., Jr., "Fire Ratings for Glass Block: What They Don't Tell You," *The Construction Specifier*, February 1991, pp. 27–29.

Klote, John, "Compartmentation and Dampers Are Essential for Life Safety," *Southern Building* March/April 1999, pp. 4, 5–7.

Leddin, Margaret M., "Carbon Monoxide," *Southern Building*, March/April 1995, pp. 14–18.

National Fire Protection Association, *NFPA 80: Fire Doors and Fire Windows*, NFPA, Quincy, MA, 1999.

National Fire Protection Association, *NFPA 251: Fire Tests of Building Construction and Materials*, NFPA, Quincy, MA, 1999.

Parker, John W., "Changes in Science and Standards Open Door to High-Tech Detection," *NFPA Journal*, September/October 1995, pp. 43–47.

Pierce, Michael and Gerald M. Cordasco, "Smarter Detectors," *NFPA Journal*, November/December, pp. 79–82.

Puchovsky, Milosh, "NFPA 13: What You Need to Know about the 1999 Edition," *NFPA Journal*, September/October 1999, pp. 73–76.

Puchovsky, Milosh, "Strengthening the Standards," *NFPA Journal*, January/February 1998, pp. 26–27.

Puchovsky, Milosh, "Fast Responses," *NFPA Journal*, September/October 1997, pp. 26–27.

Reese, Shelly, "Decisions, Decisions," *NFPA Journal*, November/December 1998, pp. 76–79.

Rossiter, W.J. and J.A. Ventrella, "Site Testing Smoke Detectors in Commercial Occupancies," *NFPA Journal*, May/June 1998, pp. 110–115.

Scott, David, "Halon; The Hunt for Alternatives," *NFPA Journal*, July/August 1997, pp. 62, 64–65.

Seaton, Michele, "Halon Searching for Solutions," *NFPA Journal*, November/December 1995, pp. 45, 47–53.

Underwriters Laboratories Inc., *The Code Authority*, 1997.

Underwriters Laboratories, Inc., *Fire Resistance Directory, Vol. I and II, UL, Inc.*, Northbrook, IL, 2000.

HISTORICAL BUILDINGS

Fisher, Charles E., III, Michael Auer, and Anne Grimmer, *The Interiors Handbook for Historic Buildings*, Historic Education Foundation, Washington, DC, 1988.

International Conference of Building Officials, *The Uniform Code for Building Conservation*, ICBO, Whittier, CA, 1997.

Kass, Stephen L., Judith M. LaBelle, and David A. Hansell, *Rehabilitating Older and Historic Buildings*, 2nd ed., John Wiley & Sons, New York, NY, 1992.

Kay, Gersil N., "Making Historical Buildings Accessible," *The Construction Specifier*, August 1992, pp. 33–34.

U.S. Department of the Interior, The Secretary of the Interior's Standards for Rehabilitation, Washington, DC, 1990.

MEANS OF EGRESS

Allen, Edward and Joseph Iano, *The Architect's Studio Companion*, John Wiley & Sons, New York, NY, 1995.

Brummett, William J. and Alec W Johnson, *Building Code Quick Reference Guide: A Schematic Building Design Timesaver*, Professional Publications, Belmont, CA, 1993, pp. 88–107.

Cote, Ron, P.E., *Life Safety Code Handbook*, 7th ed., National Fire Protection Association, Inc., Quincy, MA, 1997.

International Conference of Building Officials, *Handbook to the Uniform Building Code*, ICBO, Whittier, CA, 1998.

Koffel, William, P.E., "Once You're Out...," *NFPA Journal*, September/October 1998, p. 22.

Koffel, William, P.E., "Renovation by the Book," *NFPA Journal* , July/August 1997, p. 26

Koffel, William, P.E., "Using Elevators as a Means of Egress," *NFPA Journal*, January/February 1996, p. 30.

MECHANICAL CODES

Ballast, David K., *Interior Design Reference Manual*, Professional Publications, Inc., Belmont, CA, 1992, pp. 175–177.

International Code Council, *International Mechanical Code*, ICC, Falls Church, VA, 2000.

OCCUPANCY CLASSIFICATION

Allen, Edward and Joseph Iano, *The Architect's Studio Companion*, John Wiley & Sons, Inc., New York, NY, 1995.

Cote, Ron, P.E., *Life Safety Code Handbook*, 7th ed., National Fire Protection Association, Inc., Quincy, MA, 1997.

International Conference of Building Officials, *Handbook to the Uniform Building Code*, ICBO, Whittier, CA, 1998.

Koffel, William, P.E., "Are Occupancy Classifications Outdated?," *NFPA Journal*, September/October 1997, p. 28.

Koffel, William, P.E. , "Classifying Assisted-Living Facilities," *NFPA Journal*, July/August 1999, p. 32.

Koffel, William, P.E., "Five Myths of Occupant Load Calculations," *NFPA Journal*, September/October 1997, p. 30.

PLUMBING CODES

International Code Council, *International Plumbing Code*, ICC, Falls Church, VA, 2000.

Massey, Howard C., *Basic Plumbing with Illustrations*, Craftsman Book Company, Carlsbad, CA, 1992.

Perry, Lawrence, AIA and Soy L. Williams, AIA, "Unisex Toilet and Bathing Rooms: A Clear Need, a Clearer Opportunity," *Southern Building*, July/August 1996, pp. 20–21.

Puchovsky, Milosh, "The International Plumbing Code: Essential to the Solution," January–February 1999, http://www.icbo.org.

RESIDENTIAL—ONE AND TWO FAMILY

Barrier Free Environments, *The Accessible Housing Design File*, Van Nostrand Reinhold, New York, NY, 1991.

Mullin, Ray C., *Electrical Wiring Residential*, Delmar Publishers, Inc., Albany, NY, 1993.

International Code Council, *International Residential Code*, ICC, Falls Church, VA, 2000.

National Fire Protection Association, *NFPA 73: Electrical Maintenance Code for One and Two Family Dwellings*, NFPA, Quincy, MA, 1996.

National Fire Protection Association, *NFPA 13D: Installation of Sprinkler Systems in One and Two Family Dwellings and Manufactured Homes*, NFPA, Quincy, MA, 1999.

National Fire Protection Association, *NFPA 720: Installation of Household Carbon Monoxide (6) Warning Equipment*, NFPA, Quincy, MA, 1998.

U.S. Department of Housing and Urban Development, *Fair Housing, Its Your Right*, Washington, DC, April 1993.

GLOSSARY

ACCESSIBLE A building or space that can be approached, entered, and used by persons with disabilities.

ACCESSIBLE ROUTE A continuous and unobstructed path connecting all accessible elements and spaces of a building including corridors, floors, ramps, elevators, lifts, and clear floor spaces at fixtures.

ADDITION An expansion, extension, or increase in the gross floor area of a building.

AFTER FLAME When an item continues to hold a flame after the source of ignition is removed.

AISLE The space between elements such as furniture and equipment that provides clearances to pass by and/or use the elements.

AISLE ACCESSWAY The portion of an exit that leads to an aisle.

ALTERATION A change to a building that affects the usability of the building, including remodeling, renovation, rehabilitation, reconstruction, historic restoration, and changes or rearrangement of structure elements (i.e., walls).

ANNUNCIATOR A device with one or more types of indicators that provide status information about a circuit, condition, or location.

APPROVED Acceptable to the authority having jurisdiction.

AREA, GROSS FLOOR The area within the inside perimeter of a building's exterior walls, exclusive of vent shafts and interior courts, with no deduction for corridors, stairs, closets, wall thicknesses, columns, toilet rooms, mechanical rooms, or other unoccupiable areas. (Shall not include shafts with no openings or interior courts.)

AREA, NET FLOOR The area actually occupied within a building *not* including accessory unoccupied areas such as corridors, stairs, closets, wall thicknesses, columns, toilet rooms, and mechanical rooms.

AREA OF REFUGE An area protected by fire-rated walls to provide protection from fire or smoke where persons who are unable to use the stairways can remain temporarily to await assistance during an emergency evacuation. (Code term.)

AREA OF RESCUE ASSISTANCE An area that has a direct access to an exit where people who are unable to use stairs may remain temporarily in safety to await further instructions or assistance during emergency evacuations. (Accessibility term.)

ASSEMBLY, CONSTRUCTION Building materials used together to create a structural element.

ASSEMBLY, FIRE-RATED A combination of parts (including all required construction materials, hardware, anchorage, frames, sills, etc.) that when used together make up a structural element that has passed various fire tests and has been assigned a fire rating.

ATRIUM A roofed, multistory open space contained within a building that is intended for occupancy.

AUTOMATIC DOOR CLOSER A door closure that is activated by smoke or heat, causing the door to close in an emergency to prevent the spread of fire and smoke.

AUTOMATIC SPRINKLER SYSTEM A system using water to suppress a fire when activated by a smoke or fire detector system.

BACKCOATING The process of coating the underside of a fabric or finish to improve its durability and/or serve as a heat barrier.

BACK DRAFT See Flashover.

BALLAST A magnetic coil that adjusts current through a fluorescent tube, providing the current surge to start the lamp.

BARRIERS Any building element, equipment, or object that restricts or prevents the intended use of a space.

BASEMENT Any story of a building that is partially or completely below grade level.

BORROWED LIGHT An interior stationary window that allows passage of light from one area to the next.

BOX, ELECTRICAL A wiring device that is used to contain wire terminations where they connect to other wires, switches, or outlets.

BOX, JUNCTION An electrical box where several wires are joined together.

BRANCH A horizontal pipe that leads from a main, riser, or stack pipe to the plumbing fixture or sprinkler head.

BUILDING A structure that encloses a space used for sheltering any use or occupancy.

BUILDING CODE Regulations that stress the construction of a building and the hazardous materials or equipment used inside.

BUILDING CORE A building element that is vertically continuous through one or more floors of a building for the vertical distribution of building services.

BUILDING ELEMENTS See Structure Elements.

BUILDING, EXISTING Any structure erected and occupied prior to the adoption of the most current building code, or a structure for which a construction permit has been issued.

BUILDING OFFICIAL See Code Official.

BUILDING TYPE A specific class or category within an occupancy classification.

CABLE A conductor, consisting of two or more wires combined in the same protective sheathing and insulated to keep the wires from touching.

CHILDREN People below the age of 12 (elementary school and younger).

CIRCUIT The path of electrical current that circles from the electrical source to the electrical box or fixture and back to the source.

CIRCUIT, BRANCH A circuit that supplies electricity to a number of outlets or fixtures.

CIRCUIT BREAKER A safety device that opens or disconnects a circuit to stop the flow of electricity when an overload or fault occurs.

CLEAN OUT An access opening in the drainage system to remove obstructions.

CLEAR FLOOR SPACE The minimum unobstructed floor or ground space required to accommodate a single, stationary wheelchair and its occupant.

CLOSED CIRCUIT TELEPHONE A telephone with a dedicated line, such as a house phone, courtesy phone, or phone that must be used to gain entrance to a facility.

CODE A set of safety criteria made mandatory by a state or local legislative body and enforced by a building or code official.

CODE DEPARTMENT A local government agency that enforces the codes and standards within a jurisdiction.

CODE OFFICIAL An officer or other designated authority charged with the administration and enforcement of the codes, standards, and regulations with a jurisdiction; also known as building official.

CODE VIOLATION Not complying with a code as stated in a code book or required by a jurisdiction, whether the noncompliance is deliberate or unintentional.

C.O.M. An acronym for "customer's own material"; refers to fabrics that are ordered separately from the furniture that they will cover.

COMBUSTIBLE Refers to materials, such as building materials or finishes, that are capable of being ignited or affected by excessive heat or gas in a relatively short amount of time.

COMMON PATH OF TRAVEL That portion of an exit access that leads up to two separate and distinct paths of egress travel or two separate exits. Paths that merge are also considered common paths of travel.

COMPARTMENTATION The process of creating confined spaces or areas within a building for the purpose of containing a fire and creating safe areas of refuge.

COMPARTMENT, FIRE A space within a building enclosed by fire barriers on all sides, including the top and bottom.

COMPARTMENT, SMOKE A space within a building enclosed by smoke barriers on all sides, including the top and bottom.

CONDUCTOR A cable or wire that carries and distributes electricity.

CONDUIT, ELECTRICAL A raceway or pipe used to house and protect electrical wires and cables.

CONDUIT, PLUMBING A pipe or channel for transporting water.

CONSTRUCTION DOCUMENTS A complete set of drawings that includes floor plans, notes, schedules, legends, and any required details, as well as written specifications and any other code required information needed to convey what is being built.

CORRIDOR A passageway that creates a single path of travel that is enclosed by walls, a ceiling, and doors that lead to other rooms or areas or provides a path of egress travel to an exit.

DAMPER See Fire Damper and Smoke Damper.

DEAD END CORRIDOR A hallway in which a person is able to travel in only one direction to reach an exit.

DEAD LOAD The weight of permanent construction such as walls, partitions, framing, floors, ceilings, roofs, and all other stationary structure elements and the fixed service equipment of a building.

DELUGE SYSTEM An automatic sprinkler system that delivers a large amount of water to an area upon detection of fire by a separate automatic detection system.

DETECTABLE WARNING A standardized surface texture applied to or built into a walking surface to warn visually impaired people of hazards in the path of travel.

DISABLED Includes the inability and difficulty to walk, reliance on walking aids, blindness and visual impairment, deafness and hearing impairment, incoordination, reaching and manipulation disabilities, lack of stamina, difficulty in interpreting and reacting to sensory information, and extremes in physical size.

DRAFT STOP A continuous membrane used to subdivide a concealed space within a building to restrict the passage of smoke, heat, and flames.

DRAIN PIPE Any pipe that carries waste water in a building.

DUCT An enclosed rectangular or circular tube used to transfer hot and cold air to different parts of a building.

DWELLING Any building that contains one or more dwelling units to be built, used, rented, leased, or hired out and intended for living purposes.

DWELLING UNIT A single unit providing complete independent living facilities for one or more persons, including permanent provisions for living, sleeping, eating, cooking, and sanitation.

EGRESS A way out or exit.

ELEVATOR A hoistway and lowering mechanism equipped with a car or platform that moves on glides in a vertical direction through successive floors or levels.

ENTRANCE Any access point into a building or portions of a building used for the purpose of entering.

EXHAUST AIR Air removed from a conditioned space through openings, ducts, plenums, or concealed spaces to the exterior of the building.

EXIT The portion of a means of egress that leads from an exit access and to an exit discharge and is separated from other interior spaces by fire rated construction and assemblies.

EXIT ACCESS The portion of a means of egress that leads to an exit.

EXIT COURT An outside space with building walls on at least three sides and open to the sky that provides access to a public way.

EXIT DISCHARGE The portion of a means of egress between the termination of an exit and the public way.

EXIT PASSAGEWAY A fire-rated portion of a means of egress that provides a protected path of egress in a horizontal direction to the exit discharge or public way.

EXIT, SECONDARY An alternative exit, not necessarily required by codes.

FAUCET A fitting that controls the flow of water at the end of a water supply line.

FEEDER A conductor that supplies electricity between the service equipment and the branch circuits.

FIRE AREA The aggregate floor area enclosed and bounded by fire walls, fire barriers, exterior walls, or fire-rated horizontal assemblies of a building.

FIRE BARRIER A continuous membrane with a fire resistance rating that will resist flame and limit the spread of fire in which openings are protected.

FIRE BLOCKER Fire-rated material used to protect materials that are not fire rated.

FIRE DAMPER A listed device installed in ducts or air transfer openings that automatically close upon detection of heat to interrupt airflow and restrict the passage of flame.

FIRE DEPARTMENT CONNECTION A hose connection at grade or street level for use by the fire department for the purpose of supplying water to a building's standpipe and/or sprinkler system.

FIRE DETECTOR A device that detects one of the signatures of a fire.

FIRE EXIT HARDWARE Similar to panic hardware but additionally provides fire protection since it is tested with and included as part of a fire door.

FIRE LOAD The amount of combustible material present that can feed a fire.

FIRE PROTECTION Refers to assemblies and opening protectives that have been chemically treated, covered, or protected so that they prevent or retard the spread of fire and smoke.

FIRE RATING The time in minutes or hours that materials or assemblies have withstood a fire exposure as established by a standard testing procedure; includes fire resistance and fire protection ratings.

FIRE RESISTANT Refers to construction materials, assemblies, and textiles that prevent or retard the passage of excessive heat, hot gases, or flame.

FIRE RISK The probability that a fire will occur with the accompanying potential for harm to human life and property damage.

FIRESTOP An assembly or material used to prevent the spread of fire and smoke through openings in fire resistive assemblies.

FIRE SUPPRESSION SYSTEM A system using carbon dioxide, foam, wet or dry chemical, a halogenated extinguishing agent, or an automatic sprinkler system to suppress a fire when activated by a smoke or fire detector system.

FIRE WALL A rated wall having protected openings, which restricts the spread of fire and extends continuously from the foundation to or through the roof with sufficient structural stability under fire conditions to allow collapse of construction on either side without collapse of the wall.

FLAME RESISTANT Refers to finishes or furniture that prevent, terminate, or inhibit the spread of a flame upon application of a flame or nonflaming ignition source with or without removal of the ignition source.

FLAME RETARDANT A chemical or other treatment used to render a material flame resistant.

FLAME RETARDANT TREATMENT A process for incorporating or adding flame retardants to a finish or other material.

FLAMMABILITY The relative ease with which an item ignites and burns.

FLAMMABLE Capable of being ignited.

FLASHOVER A back draft, the dangerous explosion of fire that occurs as a fire begins to develop, resulting in simultaneously igniting surrounding areas.

FLOOR AREA The amount of floor surface included within the exterior walls. (See Area, Net Floor and Area, Gross Floor.)

FULL SCALE TEST The simulation of an actual fire condition, such as for a full size room or a full size piece of furniture with all its contents.

FUSE A safety device that contains metal that will melt or break when the electrical current exceeds a specific value for a specific time period, causing the flow of electricity to stop.

FUSIBLE LINK A connecting link of a low-melting alloy that melts at a predetermined temperature causing separation.

GLAZING The process of installing glass into frames.

GRADE The finished ground level where it adjoins the building at the exterior wall.

GUARD or **GUARDRAIL** A system of rails or other building components located near open sides of elevated walking surfaces that minimizes the possibility of a fall.

HABITABLE A room or enclosed space in a building for living, sleeping, eating, or cooking. Bathrooms, toilet rooms, closets, halls, storage or utility spaces, and similar areas are not considered habitable spaces.

HANDICAPPED See Disabled.

HANDRAIL A horizontal or sloping rail intended for grasping by the hand for guidance or support.

HAZARDOUS MATERIAL A chemical or other substance that is a physical or health hazard whether the material is in usable or waste condition; includes low, medium, and high hazards.

HEAT BARRIER A liner or backcoating used between upholstery and the filling underneath to prevent the spread of flame or smoldering heat.

HEIGHT, BUILDING The vertical distance from the grade plane to the average height of the highest roof surface.

HEIGHT, CEILING The clear vertical distance from finished floor to finished ceiling.

HEIGHT, STORY The clear vertical distance from finished floor to the finished floor above or finished floor to the top of the joists supporting the roof structure above.

HIGH-RISE BUILDING A structure with a floor used for human occupancy exceeding 75 feet above the lowest level of access by a fire department vehicle.

HISTORICAL BUILDING A building or facility that is either listed in or eligible for listing in the *National Register of Historic Places*, or that is designated as historic under a state or local law.

HOISTWAY A vertical shaft for an elevator or dumbwaiter.

HORIZONTAL EXIT A fire-rated passage that leads to an area of refuge on the same floor within a building or on the same level of an adjacent building.

HORIZONTAL PASSAGE Allows movement between rooms or areas on the same floor or story, for example, a door, archway, or cased opening.

INGRESS An entrance or the act of entering.

INTERIOR FINISH Any exposed interior surface of a building, including finished ceilings, floors, and walls.

INTERIOR ROOM Any enclosed space or room within the exterior walls of a building.

JURISDICTION A geographical area, such as a state, city, or municipality, that uses and enforces the same codes, standards, and regulations.

LABELED Refers to any equipment or building material and assemblies that include a label, symbol, or other identification mark by an organization acceptable to the jurisdiction concerned with product evaluation.

LANDING, DOOR A level floor surface immediately adjacent to a doorway or threshold.

LANDING, INTERMEDIATE A level floor surface between two flights of stairs or ramps.

LIMITED-COMBUSTIBLE Refers to material that is not considered noncombustible, yet that still has some fire resistive qualities.

LINTEL The member that is placed over an opening in a wall to support the wall construction above.

LISTED Refers to equipment or building materials included in a list published by an organization acceptable to the jurisdiction concerned with product evaluation.

LIVE LOAD Any dynamic weight within a building, including the people, furniture, and equipment, and not including dead load, earthquake load, snow load, or wind load.

LIVING AREA See Dwelling Unit.

MAIN The principal artery of any continuous piping system to which branch pipes may be connected.

MASONRY The form of construction composed of stone, brick, concrete block, hollow clay tile, glass block, or other similar building units that are laid up unit by unit and set in mortar.

MEANS OF EGRESS A continuous and unobstructed way of exit travel, both horizontally and vertically, from any point in a building to a public way; it consists of the exit access, the exit, and the exit discharge.

MEANS OF ESCAPE An alternative way out of a building that does not conform to the strict definition of a means of egress.

MEMBRANE PENETRATION An opening created in a portion of a construction assembly that pierces only one side (or membrane) of the assembly.

MEZZANINE An intermediate floor level placed between a floor and the ceiling above in which The flour area is not more than one-third of the room in which it is located.

MOCK-UP, FURNITURE A full or partial representation of a finished piece of furniture that utilizes the same frame, filling, and upholstery as the finished piece.

NATURAL PATH OF TRAVEL The most direct route a person can take while following an imaginary line on the floor, avoiding obstacles such as walls, equipment, and furniture to arrive at the final destination.

NOMINAL DIMENSION Not the actual size, it is the commercial size by which an item is know. For example, the nominal size of a stud is 2×4 and the actual size is $1\frac{1}{2} \times 3\frac{1}{2}$ inches.

NONCOMBUSTIBLE Refers to material, such as building materials and finishes, that will not ignite, burn, support combustion, or release flammable vapors when subject to fire or heat.

NOSING The leading edge of the tread on a stair and of the landing within a stairwell.

OCCUPANCY The use or intended use of a building, floor, or other part of a building.

OCCUPANCY, MIXED A building used for two or more occupancy classifications.

OCCUPANT The person or persons using a space, whether they are tenants, employees, customers, or whatever.

OCCUPANT CONTENT The actual number of total occupants for which exiting has been provided. This is the maximum number of people that can occupy the space.

OCCUPANT LOAD Refers to the (minimum) number of people or occupants for which the code will require you to provide means of egress or existing in your design.

OCCUPIABLE Refers to a room or enclosed space designed for human occupancy that is equipped with means of egress, light, and ventilation.

OPENING PROTECTIVE Refers to a rated assembly placed in an opening in a rated wall assembly, such as a door or window, designed to maintain the fire resistance or the wall assembly.

OUTLET, FIXTURE An electrical box in which electrical wiring is connected to a light fixture or the light switch.

OUTLET, RECEPTACLE An electrical box in which the electrical wiring allows the connection of a plug-in appliance or other equipment.

OWNER Any person, agent, firm, or corporation having a legal or equitable interest in the property.

PANIC HARDWARE A door latching assembly that has a device to release the latch when force is applied in the direction of exit travel. (See also Fire Exit Hardware.)

PARTITION An interior space divider such as a wall.

PARTITION, PARTIAL A wall that does not extend fully to the ceiling and is usually limited by the codes to a maximum height of 72 inches.

PASSAGEWAY An enclosed path or corridor.

PATH OF TRAVEL A continuous, unobstructed route that connects the primary area of a building with the entrance and other parts of the facility.

PERFORMANCE TEST The check of a component for conformity to a performance criteria or standard, performed during manufacturing, at the site during or after installation, or at a certified testing agency.

PERMANENT SEATING Any multiple seating that remains at a location for more than 90 days.

PERMIT An official document issued by the code jurisdiction that authorizes performance of a specified activity.

PHYSICALLY DISABLED or **CHALLENGED** See Disabled.

PLATFORM LIFT A type of elevator, typically used when a ramp is not possible, to transport people short vertical distances.

PLENUM SPACE A chamber that forms part of an air circulation system other than the occupied space being conditioned; includes the open space above the ceiling, below the floor, or in a vertical shaft.

PLUMBING CHASE An extra thick wall consisting of studs with a space between them to create a wall cavity allowing for wide plumbing pipes.

PLUMBING FIXTURES Installed receptacles, devices, or appliances that are supplied with water or that receive or discharge water or waste.

POTABLE WATER Water that is satisfactory for drinking, cooking, and cleaning and that meets the requirements of the local health authority.

PROTECTED Refers to construction materials that have been chemically treated, covered, or protected so that they obtain a fire resistance rating.

PUBLIC USE AREAS Interior or exterior rooms or spaces that are made available for the general public.

PUBLIC WAY Any street, alley, or other parcel of land open to the outside air, meant for public use, and having a clear and unobstructed width and height of no less than 10 feet.

RACEWAY An enclosed channel designed to hold wires and cables.

RADIANT HEAT The heat that is transmitted through an object to the other side.

RAMP A walking surface that has a continuous slope.

RAMP, CURB A short ramp cutting through a curb or built up to it.

READILY ACHIEVEABLE A term used by the *Americans with Disabilities Act* to indicate a change or modification that can be done without difficulty or expense.

REFLASH The reignition of a flammable item by a hot object after the flames have been extinguished.

RETURN AIR The air removed from a conditioned space through openings, ducts, plenums, or concealed spaces to the heat exchanger of a heating, cooling, or ventilation system.

RISER, PLUMBING A water pipe that runs vertically one full story or more within a building to supply water to branch pipes or fixtures.

RISER, STAIR The vertical portion of a stair system that connects each tread.

SECURITY BALLARDS Any device used to prevent the removal of products and/or shopping carts from store premises.

SECURITY GRILLE A metal grating or a gate that slides open and closed, either vertically or horizontally, for security and protection.

SEISMIC Refers to that which is a result of an earthquake.

SELF-CLOSING As applied to a fire door or other opening, equipped with an approved device that will ensure closing after having been opened.

SHAFT An enclosed vertical opening or space extending through one or more stories of a building.

SIDE LIGHT A frame filled with glass or a solid panel that is attached to the side of a door frame.

SIGNAGE Displayed verbal, symbolic, tactile, and pictorial information.

SILL The horizontal member forming the base of a window or the foot of a door.

SMOKE BARRIER A continuous membrane, such as a wall, floor, or ceiling assembly, that is designed and constructed to resist the movement and passage of smoke, requiring protection at all openings.

SMOKE COMPARTMENT A space within a building enclosed by smoke barriers on all sides, including the top and bottom.

SMOKE DAMPER A listed device installed in ducts and air transfer openings that is design to resist the passage of air and smoke during an emergency.

SMOKE DETECTOR A device that detects the presence of smoke as an indicator of fire.

SMOKEPROOF ENCLOSURE An exit consisting of a vestibule and/or continuous stairway that is fully enclosed and ventilated to limit the presence of smoke during a fire.

SMOLDERING The combustion that occurs without a flame but that results in smoke, toxic gases, and heat, usually resulting in a charred area.

SOIL PIPE A pipe that carries sewage containing solids.

SPACE A definable area such as a room, corridor, entrance, or alcove.

SPECIFICATIONS Written information that is a part of or an addition to construction drawings that logically communicate the requirements of the construction and installation.

SPRINKLERED Refers to an area or building that is equipped with an automatic sprinkler system.

SPRINKLER HEAD The part of a sprinkler system that controls the release of the water and breaks the water into a spray.

STACK PIPE A vertical main that can be used as a soil, waste, or venting pipe.

STAIR A change in elevation, consisting of one or more risers.

STAIRWAY One or more flights of stairs with the required landings and platforms necessary to form a continuous and uninterrupted vertical passage from one level to another.

STANDPIPE A fixed, manual extinguishing system, including wet and dry systems, with outlets to allow water to be discharged through hose and nozzles for the purpose of extinguishing a fire.

STORY See Height, Story.

STRUCTURE ELEMENTS The various building components that make up a building, such as walls, columns, floors, and beams; also known as building elements.

STRUCTURE See Building.

SUPPLY AIR The air delivered to a conditioned space through openings, ducts, plenums, or concealed spaces to the heat exchanger of a heating, cooling, or ventilation system.

TELEPHONE BANK Two or more adjacent public telephones, often installed as one unit.

TENANT A person or group of people that uses or occupies a portion of a building through a lease and/or payment of rent.

TENANT SEPARATION A wall or floor–ceiling assembly between tenants.

TEXT TELEPHONE Similar to computers with modems, a type of keyboard input and visual display output that provides telephone communications for persons with hearing or speech impairments; also known as a TDD or TTY.

THROUGH-PENETRATION An opening created in a portion of a construction assembly that is a complete opening on both sides of the assembly.

THROUGH-PENETRATION PROTECTIVE A system or assembly installed in or around a through-penetration to resist the passage of flame, heat, and hot gases for a specified period of time.

TRANSIENT LODGING Facilities other than medical care facilities that provide sleeping accommodations.

TRANSOM An opening above a door that is filled with glass or solid material.

TRAP A fitting or device that creates a liquid seal at a plumbing fixture to prevent the passage of odors, gases, and insects back into the fixture.

TREAD, STAIR The horizontal portion of a stair system that connects each riser.

TRIM Picture molds, chair rails, baseboard, handrails, door and window frames, and similar decorative or protective materials used in fixed applications.

TURNSTILE A device used to control passage from one area to another, consisting of revolving arms projecting from a central post.

UNDUE HARDSHIP A term used by the *Americans with Disabilities Act* to mean "significantly difficult or expensive"; also known as undue burden.

UNPROTECTED Refers to materials in their natural state that have not been specially treated.

USE GROUP Sometimes referred to as building type, use group usually gets more specific and can be a subclassification within a building type. (See also Building Type.)

VALVE A device used to start, stop, or regulate the flow of liquid or gas into piping, through piping, or from piping.

VENEER A facing attached to a wall or other structural element for the purpose of providing ornamentation, protection, or insulation, but not for the purpose of adding strength to the element.

VENTILATION The process of suppling or removing conditioned or unconditioned air by natural or mechanical means to or from a space.

VENTILATION AIR The portion of supply air that comes from the outside plus any recirculated air that has been treated to maintain the desired quality of air within a space.

VENT, MECHANICAL The part of the air distribution system that dispenses and collects the air in a space, including supply diffusers and return grilles.

VENT PIPE (also called a flue) A pipe that provides a flow of air to the drainage system and allows the discharge of harmful gases to prevent siphonage or backpressure.

VERTICAL OPENING An opening through a floor or roof.

VERTICAL PASSAGE Allows movement from floor to floor, for example, a stairway or an elevator.

WALL, BEARING A wall supporting any vertical structural element in addition to its own weight.

WALL, CAVITY A wall, typically built of masonry or concrete, arranged to provide a continuous air space within the wall.

WALL, DEMISING A wall that separates two tenant spaces in the same building, typically requiring a fire rating.

WALL, EXTERIOR A fire-rated wall that is used as an enclosing wall for a building other than a party wall or fire wall.

WALL, FIRE A fire-rated wall that extends continuously from the foundation of a building to or through the roof with sufficient structural stability to allow collapse of one side while leaving the other side intact, requiring a three- to four-hour-fire rating.

WALL, FIRE SEPARATION A fire-rated wall used to create compartments and enclosures within a building and designed to restrict the spread of fire, requiring a one- to three-hour fire rating.

WALL, NON-LOAD-BEARING A wall that supports only its own weight.

WALL, PARAPET The part of any wall that extends above the roof line.

WALL, PARTY See Fire Wall.

WASTE The discharge from any plumbing fixture that does not contain solids.

WHEELCHAIR LIFT See Platform Lift.

WHEELCHAIR SPACE A space for a single wheelchair and its occupant. (See also Area of Refuge.)

WIRELESS SYSTEM A system or part of a system that can transmit and receive signals without the aid of a wire.

WORKSTATION An individual work area created by the arrangement of furniture and/or equipment for use by occupants or employees.

ZONE A space or group of spaces within a building with heat or cooling requirements that are similar and are regulated by one heating or cooling device/system.

INDEX

A

Access Board, 17, 45, 277, 298, 302
Accessibility requirements, *see also* Wheelchair
  aisles, 46, 90
  alarms, 158, 159
  assistive listening devices, 45, 47, 207
  clearance:
    floor space, 45, 46, 47, 81, 82, 94, 179–184, 211
    toe space, 180, 183, 184
    knee space, 180, 181, 243
  communication systems, 85, 94, 207
  corridors, 90
  doors, 46, 81–84
  elevators, 85
  finishes:
    detectable warnings, 45, 243
    visual aids, 243
  furnishings:
    counters, 45, 46, 243
    seating, 46, 243
    tables, 46, 243
    worksurfaces, 46, 243
  occupancy classifications, *see* Occupancy
  plumbing fixtures, 178–183. *See also* Plumbing
    fixture(s)
  by project type, 299–301
  ramps, 88, 89
  rooms, 46, 47
  route, 45, 46, 182, 299
  signage, 85, 185
  stairs, 87
  storage, 46
  telephones, 182, 211
  toilet facilities, 46, 178–185

Accessible warning systems, *see* Detection
  system(s)
ACT, *see* Association for Contract Textiles
ADA, see Americans with Disabilities Act
ADAAG, see Americans with Disabilities Act Accessibility
  Guidelines
Additions, building, *see* Building(s)
Adjoining rooms, *see* Room(s)
Air circulation, *see* Ventilation
Aisle accessway, *see* Aisles
Aisles, 90, 101. *See also* Assembly occupancies;
  Accessibility requirements
Alarm systems, *see* Detection system(s)
Alley, *see* Exit discharge(s)
Alterations, *see* Building(s)
American Furniture Manufacturers Association,
  228
American National Standard, see ANSI standards
American National Standards Institute (ANSI), 18,
  20–22, 144, 186, 195, 273
American Society of Heating, Refrigeration, and Air-
  Conditioning Engineers (ASHRAE), 22, 186
American Society for Testing and Materials
  (ASTM), 21, 22, 144, 222
Americans with Disabilities Act (ADA), 4, 17, 45, 273,
  276, 277, 297–302
  compliance with, 302
  enforcement, 301, 302
  levels of compliance:
    alterations, 299, 300
    existing facilities, 276, 300
    historical, 277
    new construction, 299
Americans with Disabilities Act, Accessibility Guidelines
  (ADAAG), 4, 17, 18, 41, 45, 276, 277, 297–302

ANSI standards, 18, 20–22. *See also* Testing, summary of
Appeals process, code, 54, 256, 257
Appliance(s), 196, 197, 204, 214. *See also* Plumbing fixtures
Architectural and Transportation Compliance Board (ATCB), *see* Access Board
Area(s) of refuge, 72, 75, 76, 84, 86, 92, 94, 102, 103, 121, 128
Area of rescue assistance, *see* Area(s) of refuge
Area:
    building, 51, 68, 70, 71, 126, 270
        calculation of, 51, 68, 69, 70, 71
        code tables, 69
        limitations of, 68–72
    floor, 48, 50, 57, 58
    gross area, 50, 52
    net area, 50, 51
    per occupant, 48
    occupiable, 176
    separation, *see* Room(s)
Arrangement of exits, *see* Exit(s)
Arrangement of rooms, *see* Room(s)
Assemblies:
    construction, 121, 124, 134, 140, 144, 149
    fire-rated, 121, 124, 143
    selection and specification of, 146–149
    types of:
        door, 134–138
        floor/ceiling, 59, 65, 74, 130, 132, 142–144, 146, 147
        roof/ceiling, 59, 130, 146
        wall, 59, 74, 124–130
        window, 134, 135, 138–140
Assembly occupancies:
    accessibility requirements, 45, 90
    aisles in, 90
    classification of, 27, 29, 31–33, 38, 44, 45, 48, 52
    communication systems in, 45, 46
    electrical requirements in, 206
    finish selection for, 234
    hazards in, 31
    means of egress in, 88, 99, 101,
    plumbing requirements in, 177, 181
    seating for, 31, 32. *See also* Seating types of
Assistive listening devices, *see* Accessibility requirements
Association for Contract Textiles (ACT), 236, 239
ASTM Annual Book of Standards, 22
ASTM standards, *see also* Testing, summary of
    ASTM D6413, 225
    ASTM E84, 222, 238
    ASTM E119, 141, 144, 145
    ASTM E152, 145

ASTM E163, 146
ASTM E648, 224
ASTM E662, 227
ASTM E814, 141
ASTM E1590, 229
ASTM F84, 273
ASTM 257, 145
ASTM 1353, 226
ASTM 1474, 228
ASTM 1537, 228
Attics, 142
Atriums, 66
Audible alarms, *see* Accessible warning systems
Authority having jurisdiction, *see* Jurisdiction(s)
Automatic detection, *see* Detection system(s)
Automatic sprinkler systems, *see* Suppression system(s)

B

Back flash, *see* Flashover
Backing and back coating, 218, 226, 228
Backup system, *see* Electrical, emergency system
Barriers, *see* Fire barrier(s); Smoke barrier(s)
Basement(s), 73, 102, 208
Bathroom, *see* Toilet facilities
Bathtubs, *see* Plumbing fixture(s)
Block liner, *see* Fire, block
Board of Appeals, 257
Board for the Coordination of Model Codes, 281
BOCA, *see* Building Officials and Code Administrators International
BOCA National Building Code (NBC), 9–13
BOCA National Mechanical Code (NMC), 13, 186. *See also* *International Mechanical Code*
BOCA National Plumbing Code (NPC), 13, 172. *See also* *International Plumbing Code*
Booth seating, *see* Seating
Box, electrical, *see* Electrical; Outlets
Bridges, *see* Exit(s), types of
Building(s):
    accessible, 4
    additions to, 41, 276
    adjacent structures, 73
    alterations to, 41, 257, 299, 300
    area, *see* Area, building
    core, 76, 193
    existing, 41, 61, 231
    federal, 16, 298
    height, *see* Height(s)
    high-rise, *see* High-rise buildings
    historic, 275, 277–278
    location, 73

materials, 12, 16, 21, 58, 61, 63, 64, 122, 124, 154, 169, 217– 222, 224–229, 236, 238, 239
mixed use, *see* Occupancies
multi-story, 52, 81, 98–100, 198
new, 29, 41, 61, 70, 174, 231, 299
permit, *see* Permit
renovation to, 276, 299, 300
size of, 51, 57, 68, 70–73
story(s), 72, 73
type(s), 27, 31– 40, 45
Building Elements, *see* Structural elements
Building inspector, 250, 261
Building official, *see* Code official(s)
Building Officials and Code Administrators International (BOCA), 9, 250
Business and Institutional Furniture Manufacturers Association (BIFMA), 20, 228, 297, 298
Business occupancies:
accessibility requirements, 45, 46
classification of, 31, 32, 33, 35, 44, 48, 51, 52
means of egress in 103–105, 110, 111
tenant spaces in, *see* Tenant space
types of, 33

C

Cabinetry, 242
Cable tray, 210
Cabling:
electrical, 196–200, 203, 207
low-voltage, 209–210
CABO, *see* Council of American Building Officials
CABO Common Code Format, 11, 16
California Technical Bulletin #133, see CAL 133
CAL 116, 226
CAL 117, 226
CAL 129, 229
CAL 133, 228, 229
Carpeting, *see* Floor(s), finishes for
Casework, *see* Millwork
Ceiling(s):
assembly, *see* Assemblies, types of; Fire barrier
cove, 205
finishes, 219, 225, 227, 231, 234, 273
suspended, 130, 132, 190, 193
Certificate, *see* Testing
Certificate of completion, 262
Certificate of Occupancy, 261, 262
Chamber Test, 224
Char, 63, 64, 141, 226
Checklists:
electrical and communication, 214–216
finishes and furniture, 245–248

fire protection systems, 167–169
fire resistant materials and construction, 149–151
interior codes, 24–26, 35
interior projects, 263, 264
means of egress, 115–118
occupancy, 54–56
plumbing and mechanical, 191–193
Chutes, 129, 133
Cigarette Ignition Test, 226, 227
Circuit(s), electrical, 196
branch circuits, 196
circuit breakers, 196
dedicated circuits, 201
short circuits, 204
Coatings, *see* Fire, retardant coatings and treatments
Code(s), *see also* Jurisdiction(s)
adoption of, 8, 9, 250, 252
amendments to, 8, 22
background, 7, 8
compliance with, 255–257, 259
department, 250, 251
enforcement of, 22, 252
fire, 14, 20, 119–121, 127, 220, 250
future of, *see* Future technology
health, 24, 171
historical, 7, 217
interpretation of, 256, 257
model, *see* Model codes
review, 253, 255, 256
revisions to, 9
standards in, *see* Standards
tables, 52
variance, 257
where to obtain, 254
Code of Federal Regulations (CFR), 16
Code official(s):
approval, 12, 140, 149, 177, 259, 261
consult with, 12, 29, 54, 56, 65–67, 97, 112, 140, 157, 253, 254, 267, 276
department of, 2, 250, 252
plan review, 255, 256
qualifications, 250–253
site visits, *see* Inspection, code
types of:
fire marshal, 250
inspector, 250, 261
plans examiner, 250, 255, 259
Code research:
documentation of, 12, 26, 247, 262–266
liability for, 12, 235, 247, 248, 262, 263
Combustible, 58, 63, 64, 134, 138, 142, 190, 205, 266
Common Code Format, *see CABO Common Code Format*

Common path of travel, *see* Path of travel
Communication system(s), 207–214. *See also*
　　Telephone system(s); Security systems
　accessibility of, *see* Accessibility requirements
　assistive listening devices, *see* Accessibility
　　requirements
　installation of, 207
　room types, 208–209
　types of, 207
　wiring of, *see* Cabling, low-voltage
Compartmentation, 72, 73, 127, 129. *See also* High-
　rise buildings
Computers, 207–209, 211, 213
Concealed spaces, fire protection of, 130, 142
Conduit, electrical, 200
Construction documents, 66, 249, 253, 254, 255,
　259, 265
Construction types, *see also* Combustible; Heavy
　timber; Limited combustible;
　Noncombustible
　code tables, 62, 69, 127, 129, 131, 155
　description of, 57–59
　determination of, 61, 65–67
　materials in, 63, 64
　mixed, 67
　by occupancy, 67, 73, 269, 270
Consumer Product Safety Act, 13, 173, 179
Consumer Product Safety Commission (CPSC), 8
Conveyer walkways, *see* Moving walks
Cooling loads, *see* loads
Corner Test, 229
Corridors, 76, 79–82, 95, 96, 100–102, 104, 105, 107,
　109, 110–112. *See also* Fire barriers
　accessibility of, *see* Accessibility requirements
　calculation of, *see* Means of egress, capacity of
　dead end, 111–114
　exit access requirements, 81, 89, 90
　exit discharge requirements, 95, 96
　exit requirements, 91, 93–95, 102
　finishes for, 232, 234, 235
　fire rated, 93, 95
　fire rating of, 81, 91, 95
Council of American Building Officials (CABO), 11,
　15, 251, 269
Counters, *see* Furnishings
Cove ceilings, *see* Ceiling(s)
Critical radiant flux, 224
Curb ramp, 89

D

Dampers, *see* Through-penetration protectives
Dead end corridors, *see* Corridors
Dead load, *see* Loads

Decoration, *see* Finishes, trim and incidental
Demising walls, *see* Wall(s)
Department of Housing and Urban Development
　(HUD), 18, 275
Department of Interior (DOI), 275
Department of Justice (DOJ), 17, 298, 302
Department of Labor (DOL), 19
Department of Transportation (DOT), 17
Detectable warnings, *see* Accessibility
　requirements, finishes
Detection systems, 153, 155, 156
　accessible warning systems, 159
　audio systems, 159
　carbon monoxide, 156
　fire alarms, 158, 159
　smoke detectors/alarms, 157, 158
Detentional/correctional occupancies, 36–37. *See
　also* Institutional occupancies
Disabled requirements, *see* Accessibility
　requirements
Discharge, exits, *see* Exit discharge(s)
Documentation, *see* Code research; Construction
　Documents
Door(s), 81, 82, 83
　accessibility of, *see* Accessibility requirements
　assembly, *see* Assemblies, types of
　classes of, 137, 138
　exit access requirements, 81– 83
　exit requirements, 91, 92, 135, 136, 270
　fire barrier, 125
　fire-rated, 91, 133, 134, 136, 138. *See also* Opening
　　protectives
　frame for, 136
　glass in, 138
　hardware for, 83, 84, 136, 137
　sizes of, 102, 137
　swing of, 82, 84, 92, 183
　testing of, 144, 145
　threshold, 83
　types of, 82, 83
Door closure(s), *see* Door, hardware
Draftstop, *see* Through penetration protectives
Draperies, *see* Window(s), treatments
Drawings, *See* Construction Documents; Plans
　check
Drinking Fountain, *see* Plumbing fixtures
Drywall, *see* Gypsum board
Ducts, *see* Mechanical system(s)
Dumbwaiters, 128. *See also* Shaft(s)
Duplex Houses, *see* One and two family dwellings
Dwellings or dwelling units, *see* Residential
　occupancies; Transient lodging

E

Educational occupancies:
  classifications of, 33, 34
  finish selection for, 232, 234, 235
  mixed occupancies of, 33
  smoke dampers in, 132
  types of, 34
Egress, *see* Means of egress
Electrical system(s), 156, 197–207, 261, 272, 273. *See also* Outlet(s); Ground
  box, electrical, 196, 201–203
  emergency systems, 205, 206, 207
  equipment, 23, 195, 196
  junction box, 196, 203–204, 210
  panels, 198
  room, *see* Room(s)
  standby power, 207
  transformers, 197
  uninterrupted power supply, 207
  utilities, 197
  wiring, *see* Cable; Conduit
Elevator(s), 75, 84, 85. *See also* Lifts
Emergency lighting, 115, 206
Emergency systems, *see* Electrical system(s)
Enclosure, *see* Shaft(s); Elevator(s); Stairs
Engineers, 12, 13, 61, 65–67
  electrical, 179, 196, 198, 199, 204, 206, 207, 208, 214
  mechanical, 13, 75, 163, 171, 172, 179, 186–188, 191
  structural, 47, 57, 66, 67
Equipment, *see also* Mechanical system(s); Electrical system(s)
  loads for, 47
  placement of, 50, 90, 196
  travel distance around, 109
Escalators, 88
Evacuation, *see* Occupants, evacuation of
Exhaust, *see* Ventilation
Existing buildings, *see* Building(s)
Exit(s),
  accessibility of, *see* Accessibility requirements
  calculations for, *see* Means of egress, capacity of
  enclosure of, 91, 92, 107
  finish requirements for, 234, 244
  fire ratings of, 91–93, 95
  marking of, *see* Exit signs
  types of:
    exit passageways, 93– 95, 128
    exit stairs, *see* Stairs
    exterior doors, *see* Door(s)
    horizontal exits, 84, 92, 93, 100. *See also* Fire barriers
Exit access(es), 78–91, 128, 206

  accessibility of, *see* Accessibility requirements
  calculations for, *see* Means of egress, capacity of
  finish requirements for, 234
  fire ratings of, 89, 128
  types of:
    adjoining or intervening rooms, *see* Room(s)
    aisles, *see* Aisles
    corridors, *see* Corridors
    doors, *see* Door(s)
    ramps, *see* Ramps
    stairs, *see* Stairs
Exit court, *see* Exit(s), types of
Exit discharge(s), 79, 90, 95, 96
  accessibility of, *see* Accessibility requirements
  calculations for, *see* Means of egress, capacity of
  fire ratings of, 83, 87
  types of:
    alley, 95, 96
    corridors, *see* Corridors
    exit court, 96
    foyer, 91, 95
    lobby, 95, 90, 114
    sidewalk, 95, 96
    vestibule, 82, 95, 114, 162, 181, 182, 189, 190
Exiting systems, 120. *See also* Signage and Emergency lighting
Exit lighting, *see* Emergency lighting
Exit passageways, *see* Exit(s), types of
Exit signs, 85, 114, 115, 206, 244. *See also* Signage
Extinguishers, *see* Suppression system(s)

F

Fabric, *see* Finishes, textiles
Factory Mutual, 147
Factory occupancies, *see* Industrial occupancies
Fair Housing Act (FHA), 18, 19, 273
Family residences, *see* One and two family dwellings
Fans, *see* Ventilation
Federal buildings, *see* Building(s)
Federal Flammability Standard, see Pill Test
Federal Register (FR), 16
Federal regulations, 16–17, 19
  compliance with, 4
  regulated by, 252
  where to obtain, Appendix D
Feeder, electrical, 197
Fees, *see* Permit
Finishes, *see also* Testing
  accessibility of, *see* Accessibility requirements
  classification of, 222, 224
  code tables, 233
  determination of, 239, 241, 242

Finishes (*cont'd*)
  foam/plastics, 244, 245
  ratings for, *see* Ratings
  restriction on, 243, 244, 245
  selection of:
    nontested, 238, 239
    pretested, 235, 236, 238
  testing of, 221–227, 238, 262
  textile/upholstery, 217, 226, 227, 228, 229
  treatment of, 239, 242
  trim and incidental, 103, 244
  types of:
    ceiling, *see* Ceiling(s)
    floor, *see* Floor(s)
    wall, *see* Wall(s)
    window treatments, *see* Window(s)
Fire:
  alarm systems, *see* Detection system(s)
  barrier(s), 124, 126, 127, 128, 129, 130, 131. *See also*
    Fire barrier
  compartments, *see* Compartmentation; High-rise
    buildings
  dampers, *see* Through-penetration protectives
  department, 72, 156, 161, 163, 250
  detection systems, *see* Detection system(s)
  development, stages of, 220
  doors, *see* Door(s)
  escapes, 95
  exit hardware, 136
  extinguishers, *see* Suppression system(s)
  hose, *see* Suppression system(s)
  protection, *see* Prevention system(s); Detection
    system(s); Suppression system(s)
  ratings, *see* Ratings, fire
  resistive, 64, 65, 122, 124. *See also* Flame,
    resistance
  retardant coatings and treatments, 63– 65, 239, 242
  walls, *see* Walls, fire walls
  windows, *see* Window(s)
Fire barriers, 124–132
  corridor wall, 128
  fire walls, 126–127
  floor/ceiling assembly, 130
  horizontal exit, 128
  occupancy separation, wall, 127
  room separation, 130, 147
  tenant separation wall, 128
  vertical shaft enclosure, 129–130
Fire marshal, *see* Code official, types of
Fire Resistance Design Manual, 147
Fire Resistance Directory, 147
Firestops, *see* Through-penetration protectives
Fixed seats, *see* Seating
Fixtures, *see* Light fixtures; Plumbing fixture(s)

Flame, *see also* Testing
  resistance, 218
  retardant requirements, 218
  spread, 218, 222, 224
Flammable, 218, 226
Flashover, 220, 228
Floor(s):
  assemblies, *see* Assemblies, types of; Fire barriers
  finishes for, 85, 86, 219, 221, 224, 225, 227, 231,
    234, 243
  means of egress for, 96–101, 103, 105
Floor area, *see* Area
Flooring Radiant Panel Test, 224
Floor plans, *see* Drawings
Foam, *see* Finishes; Seating
Foyer, *see* Exit discharge(s)
Furnishings, 217, 219, 239, 241. *See also* Seating
    accessibility of, *see* Accessibility requirements
  determination of, 239, 241, 242
  loads for, 47
  mock-up of, 218, 226, 228
  placement of, 90, 109, 239, 241, 242
  restriction on, 243, 244, 245
  testing of, 23, 227–230. *See also* Testing
  travel distance around, 109
  types of:
    bedding/mattresses, 229, 230
    counter, 45, 46, 243
    panel systems, 219
    seating, *see* Seating
    table, 46, 243
    worksurfaces, 46, 243
Furniture, *see* Furnishings
Furring strips, 244
Fuse(s), electrical, 197
Fusible link, 143, 154
Future technology, *see* Technology

G

Gates, *see* Stairs
GFI or GFCI, *see* Ground fault circuit interrupters
Glass, *see* Glazing
Glazing, *see also* Door(s); Window(s)
  fire-rated glazing, 140
  glass block, 139, 145
  wire glass, 139
Grab bars, *see* Toilet facilities
Ground(ing), electrical, 199, 200, 204
Ground fault circuit interrupters (GFCI or GFI),
    204, 214
Guardrails, 88
Gypsum Association, 147
Gypsum board, 58, 64, 130, 201, 244, 261

H

Habitable, *see* Occupiable
Half Diagonal rule, 106, 107, 117
Handicap requirements, *see* Accessibility
    requirements
Handrails, 86, 87, 103
Hardware, *see* Door(s)
Hazardous materials/contents, 30, 34–36, 130
Hazardous occupancies:
    area limitations, 73
    classification of, 29, 30, 35, 36
    means of egress in, 108
    types of, 36
Hazards, 29, 30, 163, 200
Headroom, *see* Height(s)
Health care occupancies, 36, 37, 231, 245. *See also*
    Institutional occupancies
Heat barrier, 218
Heat transfer, 129
Heavy timber, *see* Wood
Height(s):
    building, 58, 68, 70–73, 270
        code tables, 69
        limitations of, 71–73
    ceiling, 81, 134, 188, 270
    door, 81
    furniture, 243
    guardrails, 88
    handrails, 86–88
    headroom, 81
    signs, *see* Signage
    stairs, 86
    story, 50
High hazard, *see* Hazardous occupancies
High-rise buildings, 40, 58, 72, 92, 127, 162. *See also*
    Compartmentation
Historic buildings, *see* Building(s)
Historic preservation, 24, 277
Hoistway enclosure, *see* Shaft(s)
Horizontal exits, *see* Exit(s), types of
HVAC, *see* Mechanical system(s)

I

ICC Electrical Code (IEC), 15, 195
Illumination, *see* Emergency lighting; Exit signs
Industrial occupancies:
    allowed hazards, 35
    classification of, 34
    finishes in, 232
    sprinklers for, 163
    types of, 34
Inspection, code, 251, 259–261

Inspectors, *see* Code official, types of
Installers, *see* Contractor(s)
Institutional occupancies:
    accessibility requirements, 45
    classification of, 36–37, 44, 67
    evacuation of, 36, 67
    finish selection for, 231, 245
    fire separation in, 132
    means of egress in, 83, 92, 99
    plumbing requirements for, 178
    sprinkler heads for, 166
    types of, 37
Interior finishes, *see* Finishes
International Building Code (IBC), 9–13
International Code Council (ICC), 9, 12, 13, 15, 251,
    269
International Conference of Building Officials
    (ICBO), 9, 250, 275
International family of codes, 3–4, 10, 15. *See also*
    International Code Council
International Mechanical Code (IMC), 13, 171, 186
International Performance Code, 12. *See also*
    Performance type codes
International Plumbing Code (IPC), 12, 171, 172, 174–176
International Residential Code (IRC), 15, 38, 202, 269–
    272, 274
International Symbol of Accessibility, 185
Intervening rooms, *see* Room(s)

J

Junction box, *see* Electrical, box
Jurisdiction(s), 2, 12, 24, 26, 249, 250, 252, 253,
    255, 262, 265

L

Label(s), *see* Testing; UL labels
Laboratory testing, *see* Testing
Lamp(s), 205
Landings, *see* Stairs; Ramps
Laundry chutes, *see* Chutes
Lavatories, *see* Plumbing fixture(s)
LC50 (Test), 227, 235
Liability, *see* Code research
Life Safety Code (LSC), 14–15, 20
Lifts, platform, 84
Light fixtures, 115, 120, 188, 197, 204–205, 207
Lighting, *see* Emergency lighting; Exit signs
Limited-combustible, 58, 64
Live loads, *see* Loads
Load(s):
    cooling loads, 188
    dead loads, 47

Loads(s) (*cont'd*)
 live loads, 47
 occupancy loads, *see* Occupancy loads
Load factor, 48–52, 54
Lobby, *see* Exit discharge(s), types of
Locks, *see* Door(s), hardware
Low voltage wiring, *see* Cabling
LSC, see Life Safety Code

M

Mattresses, 219, 229
Means of egress, 48, 53–54, 75–76, 117, 118, 231, 232
 accessibility of, *see* Accessibility requirements
 capacity of, 96–114. *See also* Occupancy load
  arrangement of, 106–108
  number of, 97–100
  widths of, 100–105
 changes in floor level, *see* Stairs; Ramps
 common path of travel, *see* Path of travel
 dead end corridor(s), *see* Corridor(s)
 finishes in, 231, 244
 headroom in, *see* Height(s)
 lighting of, *see* Emergency lighting
 marking of, *see* Exit lighting; Exit signs; Signage
 occupancy load requirements, *see* Occupancy
  loads
 travel distance in, 95, 96, 98, 112, 108–111, 177
 types of, 78–80
  exit, *see* Exit(s)
  exit access, *see* Exit access(es)
  exit discharge, *see* Exit discharg(es)
  public way, *see* Public way
Means of escape, *see* Occupancy, evacuation of
Mechanical system(s), 160, 171, 186–190
 access to, 190
 controls, 189
 cooling loads, *see* Loads
 dampers, *see* Through-penetration protectives
 ducts, 186, 188, 190, 142, 143
 equipment, 187
 exhaust requirements, 189
 plenum, 190 199
 return air grilles, 187, 188, 190
 room, *see* Room(s)
 supply diffusers, 187, 188. 190
 types of, 188
 ventilation, 189–190
 zoning of, 187, 189
Membrane penetrations, *see* Penetrations
Mercantile occupancies:
 accessibility requirements, 45–46
 classification of, 38, 44
 means of egress in, 83, 90, 103

plumbing requirements for, 177
 sprinklers for, 163
 types of, 38
Mezzanines, 66, 73, 84
Millwork, 167, 242, 243, 298
Miscellaneous occupancies, *see* Unusual
  occupancies
Mixed occupancies, *see* Occupancies
Mock-up, *see* Furnishings
Model codes:
 building, 9–13, 251. *See also* BOCA National Building
  Code; Standard Building Code; Uniform Building
  Code
 mechanical, 13. *See also* BOCA National Mechanical
  Code; Standard Mechanical Code; Uniform
  Mechanical Code
 plumbing, 13. *See also* BOCA National Plumbing Code;
  Standard Plumbing Code; Uniform Plumbing Code
Model Energy Code (MEC), 15
Modernization, *see* Technology
Moving walks, 88

N

National Conference of States on Building Codes
  and Standards (NCSBCS), 24, 255
National Electrical Code (NEC), 15, 195, 198–207, 272,
  273
National Electric Manufacturer's Association
  (NEMA), 195
National Evaluation Services (NES), 15–16
National Fire Protection Association (NFPA), 14,
  20, 144, 155, 195, 222
National Institute of Business Sciences (NIBS), 24
National Register of Historic Places, 275
Natural path of travel, *see* Path of travel
NBC, see BOCA National Building Code
NEC, see National Electric Code
NFPA standards, *see also* Testing, summary of
 NFPA 10, 20, 160
 NFPA 13, 163, 271
 NFPA 14, 162
 NFPA 70, see National Electric Code (NEC)
 NFPA 72, 158
 NFPA 80, 14, 134, 137, 139, 140
 NFPA 90A, 143
 NFPA 90B, 143
 NFPA 92A, 132
 NFPA 92B, 132
 NFPA 101, see Life Safety Code (LSC)
 NFPA 105, 137
 NFPA 110, 207
 NFPA 220, 14, 62–63, 64
 NFPA 251, 144

NFPA 252, 137
NFPA 253, 224
NFPA 255, 222
NFPA 257, 139, 140
NFPA 260, 226
NFPA 264A, 228
NFPA 266, 228
NFPA 267, 229
NFPA 272, 228
NFPA 701, 225, 235, 238, 242
NMC, see BOCA National Mechanical Code
Nonbearing walls, *see* Wall(s)
Noncombustible, 58, 63–64, 65, 67, 72, 141, 142, 199, 244
Notification of fire department, *see* Fire department
NPC, see BOCA National Plumbing Code

O

Occupancy:
  accessibility requirements, 45–47
  allowable construction type(s), 67
  allowable height and area, 72. *See also* Height(s)
  changes in, 41, 96, 174
  classification of, 27, 28–9–31, 41, 54, 57, 67, 72, 99, 123, 125, 147, 231, 232, 245
    assembly, *see* Assembly occupancies
    business, *see* Business occupancies
    detentional/correctional, *see* Detentional/Correction occupancies
    educational, *see* Educational occupancies
    health care, *see* Health care occupancies
    industrial, *see* Industrial occupancies
    mercantile, *see* Mercantile occupancies
    residential, *see* Residential occupancies
    storage, *see* Storage occupancies
    unusual, *see* Unusual structures
  existing, 29, 41, 231
  list of, 31–40
  loads, *see* Occupant load
  minor, 30, 38, 39, 127
  mixed, 30, 32, 44–45, 52, 97, 105, 234
  multiple, 52
  new, 41, 29, 231
  separation wall, *see* Fire barrier
  sprinklers in, 163–164
  subclassification of, 31, 36, 38, 41
  use group(s), 41, 50, 54, 176
Occupant(s), *see also* Occupancy load(s)
  content, 28, 76
  evacuation of, 38, 67, 72, 103, 119, 120, 134, 156, 157, 245, 266
  location of, 79
  number of, 29, 70, 72, 91, 98, 176

Occupant load(s), 27, 48–52, 53, 96, 97, 174, 101. *See also* Area
  calculation of, 50–52, 52–53, 71, 197
  code tables, 71, 48–50, 56
  fixed seats, *see* Seating
  formula, 50–51, 52, 71
  load factor, 48–52, 54, 56
  means of egress use, *see* Means of egress
  mixed use requirements, 52
  multiple use requirements, 52
  for plumbing fixture quantities, 174–176, 177
  posting of, 54
Occupational Safety and Health Act (OSHA), 19
One and Two Family Dwelling Code (OTFOC), 15, 269, 274. *See also International Residential Code (IRC)*
One and two family dwellings, 15, 38, 99, 202, 269–274, 298. *See also* Residential occupancies
$\frac{1}{28}$ Inch Rule, 244
Opening protectives, 120, 122, 134–140
  fire doors, 134–138
  fire windows, 138–139
  rated glazing, 139–140
Outlet(s), *see also* Box
  dedicated, 201
  electrical, 147, 197, 201–203, 205, 210, 211
  fixture, 205
  mounting height of, 203, 205
  switch, 147, 202, 203
  voice/data, 211

P

Paint(s), 156, 244
Panic hardware, 136
Parapet walls, *see* Wall(s)
Partitions, *see* Wall(s)
Party walls, *see* Wall(s), fire wall
Passageways, *see* Exit(s), types of
Path of travel, 82, 100, 108, 111
  common path, 76, 111, 114
  natural path, 76, 109
Penetrations, 65, 122, 124, 126, 134, 140. *See also* through-penetration protectives
Performance type codes, 11, 12, 14, 139, 140, 149, 252, 257, 266
Permit, 257–259
Perscriptive type codes, 11, 252
Pill Test, 225
Pitts Test, see LC50
Plans check, *see also* Construction Documents
  final, 250, 259
  preliminary, 250, 255–256, 259
Plans examiner, *see* Code official, types of
Plastics, *see* Finishes, foam/plastics

Platforms, *see* Lifts, platform
Plenums, *see* Mechanical system(s)
Plumbing fixture(s), *see also* Toilet facilities
   accessibility percentages, 178–179. *See also*
      Accessibility requirements
   code tables, 173, 174–176, 177, 179
   controls for, 173, 180, 181
   potty parity, 177
   quantity of, 174–179
   types of, 179–182
      bathtubs, 181, 185
      clothes washers, 182
      dish washers, 182
      drinking fountains, 181, 298, 299
      lavatories, 180, 176, 182
      showers, 181–182, 185
      sinks, 180–181
      urinals, 180, 183, 184
      waterclosets, 179–180, 176, 178, 185
Plumbing system, 172, 178
Prevention systems, 120, 153. *See also* Wall(s)
   fire barriers, *see* Fire barriers
   opening protectives, *see* Opening protectives
   smoke barriers, *see* Smoke barriers
   test ratings of, *see* Test ratings
   through-penetration protectives, *see* Through-
      penetration protectives
Public telephone systems, *see* Communication
      system(s)
Public way, 79, 92, 101

R

Raceway, *see also* Cable tray
   communication, 210
   electrical, 197
Radiant heat, 145, 224
Radiant panel test, *see* Flooring Radiant Panel Test
Railings, *see* Handrails; Guardrails
Ramps, 79, 88–89, 101, 147, 243. *See also*
      Accessibility requirements
Ratings:
   finish, 222, 224, 226, 227
   fire, 58, 59, 61, 63, 121, 124, 126–130, 132, 134
      F-rating, 141
      protective ratings, 140–144
      resistant ratings, 58, 134, 136–140
      T-ratings, 141
   furnishing, 219, 229, 230, 235
   testing for, 124, 144–145, 222, 235
Receptacles, *see* Outlet(s)
Rehabilitation Guidelines, 275
Renovation, *see* Building(s)
Research recommendations, *see* Code research

Residential occupancies:
   accessibility requirements, 19, 45, 46, 273
   classification of, 38
   electrical requirements for, 203, 272–273
   family dwellings, *see* One and two family
      dwellings
   finish selection for, 231, 245, 273
   means of egress in, 99, 270–271
   plumbing requirements, 181, 182, 178, 271–272
   smoke detectors in, 157, 271
   sprinklers in, 163
   types of, 39
Restroom(s), *see* Toilet facilities
Return grilles, *see* Mechanical system(s)
Room(s):
   accessibility of, *see* Accessibility requirements
   adjoining and intervening, 90–91
   arrangement of, 91, 96, 112
   dress/fitting, 46
   electrical, 198
   exit width for, 100
   incidental, 130
   mechanical, 187, 208
   separation, *see* Fire barrier
   sprinklers in, 164
Rubbish chutes, *see* Chutes

S

SBC, see Standard Building Code
Seating, 219, 228, 242
   accessibility of, *see* Accessibility requirements
   arrangement of, 90, 243
   booths, 53, 242
   continuous, 52–53, 90, 243
   fixed seats, 52–53
   foam in, 219, 229
   testing for, 228–229
Secretary of the Interior's Standards for Rehabilitation,
      275
Security systems, 46, 136, 156, 211–214
Self-closing, *see* Door(s), hardware
Separation walls, *see* Wall(s)
Shaft(s), *see also* Elevator(s); Chutes
   enclosures for, 59, 65, 128–130, 133
   fire ratings of, *see* Fire barriers
   penetrations in, 129
   smoke barriers of, *see* Smoke barriers
   uses for, 129
Showers, *see* Plumbing fixture(s)
Sidewalk, *see* Exit discharge(s)
Signage, 106, 114, 155, 181. *See also* Exit signs;
      Accessibility requirements
Sinks, *see* Plumbing fixture(s)

Slope ratio, *see* Ramps
SMC, *see Standard Mechanical Code*
Smoke:
  dampers, *see* Through-penetration protectives
  danger of, 119, 133
  detectors, *see* Detection system(s)
  developed ratings, 222
  enclosure, 132
  proof enclosures, 132. *See also* Ventilation;
    Shaft(s); Smoke barriers
  travel of, 119, 132, 133, 152
Smoke barriers, 120, 122, 132–134, 141, 142
  vertical shafts, 133
  vestibules, 133–134. *See also* Exit discharge(s)
  wall assemblies, 132
Smoldering, 218, 226
Smolder resistance test, *see Cigarette Ignition Test*
Southern Building Code Congress International
  (SBCCI), 9, 250, 275
Spaces, *see* Room(s)
SPC, *see Standard Plumbing Code*
Specifications, *see* Construction documents
Specification Tested Product Guide, 147
Sprinkler systems, *see* Suppression system(s)
Stairs, 77, 84–88, 91–92, 129
  accessibility of, *see* Accessibility requirements
  dimensional criteria, 86. *See also* Means of egress,
    capacity of
  enclosures for, 92, 128–130, 138
  exit access requirements, 84–88, 129
  exit requirements, 91–92, 129
  fire rating of, 85, 92, 129
  gate for, 92
  guardrails, *see* Guardrails
  handrails, *see* Handrails
  landings for, 86, 94
  nosings, 86
  surface application, 243
  types of, 85
Stairway, *see* Stairs
Stairwell(s), *see* Stairs, enclosure
Stalls, *see* Toilet facilities
Standard and Existing Building Code, 275
Standard Building Code (SBC), 9–13
Standard for the Flammability of Mattresses (FF4–72),
  229
Standard Mechanical Code (SMC), 13, 186. *See also*
  International Mechanical Code (IMC)
Standard Plumbing Code (SPC), 13, 172. *See also*
  International Plumbing Code (IPC)
Standards, *see also* ANIS standards; NFPA
  standards; UL standards
  adoption of, 20
  compliance with, 21

  defined, 19–23
  development of, 8, 19, 22
  organizations, 20–23
  referencing of, 7, 13, 20
  where to obtain, Appendix D
Standby power systems, *see* Electrical system(s)
Standpipe and fire hoses, *see* Suppression system(s)
Steps, 86, 147
Steiner Tunnel Test, 221, 222–224, 231, 235, 238, 239
Storage occupancies:
  allowed hazards, 40
  classification of, 39
  finishes in, 232
  sprinklers in, 163
  types of, 39
Story, *see* Building(s); Height(s)
Structure, *see* Building(s); Wood
Structure elements, 58–61, 63, 64, 65, 120, 124, 128,
  144, 217, 248
Subcontractor(s), *see* Contractor(s)
Supply diffusers, *see* Mechanical system(s)
Suppression system(s), 156–167, 120
  fire extinguisher(s), 160
  sprinkler system(s), 163–167, 244
    clearance at, 167
    coverage of, 167
    design issues for, 165–166
    head/escutcheon types, 153, 163, 166–167
    restrictions, 163–164, 166
    trade-offs allowed, 73, 101, 107, 123, 126, 154,
      162, 165–166, 232, 244
    types of, 164–165
  standpipe and fire hoses(s), 160–163
Suspended ceiling, *see* Ceiling(s)
Switches, *see* Box; Outlet

T

TB 133, see CAL 133
Technology, 158, 168, 169, 208, 266
Telephone system(s), *see also* Communication
  system(s)
  accessibility of, 299
  public telephones, 211
Tenant separation, *see* Wall(s)
Ten (10) Percent Rule, 242, 244, 245
Testing, *see also* Fire, ratings; Flame, tests
  agencies/companies, 22, 144, 238
  certificate(s), 23, 239
  classification of, 137, 222, 238
  future of, *see* Technology
  label(s), 23, 137, 139, 140, 145, 228, 236–238, 247.
    See also UL labels
  laboratories, 22

Testing (cont'd)
  obtaining results, 147, 155, 221, 235
  positive pressure in, 137, 145
  ratings, *see* Ratings, testing for
  summary of, 145, 222
  using rated materials, 144
Textile(s), *see* Finishes
Thermostat, *see* Mechanical systems, controls
Through-penetration protectives, 91, 120, 122, 140–144
  ceiling dampers, 144
  draftstops, 120, 142
  fire dampers, 142–143, 190
  fire rated, 140
  firestops, 122, 141–142, 190, 199, 261, 271
  glazing, *see* Glass
  smoke dampers, 143–144
Through-penetrations, *see* Penetrations
Toilet facilities, *see also* Plumbing fixture(s)
  accessibility of, *see* Accessibility requirements
  accessories in, 184–185
  counter tops in, 180
  grab bars in, 183, 184–185
  multiple, 183–184
  privacy in, 182
  signage in, *see* Signage
  single, 182–183
  sizes of, 183, 184
  stalls in, 183–184
  unisex, 177–178, 179
  ventilation of, *see* Ventilation
Town houses, *see* One and two family dwelling
Transformers, *see* Electrical
Transient lodging, 45, 46
Trap, *see* Plumbing, parts of
Travel distance, *see* Means of egress
Tread finishes, *see* Stairs
Treatment companies, 239, 247
Trim, *see* Finishes
Tufted textiles, *see* Finishes
Tunnel test, *see* Steiner Tunnel Test
Turning space, *see* Wheelchair

U

UBC, *see* Uniform Building Code
UL Catalog of Standards, 23
UL label, 23, 205. *See also* Testing, labels
UL standards, 23. *See also* Testing, summary of
  UL 155, 143
  UL 263, 144
  UL 723, 222
  UL 992, 224
  UL 1056, 228

UMC, *see Uniform Mechanical Code*
Underwriters Laboratories (UL), 22–23, 144, 147, 195, 204, 222
Uniform Building Code (UBC), 9–13
Uniform Code for Building Conservation, 275
Uniform Federal Accessibility Standards (UFAS), 17, 18
Uniform Mechanical Code (UMC), 13, 186. *See also International Mechanical Code (IMC)*
Uniform Plumbing Code (UPC), 13, 172. *See also International Plumbing Code (IPC)*
Unusual Structures, 30, 40
UPC, see Uniform Plumbing Code
Upholstered furniture, *see* Furnishings; Seating
Upholstered Furniture Action Council (UFAC), 16
Upholstery, *see* Finishes
Urinals, *see* Plumbing fixture(s)
Use group(s), *see* Occupancies
Utilities, *see* Electrical System(s)

V

Variance, *see* Code(s)
Veneer, *see* Wood
Vent(s), *see* Mechanical system(s); Plumbing system
Ventilation, 132, 134, 189–190. *See also* Smoke, proof enclosures
  exhaust, 134, 189
  mechanical, 134
  natural, 134
  when required, 129, 189–190, 198
Vertical shafts, *see* Shaft(s)
Vestibule, *see* Exit discharge(s)
Visual alarms, *see* Accessible warning systems
Voice/data outlets, *see* Outlets

W

Wallcoverings, *see* Wall(s), finishes/coverings
Wall openings, *see* Through-penetration protectives
Wall(s), 7, 11, 59, 225. *See also* Compartmentation; Fire barriers; Shafts; Smoke barriers
  assembly of, 146–149
  corridor, 128
  demising, 65, 128
  finishes/coverings, 217, 219, 222, 225, 230–232, 234, 236, 239, 244
  fire-rated, 44, 91, 124, 132, 144, 147, 190, 198
  fire resistive rating, *see* Fire, ratings
  fire walls, 59, 65, 67, 73, 124, *see also* Fire barriers
  load bearing, 59, 63, 65, 145
  nonload bearing, 59, 61, 63, 65
  occupancy separation, 127

parapet, 67
party, *see* Walls, fire walls
tenant separation, *see* Fire barriers
Waterclosets, *see* Plumbing fixture(s)
Water fountain, *see* Plumbing fixture(s)
Way, public, *see* Public way
Wheelchair, *see also* Accessibility requirements;
    Area of refuge
lift, *see* Lift, platform
size, 94
turning space, 105, 183, 184
Window(s), 65, 189
assembly, *see* Assemblies, types of
fire rated, *see* Opening protectives
treatments, 219, 225, 230, 236, 242, 244

Wire(ing), *see* Cabling
Wire glass, *see* Glass
Wood, 64, 65
fire retardant, 64
heavy timber, 61, 64, 65
structures, 65, 269
testing with, 222, 227
veneer, 219, 242
Working drawings, *see* Construction documents
Work surfaces, *see* Furnishings, types of

Z

Zoning ordinances, 24, 252